From Main Street to Wall Street

From Main Street to Wall Street

How the economy influences stock markets and what investors should know

JESPER RANGVID

OXFORD
UNIVERSITY PRESS

OXFORD
UNIVERSITY PRESS

Great Clarendon Street, Oxford, OX2 6DP,
United Kingdom

Oxford University Press is a department of the University of Oxford. It furthers the University's objective of excellence in research, scholarship, and education by publishing worldwide. Oxford is a registered trade mark of Oxford University Press in the UK and in certain other countries

First Edition published in 2021

Published in the United States of America by Oxford University Press
198 Madison Avenue, New York, NY 10016, United States of America

British Library Cataloguing in Publication Data
Data available

Library of Congress Control Number: 2020950664

ISBN 978–0–19–886640–4

DOI: 10.1093/oso/9780198866404.001.0001

Acknowledgements

A number of people have helped me in the writing of this book. My deepest thanks go to my colleague at Copenhagen Business School, Henrik R.-Hansen, who carefully read the complete manuscript, and reread many parts, providing a number of great comments. Another good colleague at CBS, Lasse H. Pedersen, also helped me at different stages of the process with suggestions and advice. Three anonymous reviewers at Oxford University Press gave useful feedback that helped improve the manuscript. I would also like to thank my coauthors on research papers that I cite in this book, but also my many other coauthors. The cooperation I have had with you throughout the years have helped me sharpen my arguments and my understanding of finance.

This book relies on the data. I decided early on that would I strive to base the book mainly on freely-available data, such that all readers can source the underlying data should you wish to do so. Thanks go to academics who collect data and make them available to the rest of us. It is a tremendous and highly valuable work that is sometimes not appreciated enough. In this book, I rely particularly on data from the Robert J. Shiller database, the Jorda et al. (2019) database, the Barro-Ursua (2008) database, and the Kenneth R. French database, as well as data from the St. Louis Fed, the World Bank, OECD, and other public authorities that make macroeconomic and financial data available.

I would also like to thank the staff at Oxford University Press for answering all my questions and helping me turn this into a real book.

Finally, a huge hug to my nearest ones—Bea, Marie, and Mathias—for all your constant support. Without you, life would not be even remotely as fun and enjoyable as it is.

Contents

II. ECONOMIC GROWTH AND STOCK RETURNS IN THE LONG RUN

III. ECONOMIC GROWTH AND STOCK RETURNS DURING THE BUSINESS CYCLE

V. THE PROSPECTS FOR RETURNS

List of Figures

List of Tables

1
Introduction

From Main Street to Wall Street analyses the relation between economic activity and stock returns. Its main point is that economic activity is an important driver of returns.

Economic activity contains a long-run and a short-run component. The long run refers to many years, even decades. The short run to days, months, quarters, or a couple of years. In its discussion of the relation between economic activity and financial markets, *From Main Street to Wall Street* distinguishes between the long-run relation and the short-run relation.

In the long run, economies grow. The rate at which an economy grows in the long run is *the* determinant of whether a country becomes rich or poor, whether an economy prospers or not. Expectations of developments in economic activity in the long run will also help us in formulating expectations for returns from financial assets in the long run. When twenty years old Sarah asks how much she should save for retirement, i.e. after many years, the answer will depend on the returns she can expect from her savings. And, these returns will in turn depend on how fast we expect the economy to grow in the long run. Parts I and II of the book describe the historical long-run relations between economic activity and stock returns.

In the short run, economic activity fluctuates. Sometimes even substantially so. There are years when the economy is booming, unemployment is low, and times are good. At other times, in recessions, economic activity contracts, people are laid off, and times are bad. The recurrent alternations between good and bad times is the business cycle.

Economic activity and the stock market share common business-cycle characteristics. The level of economic activity and the value of stocks rise and fall jointly through the business cycle. In order to understand why stock returns are sometimes high and why they are sometimes low, we need to understand business-cycle fluctuations in economic activity. Part III deals with this.

When we understand how economic activity relates to financial assets in the long run and across business cycles, we are in a better position to formulate reasonable expectations for future movements in economic activity and returns on financial assets. Parts IV and V deal with this, i.e. how we can use our knowledge of the historical facts to forecast economic activity and returns in the short and the long run.

The final part, a short one, summarizes a few practical implications for investors.

From Main Street to Wall Street. Jesper Rangvid, Oxford University Press (2021). © Jesper Rangvid.
DOI: 10.1093/oso/9780198866404.003.0001

Table 1.1 *From Main Street to Wall Street*: Outline

Part I:	Growth and returns: Basic definitions and stylized facts
Part II:	Economic growth and stock returns in the long run
Part III:	Economic growth and stock returns during the business cycle
Part IV:	The prospects for economic growth
Part V:	The prospects for returns
Part VI:	Practical investment advice

Table 1.1 presents the outline of the book. The following sections of this Introduction describe the content of the individual chapters in Parts I–VI.

Part I. Growth and returns: Basic definitions and stylized facts

The first part of the book, outlined in Table 1.2, introduces key concepts, definitions, and stylized facts regarding long–run economic growth and stock returns. Chapter 2 analyses the rate at which economies have grown in the past, distinguishing between aggregate economic growth and growth in per capita economic activity. Economic growth is important because it influences peoples' standard of living. People living in rich countries, i.e. countries that have experienced many years of high economic growth, on average live longer and are better educated. Economic growth is also important because it affects asset markets, the theme of this book.

Chapter 3 describes stylized facts regarding long-run historical stock returns. The historical long-run returns to stocks have been amazing. One dollar invested in the stock market hundred years ago would have turned into several thousand dollars today. Stock markets are also risky, however. The chapter illustrates this by comparing stock returns to bond returns.

Chapter 4 explains how stock returns can be decomposed into underlying drivers of stock returns: yield, growth, and valuation change. It also shows the relative importance of each of these components for historical stock returns.

Part I deals with long-run economic growth and stock returns one by one, leaving it to Part II to describe how they are related in the long run.

Table 1.2 Part I: Long-run growth and returns: Definitions and stylized facts

Chapter 2 Long-run economic growth	Chapter 3 Long-run stock market returns	Chapter 4 Drivers of stock returns

Part II. Economic growth and stock returns in the long run

The second part of the book analyses the relation between economic growth and stock returns in the long run. The long run means many years, e.g. several decades. Table 1.3 illustrates Part II. Chapter 5 describes why one should expect a relation between drivers of stock returns and economic activity in the first place. The underlying idea is simple. Stock prices are discounted dividends. Dividends depend on firms' profits. Profits depend on economic activity. The chapter shows that, in the long run, profits and stock prices follow economic activity. Chapter 5 illustrates the concepts and ideas using US data.

Chapter 6 discusses whether countries that have historically experienced high growth in economic activity are also countries that have historically delivered high stock returns. The conclusion is clear. The relation between economic growth and stock returns across countries is weak. Stock market returns have exceeded the rate of economic growth by a wide margin. On the other hand, the chapter shows that economic growth is linked to growth in stock prices and interest rates in the long run.

Chapter 7 shows that the average annual return to equities has exceeded the average annual return to safe assets by a factor of three to four. This difference is the equity premium. The fact that the average return to equity is so high has puzzled economists. They call it an 'equity premium puzzle'. Scrutinizing what determines the equity premium will help us understanding the conclusion from Chapter 6 that there is no clear relation between economic growth and returns across countries in the long run.

Part III. Economic growth and stock returns during the business cycle

Part III examines the shorter-horizon relation between economic growth and stock returns: the relation over the business cycle. The business cycle refers to recurrent shifts between contractions in economic activity, i.e. recessions, and expansions in economic activity. An expansion in economic activity starts at the trough of a business cycle, i.e. after a recession. After some time, the level of

Table 1.3 Part II: The relationship between economic growth and stock returns in the long run

Chapter 5 Economic growth and drivers of stock returns	Chapter 6 Growth and returns across countries	Chapter 7 The equity premium puzzle

Table 1.4 Part III: The relationship between economic growth and stock returns over the business cycle

Chapter 8 Business-cycle fluctuations in economic activity	Chapter 9 The stock market over the business cycles	Chapter 10 Monetary policy and the business cycle
Chapter 11 Monetary policy, interest rates, and stock markets	Chapter 12 The 2008–2009 financial crisis and its aftermath	Chapter 13 Value, size, sector, and momentum stocks

economic activity reaches a (temporary) peak.[1] The economy enters a recession. And, then it all starts over. Expansions and contractions define the business cycle. Business-cycle fluctuations are fluctuations in economic activity around the long-term growth trend. Part III of this book describes the business cycle and how it relates to stock markets. We will see that stock markets react strongly to the business cycle. Stocks do great when economic activity expands, but poorly when the economy contracts.

The composition of Part III is outlined in Table 1.4. Chapter 8 explains what the business cycle is. How it is defined, what characterizes it, what causes it, etc. The chapter also describes the typical business cycle, i.e. the duration of the typical expansion and recession and how much economic activity typically contracts during recessions and increases during expansions.

Chapter 9 examines the relation between the business cycle and stock returns. We will see that business-cycle fluctuations in economic activity have first-order impact on stocks and bonds. Stocks perform badly during recessions, but well during expansions. Chapter 9 also looks at bond returns. Bonds provide safe havens during recessions, i.e. perform better than stocks during recessions. On the other hand, bond returns are considerably lower than stock returns during expansions.

One of the important factors influencing the business cycle is monetary policy. Monetary policy can both induce a recession and help in softening and shortening the impact of a recession. Chapter 10 describes what monetary policy is and Chapter 11 explains how monetary policy affects the stock market, via its impact on the business cycle and in itself.

Chapter 12 provides a 'case study'. To get a deeper feeling for how a business cycle develops, the chapter analyses one particular business cycle, the one surrounding the financial crisis in 2008–2009. The financial crisis was a

[1] It is a temporary peak because there is long-run growth, i.e. later this temporary peak will be surpassed by another, higher, temporary peak.

fascinating—and scary—episode. The chapter describes what caused it, what was done to reduce its impact, and how it influenced the stock market.

The book mainly deals with the aggregate stock market. Chapter 13 recognizes that some stocks tend to do better than the general stock market in the long run, i.e. across multiple business cycles, and some tend to do worse. Stocks that tend to do better are value, small-cap, and momentum stocks. The chapter shows that these better-performing stocks suffer particularly much during recessions. To compensate for the higher risk during recessions, these stocks provide so much higher returns during expansions that they outperform in the long run.

Part IV. The prospects for economic growth

What should we expect stocks to return going forward? If we are interested in long-run returns, the answer will depend on our expectations for long-run growth in economic activity. If we are interested in returns over the shorter run, the answer will depend on how we expect the business cycle to develop over our investment horizon. But how should we then come up with reasonable projections for economic activity, both for the short and the long run? The fourth part of the book, outlined in Table 1.5, discusses this. Chapter 14 describes the outlook for long-run economic growth. Long-run growth depends on long-run developments in productivity and population dynamics. The chapter argues that productivity growth and population growth will most likely be lower going forward compared to their historical norms. This implies that economic growth will most likely be lower going forward, too. Regarding the shorter run, Chapter 15 deals with methods one can use to judge the stance of the business cycle. Economists study a number of indicators when they evaluate the business cycle and its turning points. The chapter describes these indicators and how to understand them.

Part V. The prospects for returns

Based on knowledge gained in Part IV on the outlook for economic activity, and the earlier parts of the book on the historical relation between economic activity and returns, Part V deals with expected future stock returns. Table 1.6 shows that

Table 1.5 Part IV: The prospects for economic growth

Chapter 14 The outlook for long-run economic growth	Chapter 15 Judging the stance of the business cycle

Table 1.6 Part V: The prospects for returns

Chapter 16 Predicting returns: Theory	Chapter 17 Predicting short-to-medium horizon returns	Chapter 18 Predicting long-horizon returns
	Chapter 19 Predicting returns over several decades	

Part V starts out describing in Chapter 16 why there is hope that we might be able to say something about expected stock returns in the first place, i.e. the chapter describes the underlying theory. The following three chapters present empirical methods one can use to judge the outlook for stocks. It turns out that the forecast horizon matters for how to proceed. If one is interested in the shorter horizons, the outlook for stocks depends on the outlook for the business cycle. Chapter 17 describes this. Over medium-term horizons, such as a decade or similar, valuations and valuation changes matter a lot, as explained in Chapter 18. Finally, if one is interested in the very long run, say multiple decades, it depends on expectations for long-run average growth. This is in Chapter 19.

The book knows and emphasizes that formulating return expectations is a difficult task. In fact, we can only hope to capture a small fraction of stock-market fluctuations. This means that we should approach the issue of forecasting stock returns with a useful does of humility. But saying that economic activity and financial markets are difficult to forecast—which is true—is not the same as saying that we do not know anything. After reading *From Main Street to Wall Street*, investors should know how business cycles and long-run economic growth trajectories influence stock markets. This should help readers formulate realistic return expectations and improve performance.

Part VI. Practical investment advice

A final short part of the book, including Chapter 20 only, explains how we can use the insights from the book when making investments. It also touches upon a number of additional questions the investor faces. The chapter lays out what the academic literature has to say about these questions in easy-to-understand language.

PART I

GROWTH AND RETURNS: BASIC DEFINITIONS AND STYLIZED FACTS

2
Long-run economic growth

Long-run economic growth is a truly fascinating subject. After noticing that the Indonesian economy outpaced the Indian over the 1960–1980 period, Nobel Laureate in Economics Robert E. Lucas (1988) wondered:

> Is there some action a government of India could take that would lead the Indian economy to grow like Indonesia's or Egypt's? If so, what, exactly? If not, what is it about the 'nature of India' that makes it so? The consequences for human welfare involved in questions like these are simply staggering: Once one starts to think about them, it is hard to think about anything else.

You can almost feel his fascination.

Lucas' point was not that there is anything special about Indonesia, India, or Egypt. His point was that sustained economic growth is what determines peoples' standards of living, and peoples' standards of living determine many of their possibilities in life. It is not only that a higher level of income allows people to buy bigger houses, cars, etc. More important, 'quality of life' and income often go hand in hand. Populations in richer countries, i.e. countries that have enjoyed long periods of sustained economic growth, on average live longer, are healthier, better educated, and—some studies show—happier than people in poorer countries.

This chapter starts out introducing what we understand by 'aggregate economic activity'. This will allow us to explain Gross Domestic Product, per capita income, and related concepts that will be used repeatedly throughout this book. The chapter then turns to its main point: how economic activity has developed historically. We first use US data to illustrate the different concepts, after which we turn to international data.

This chapter will not go into detail with what causes long-run economic growth to be high or low. Chapter 14 deals with this. Instead, here, we deal with the concepts and stylized facts that we can use these when analysing their implications for asset markets in the chapters that follow.

2.1 What is aggregate economic activity?

This book studies the relation between financial markets and economic activity. Consequently, the level of and development in economic activity are key concepts.

From Main Street to Wall Street. Jesper Rangvid, Oxford University Press (2021). © Jesper Rangvid.
DOI: 10.1093/oso/9780198866404.003.0002

Total/aggregate level of economic activity in a country is labeled Gross Domestic Product or Gross National Product. Shorthand notations are GDP and GNP. Given that these concepts are central to the rest of this book, it is useful to understand the basic mechanisms and interpretations.

Gross Domestic Product measures the total value of all goods and services produced in an economy within a certain period (within a quarter, within a year, etc.), expressed in some currency (US dollar, Japanese Yen, etc.). Gross Domestic Product can be viewed, calculated, and interpreted in three different ways:

- The total value of production in an economy, measured by the value of final goods and services sold.
- Total income generated in the economy.
- The sum of value added in the economy.

GDP can also be measured by the spending side. This means that one can distribute income into the sectors that spend it. There are four main sectors in the economy: households; the private firms; the government; and the contribution of international trade to the domestic economy (the difference between exports and imports).[1] We can split GDP into its different components. How much has been spend by households for consumption? How much has been spend by firms on investments? How much by the government? And, how much has been sold abroad net, i.e. exports to foreign countries minus imports from foreign countries. In economic textbooks, GDP is often expressed as $Y = C + I + G + X - Z$, where Y is GDP, C measures private consumption, I investments of firms, G government consumption, X exports, and Z imports. As an example, imagine an economy with a GDP of 100 (= Y). Say households use 50 for consumption (C), the government uses 20 for government expenditures (G), firms use 10 for investments (I), and 20 are exported net to other countries ($X - Z$). This is the second way to look at GDP.

Calculating GDP is a formidable task. To calculate it, one needs the value of all final goods and services sold in the economy, the sum of all value added, and the sum of all factor incomes. Box 2.1 provides a stylized explanation of how to calculate GDP. Statistical bureaus have to calculate this for the whole economy. And, they have to calculate the distribution of income according to who spends it. This means that GDP numbers are typically published with a lag. It simply takes time to collect the data and ensure they are correct. Most countries produce quarterly GDP figures. Statistical bureaus publish them a month or two after the

[1] Exports are the value of sales from domestic sectors to the rest of the world. Imports are the value of purchases from the rest of the world by domestic sectors.

Box 2.1. Stylized theroretical example of a GDP calculation

To illustrate the calculation and interpretation of GDP in the simplest way possible, consider the following example. Imagine an economy where, to begin with, nothing is produced. Then, gold is discovered. A company employs some workers to dig up the gold. It sells the gold for 40 (of whatever currency we measure this in). The company has now earned 40. It uses some of it to pay workers. Workers are paid 30. The owners of the gold mine keep 10 in profits.

If no further economic activity takes place, what is GDP in this country? The total value of production is 40 (only gold is produced, and it is sold on the market for 40). The value added is also 40, because the economy started out producing nothing and now produces goods worth 40, i.e. products valued at 40 have been added to the economy. Total income in the country is also 40, consisting of 30 to workers and 10 to owners of firms. I.e., the total value of production, total income, and total value added are all equal to 40. GDP is 40.

Let us continue one step further. Imagine that the gold is sold to a jeweler. He produces jewelry that he can sell for 75. Now, gold is not the final good any more, but an intermediate good used in the production of jewelry. Instead, jewelry is the final good. The value of final goods is now 75. The jeweler bought gold for 40, but can sell the new product (the jewelry) for 75, i.e. 75 − 40 = 35 has been added to the value of the economy. What is the total value added in the economy? The gold mine added value of 40 and the jeweler has added an additional 35, i.e. the total/aggregate value added is 40 + 35 = 75. This is the same as the value of the final good. Finally, the jeweler works for himself, i.e. he can keep the value added by the jewelry for himself as income (he is paid 75 for the jewelry, but paid 40 for the gold, i.e. profits are 35). Total income in the economy is thus the 30 earned by the workers in the gold mine, 10 in profits to the owners of the gold mine, and 35 to the jeweler, in total 75. The same as the value of the final goods sold, and the same as the sum of value added. GDP is 75. Hence, GDP measures the value of final goods and services produced in an economy, the total value added in the economy, and the sum of all factor payments (incomes and profits) in the economy.

end of the quarter. Furthermore, GDP figures are typically revised after some time, as more and better data have been collected.

Gross National Product is equal to Gross Domestic Product plus net income from abroad accruing to the residents of the country. If somebody owns a firm abroad, and transfers profits from that foreign firm to our economy, GNP will exceed GDP. When we talk about overall economic developments and their consequences for financial markets, we often get basically the same conclusion whether we look at GNP or GDP.

GDP/GNP measure recorded market transactions. GDP/GNP do not include activities in informal markets. This could be the street vendor selling the same goods as the supermarket, but only taking cash, not reporting his/her sales, and not paying taxes. Schneider (2007) estimates that the informal economy accounts for 15% of official GDP in developed economies and 37% in developing economies.[2]

GDP or GNP at a given point in time tells us how much is produced in the country at that point in time. Often, and particularly in this book, we are interested in the growth rate of GDP throughout time: How much has production increased from year to year?

2.2 US aggregate economic activity throughout time

2.2.1 Nominal versus real

GDP and GNP are measured in real terms and in nominal terms. Nominal GDP refers to the value of production measured in current prices. For instance, nominal GDP for 1900 is calculated using the actual prices of goods and services in 1900. And, nominal GDP for 2020 is calculated using prices prevailing in 2020. Prices of goods and services change, however. The price of an apple today is very different from what you had to pay for an apple in 1900. An increase in nominal GDP can thus be due to a price increase and to an increase in the amount of goods and services produced. We need to be able to separate the two.

To measure real economic activity, we use 'real GDP'. 'Real' means that price changes have been accounted for. When using real GDP, the values of goods and services are calculated using their values in a base year, for instance 2013. As an example, the U.S. Bureau of Labor Statistics reports that one pound of flour costs USD 0.524 on average across the US in 2013. A century earlier, in 1913, the price of one pound of flour was USD 0.033. Over 100 years, the price of flour has increased by a factor of 16.[3] When calculating GDP in real terms, measured in 2013 prices, the value of flour production (in this case) in any year is calculated assuming that the price of flour was USD 0.524 every year, i.e. assuming that the

[2] Schneider (2007) does not include the value of classic criminal activities, such as robbery, drug dealing, etc., in his calculations, nor the value of household production.

[3] Similarly, a pound of bread has increased from USD 0.056 in 1913 to USD 1.422 in 2013, i.e. a factor of 25, cheese from USD 0.222 to USD 5.832, rice from USD 0.086 to USD 0.715, etc.

price was USD 0.524 in 1913, in 1914...in 2013, in 2014, and so forth. In this way, any change in the real value of flour production implies that there has been a change in the amount of flour produced, not that the price of flour has changed. As we are interested in real economic growth in this book, we will primarily study developments in real quantities.

There will be sections in the book that focus squarely on inflation, i.e. the rate at which prices of goods and services increase. Inflation is an important concept in economics and finance. In itself, inflation might even influence production and asset returns. But this is for later. When measuring whether and to what extent economies grow, we are interested in whether more goods and services are produced. Basically, are more apples produced?

An apple today is pretty much the same as an apple hundred years ago. The same with a pound of flour. But the cars of today are very different from the cars driving around the streets hundred years ago, a telephone today is very different from the ones used hundred years ago, etc. The quality of most products improve over time. In addition, some products were not even available hundred years ago, such as computers, cell phones, and many others. Statistical bureaus spend a great deal of time thinking about how to account for quality changes and new products in their calculations of price indices and measures of aggregate economic activity, such that we can properly measure growth in economic activity.

2.2.2 Real US activity

Figure 2.1 shows the evolution of US Gross National Product from 1871 through 2018.[4] The numbers shown in Figure 2.1 are in 'constant 2012 prices', i.e. 'real prices'. Hence, the figure shows the evolution of aggregate income accruing to residents in the United States throughout the last app. 150 years.

Total income accruing to residents of the United States in 1871 (measured in 2012 dollars) was USD 139 billion. It 2018, it was USD 18,750 bn. This means that aggregate income in the US was one hundred and thirty-five times larger in 2018 than it was in 1871. This is truly an impressive increase in economic activity. The US economy has grown considerably, and the US economy is today the largest economy in the world. But, does this economic growth also mean that the average American is richer today compared to 150 years ago?

[4] The data consist of 'official' GNP data available from 1929. These can be downloaded from the St. Louis Fed Database (FRED), for instance. The pre-1929 data are from Balke & Gordon (1989). We show GNP instead of GDP in Figure 2.1 because the pre-1929 total production data are GNP data; see Balke & Gordon (1989).

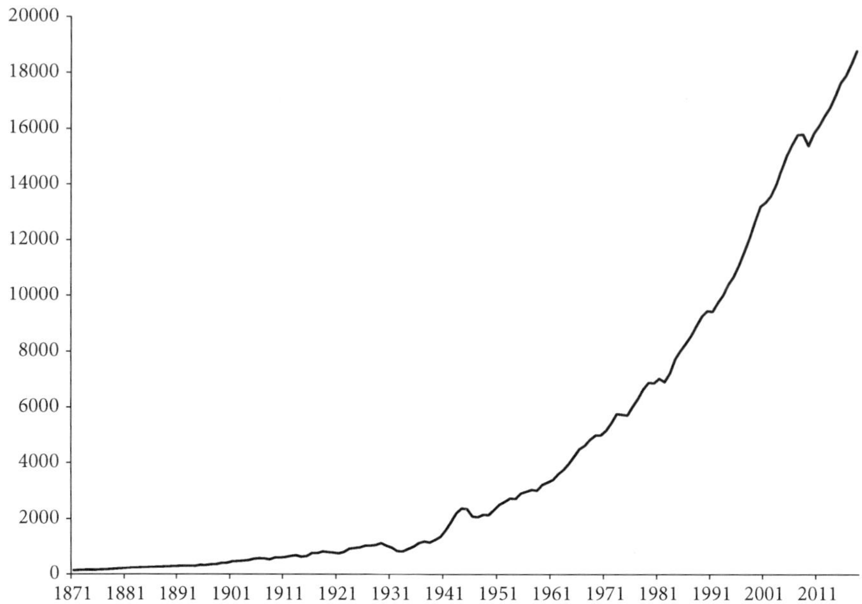

Figure 2.1 US Gross National Product in constant 2012 prices. USD bn. 1871–2018.
Data source: FRED database and Balke & Gordon (1989).

2.2.3 Per capital GNP

The total value of what is produced in the US is much larger today than it was in the late nineteenth century. But there are also more people living in the US today. Growth in the US population is visualized in Figure 2.2. There were 41 million residents in the US in 1871 whereas there are 329 million in 2018. This means that part of the increase in total production seen in Figure 2.1 can be traced back to the simple fact that more people participate in production today. If one person produces 100 widgets per day, adding one more person to the economy increases total production.

An important stylized fact is that total income has expanded faster than the size of the population. Total income has, as mentioned, increased by a factor of 135 over the last app. 150 years. The size of the population has increased by a factor of eight (from 41 million to 329 million). This means that growth in the US economy has not been due to population growth only. Population growth is a contributing factor to growth in total income, but the economy grows faster than the size of its population, over long periods of time. Developments in GNP per capita show this directly. With total income equaling app. USD 139bn in 1871 and the number of residents equalling 41 million, per capita GNP was app. USD 3,400 in 1871. In

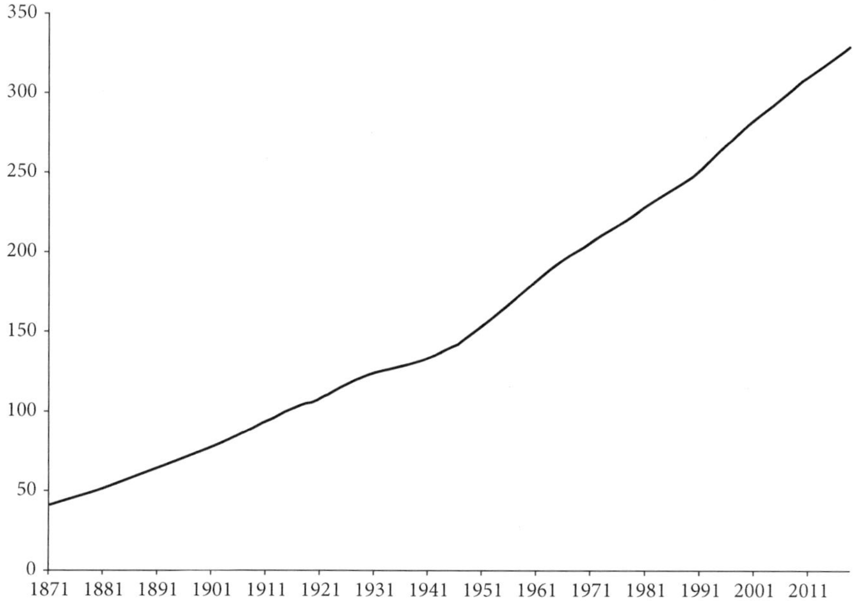

Figure 2.2 US total population in millions. 1871–2018.
Data source: Maddisson database: www.ggdc.net/maddisson.

2018, it was USD 57,000. This means that income earned by the average American has increased by a factor of 17 since 1871. Growth in per capita GNP is illustrated in Figure 2.3.

As we will see in Section 2.4, all advanced economies have experienced long-run growth in per capita income. When people have higher incomes, they have higher standards of living. Growth in per capita income implies that citizens in advanced economies today live in bigger and better-isolated houses, have access to water and shower, own and drive cars, have a diverse range of food products at their daily disposal, have enough food, have access to medical services to a far greater extent than in 1871, helping to increase health standards, attend more years of schooling, i.e. are better educated, and so on. It is no coincidence that we live longer today than we did a century ago. Average life-expectancy of a new-born American was around 50 years in year 1900 (Human Life Table Database). Today, it is close to 80 years, a dramatic improvement in life expectancy. Improvements in life expectancy have occurred not only in the US, but in all advanced countries. As a result of economic improvements that have led to better health-care systems, nutrition, etc., most people in advanced countries live better and longer lives than the average citizen did 150 years ago.

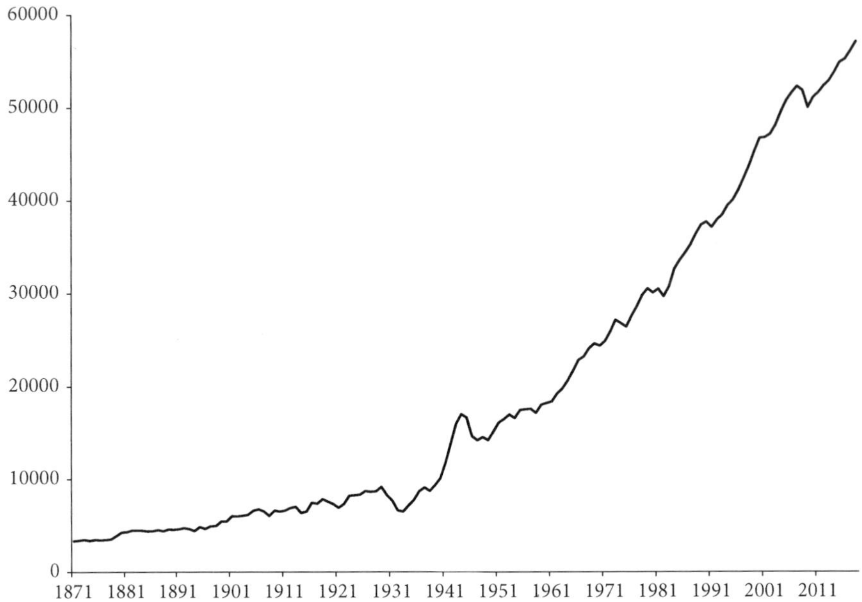

Figure 2.3 US per capita GNP in 2012 dollars. 1871–2018.
Data source: See Figures 2.1 and 2.2.

Figure 2.4 provides an illustration that higher levels of income typically lead to higher levels of 'quality of life'. The figure shows for a large number of countries the level of GDP per capita in USD in 2011 versus the so-called Human Development Index, developed by United Nations. The Human Development Index measures 'average achievement in key dimensions of human development: a long and healthy life, being knowledgeable and have a decent standard of living'. Figure 2.4 contains a clear message. People in richer countries are not only richer but live healthier lives and are more knowledgeable. Economic progress helps people improve their standards of living.

2.2.4 Happiness

When income is high, we can better afford many of the really important things in life, such as education, health care, leisure activities, etc. Given this, one would a priori expect that people are also happier when income is high. The answer to this hypothesis is subtle, however.

We cannot directly measure how 'happy' people are. We have to ask them. To measure happiness, economists and sociologists conduct surveys and ask

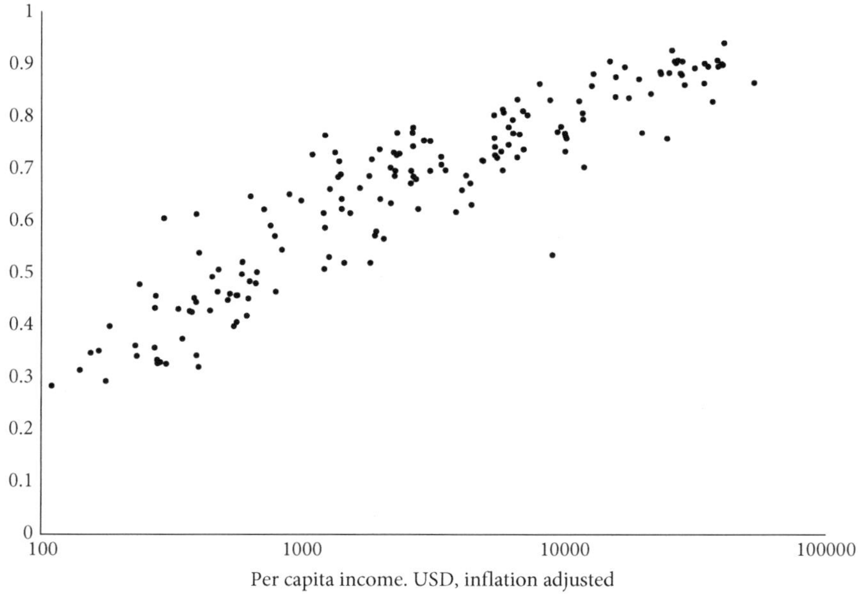

Figure 2.4 Income per capital in USD and Human Development Index (y-scale). 2011 data.
Data source: gapminder.org.

questions of individuals such as: 'On a scale from 0 to 10, how happy would you say you are, with 10 being very happy and 0 not happy at all?'. Alternatively, one can ask about peoples' life satisfaction, i.e. 'on a scale from 0 to 10, how satisfied are you with the life you live?'. In 1974, the then Professor of Economics at the University of Pennsylvania Richard Easterlin discovered that the answers to such questions differ depending on whether we look within a country at a given point in time or whether we look across time or across countries. This is labelled the 'Easterlin Paradox'.

Within a country at a given point in time, Easterlin found that people with higher levels of income report higher levels of happiness. I.e., at a given point in time, rich people in a country are typically happier than people with lower income. But Easterlin also discovered that across countries, there is no association between the level of income in a country and the average degree of happiness of the residents in that country. People in poor countries seem to be as happy as people in rich countries. Finally, when looking at one country over time, Easterlin found no evidence that people become happier when income levels grow. So, in spite of an increasing level of GDP per capita in a country, people in that country do not report a higher level of happiness. The Easterlin paradox is that, within a country at a given point in time, people look at their own income in relation to that of others, and those with high income are happier, but over time, the average person in a country does not get happier when income grows.

Subsequent research has shown that when extending the data to many countries, there is a non-linear relation between income and happiness across countries. For instance, Inglehart & Klingemann (2000) show that among poor nations, people in very poor nations are less happy than people in still poor, but not that poor, nations. I.e., there is a relation between happiness and income across poor countries. At the same time, Inglehart & Klingemann (2000) show that among richer countries, the Easterlin finding prevails, i.e. across relatively rich countries, happiness does not correlate with income.

2.2.5 Inequality

Another aspect worth paying attention to when discussing income levels and income growth is inequality. Today, income is considerably higher for the average person in an advanced economy, compared to what the average person earned 150 years ago. Income has not increased equally much for everybody, though. Some groups of the population have seen their incomes rise faster than other groups, in particular during the last couple of decades.

In an influential report, the US Congressional Budget Office (CBO) in 2011 reported that 'between 1979 and 2007, income grew by: 275 percent for the top 1 percent of households; 65 percent for the next 19 percent; just under 40 percent for the next 60 percent; and 18 percent for the bottom 20 percent.' In other words, most of the benefits of economic growth during recent decades have helped the already well-off the most, whereas those with low incomes have only experienced small improvements. The increase in inequality is particularly pronounced in the US, i.e. the US is an outlier, but inequality has increased within many countries, even if not as dramatic as in the US.

One way to illustrate the increase in inequality in the US is provided in Figure 2.5. The figure shows developments in real incomes of US families since 1966. The figure plots the development in incomes for the bottom 20% of the income distribution and for the top 5%. Figure 2.5 tells a story of a dramatic change in the income distribution in the US. During the 1960s, and 1970s, real incomes of the lowest and highest earning families basically followed each other. The benefits of economic growth were equally shared across the population. Then something changed. The incomes of the highest-earning families started increasing faster than the incomes of the lowest-earning families, and they have continued to do so. In fact, the figure shows that real incomes of the 20% of US families with the lowest incomes have practically not increased during the last five decades. This implies

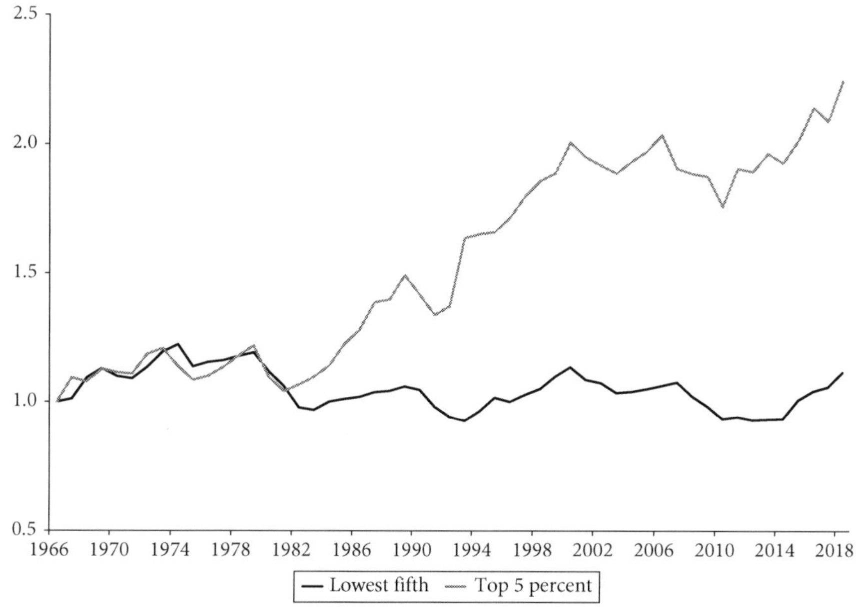

Figure 2.5 Developments in US family real incomes. The bottom 20% and top 5% of the income distribution. 1966–2018.
Data source: US Census Bureau.

that the purchasing power of the 20% of US families that earn the least in 2018 is more or less the same as the purchasing power of the 20% of US families that earned the least in 1966. These are not necessarily the same families (rather, most of them are not), but the developments nevertheless indicate that economic growth has not 'trickled down'. This is not because income in the US has not increased. It has increased a lot. But it has gone to that fraction of the population that already earns the most. For instance, the 5% of US families that earn the most have seen their incomes increase significantly. In 2018, the real incomes of the 5% highest-earning US families were more than twice as large as the real incomes of the highest-earning families in 1966.[5]

One can tell a similar story regarding wealth. Figure 2.6 shows the share of wealth held by the bottom 90% of the wealth distribution in the US and the share held by the top 0.1%. Around the late 1970s, the 90% of the US population who owned the least wealth owned around 40% of all wealth in the US. By 2013 that fraction had dropped to 28%. On the other hand, the 0.1% of the population

[5] Again, the 5% richest families in 2018 are not necessarily the same as the 5% richest families in 1966.

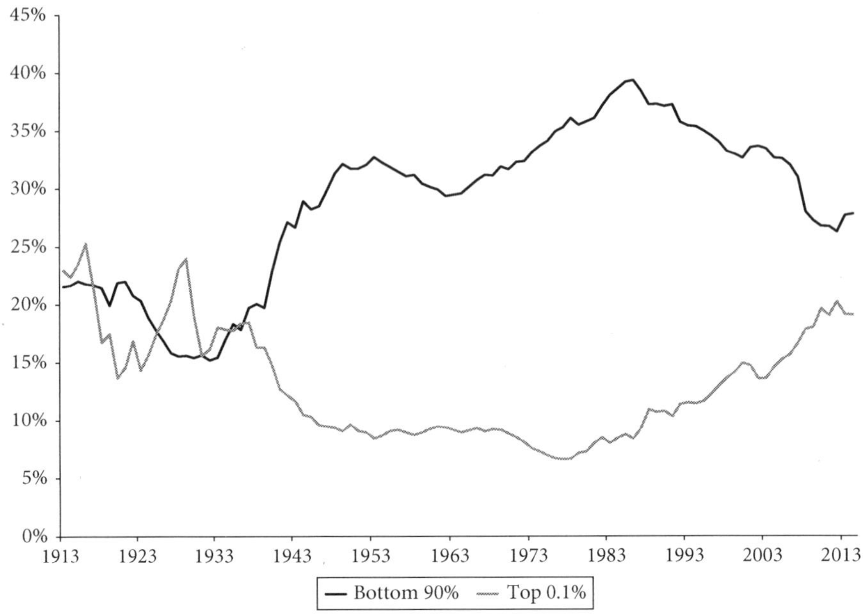

Figure 2.6 Wealth distribution in the US. 1913–2014.
Data source: Saez & Zucman (2016).

that had accumulated most wealth, increased their ownership fraction of total US wealth from around 7% in the late 1970s to around 20% in 2013. Wealth has been concentrated even more. Inequality has increased in the US, whether we look at income or wealth inequality.

It is important to stress that the US development is extreme. Inequality has increased in many countries during the last couple of decades, but generally considerably less than in the US, see OECD (2015).

Increases in inequality imply that the average tells less about the situation for the typical individual. When talking about income growth for the 'average' citizen, we should thus bear in mind that this income growth has been unevenly distributed during the last couple of decades, in particular in the US. It would, however, take us too far afield if we devote too large a fraction of the chapter to inequality. For this reason, we continue to look at averages in this chapter, but urge readers to bear in mind that inequality has increased in some countries over the last couple of decades. In spite of this cautioning remark, it is at the same time fair to conclude that most Americans have considerably better economic conditions today than Americans had 150 years ago as a result of long-term economic growth. We should not forget that either.

2.2.6 Logarithmic scale

The visual impression one gets from Figures 2.1 and 2.3 is that the line in the figures is more or less flat during the first decades and much steeper during the latter. I.e., one might—falsely—interpret this as evidence that GNP (Figure 2.1) and GNP per capita (Figure 2.3) have grown faster in recent decades. The reason why Figures 2.1 and 2.3 cheat the eye is due to compounding. A 5% increase from 100 gives 105, i.e. an increase of 5, whereas a 5% increase from 1,000 gives 1,050, an increase of 50. Hence, equal-sized percentage increases cheat the eye in graphs such as Figures 2.1 and 2.3 .

Figure 2.7 shows total US real GNP and real GNP per capita on a 'logarithmic scale with base 10'. Logarithmic scales provide better visual impressions of growth. An equal-sized move on the vertical logarithmic axis corresponds to an equal-sized percentage change. The vertical scale has an easy interpretation: When the series shown in the figure increases by ten, the underlying series has increased by a factor of ten. In Figure 2.7, this means that aggregate real US GNP had increased by a factor of ten in 1941, compared to its starting level in 1871, i.e. total production in the US was ten times larger in 1941 than it was in 1871. Likewise, in 2003, US

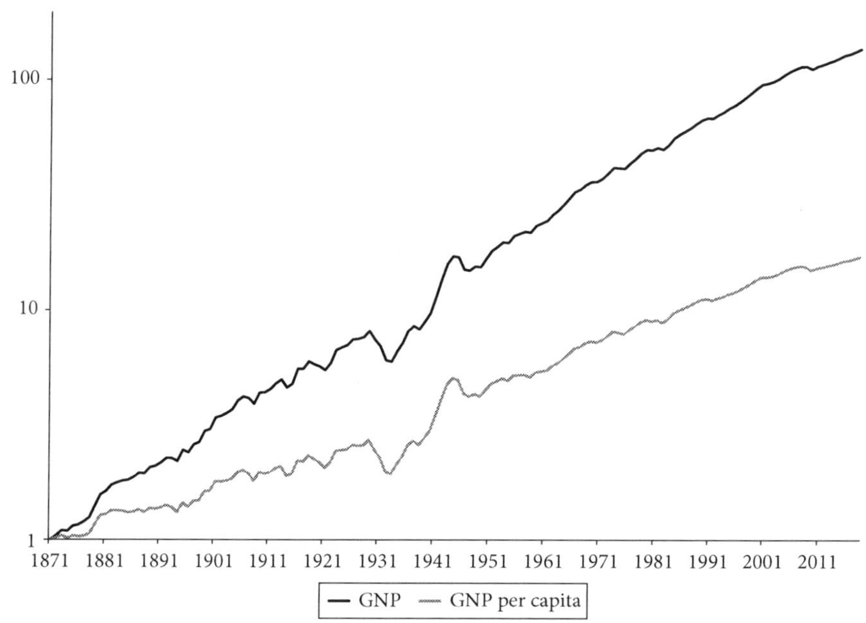

Figure 2.7 US real GNP and GNP per capita. Logarithm with base 10 scale. 1871–2018.

Data source: See Figures 2.1 and 2.2.

real GNP was 100 times larger than it was in 1871. In 1986, per capita GNP was ten times larger than it was in 1871.

When shown on a logarithmic scale, as in Figure 2.7, the graph rightly does not indicate that GNP grew faster in the later part of the sample. Logarithmic graphs better visualize long-term growth rates. This book will often use logarithmic scales.

Figure 2.7 paints a picture of remarkable steady growth over the last 150 years. Given this, the figure could lead one to expect that there always has and thus always will be economic growth. We will return to this in Chapter 14 when we discuss whether the rates of economic growth that we have been used to can be expected to continue.

2.2.7 Average annual growth numbers

US total income has increased by a factor of 135 from 1871 to 2018, the size of the US population is eight times larger in 2018 than it was in 1871, and the average American produce approximately 16 times more goods and services in 2018 than he/she did in 1871. These are overall long-run growth rates. Often, we are interested in the average annual growth rate over a certain period.

Over the full 1871–2018 period, the average annual growth rate of real US GNP is 3.5%. The average annual growth rate of the size of the US population is 1.4%. This implies that the average annual growth rate of real GNP per capita is 2.1%. In numbers that are easy to remember, over the last 150 years, US real GNP has increased by app. 3.5% per year on average and the US population has increased by app. 1.5% per year on average. This implies that the value of production of an average individual in the US has increased by app. 2% per year on average.

2.3 Annual growth rates of economic activity

The average annual long-run rate of growth in the US economy is 3.5%. This does not mean that GNP has increased by 3.5% every year. In fact, annual growth has been considerably below 3.5% in some years. In other years, it has been considerably above. We will return to a thorough description of these fluctuations in Part III of the book that deals with the business cycle. We can illustrate the fact that there are fluctuations in economic activity already here, though. Figure 2.8 does so. It shows the year-by-year growth rate of aggregate US GNP and per capital GNP.

Annual growth is volatile. There are years when economic activity grows a lot, such as 1941, when GNP grew by almost 19%. In just one year, total economic

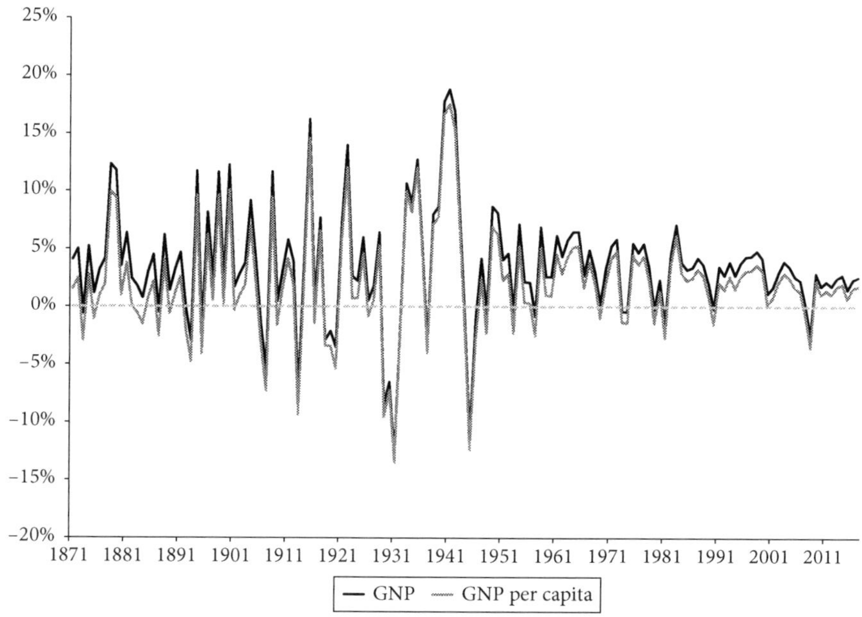

Figure 2.8 Annual growth rates of US aggregate real GNP and US GNP per capita. 1871–2018.

Data source: See Figures 2.1 and 2.2.

activity in the US increased by almost a fifth. More or less the same goes for years such as 1915 and 1922 when GNP increased by 16% and 14%, respectively. But there are also years such as 1931, when GNP contracted by 13.5%, and 1945 when it contracted by 12%. Annual growth rates fluctuate substantially.

Figure 2.8 demonstrates that since 1945 growth has been smoother, i.e. fluctuating less. The US has not experienced years with double-digit growth since 1945, but neither has it experienced years where the economy has contracted by double-digit figures. In Chapter 8, we return to explaining why growth has been smoother since 1945.

A clear conclusion from Figure 2.8 is that fluctuations in aggregate GNP and GNP per capita are very similar. This means that fluctuations in population growth are small compared to fluctuations in GDP growth.[6]

Table 2.1 shows average growth rates in per capita GNP during different subperiods. Since 1974, average per capita GNP growth has been 1.7% which is both below the long-term average of 2% growth per year and below the 1945–1973 average. Growth during the 1945–1973 period, i.e. between the end of WWII and

[6] Figure 2.2 also showed that population size develops smoothly over time.

Table 2.1 Average annual growth in US real per capita GNP during different subperiods

Period	Average growth
1871–2018	2.1%
1871–1945	2.2%
1946–2018	1.9%
1945–1973	2.2%
1974–2017	1.7%
1974–2007	2.1%
2007–2018	0.6%

the oil-price shocks of the early 1970s, was particularly high. During the last ten years, i.e. including and since the financial and economic crisis of 2007–2008, there has been almost no economic growth in per capita terms. This illustrates the cost of financial and economic crises. We explain what caused the financial crisis of 2008 in Chapter 12 where we also deal more explicitly with its costs. In Chapter 14, we discuss whether long-run growth will most likely be high or low going forward.

2.4 Long-run international economic growth

The conclusions drawn for the US economy largely describe other advanced economies, too. Barro & Ursua (2008) compiled an impressive data set covering long-term economic growth rates for a large set of countries. Barro & Ursua provide figures for per capita real GDP growth. As just mentioned, population growth is generally smooth, so the fluctuations in GDP and GDP per capita will generally be quiet similar. Figure 2.9 shows the average annual growth rates of real GDP per capita for a number of today's advanced economies.[7]

US GNP per capita has been growing with app. two percent per year on average over the last app. 150 years, as mentioned. US is not an outlier. The average annual per capital GDP growth rate across 15 countries for the 1900-2017 period is 2.1%. Two percent per capita GDP growth is a good rule-of-thumb for historical long-term real per capita economic growth.

There are large year-by-year swings in economic activity in all countries. Figure 2.10 shows for every year the growth rate of the country (out of the fifteen countries in Figure 2.9) with the highest growth rate that year, as well as the growth rate of

[7] Chapter 14 discusses outlooks for emerging and developing countries. For these countries, however, we do not have as good long-term historical data as for advanced economies.

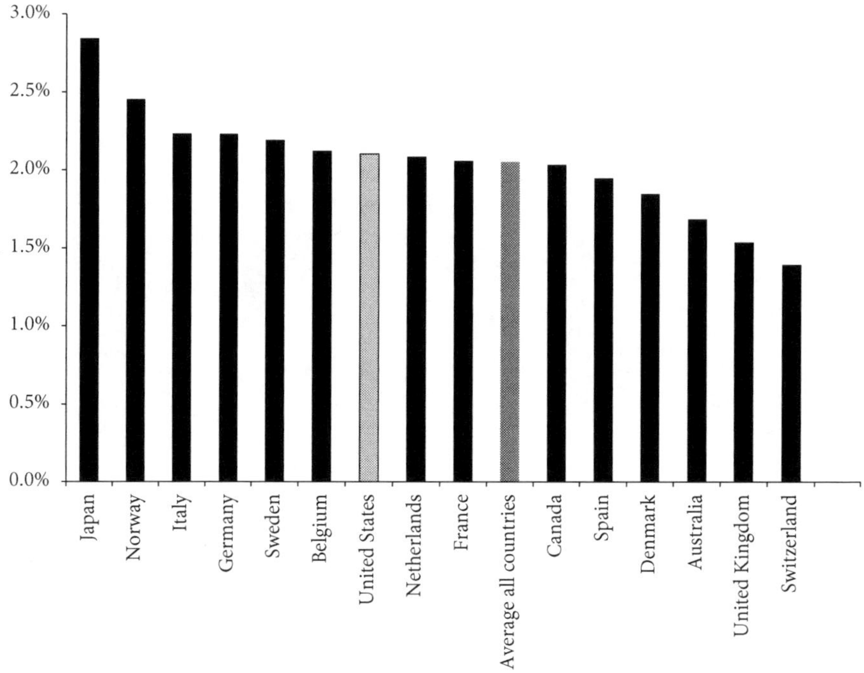

Figure 2.9 Average per capita real GDP growth rates for 15 countries. 1900–2017.
Data source: Barro & Ursua (2008).

the country with the lowest growth rate that year, and the average growth rate across countries. There are large fluctuations in annual GDP growth rates, and there are large differences between the growth rates of countries in different years, even when the long-run average growth rate for most countries is close to 2%. As the most extreme example, Germany saw its GDP per capita fall by 66% in 1944. Two thirds of economic activity was wiped out in one year. The second world war (WWII) was very costly for Germany. Netherlands saw theirs increase by 67% in 1945.

An important conclusion from Figure 2.10 is that cross-country differences in annual growth rates have been markedly smaller since 1945, and in particular since 1970s. Before 1945, the difference between the country with the highest and the lowest GDP growth rate in a given year generally exceeded ten percentage points, and sometimes exceeded twenty and thirty percentage points. The average difference between the country with the highest and the lowest GDP growth rate was 22% before 1945. After 1945, this difference has been seven percentage points, and since 1970 five. A big-picture conclusion, thus, is that fluctuations in economic

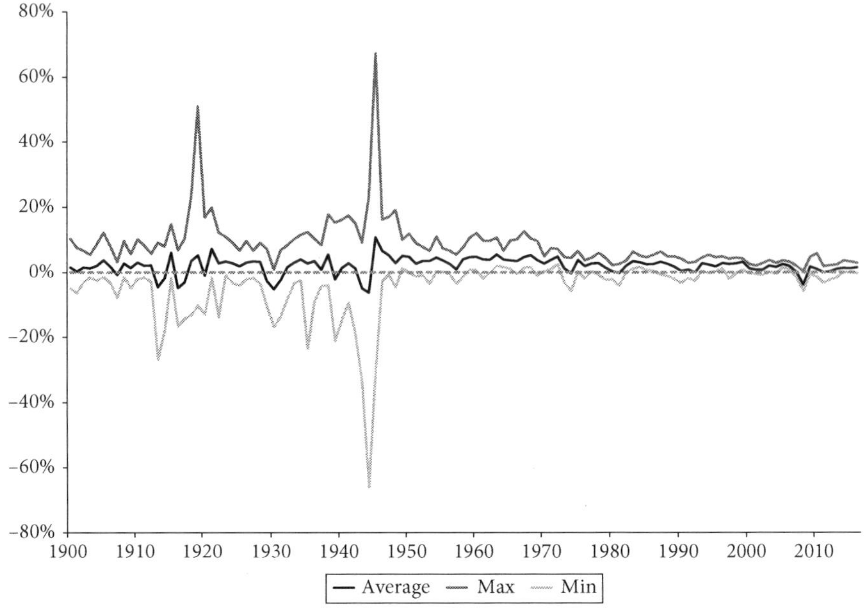

Figure 2.10 The country experiencing the highest and the lowest growth in a given year among a group of 15 countries, as well as the average growth rate across 15 countries.
Data source: Barro & Ursua (2008).

growth, country-by-country, have been reduced since 1970, and the differences between rates of economic growth across advanced economies have been reduced, too. There are still differences in growth rates across countries, but they are smaller than they were earlier in history. Economic growth has become smoother and more similar across advanced countries.

2.5 Checklist

This chapter has described developments in GDP over long periods. The main conclusions to remember are:

- US real GNP, a measure of total real economic activity in the US, has increased by 3.5% per year on average during the last app. 150 years. In 2018, the aggregate US economy is more than hundred times larger than it was in 1871.

- The size of the US population has increased by around 1.5% per year on average.
- Per capita real economic activity has grown by around 2% (= 3.5% − 1.5%) per year on average over the last app. 150 years.
- The US is not special. Today-advanced countries have seen their GDP per capita increase by around 2% per year on average over the last century or so. Two percent growth is a good number to remember when talking about long-run growth in real per capita economic activity.
- Not everybody has benefitted equally from economic growth. Inequality has increased within many countries, in particular during recent decades, and in particular in the US. In the US, the median household has seen only a little income growth during the last three to four decades. This is not because there has been no income growth, but because income growth has been captured by those who already earn the most. Inequality in wealth has also increased during the last couple of decades.
- In spite of increased inequality, most people in advanced economies live considerably better lives today than people did 150 years ago. Health and life expectancy correlate positively with income.
- GDP fluctuates considerably from year to year. Fluctuations in economic activity are smaller today than they were before 1945, though.
- Today, across advanced countries, GDP growth rates typically do not differ by more than five percentage points. Before 1945, cross-country differences in GDP growth sometimes exceeded twenty percentage points. Growth has become more stable and more similar across countries, compared to the period before 1945.
- Growth has been low since the mid–1970s, in particular during the last decade that includes the economic crisis of 2007–2008.

3

Long-run stock market returns

The previous chapter presented stylized facts regarding long-run economic growth. This chapter presents facts and concepts regarding long-run stock market returns.

The chapter starts out briefly defining stock returns. Like the previous chapter primarily dealt with real economic activity, this chapter (and, in fact, the remainder of this book) primarily deals with real stock market returns, i.e. returns after inflation. The reason is that real stock returns tell us how savings in stocks influence our future consumption possibilities.

Chapter 2 started looking at US economic activity before continuing to other countries. This chapter does the same, i.e. starts out looking at returns to US stocks before describing other stock markets. There are good reasons. The US stock market is the dominant stock market in the world, the largest in terms of market value, and the market for which we can get the best long-run data. In addition, it is easier to understand concepts when focusing on one country.

The chapter also introduces concepts that will be used repeatedly throughout the book, such as different kinds of averages (arithmetic and geometric), standard deviations, variances, and other important concepts in finance.

We measure stock-market returns by returns to broad stock-market indices, i.e. the general stock market. Chapter 13 describes and explains other kinds of stock-market indices, such as indices of value stocks, growth stocks, small cap stocks, etc.

This chapter presents stylized facts about long-run stock returns. It does not try to explain what generates these returns. This is the topic of subsequent chapters. In the next chapter, we break stock market returns into their underlying drivers. Part II of the book relates long-run stock returns to long-run economic growth.

3.1 Defining stock returns

Returns to stocks originate from two sources: The change in the stock price during the holding period and the dividend yield. The percentage increase (fall) in the stock price during the holding period is the capital gain (loss). The dividend received during the holding period relative to the price at which you bought the stock is the dividend yield:

From Main Street to Wall Street. Jesper Rangvid, Oxford University Press (2021). © Jesper Rangvid.
DOI: 10.1093/oso/9780198866404.003.0003

$$\text{Stock return} = \underbrace{\frac{\text{Price at which the stock is sold} - \text{Price at which the stock was bought}}{\text{Price at which the stock was bought}}}_{\text{Capital gain}} + \underbrace{\frac{\text{Dividends paid out during the holding period}}{\text{Price at which the stock was bought}}}_{\text{Dividend yield}}$$

For instance, if you bought the stock for USD 95, it is now worth USD 101, and we have received USD 4 in dividends during the holding period, the return is:

$$\frac{101-95}{95} + \frac{4}{95} = \underbrace{6.3\%}_{=\text{ Capital gain}} + \underbrace{4.2\%}_{=\text{ Dividend yield}} = 10.53\%.$$

We are often interested in a string of returns, i.e. a time series of returns. Continuing the example, imagine that the stock price increases to 105 during the next period, and dividends are USD 3 during that period. Returns during period two are $(105 + 3 - 101)/101 = 6.93\%$, as the stock price is 101 when entering the second period. When returns in two successive periods are 10.53% and 6.93%, the cumulative net return is $(1+0.1053)\cdot(1+0.0693)-1 = 18.2\%$. This assumes that dividends are reinvested.[1]

As in the previous chapter, we can deflate nominal stocks prices and dividends with a price index such that we measure stock prices and dividends in real terms, i.e. after inflation.

We deal with before-tax returns in this book. You have to pay taxes on your returns, but tax rules differ from country to country, and over time. We thus leave taxes aside.

3.2 Stock market returns over the long run

The long-run returns to the stock market have been truly breathtaking. Figure 3.1 shows how an investment of one dollar in the US stock market in 1871 would have developed over time in real terms, i.e. inflation-adjusted.[2] The figure

[1] To see the effect of reinvesting dividends, let us relate what we end up with after period two to what we invested in the beginning of period one (95). When we receive 4 in dividends during period one, we can use those to buy 4/101 of a stock when entering period two. This means that after two periods, we end up with $(105 + 3 + 105 \cdot (4/101) + 3 \cdot (4/101)) = 112.28$. We invested 95 in the beginning, i.e. over two periods we have obtained a return of $112.28/95 = 18.2\%$.

[2] The data for the US stock market used in this and many of the subsequent chapters are provided by Nobel Laureate Robert J. Shiller on his webpage. Thanks to the impressive work of Shiller, we now have freely-available data going back as far as 1871. The stock-market data cover what is today the S&P 500.

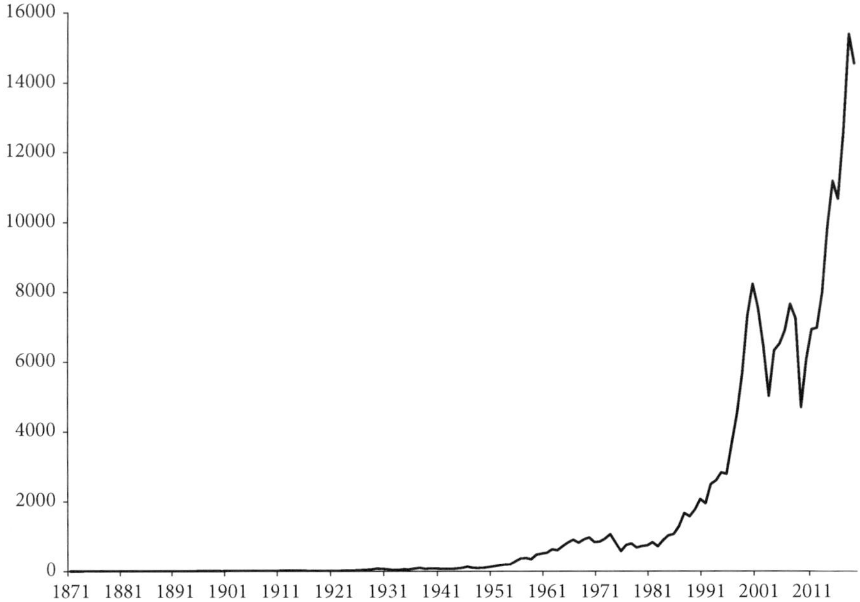

Figure 3.1 Development in the cumulative value of an investment of one dollar in the US stock market in 1871. Inflation-adjusted.
Data source: Webpage of Robert J. Shiller.

illustrates the development in the cumulative value of an investment strategy that invests one US dollar in the US stock market in January 1871 and reinvests all dividends. The figure represents the cumulative real return to the US stock market in the long run.

One dollar invested in the US stock market in 1871 would have turned into ten dollars in real terms in 1899, hundred dollars in 1937, thousand dollars in 1973, and surpassed ten thousand dollars in 2015. In January 2018, one dollar invested in 1871 had turned into app. 15,400 dollars. This is amazing.

The previous chapter showed that the US economy has increased by a factor of 130 since 1871. An investment in the US stock market has increased by a factor of 15,400. Stock market returns have by far exceeded the rate of economic growth. We return to this later.

Figure 3.1 plots the cumulative value of an investment of USD 1 in the US stock market in 1871. Like initial graphs in Chapter 2, Figure 3.1 seems to indicate that the stock market did not provide any return in the early part of the sample, but all returns were realized in the later part of the sample. This is not the case. We return to this in Section 3.3.

3.2.1 Arithmetic and geometric averages

How much has the US stock market returned per year on average? We now introduce a distinction between two kinds of averages: The arithmetic and the geometric average. Chapter 2 discussed average annual rates of growth in economic activity. In Chapter 2, it was not very important to distinguish between these two ways of calculating an average. Below, we explain why. When it comes to returns, it is important.

If calculating stock returns year-by-year and then taking the average, we find that the average annual real stock return over the 1871 to 2018 period is 8.3%. This is the *arithmetic* average annual real return.

The reason we need to distinguish between two kinds of averages is that the arithmetic average does not represent the value by which an investment in the stock market has increased year by year to reach its cumulative end-value. If—counterfactually—an investment of USD 1 in the stock market in 1871 had increased by 8.3% per year, it would have turned into USD 123,135 ($= 1.083^{147}$) after 147 years. This is obviously much more than the 15,400 that the investment strategy has in fact turned into. This might be confusing at first sight, but it is the reason why we calculate average returns in two different ways.

The *geometric* average, in contrast to the arithmetic average, tells us how much USD 1 invested in 1871 on average has increased year-by-year to reach the cumulative value of 15,400 in January 2018. The geometric average annual real return from the stock market has been 6.78% over the 1871 to 2018 period. An investment of USD 1 that increases 6.78% per year turns into 15,400 after 147 years. Box 3.1 explains how to calculate arithmetic and geometric average.

So, the arithmetic average is 8.3% and the geometric is 6.8% (6.78%). What might appear as a small difference between the geometric (6.8%) and the arithmetic (8.3%) average return has dramatic consequences when accumulated over long periods of time. A return of 6.8% per year over 147 years turns into 15,400, whereas 8.3% per year turns into more than 123,000. It is important that we make clear whether we are talking about arithmetic or geometric averages.

Arithmetic and geometric average returns are both fine and good, as they serve different purposes. Whether you should rely on the arithmetic or the geometric average depends on the question posed. If you want to know the average of a string of returns, you should use the arithmetic average. If you want to know how much the value of an investment has increased on average year-by-year, you should use the geometric average. This also means that if you use historical returns to forecast future returns, your best estimate of future returns will depend on the question asked. For instance, if you are asked about your best estimate for the return obtained

Box 3.1. Arithmetic vs. geometric average return

To see how the different averages are calculated, let us look at an example. A stock is worth USD 100 today. Over the next year, it returns a negative 50%. The following year, it returns a positive 50%. After two years, the value of the stock investment is thus USD 75 (= 100 · (1 – 0.5) · (1 + 0.5)). The investor has lost USD 25.

The *arithmetic* average return is (– 0.5 + 0.5)/2 = 0%. This is the average of the annual returns. This average, however, does not reveal that the investor has in fact lost money over the investment horizon.

The *geometric* average is $\sqrt{(1-0.5)\cdot(1+0.5)}-1=-13,4\%$. Two consecutive years with a negative return of 13.4% per year exactly shows that the value of the investment has fallen by 25% after two years. The geometric return shows the rate at which the investment has grown/fallen over the investment horizon on average.

over any single individual year during your forecast horizon, your answer is the arithmetic average. E.g., it is your answer to the question: 'Over the next ten years, what is your best estimate of the return in any one of these ten years?' If, on the other hand, you are asked about your best estimate of the rate at which your investment will grow over a longer period of time, your answer is the geometric average return.

Chapter 2 mentioned that the average annual growth rate of US real GNP from 1871 to 2018 is 3.5%. This is the arithmetic average. If calculating the geometric average, it turns out to be 3.4%. The difference between the geometric and the arithmetic average annual growth rate of GNP is small (3.5% versus 3.4%). The difference between the arithmetic (8.3%) and the geometric (6.8%) average stock return is larger. The reason why the difference between geometric and arithmetic average returns is larger than the difference between geometric and arithmetic average GNP growth rates is that stock returns are more volatile than GNP growth. The difference between a geometric and an arithmetic average increases with the volatility of the series that the averages are based upon. Something that is more volatile (such as returns) will see a larger difference between the arithmetic and geometric average.

A geometric average is approximately equal to the arithmetic average minus a half times its variance. Variance is explained in the next section. For now, just note that the variance of US real stocks returns from 1871 to 2018 is 3.1%. The arithmetic average is 8.3%, as mentioned. The geometric average is 6.8%. This is basically equal to $8.3\% - 0.5 \cdot 3.1\% = 6.8\%$. Geometric averages will always be lower than arithmetic averages (or the same, if variance is zero). Furthermore, the larger is the variance, the smaller is the geometric average compared to the arithmetic average. This also explains why the difference between the geometric and arithmetic average of GNP growth is so small. The variance of GNP growth is only 0.2%, i.e. half variance is 0.1%.

3.3 Volatility of returns

The arithmetic-average US annual real stock return is 8.3%. When zooming in on individual years, it is seldom that a return of 8.3% is realized, however. Returns fluctuate around 8.3%.

Figure 3.2 shows annual real stock returns from 1871 to 2018, year-by-year. Returns can be 30% one year, only to be negative the next year, and then positive again the year after. There is a lot of variation in annual returns.

We characterize the size of return fluctuations by 'standard deviation', or volatility, and its related concept 'variance'. Loosely speaking, standard deviation tells us

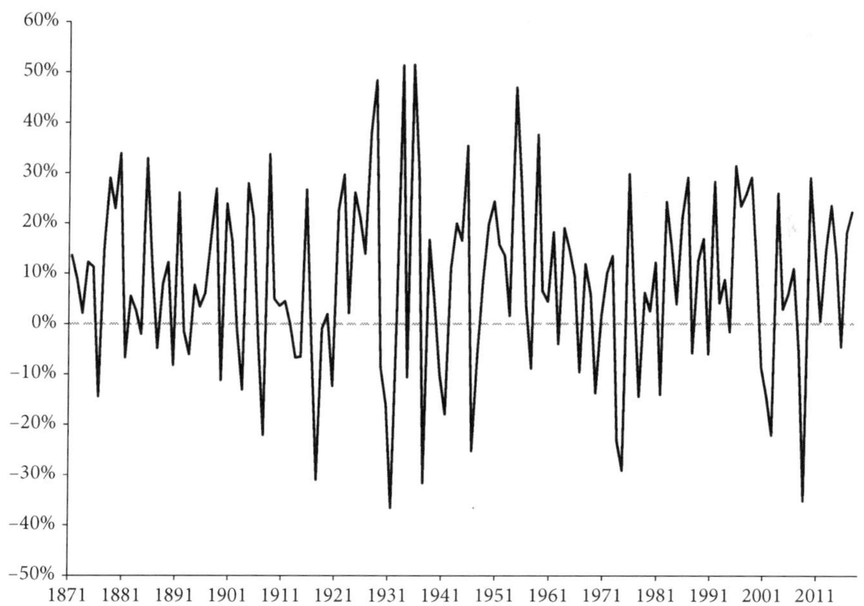

Figure 3.2 Annual real returns from US stocks. 1871–2018.
Data source: See Figure 3.1.

how far from the average return, returns typically are on average. Tongue twisting, but this is what it is. Box 3.2 describes how to calculate standard deviation.

The standard deviation of annual real returns over the period from 1871–2018 is 17.6%. The arithmetic average is 8.3%. Average return together with

Box 3.2. Variance and standard deviation

Standard deviation measures the average degree to which returns fluctuate around an average. Standard deviation is also called volatility. Volatility can be used to compare different investment strategies in terms of how much returns have fluctuated around their average, i.e. how risky is the investment strategy. A related concept is variance.

Variance is the average of each period's squared distance from the average returns; we square as returns in a given period can be above or below the average. For example, for a 7%, 5%, and 9% string of returns, the return in the first month (7%) is equal to the average (also 7%), so the difference is 0. The next month, the return is 2%-points below the average, so the squared difference from the average is $(0.05 - 0.07)^2 = 0.0004$. The third month, the return is 2%-points above the average, so the squared difference is $(0.09 - 0.07)^2 = 0.0004$. The variance is the average squared difference, or:

$$\frac{(0.07-0.07)^2+(0.05-0.07)^2+(0.09-0.07)^2}{3} = 0.000267 = 0.0267\%$$

Variance is thus an estimate of 'how far away returns on average have been from the average return, squared'.

If returns had been 7% in the first month, but 3% in the second, and 11% in the third, i.e. still a 7% average return, but with larger fluctuations, variance would have been 0.107%. Returns have in this case fluctuated more around their mean. This is reflected in a higher variance: variance is almost 5 times higher in this case. And, on the other hand, if the string of returns is 7%, 7%, and 7%, variance is zero, rightly indicating no variation around the average.

Often, we are interested in how far returns on average have been from their average, not how far away they have been in terms of the squared difference. We convert the squared difference to the same base by taking the square root of the variance. The result is standard deviation. Standard deviation is a common measure of volatility. It is also the measure of volatility we will use in this book.

Standard deviation for a 7%, 5%, and 9% string of returns is $\sqrt{0.000267} = 0.0163$, or 1.63%. For the 7%, 3%, and 11% string, it is 3.27%.

standard deviation tells us something about the range within which returns have fluctuated. It turns out that there is a 95% probability that returns have been within the range:

average return minus two times standard deviation
to
average return plus two times standard deviation.[3]

This means that over the 1871–2018 period, approximately 95% of all annual returns were within the range −26.2% to 42.8% (8.3% $\pm$ 1.96 $\cdot$ 17.6%). Similarly, if future returns behave like they have done throughout the last 147 years, we can expect 95% of all annual returns to fall within the −26.2% to 42.8% interval. Another way of expressing this is that the chance that returns will be lower than −26.2% in a given year is small at 2.5%, and the chance that returns will be higher than 42.8% in a given year is also only 2.5%.

Figure 3.3 plots annual returns in a histogram. The figure collects the number of years where annual returns fell within five-percentage points brackets, starting from the lowest annual real return of −36.5% in 1931. The figure reveals that annual returns typically fall within the 3.5% to 18.5% brackets, i.e. centered around the average. At the same time, the figure shows that there are a few years with extreme returns, either very low or very high. If history repeats itself, you are more likely to receive a return around the average than receiving an extremely high or an extremely low return. Returns are often said to be approximated by a 'normal distribution', see Box 3.3.

Box 3.3. Normal distribution

The normal distribution is fully characterized by two moments, the mean and the standard deviation. Figure 3.4 shows the theoretical normal distribution when the mean is 8.3% and standard deviation 17.6%, as in the data. When returns are normally distributed, they are symmetrically distributed around the mean, i.e. there are the same number of observations to the right of the mean as to the left. The height of the figure shows the number of observations. In a normal distribution, there are most observations at the mean and fewer observations further away from the mean. 2.5% of observations of returns are below −26.2% and 2.5% above 42.8%. Figure 3.4 is the theoretical counterpart of the actual distribution of returns that Figure 3.3 contains.

[3] The exact number is not 'two times' but 1.96 times, but this is for *feinschmeckers*.

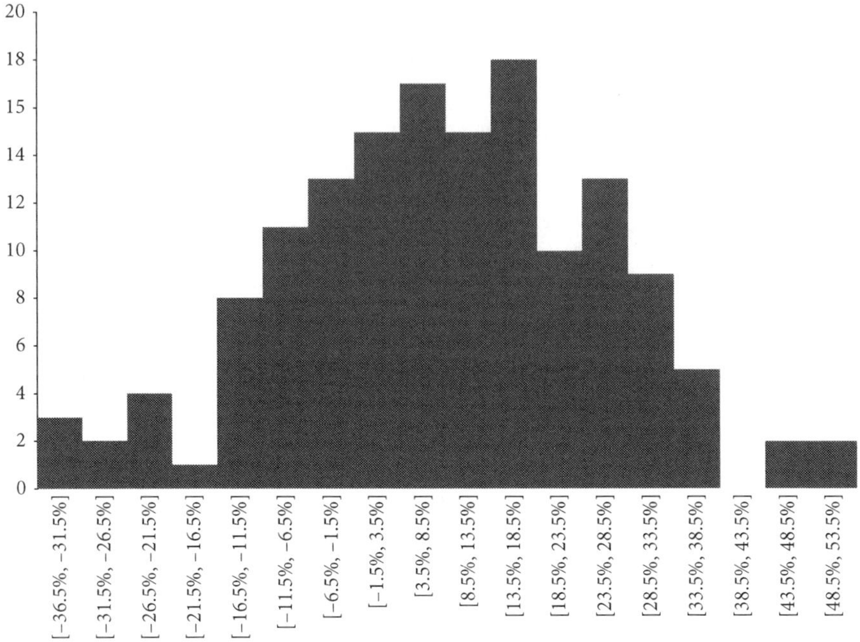

Figure 3.3 Histogram of real annual returns from US stocks. 1871–2018.
Data source: See Figure 3.1.

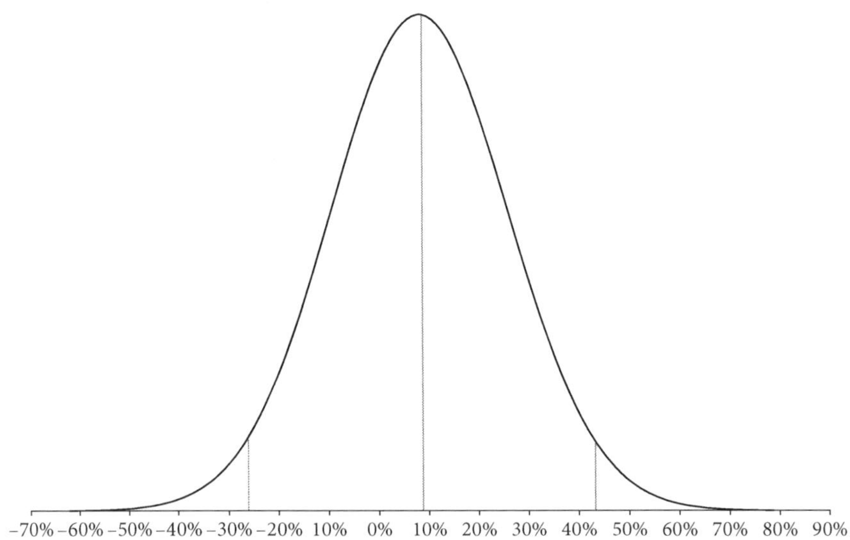

Figure 3.4 Normal distribution with mean = 8.3% and standard deviation = 17.6%.

Table 3.1 Averages (arithmetic) and standard deviation of US real returns

	1871–2018	1871–1945	1946–2018
Arithmetic mean	8.3%	8.3%	8.2%
Standard deviation	17.6%	18.7%	16.4%
Variance	3.1%	3.5%	2.7%
Arith. mean / Std.	0.47	0.45	0.50

Table 3.1 splits the 1871–2018 period into two almost equal-sized periods (before and after 1945) to see if there are differences across time. It appears that average returns and standard deviations of returns have been remarkable stable over these long periods. Average annual arithmetic returns have been around 8%, and the standard deviation around 16%–19%, both before and after 1945. When average annual real returns have been around 8% both before and after 1945, Figure 3.1 should be interpreted in this light, as also mentioned in Section 3.2.

Standard deviation is a measure of the riskiness of stocks. The larger is the standard deviation, the more returns will fluctuate around their average. Variance is standard deviation squared.

Sometimes we divide the average return by the standard deviation to find the risk-return ratio. As Table 3.1 shows, this is around 0.5. Also this is rather stable across these long periods.

3.3.1 Stock price and dividend volatility

Figure 3.5 shows annual changes in real stock prices and dividends, the two components making up stock returns. Stock prices are more volatile than dividends, in particular after 1945. Across the whole sample period, the standard deviation of annual stock-price changes is 17.4% versus 11.7% for dividends. For the post-1945 period, the difference is even larger: 16.7% volatility of capital gains versus 6.7% volatility of dividend growth. Since 1945, stock prices have fluctuated more than twice as much as underlying dividends.

Stock prices are sensitive to changes in expectations to future dividends and stock returns. To see this, let us refer to a well-known model for determining stock prices. Start from the fact that ownership of stocks gives right to dividends. Dividends are the payoffs we receive from holding stocks. The stock price today is given by the dividends we receive today plus the discounted value of all future dividends:

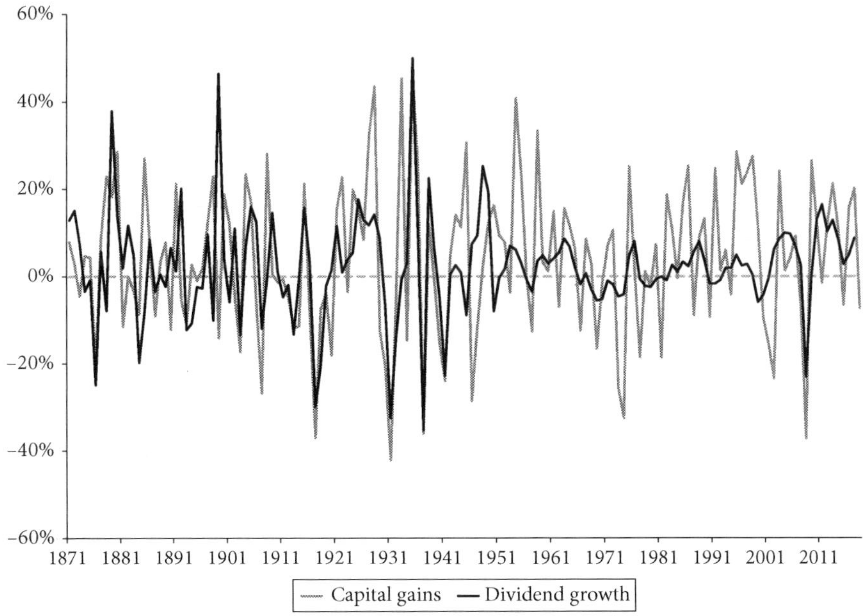

Figure 3.5 Annual changes in real stock prices and real dividends.
Data source: See Figure 3.1.

Stock price today =
Current dividends +
Expected dividends next period discounted back to today +
Expected dividends after two periods discounted back to today + ...

Professor Myron J. Gordon from the University of Toronto showed in the 1950s that if dividends grow by a constant factor from period to period, and the discount rate, and hence, expected returns are constant, too, then the stock price today becomes:[4]

$$\text{Stock price today} = \frac{\text{Current dividends}}{\text{Expected stock returns} - \text{Expected dividend growth}} \tag{3.1}$$

[4] In mathematical terms, this is written as $P_t = D_t + \frac{D_{t+1}}{1+r} + \frac{D_{t+2}}{(1+r)^2} + \frac{D_{t+3}}{(1+r)^3} + ... = \sum_{i=0}^{\infty} \frac{D_{t+i}}{(1+r)^i}$, where P_t is the stock price today, D_{t+i} represents dividends paid out in period $t + i$, r is the discount rate (the return on the stock), and $\sum_{i=0}^{\infty}$ means that we summarize over all future periods. When dividends grow by some constant growth rate g from period to period, another way to write this is $P_t = \sum_{i=0}^{\infty} \frac{D_t(1+g)^i}{(1+r)^i}$, where D_t are current dividends. Solving this gives that the stock price today is $P_t = \frac{D_t}{r-g}$. This is the 'Gordon growth formula'. The crucial assumption needed to derive this is that returns (r) and dividend growth rates (g) are constant.

Today, Eq. (3.1) is known as the 'Gordon growth formula'. Eq. (3.1) can be rearranged such that it shows stock prices in relation to dividends:

$$\frac{\text{Stock price today}}{\text{Current dividends}} = \frac{1}{\text{Expected stock returns} - \text{Expected dividend growth}}. \tag{3.2}$$

Equation (3.2) tells us that movements in the ratio of stock prices to dividends result from movements in expected returns or expected dividend growth, or both. We do not need large changes in expected returns or dividend growth to generate large stock price movements relative to dividends. For instance, if expected real stock returns are 3.5% and dividend growth 1.5%, then the stock price-dividend ratio is 50 (= 1/(0.035 − 0.015)). Imagine now that investors for some reason increase their expectations of returns, from 3.5% to 4.5%, i.e. by one percentage point. Nothing else happens. In this case, the stock-price dividend ratio drops to 33. This is a 34% drop in stock prices relative to dividends. Or, in other words, even if dividends drop, stock prices would drop by 33% more. Similarly, if expected dividend growth falls by half a percentage point, from 1.5% to 1% (and stock returns remain at their initial level of 3.5%), the stock-price dividend ratio drops to 40, i.e. a stock price drop 20% larger than any change in dividends. Investors do not need to change their expectations a lot before stock prices react wildly. This helps us understand why stock prices are so volatile. Stock prices are sensitive to changing market expectations.

So, stock prices react dramatically to small changes in expectations. But can we reconcile the magnitude of stock price changes (in relation to dividend changes) that we see in the data (Figure 3.5) with the extent to which expectations change? Academics have investigated this. In turns out that it is difficult to understand what underlying economic forces cause stock prices to fluctuate so wildly. In fact, academics find it so puzzling that they have even labelled it the 'excess volatility puzzle' (Shiller, 1981). We will return to this in Chapter 16. For the investor, two points should be remembered. First, stock prices fluctuate more than dividends. As a consequence, second, the main reason stock returns fluctuate wildly is that stock prices fluctuate wildly, not that dividends are volatile.

3.4 Compounding

Average annual GDP growth is 3.5%, as Chapter 2 showed. If something grows by 3.5% per year on average over 147 years, it in total increases by a factor of around 130 over 147 years. The geometric average real return from the stock market is basically double, 6.8%. If something increases by 6.8% per year on average, it increases by a factor of more than 15,000 over 147 years. This is obviously much more than the double of 130. These small calculations tell us something about the importance of the size of the annual growth rate/return for the cumulative value you end up with. The important concept here is compounding. Compounding implies that if you double the annual growth rate (or monthly, or quarterly, or whatever horizon you look at), you more than double the increase in the cumulative end-value of the investment, assuming all dividends are reinvested. A return of 2% per month makes an investment of USD 1 end at 1.0404 after two months, whereas a return of 4% per month (i.e., double of 2%) over two months makes an investment of USD 1 end at 1.0816 after two months. 0.0816 is more than double 0.0404. If such compounding takes place over many periods, the effect becomes dramatic.

Figure 3.6 shows the cumulative value after 50 periods when a growth rate is 1%, 2%, 4%, and 8% per period. 50 periods could be fifty years. It could represent the return to a young person who starts saving when she is 20 and who would like to know the value of her savings at retirement. If returns are 1% per year on average, USD 1 invested today turns into 1.63 after 50 years, i.e. an increase of 63%. If returns are 2% per year (twice 1%), USD 1 turns into 2.7 after 50 years. This is an increase of 160%. 160% is more than the double of 63%. Doubling the annual growth rates leads to more than a doubling of the cumulative value. If returns are 8% per year, USD 1 turns into USD 47 after 50 years. The annual growth rate matters a lot for how long-term savings evolve.

There is another way to illustrate the importance of compounding, 'doubling-time'. If the annual growth rate is 1%, it takes approximately 70 years to double the starting value. If you invest USD 1, and it increases by 1% per year, you have USD 2 after 70 years. When growth is 2% per year, it takes 36 years, with 4% growth 18 years, and with 8% annual growth it only takes 9 years to double the value of your investment. The 'Rule of 72' is an easy way to calculate 'doubling-time', see Box 3.4.

Box 3.4. Rule of 72

The 'rule of 72' is a simple way to find the time it takes for your investment to double in value. It turns out that doubling time is well-approximated by:

$$\text{Doubling time} = \frac{72}{\text{Rate of return}}.$$

For instance, if you expect the rate of return on your investment to be 4% per year, the doubling time is approximately equal to 72/4 = 18 years.

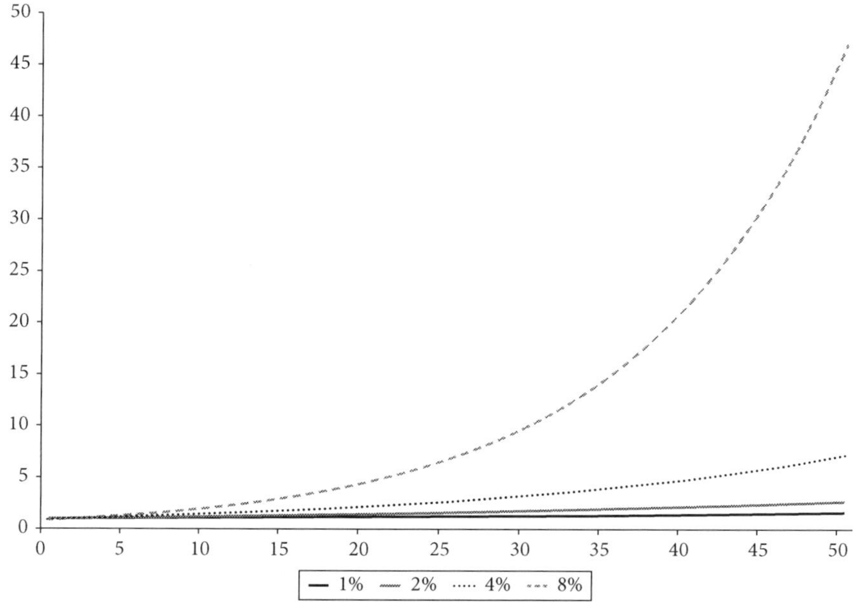

Figure 3.6 Development in cumulative value over 50 years of an investment of USD 1 in year 0. Different annual growth rates.

3.5 Risk-free rate and risk premium

Per definition, stock returns are given by the sum of capital gains and the dividend yield. Sometimes stock returns are expressed in a different way, though, as the risk-free rate plus a risk premium. The idea is that stock returns are risky, as explained in the previous section, and that investors require compensation for taking on this risk.

Imagine that you face two investment possibilities. In the first, you are sure to get a return of, say, 3% per year. Given that you are sure to receive 3% per year, this is a risk-free investment. The other investment, we imagine, will provide you with a return of either 0% or 6%, with equal probabilities. When probabilities are equal, the expected return on this investment is 3%, the same as the return from the risk-free investment. But, the realized return from the second investment is not going to be 3%. It will either be 0% or 6%. Hence, the second investment is risky.

Lots of research shows that investors dislike risk. We say that investors are risk averse. Risk aversion means that your loss of happiness (or, in the language of economists, your loss of utility) if you get a return of 0% instead of 3% exceeds your gain of happiness if your return is 6% instead of 3%.

When investors are risk averse, they will require a risk premium. When facing the choice between the risk-free investment yielding a return of 3% and the risky investment yielding the same *expected* return (3%), but uncertainty surrounds the return that will be realized, investors will refuse to buy the asset providing 3% expected, but risky, return. Why should you buy something that you expect will return 3% but may end up giving you nothing (and may end up giving you 6%), when you can buy something that gives you 3% for sure?[5] When investors will not buy the risky asset, its price fall. And when the price falls, expected return increases, perhaps to 5%, 6%, or whatever. In other words, if investors are willing to buy a risky asset instead of a risk-free asset, they will require a risk premium over and above the return of the risk-free asset. Returns on risky assets are returns on safe assets plus a risk premium.

What has been the historical risk-premium on stocks? To answer this, we must first find a risk-free investment. Government bonds have historically been practically risk-free. The US government pays back its creditors, i.e. investors in US government bonds are pretty sure to get their promised payments. If we consider annual returns, which we do here, the risk-free rate will be the yield on a one-year government bond. This is the one-year risk-free return in nominal terms. To calculate the historical risk-free real rate, we take a short interest rate and subtract annual inflation.[6]

The average annual real risk-free rate over the 1871–2018 period is 2.6% per year. It is risk-free over one year, but varies from year to year. The standard deviation is 6.5%. Table 3.2 shows the average real risk-free rate and equity risk-premium over different periods, together with associated standard deviations. The risk-free rate was higher before WWII, around 4% per year on average, versus 1% per year afterward.

When stocks have provided 8.3% per year (arithmetic average) and the risk-free rate is 2.6% per year, the risk premium—the extra return investors have obtained

Table 3.2 Risk-free real interest rate and risk premium

	1871–2018	1871–1945	1946–2018
Risk-free rate	2.6%	4.0%	1.1%
Standard deviation	6.5%	8.2%	3.5%
Risk premium	5.7%	4.3%	7.1%
Standard deviation	18.1%	19.9%	15.6%

[5] You might say that if you have an equal chance of gaining 6% or nothing you are indifferent between this and the 3% risk-free return. But this is only if you are risk-neutral, i.e. do not care about risk. Very few of us, if any, do not care about risk.

[6] Future inflation is risky, but we disregard inflation risk here.

over and above the risk-free rate—has been 5.7% per year on average. Investors have been handsomely rewarded for taking on the extra risk that the stock market contains in comparison to putting their money in a risk-free investment. The risk premium has been even higher after WWII. The risk-premium is approximately as volatile as stock returns, i.e. the risk premium fluctuates considerably from year to year.

In Chapter 7, we return to the question of whether we can explain the size of the equity risk premium. For now, we simply notice that there is a considerably premium to be earned if investing in risky stocks instead of safe bonds.

3.6 Are stocks safer in the long run?

Two conclusions emerge from the discussion so far: (i) Over very long periods, average real stock returns are reasonably stable (Table 3.1 showed that average annual returns from 1871–1945 has been the same as average annual returns from 1945–2018), but also that (ii) fluctuations in stock returns are large from year to year. These important conclusions will reappear later in the book: In the short run, there is a lot of uncertainty about what we can expect stocks to return. In the long run, stock returns are more smooth. Do we need to go to a 70-year holding period before we feel on safer grounds?

Figure 3.7 shows the arithmetic average annual real returns investors have obtained from holdings stocks over successive ten-year holding periods. I.e., for instance, what was the average annual real return from 1871–1881? The figure reveals that this was 12.7%, the very first point in the figure. What was the annual real return from 1872–1882? 10.5%. And so on. The last ten-year period for which we can calculate the ten-year return is 2008–2018. One can do the same type of calculations for successive thirty-year holding periods. Figure 3.8 shows the results. Furthermore, Figure 3.2 showed annual returns themselves.

The first thing to notice when comparing Figures 3.2, 3.7 and 3.8 is that the range of fluctuations narrows when extending the holding period. Annual returns (Figure 3.2) fluctuate between −30% to +40%. Average annual returns over ten-year holding periods have fluctuated between −3% and +17%, as Figure 3.7 shows, whereas Figure 3.8 shows that average annual returns over thirty-year holdings periods have fluctuated between +3% and +10%. Hence, the longer the holding period, the smaller the magnitude of fluctuations. If history is any guidance, this indicates that stocks returns are less risky in the long run. This might also indicate that we can forecast returns with greater precision when our holding period is longer. We return to this in Part V.

Another interesting feature appearing from Figures 3.2, 3.7, and 3.8 is that we have a higher chance of seeing our investment growing when we have a

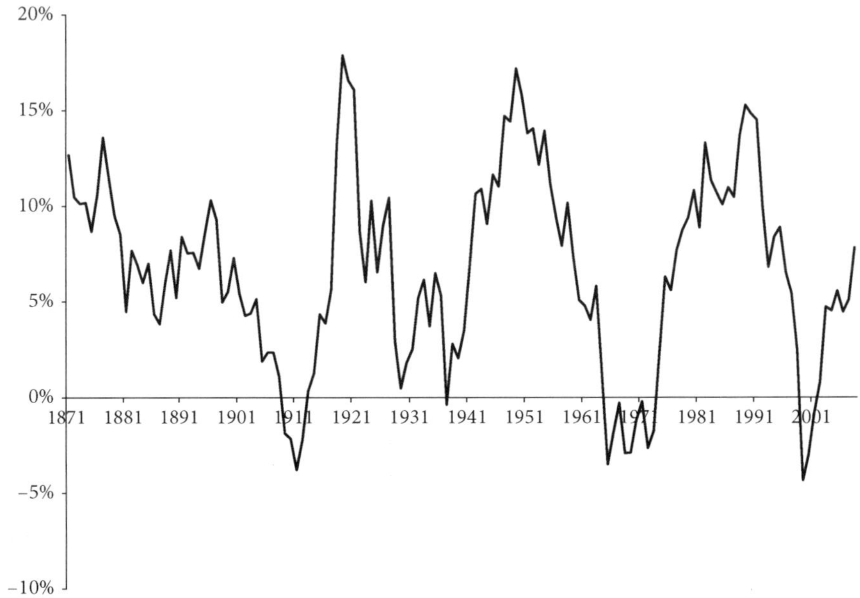

Figure 3.7 Average annual real returns obtained over 10-year holdings periods.
Data source: See Figure 3.1.

longer investment horizon. Figure 3.2 shows that there are many individual years when annual returns were negative. Figure 3.8 shows that there is no 30-year period that has resulted in a negative average annual return. Following up on this, Figure 3.9 shows the number of years when the average annual return has been negative for different investment horizons. For instance, what has been the number of years with negative one-year returns during the whole sample period from 1871–2018? Figure 3.9 shows that there were 45 individual years with negative returns. For the two-year investment horizon, what has been the number of years with negative average (over two years) annual returns, etc.?

Figure 3.9 tells a clear story: The longer the investment horizons, the more likely it is that investors will see positive average returns on their investment. During 1871–2018, there are 147 one-year holding periods. When 45 individual years saw negative returns, 45/147 = 30.6% of the one-year investment periods yielded a negative return. The (unconditional) likelihood of obtaining a negative return if holding stocks for one year is 30.6%. Consider then two-year holding periods. There were 35 two-year holding periods for which the average annual real return was negative. There were in total 146 two-year holding periods during 1871–2018. This implies that the unconditional likelihood of obtaining a negative average annual return over a two-year holding period is 24.0%. For, e.g., the ten-year holding period, the probability of obtaining a negative average (over ten

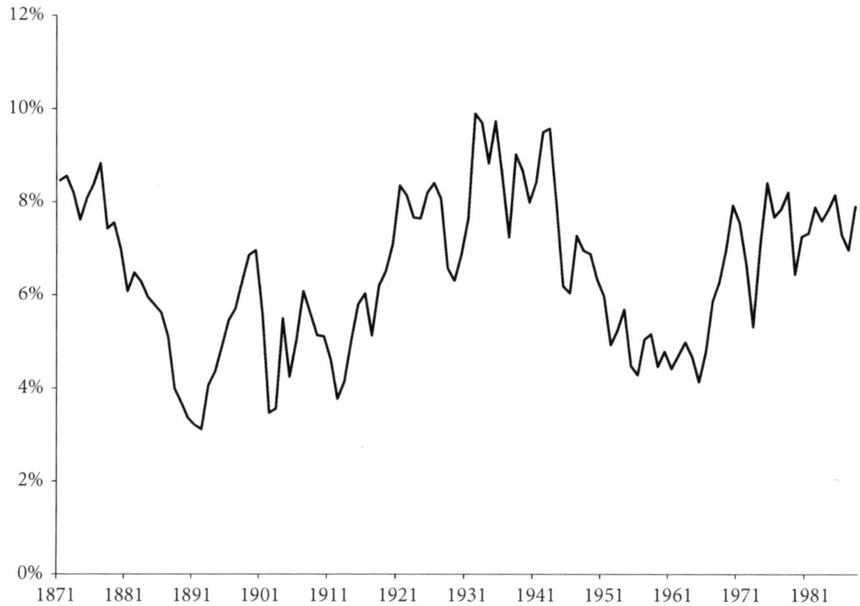

Figure 3.8 Average annual real returns obtained over 30-year holdings periods.
Data source: See Figure 3.1.

years) annual real return is 12.3%. The reduction in the probability of observing a negative average annual return declines almost monotonically with the investment horizon. For investment horizons exceeding 20 years, the average annual return has been positive in all years. Figures like Figure 3.9 have given rise to the famous investment advice that stocks are 'safer in the long run' (Siegel, 2014). There are academic quarrels about the precision with which one can make such a statement, but the impression one gets after seeing a picture like Figure 3.9 is that it seems to be a good rule-of-thumb.[7]

3.7 International returns

The US stock market has performed well compared to other stock markets, but it is not an extreme outlier. Table 3.3 shows this.[8] It contains average annual real returns, standard deviations, and the risk-return trade-off (arithmetic

[7] Pastor and Stambaugh (2012), for instance, question whether stocks really are safer in the long run.
[8] The international return data used here are from the impressive freely-available Jordà, Knoll, Kuvshinov, Schularick and Taylor (2019) dataset. German returns for 1922 and 1923 are extreme due to the German hyperinflation during these years. These two years have been disregarded for Germany.

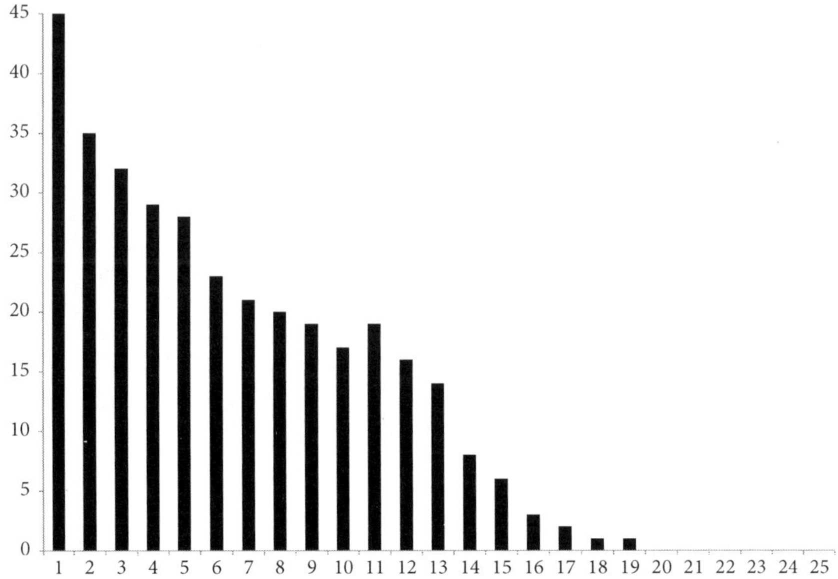

Figure 3.9 Number of years with negative returns for different investment horizons.

Data source: See Figure 3.1.

mean divided by standard deviation) for a number of countries. The period is 1900–2016.

For the 1900–2016 period, the average annual real stock return across all markets is 3.6% (average of the geometric averages). For the US, it is 6.6% over this 1900–2016 period.[9] The US has generated the highest historic average annual return, but Australia is close behind at 6.4%, as is Denmark with 6.0% and Sweden with 5.7%. I.e., the US stock market has returned the most, but others have performed almost as well. Volatility was around 18.5% for the US stock market. Table 3.3 shows that the average volatility across countries is 23.2%, i.e. in same ballpark.

There are large differences between stock markets, though. Some markets have delivered negative average real returns, with, e.g., the French stock market returning a negative 0.5% per year on average in real terms. These differences are of first order. 6.6% per year (US return) accumulated over 116 years turns USD 1 into USD 1,659 whereas a negative return of −0.5% per year (French return) leaves you with 55 cents today if you 116 years ago invested USD 1.

[9] The international data cover the 1900–2016 period, i.e. a slightly shorter period than the 1871–2018 period that the US data used in the earlier parts of the chapter cover.

Table 3.3 International annual real returns. Averages and volatility. 1900–2016

	Means			
	Arithmetic	Geometric	Stand. dev.	Mean/Std.
Australia	7.8%	6.4%	16.8%	46.4%
Belgium	5.7%	3.0%	23.4%	24.2%
Denmark	7.5%	6.0%	17.7%	42.4%
Finland	8.7%	4.9%	29.6%	29.5%
France	2.1%	−0.5%	23.7%	9.0%
Germany	7.3%	1.8%	32.8%	22.3%
Italy	4.5%	1.4%	25.4%	17.9%
Japan	6.9%	2.7%	27.1%	25.5%
Netherlands	7.0%	4.9%	21.4%	32.6%
Norway	5.6%	3.6%	20.7%	27.0%
Portugal	3.3%	−0.3%	27.5%	12.0%
Spain	5.8%	3.8%	21.0%	27.5%
Sweden	7.8%	5.7%	21.0%	37.3%
Switzerland	6.4%	4.8%	18.6%	34.4%
UK	6.8%	5.0%	20.1%	34.0%
USA	8.3%	6.6%	18.5%	44.6%
Average	6.2%	3.6%	23.2%	28.0%

Across the stock markets in Table 3.3, a stock market has on average experienced negative real annual returns 43 years. There are 116 years during 1900–2016. The unconditional likelihood of running into a year with negative returns has been 43/116 = 37.1% over this period across all countries. For ten-year holding periods, the likelihood of obtaining a negative average annual return (over ten years) has been 17%. For the 20-year holding period, it is 9.6%. For the 30-year holding period, it is 5.2%. We conclude that the likelihood of obtaining a negative average annual return declines with the holding period, also internationally. Basically, many of the features characterizing the US stock market, characterize other stocks markets from developed countries, too.

3.8 Checklist

This chapter has described developments in real stock returns over long periods. The main conclusions to remember are:

- In real terms, i.e. after accounting for inflation, US stocks have returned around 8.3% per year on average over the last approximately 150 years. This is the arithmetic average real return.
- The geometric average annual real return—which shows how the value of an investment in stocks has accumulated year by year on average—is 6.8% over

the same period. This means that an initial investment of USD 1 turns into 15,400 after 147 years when dividends are reinvested.

- Returns from stocks are volatile on a year-to-year basis. It is common to see, e.g., returns of 20% in one year followed by −10% next year. We measure fluctuations in stock returns by their volatilities. Historically, these have been around 18%.
- Volatility of US returns is more or less the same during the post-1945 and the pre-1945 periods. The same goes for average returns.
- Stock returns can also be expressed as a risk-free rate plus a risk premium. Over the 1871–2018 period, the risk-free rate has been around 2.5% per year on average and the risk-premium—the compensation that investors have obtained from investing in the risky stock market compared to the safe bond market—around 5% per year.
- Fluctuations of returns are lower when holding stocks for longer. In this sense, stocks appear 'safer in the long run'. The likelihood of having experienced a negative annual return from US stocks over the 1871–2018 period is around 30%. The likelihood of experiencing a ten-year holding period where annual returns on average have been negative is only slightly above 10%.
- To a large extent, these conclusions describe international returns as well, though the US stock market has performed well in an international comparison.

4
Drivers of stock returns

The previous chapter showed that stock returns are defined as the sum of capital gains and the dividend yield. This chapter demonstrates how we can decompose stock returns into underlying fundamental drivers. The decomposition will help us understanding how stock returns develop over time and what causes this development. It will also be useful when we—later in the book (Part V)—deal with expectations to future stock returns.

The chapter will show that stock returns can be decomposed into three underlying 'drivers':

1. **Yield**: Dividends paid out in relation to the stock price. This is the dividend yield. Yield is sometimes also called 'income'.
2. **Growth**: The growth rate of a fundamental. The 'fundamental' can be earnings of companies, dividends, GDP, or the like.
3. **Valuation change**: Growth in the ratio of stock prices to the fundamental. Stock price divided by a fundamental is also called the stock-price multiple. Or, sometimes simply the 'valuation' of stocks. Its change enters the decomposition.

The chapter starts out describing how to derive and understand the decomposition of stock returns. It then examines the relative importance of each driver for stock returns.

An important take-away is that we get somewhat different conclusions about the relative importance of each of the drivers when we analyze stock returns over very long horizons (many decades) compared to shorter horizons such as a decade or shorter. We will see that changes in valuations contribute only little to stock returns over very long horizons, but are of first-order importance for stock returns over shorter horizons. This insight will be important when we in Part V deal with expectations to future stock returns.

When valuation changes cancel out in the long run, long-run returns will be given as the sum of the first two components. In simple terms, in the long run, stock returns are 'yield plus growth'.

From Main Street to Wall Street. Jesper Rangvid, Oxford University Press (2021). © Jesper Rangvid.
DOI: 10.1093/oso/9780198866404.003.0004

4.1 Decomposing stock returns

The purpose of this section is to explain how stock returns can be decomposed as:

$$\text{Stock returns} = \text{yield} + \text{growth} + \text{valuation change} + \text{small term}.$$

The 'small term' in the decomposition is typically disregarded. It is small, as described below, i.e. typically not important for the return we receive. For this reason, we leave it aside, such that returns are approximated by:

$$\text{Stock returns} = \text{yield} + \text{growth} + \text{valuation change}.$$

The first component of the decomposition is **yield**. Yield is the dividend yield, i.e. dividends paid out during the holding period relative to the stock price at the beginning of the holding period.

The second component is **growth**. This is the rate of growth (over the holding period) of a fundamental. The 'fundamental' can be any variable that stock prices are expected to follow in the long run (in technical terms, can be expected to mean-revert towards. More on this later). This could be dividends, earnings of firms, profits, book value of assets, or GDP when talking about the entire stock market.

The third component is **valuation change**. This is the rate of change in the stock-price multiple. The stock-price multiple is the ratio of stock prices to the fundamental. We call the stock-price multiple the 'valuation of stocks', as it shows how much we have to pay for one unit of the fundamental, for instance how much we have to pay for one dollar of dividends. For instance, if the stock price is 95 in the beginning of the holding period and 4 was paid out in dividends during the holding period (the example from the previous chapter), we have paid 95/4 = 23.75 for each dollar of dividends. If, later, the stock-price dividend multiple has increased to 26, there has been growth in the stock-price multiple. We also say that the valuation of the stock has increased. In simple terms, stocks have become 'more expensive'. Box 4.1 explains how to do the decomposition.

Splitting stock returns into different components means 'decomposing' stock returns into its underlying drives. If the dividend yield is 4%, growth 2%, and growth in the stock-price multiple 1%, the return on the stock has been 4% + 2% + 1% = 7%. In this case, the most important contributor to return was yield. Yield contributed 4%/7% = 57% of the return. The remaining 43% was due to growth (29% = 2%/7%) and valuation change (14% = 1%/7%). The decomposition tells us about the relative importance of the different drivers of returns.

Box 4.1. Example of the decomposition

Imagine that we bought the stock for 95, it is now worth 101, and dividends paid out per share during the holding period are 4. This is the same example as in the previous chapter. Returns are 10.5%.

Imagine now that dividends paid out during the next period amount to 4.3 per share. There has been growth in dividends per share, from 4 to 4.3, i.e. growth has been $\left(\frac{4.3-4}{4}\right) = 7.5\%$. The stock-price multiple has also changed, from 95/4 = 23.8 to 101/4.3 = 23.5. Investors buy one dollar of dividends at a lower price next period. In this example, returns are approximately equal to

$$\underbrace{\left(\frac{4}{95}\right)}_{\text{Dividend yield}} + \underbrace{\left(\frac{4.3-4}{4}\right)}_{\text{Growth}} + \underbrace{\left(\frac{101/4.3-95/4}{95/4}\right)}_{\text{Valuation change}} = 4.2\% + 7.5\% - 1.1\% = 10.6\%$$

The decomposition provides a return that is very close to the actual return, 10.6% versus the actual return of 10.5%. The difference is due to a small adjustment term. The adjustment term is given as:

$$\underbrace{\left(\frac{4.3-4}{4}\right)\left(\frac{101/4.3-95/4}{95/4}\right)}_{\text{Product of growth and valuation change}} = -0.1\%$$

Subtracting 0.1% from 10.6% gives the actual return of 10.5%. Given that this adjustment term is typically small, in this case a tenth of a percentage point, we often disregard it. We say that returns are approximately equal to yield + growth + valuation change.

There is nothing magic about this calculation. It follows directly from the definition of stock returns. It is a mathematical identity.

If your holding period is, say, ten years, you typically annualize returns and their drivers.

4.2 Empirically decomposing stock returns

Figure 4.1 presents the results from decomposing US real stock returns using dividends as the fundamental.[1] Growth is the growth rate of real dividends and

[1] Decompositions such as these presented here were originally developed by Grinold and Kroner (2002) and Ibbotson and Chen (2003), and have more recently been used by Straehl and Ibbotson (2017).

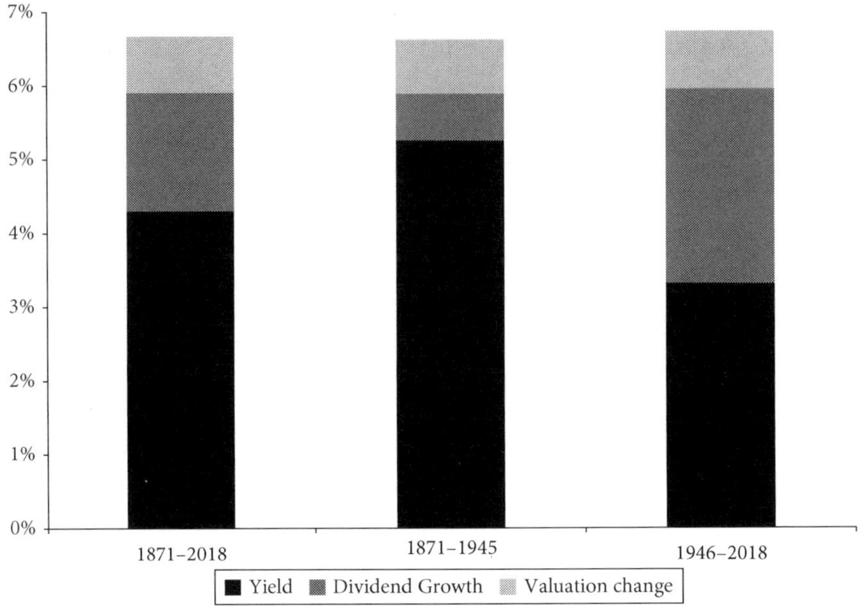

Figure 4.1 Decomposing US real stock returns into underlying drivers. Dividends as fundamental. 1871–2018.

Data source: See Figure 3.1.

valuation change is the change in the stock price to dividends multiple. The decomposition is done for every single year from 1871 to 2018. The figure presents the averages across all years, as well as averages across subperiods before, and after, 1945. The figure shows the faction of historical stock returns due to yield, growth, and valuation change.

As we know from the previous chapter, the average annual (geometric) return over the full 1871–2018 period is 6.8%. Figure 4.1 shows that yield has contributed the larger part of stock returns. The average dividend yield has been 4.4%. This means that yield has contributed two-thirds of returns, 4.4%/6.8% = 65%, on average over the 1871–2018 period. For the subperiod before 1945, yields accounted for an even larger fraction of returns, almost 80%. After 1945, the average dividend yield is 3.3%. Returns have been 6.8% after 1945, too, i.e. yields have accounted for a smaller fraction of returns after 1945, though still around 50%.

Figure 4.1 reveals that valuation changes do not influence average long-run returns to any great extent. In other words, there are no big movements in stock-price multiples over many years. Over the full 1871–2018 period, the fraction of average returns due to gains—or losses—from valuation changes is only around 10%.

When yield accounts for around two-thirds of returns and changes in stock-price multiples for around 10%, growth accounts for the remaining app. 25%. Growth has been more important for returns since 1945. Since 1945, almost half of the average stock return has been due to growth.

4.3 Decomposing returns over shorter holding periods

When measured over the very long run, valuation changes do not matter much for the return investors obtain, as just shown. This conclusion changes dramatically when we look at shorter horizons. To illustrate this, Table 4.1 shows results from the decomposition of US real stock returns for each decade from 1871 through 2018, i.e. the average annual yield, growth, and valuation change during the different decades. For each decade, the sum of the three components—dividend yield, growth in fundamentals, and growth in the stock-price multiple—equals returns. As an example, average annual real returns were 10% during 1871–1880, coming from an average 6% dividend yield, 3.3% annual growth in dividends, and 0.7% annual growth in the price-dividend multiple.

Returns are volatile, as also noticed in the previous chapter. There have been decades where the average annual real return exceeded 15%, and there have been decades where the average annual return was negative.

Table 4.1 Decomposing average annual US real stock returns decade by decade, as well as components of annual real stock returns. Yield is the dividend yield. Growth is the growth rate of real dividends. VC is valuation change, i.e. the change in the stock-price dividend multiple

	Return	Yield	Growth	VC
1871–1880	10.0%	6.0%	3.3%	0.7%
1881–1890	8.2%	4.9%	0.2%	3.0%
1891–1900	5.1%	4.2%	3.2%	−2.3%
1901–1910	7.0%	4.3%	2.7%	0.1%
1911–1920	−2.2%	5.8%	−6.4%	−1.6%
1921–1930	15.3%	5.1%	8.3%	1.9%
1931–1940	1.8%	5.4%	−2.6%	−1.0%
1941–1950	3.4%	5.5%	2.0%	−4.1%
1951–1960	14.7%	4.5%	1.2%	8.9%
1961–1970	5.0%	3.1%	1.9%	0.0%
1971–1980	−1.2%	4.0%	−1.1%	−4.1%
1981–1990	10.3%	4.0%	2.4%	3.9%
1991–2000	13.8%	2.3%	0.3%	11.2%
2001–2010	−3.1%	1.8%	1.1%	−5.9%
2011–2018	10.4%	2.0%	9.3%	−0.8%
Stand. Dev.	6.0%	1.4%	3.8%	4.7%

Section 4.2 concluded that yields account for the larger fraction of returns over long periods. Do yields also account for the shorter-run volatility of returns? No. Yields have been rather stable. Yields have fluctuated in the 2%-6% range, whereas returns, as mentioned, have fluctuated in the −3% to 15% range.

When returns are volatile, but yields are smooth, either growth or valuation changes, or both, must be volatile. It turns out that the volatility of valuation changes is high. Average annual valuation changes have been as high as 11% per year (the 1991–2001 decade), and as low as −6% per year (the 2001–2010 decade). A large part of the volatility of stock returns over ten-year periods comes from fluctuations in valuation changes.

We can illustrate these conclusions graphically. Figure 4.2 shows how yields have moved throughout time. The figure shows rolling averages of yields over the preceding decade. The main point is that yields are rather stable, i.e. do not change a lot from year to year. Movements in yields thus cannot account for the volatility of returns, as mentioned. An additional feature appearing from Figure 4.2 is that dividend yields have fallen considerably throughout the last 30+ years. We return to this stylized fact in the next chapter.

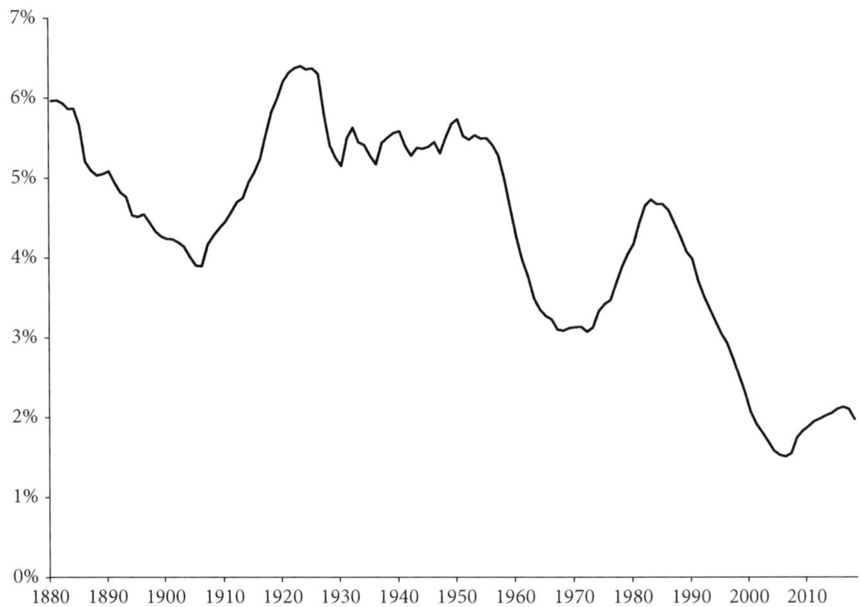

Figure 4.2 Dividend yield of US stocks. Rolling averages (ten-year periods) of annual dividend yields.

Data source: See Figure 3.1.

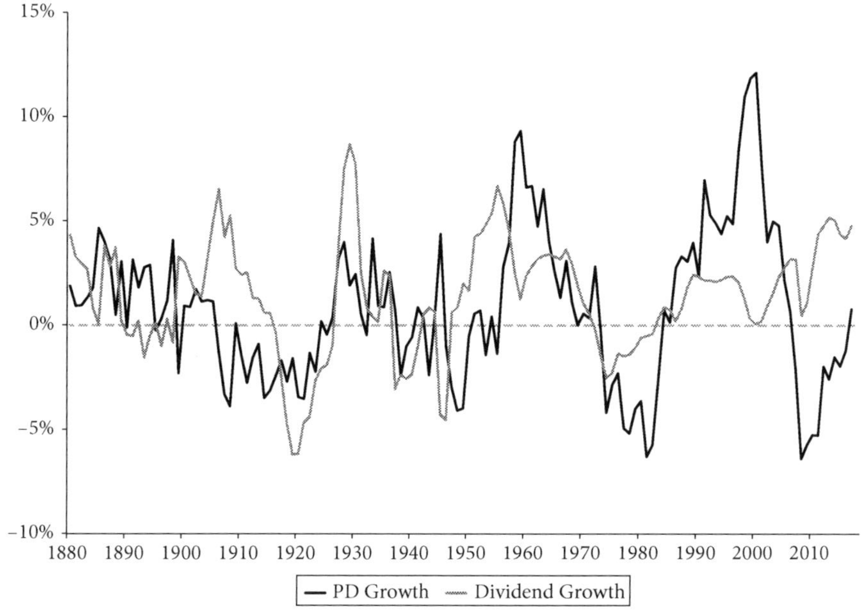

Figure 4.3 Annual growth in the stock-price dividend multiple (PD growth) and real dividends of US stocks. Ten-year rolling averages.
Data source: See Figure 3.1.

Figure 4.3 shows rolling ten-year averages of annual changes in stock price-dividend multiples and dividend growth rates. There are wild swings in valuations, in particular since 1945. Changes in stock-price valuations contributed positively to returns in the beginning of the sample period, during the 1930s, the 1960s, and the 1990s. Changes in valuations, on the other hand, harmed returns during the 1920s, 1940s–1950s, and 1970s–1980s. Figure 4.3 also shows that valuation changes fluctuate around zero. This means that over the long run, i.e. when averaging across all these valuation changes, they amount to more or less zero. This is why valuation changes contribute only little to returns over multiple decades, as shown in Figure 4.1. The conclusion is that valuation changes are of first-order importance for returns on the shorter run but almost cancel out in the long run.

Dividend growth rates are also volatile, in particular prior to 1945. Since 1945, dividend growth has not be not as volatile as valuation changes. This means that since 1945 shorter-run fluctuations in returns are mainly due to fluctuations in stock-price multiples, i.e. the valuation of stocks.

4.3.1 Why do valuation changes cancel out in the long run?

Over shorter horizons, valuation changes are important for movements in returns, but over longer horizons, they cancel out. The reason is that stock prices mean-revert towards dividends. But why, then, do stock prices mean-revert?

Mean reversion means that stock prices and dividends follow the same long-term growth path. There are good explanations. We cannot expect stock prices to soar indefinitely, compared to some fundamental determinant of stock prices, such as dividends. If the valuation of stocks soars, i.e. stock prices become very high relative to fundamentals, investors will at some point say 'now stocks are too expensive'. When investors view stocks as too expensive, investors will refuse to buy at the offered price and stock prices fall. This pushes the stock price back towards the underlying fundamental, i.e. valuations drop. And, conversely when investors view stocks as a good deal. We call this tendency for valuations to return to some 'reasonable' level mean-reversion. When prices have a tendency to return to their fundamental level, the average change in valuations over the long run is zero. In the next chapter, we examine in more detail the extent to which stock prices follow underlying fundamentals in the long run.

4.4 Other fundamentals

The decomposition is a mathematical reorganization of returns, meaning that the decomposition in itself does not specify what the fundamental is. Economic theory gives some hints, though. A fundamental driver of stocks is a variable that stocks are expected to mean-revert towards, i.e. follow in the long run. Box 4.2 shows how to do the decomposition using earnings as the 'fundamental'.

Stocks are issued by private firms. Investors buy stocks because they hope to receive dividends. Hence, dividends are a natural candidate for a fundamental that determines stock prices in the long run. As discussed more thoroughly in the next chapter, a firm can in the long run only pay out dividends if it is profitable. Profits of firms are called earnings. Earnings could be another fundamental. The aggregate earnings of all firms in the economy relate to aggregate economic activity. If the economy performs well, earnings of firms will improve. GDP is a third candidate for a fundamental when we look at the aggregate stock market. The next chapter examines these relations in more detail. The conclusions of this chapter—that yields matter much for returns and that valuation changes cancel out in the long run but are important in the shorter run—remain if using these other measures of the 'fundamental'.

Box 4.2. Earnings as fundamental

Using the example from Section 4.1, imagine that we want to calculate the decomposition of stock returns using earnings as fundamental. The stock was still bought at 95 and sold for 101, but imagine that earnings per share during the holding period are 5 and during the next period 6. In this case, the decomposition yields:

$$\underbrace{\left(\frac{4}{95}\right)}_{\text{Dividend yield}} + \underbrace{\left(\frac{5.5-5}{5}\right)}_{\text{Growth}} + \underbrace{\left(\frac{101/6-95/5}{95/5}\right)}_{\text{Valuation change}} + \underbrace{\left(\frac{6-5}{5}\right)\left(\frac{101/6-95/5}{95/5}\right)}_{\text{Product of growth and valuation change}}$$

$$= 10.5\%.$$

Returns are the same and the dividend yield is the same, but growth and valuation change have changed. The adjustment term is small in this case, too, at 0.3%, i.e. will typically be ignored.

An important point to notice when doing the decomposition is that there needs to be consistency. If you decide to examine the stock-price to earnings multiple as your favourite measure of the valuation of stocks, growth should be growth in earnings. If you decide to look at the stock-price to dividends multiple, growth is growth in dividends. This follows from the fact that the decomposition is based on a rewriting of returns. For the mathematical identity to hold, there needs to be consistency between your choice of growth and valuation variable.

4.5 Checklist

This chapter has described how stock returns can be decomposed into their underlying drivers. The main conclusions to remember are:

- The return from stocks is the sum of:
  1. **Yield**: Dividends paid out in relation to the stock price.
  2. **Growth**: The growth rate of an underlying fundamental.
  3. **Valuation change**: The growth rate of a stock-price multiple, i.e. growth in the ratio of the stock price to its fundamental.

- This is a generic decomposition. It holds for the return on a single stock, for the return on the market, for any holding period, i.e. for any stock return.
- The fundamental is a variable that stock prices are expected to mean-revert towards, such as earnings, dividends, profits in firms, book value, GDP (when we look at the entire stock market), etc. This chapter has illustrated the decomposition of stock returns using dividends as the fundamental.
- Yield is important for returns. Historically, yields have accounted for around two thirds of returns. Since 1945, growth has been almost as important as yield.
- Valuation changes are mean-reverting, implying that fluctuations in valuations cancel out in the very long run. When the average long-run change in valuations is close to zero, valuation changes are not very important for stock returns in the long run.
- Stock returns are volatile in the short run. Yields are rather stable in the short run. Since 1945, growth has been rather stable, too.
- When stock returns are volatile in the short run, but yields and growth rates are not, it logically follows from our decomposition that valuation changes must account for a large fraction of shorter-run fluctuations in stock returns ('short' here refers to holding periods of e.g., ten years, but less than many decades).
- We conclude that valuation changes are important for fluctuations in shorter-horizon returns but not for long-run returns.

PART II

ECONOMIC GROWTH AND STOCK RETURNS IN THE LONG RUN

5
Economic growth and drivers of stock returns

Chapter 4 demonstrated that yields account for around half of returns since 1945 while growth and valuation change account for the remainder. In the very long run, valuation changes cancel out and returns become yield plus growth. In the shorter run, valuation changes matter a great deal and returns become yield plus growth plus valuation change.

The previous chapter demonstrated the decomposition but did not explain what causes the underlying drivers to change. This is the topic of the current chapter. It examines how yields, growth, and valuation changes relate to economic activity in the long run.

The chapter begins by discussing reasons why there could be a relation between drivers of stock returns and economic growth in the first place. The underlying idea is simple. Economies grow in the long run, as Chapter 2 showed. When the level of economic activity increases, production of firms increases. This should tend to increase profits of firms. Firm value is determined by profits, as profits determine dividends. Thus, firm value increases when profits increase. Returns should increase.

A number of factors might affect these relations, however. First, in order for long-run economic growth to benefit stockholders, it must benefit listed firms. A significant part of economic growth is due to the creation of entrepreneurial and non-listed firms. This creates a wedge, also called dilution, between economic growth and growth in earnings of listed firms. In addition, within listed firms, the distribution of earnings between employees and owners matter. If growth in earnings is primarily used to compensate employees, owners, i.e. stock holders, benefit less from economic growth. Furthermore, for stock owners, what matters is the earnings and dividends generated per outstanding share. Share buybacks influence the number of outstanding shares. The chapter discusses these issues, and examines them using US data. The next chapter examines the international evidence.

The main conclusions of this chapter are as follows. In the US, growth in aggregate earnings has lined up with growth in total economic activity. When the economy improves, earnings of firms go up. Furthermore, GNP per capita

From Main Street to Wall Street. Jesper Rangvid, Oxford University Press (2021). © Jesper Rangvid.
DOI: 10.1093/oso/9780198866404.003.0005

has grown alongside stock prices, dividends per share, and earnings per share in the long run, i.e. growth in GNP per capita (that is closely related to the concept of productivity) has been a long-run driver of stock prices. Dilution, i.e. the part of growth in economic activity that does not lead to growth in earnings per share, was large before 1945, but has been reduced since then, most likely because the rate of creation of new firms has fallen. Since the 1980s, firms pay out a lower fraction of their earnings as dividends. Instead of using earnings to pay out dividends, firms have used earnings to buy back shares. When firms buy back shares, the number of outstanding shares decreases. This supports share prices, helping raising them in relation to earnings per share and dividends per share. It is not only buybacks that have caused share prices to rise in relation to earnings and dividends since the 1980s, however, as the aggregate value of the stock market has outpaced aggregate GDP during recent decades, too. The chapter ends by discussing potential explanations.

5.1 The theory

Fama & French (2002) present a framework that is useful for understanding how long-run average returns relate to long-run growth in underlying fundamentals. This section reviews the Fama & French ideas and relates them to the framework developed in the previous chapter.

Returns during any holding period are defined as the sum of capital gains and the dividend yield:

$$\text{Stock return} = \text{capital gain} + \text{dividend yield.}$$

Fama & French (2002) note that the *average* returns obtained over a number of years equals the sum of the *average* capital gain and the *average* dividend yield obtained over those same years. Let us call long-run average returns for $A(returns)$, average capital gain for $A(capital\ gain)$ and the average dividend yield $A(dividend\ yield)$. The starting point for our analysis can thus be stated as:

$$A(returns) = A(capital\ gain) + A(dividend\ yield). \tag{5.1}$$

5.1.1 The relation between capital gains and dividend growth

The previous chapter showed that the change in the stock-price dividend multiple is close to zero when measured over long periods of time. This means that when stock prices and dividends grow over time, the ratio of the two (the stock price-dividend multiple) will not change a lot in the long run. In the previous chapter, we said that the stock-price dividend multiple is mean-reverting. If stock prices have been growing faster than dividends for some time, the growth rate of stock prices will subsequently drop, or the growth rate of dividends will increase, such that stock prices and dividends approach each other again. When stock prices and dividends follow each other in the long run, the average growth rate of stock prices will equal the average growth rate of dividends. This implies that average returns can be written as the average growth rate of dividends plus the average dividend yield, i.e.:

$$A(returns) = A(dividend\ growth) + A(dividend\ yield). \tag{5.2}$$

This is a second way of expressing long-run average returns. In relation to Eq. (5.1), the long-run average growth rate of stock prices has been replaced by the long-run average growth rate of dividends. The assumption needed to go from Eq. (5.1) to Eq. (5.2) is that the long-run average growth rates of stock prices and dividends are more or less the same.

5.1.2 The relation between dividend growth and earnings growth

Dividends are ultimately determined by the earnings of firms. If firms are not profitable in the long run, they cannot pay out dividends in the long run. When dividends are determined by earnings, a natural hypothesis is that dividends and earnings will increase by more or less the same rate in the long run. If earnings and dividends grow by more or less the same rate in the long run, the long-run dividends-earnings ratio will be more or less constant. This is the same as saying that the fraction of earnings that firms pay out as dividends fluctuates around a constant in the long run.

There are periods when firms pay either less in dividends (as a fraction of earnings) or more. This could be because firms make investments and use a larger fraction of current and retained earnings to pay for those investments. In this case, the firm pays out less dividends in the short run. When the investments subsequently generate earnings, firms will pay out more dividends. Furthermore, the firm might have retained earnings it can use to pay out dividends now, creating a wedge between current dividends and earnings. However, these retained earnings are savings that the firm previously decided not to pay out, but pay out now. Also, the firm might borrow to pay out dividends in the short run. It cannot continuously finance dividends with loans, however, as loans need to be paid back some day. In the short run, thus, earnings and dividends might differ. In the long run, earnings will relate to dividends. This means that a reasonable hypothesis is that the fraction of earnings paid out as dividends fluctuates around a constant in the long run.

When describing stock returns, we look at the price of a share and the dividends paid out per share. Similarly, what matters here are earnings per share. Our hypothesis is that earnings per share grow by more or less the same rate as dividends per share in the long run. We now have a third way of expressing average returns. Average returns are given by average growth rates of earnings plus the average dividend yield:

$$A(returns) = A(earnings\ growth) + A(dividend\ yield). \tag{5.3}$$

The assumption needed to go from Eq. (5.2) to Eq. (5.3) is that the long-run average growth rates of dividends and earnings are more or less the same.

5.1.3 The relation between earnings growth and economic growth

Total earnings by all firms in an economy cannot exceed GDP, as total profits cannot exceed total income in an economy. This means that long-run growth in GDP places an upper bound on long-run growth in aggregate earnings. We can have individual years where the growth rate (not the level, but the growth rate) of earnings can exceed the growth rate of GDP, but this cannot continue indefinitely.

As just explained, there are good reasons to believe that long-run growth rates of dividends per share and earnings per share are more or less similar. In the same spirit, we propose the hypothesis that the long-run average growth rate of earnings per share and the long-run average growth rate of economic activity are more or less similar. As mentioned in the Introduction to this chapter, a number of assumptions needs to be fulfilled for this to be the case. In the chapter, we will discuss these assumptions. For now, this hypothesis leads to the fourth expression of average returns: average returns are equal to the average growth rate of economic activity plus the average dividend yield:

$$A(returns) = A(economic\ growth) + A(dividend\ yield). \tag{5.4}$$

The assumption needed to go from Eq. (5.3) to Eq. (5.4) is that the long-run average growth rates of earnings and economic activity are more or less the same.[1]

In total, and subject to a number of assumptions, we have four ways of expressing average long-run returns:

[1] If all theses assumptions are fulfilled, i.e. if dividends per share, earnings per share, and GDP are all growing by more or less the same rate on average, we can substitute the dividend yield by the earnings yield and/or GDP scaled by the stock price.

1. Average returns equal the average dividend yield plus the average capital gain. This is the definition of average returns. The following relations depend on assumptions.
2. Average returns equal the average dividend yield plus the average growth rate of dividends per share. For this to be true, stock prices and dividends must grow by the same rate.
3. Average returns equal the average dividend yield plus the average growth rate of earnings per share. For this to be true, dividends and earnings must grow by the same rate.
4. Average returns equal the average dividend yield plus the average growth rate of economic output. For this to be true, earnings and economic output must grow by the same rate.

The fourth way of expression average returns—average returns equal to average economic growth plus average dividend yield—is particularly interesting for this book, as it, if it holds in the data, implies a relation between average long-run returns and the average growth rate of economic activity. The next section examines whether these assumptions are fulfilled in US data.

5.2 Empirical evidence

The chain of economic relationships underlying the four relations is as follows. When the economy grows, it has the potential to improve the earnings of firms. Earnings of firms obviously matter for how much firms can pay out in dividends. Dividends in turn matter for share prices, as share prices are based on expected dividends. The chain of relations thus is:

Economic activity impacts the earnings of firms.

⇓

Earnings of firms influence dividends.

⇓

Dividends impact share prices.

⇓

Dividends and share prices determine returns.

5.2.1 Economic growth and growth in earnings

The first part of the chain relates economic growth to growth in earnings. We can split the relation between growth in earnings and growth in economic activity in

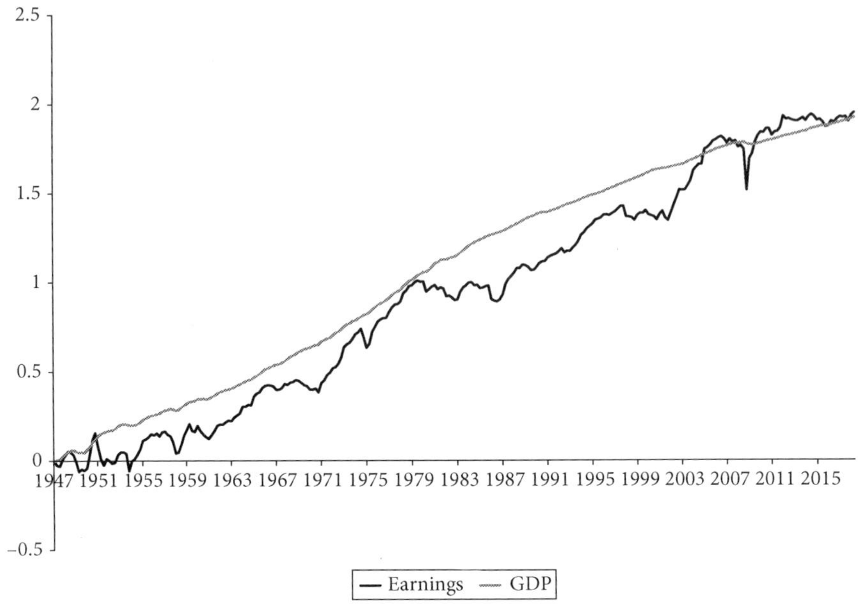

Figure 5.1 After-tax aggregate earnings in the United States and GDP. 1947–2018.
Data source: FRED.

two parts: the relation between total earnings in the economy and total output in the economy, and the relation between earnings per share and output.

The first empirical stylized fact we uncover is that—in the long run—total earnings in the economy follow total economic activity. For the US, there are data on all firms' earnings (i.e. total earnings) since 1947. Figure 5.1 plots quarterly aggregate after-tax profits (earnings) of US firms during 1947–2018 alongside quarterly GDP, both normalized to zero in 1947. Two conclusions emerge. First, in the long run, total earnings and GDP follow each other well. This is the most important conclusion here. Second, earnings are more volatile than GDP. Sometimes earnings constitute a larger part of GDP, sometimes a smaller, i.e. earnings fluctuate around the long-run growth path of economic activity. This means that earnings mean-revert towards GDP. This is illustrated in Figure 5.2 where the earnings-to-GDP ratio is shown. On average, total earnings in the economy have amounted to 6.5% of total economic activity (GDP). There are fluctuations, though, from a low of 3.3% in 1986 to a high of 10.8% in 2012. Over time, however, the earnings-to-GDP ratio returns to its average. This means that the average growth rates of earnings and GDP should be similar. Over the total period from 1947–2018, the average growth rates of earnings and GDP have been basically identical at 1.6% (nominal) per quarter. The empirical evidence clearly

Figure 5.2 Earnings-to-GDP ratio.
Data source: FRED.

supports the hypothesis that the long-run growth rates of total earnings and GDP are similar.

Earnings of private firms can be due to earnings of listed and non-listed firms. What matters for stock returns are earnings of listed firms. In other words, if aggregate earnings in the economy increase, but the earnings of listed companies do not, stock holders, i.e. the owners of listed companies, will not benefit and stock prices will not increase. It turns out that a significant part of economic growth is due to the activities of entrepreneurial and other non-listed firms. One day, if and when these firms get listed, their earnings will benefit shareholders, but until then the profits of non-listed companies will cause a wedge between the total earnings in the economy and the earnings of listed companies. If total earnings in the economy follow GDP, as we have just seen, but earnings of listed companies differ from earnings of non-listed companies, aggregate total earnings and earnings-per-share will also differ.

What do the data tell us? Table 5.1 shows the average annual growth rates of real GNP and real earnings per share for the full 1871–2018 sample, as well as the subperiods before and after 1945. Real GNP has grown by 3.5% per year on average over the 1871–2018 period, as mentioned in Chapter 2. This is considerably higher

Table 5.1 Averages (geometric) of growth in real GNP, real stock market returns, real dividend growth, and real earnings growth. US data 1871–2018

	1871–2018	1871–1945	1946–2018
GNP growth	3.5%	3.7%	3.1%
Growth in earnings per share	1.9%	0.6%	3.3%
Dilution	1.5%	3.1%	−0.2%
Growth in dividends per share	1.6%	0.6%	2.6%
Growth in GNP per capita	2.1%	2.2%	1.9%
Capital gain	2.4%	1.4%	3.4%

than the growth rate of real earnings per share. Real earnings per share have grown by 1.9% per year on average. Bernstein & Arnott (2003) call this 1.5%-point difference between GDP growth and growth in earnings-per share 'dilution'. 'Dilution' is the part of economic growth that shareholders do not reap.

An interesting conclusion arising from Table 5.1 is that dilution seems to have been a thing of the past. The wedge between the growth rate of GNP and earnings per share was a wobbling 3.1%-points before 1945, but has been reduced to basically zero since 1945. In other words, since 1945, growth in aggregate economic activity has been closer related to growth in earnings per share than before 1945.

One potential reason why dilution has been reduced over time is that fewer new businesses are created. Figure 5.3 shows the annual entry rate of new firms in the US, i.e. the number of new establishments (firms) in any given year divided by the total number of establishments in that year. In 1977, there were app. 700,000 start-ups. In 2016, there were also around 700,000 new establishments. At the same time, however, the number of total establishments in the US has increased from 4 million to app. 7 million. The rate of creation of new firms has fallen. In fact, the rate of creation of new businesses has been almost monotonically declining since the data was first compiled in 1977. When fewer businesses are created, it makes sense to expect that the share of total profits in the economy going to new and unlisted firms also decreases.

5.2.2 Growth in earnings and dividends

The next part of the economic chain is the relation between earnings and dividends. When firms make larger profits as a result of economic growth, as just shown, a reasonable hypothesis is that they pay out higher dividends. I.e., we

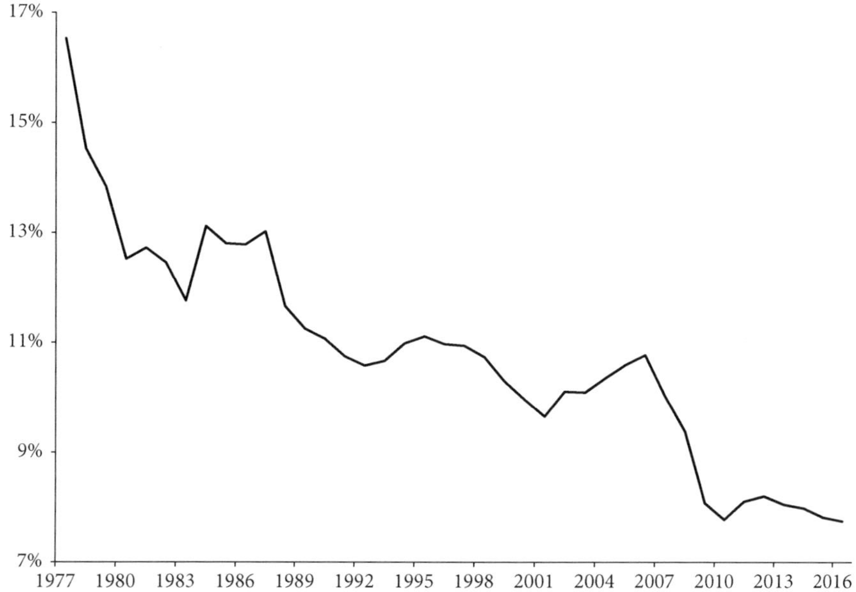

Figure 5.3 Rate of creation of new firms in the US. 1977–2016.
Data source: Business Dynamics Statistics, US Census Bureau.

expect the long-run average growth rate of earnings per share and dividends per share to be more or less the same. This part of the chain is reasonably well supported by the data, too, even when dividend growth is somewhat lower than earnings growth, in particular since 1945. Table 5.1 shows that real earnings per share have grown by 1.9% per year on average, whereas real dividends per share have grown by 1.6% per year on average. Listed firms increase dividend payments by the rate at which earnings grow, minus something like 0.3%-points. Since 1945, earnings have been growing even faster relative to dividends, though (3.3% vs. 2.6%).

Figure 5.4 shows the ratio of dividends to earnings, i.e. dividends per share divided by earnings per share, normalized to 1 in 1871, and its ten-year moving average to smooth out short-term spikes.[2] The interpretation of the figure is that when the ratio of dividends to earnings fluctuates around one (its normalized starting value in 1871), dividends and earnings grow by the same rate. Consequently, when the ratio decreases (increases), the growth rate of dividends

[2] Spikes are associated with recessions. During recessions, earnings fall dramatically but firms tend to keep on paying dividends, causing the dividends-earnings ratio to jump. We return to this in Chapter 9.

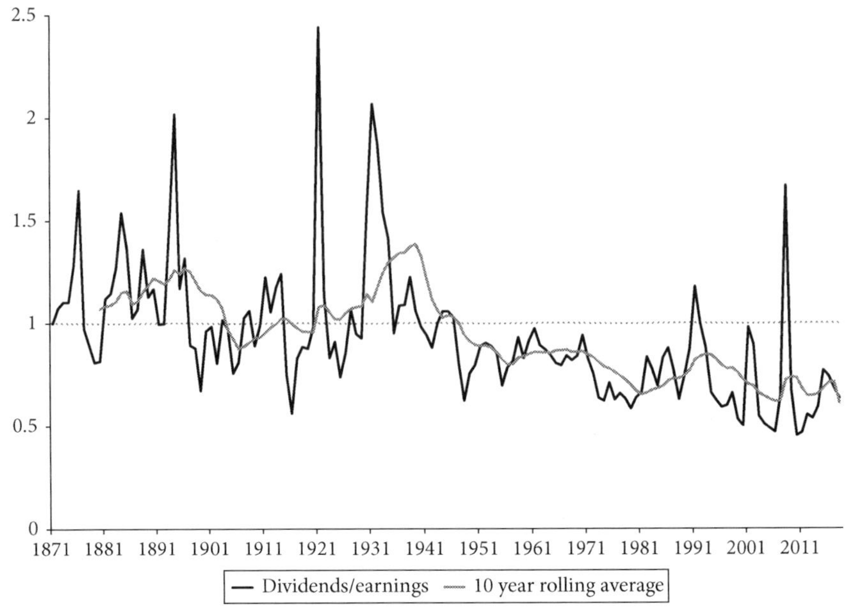

Figure 5.4 The dividends-earnings ratio normalized to 1 in 1871 and its ten-year rolling average. 1871–2018.

Data source: See Figure 3.1.

is lower (higher) than the growth rate of earnings. Earnings per share have grown faster than dividends per share, and the dividend-earnings ratio has been trending down, as the figure shows, in particular since 1945. The normalized dividends-earnings ratio is 0.6 at the last observation in 2018. This means that in 2018 the dividends-earnings ratio is 60% of its value in 1871. In 1871, firms paid out 65% of their earnings as dividends. In 2018, firms paid out 40% of their earnings (which is 60% of the 1871 value). Since the 1980s, the fraction of earnings that firms pay out as dividends seems to have stabilized at, but fluctuated around, a lower level than previously. Since 1980, the average annual payout ratio (dividends to earnings) has been 45%. Before 1980, it was 65%.

One reason firms pay less dividends (as a fraction of earnings) is that firms have started distributing profits in terms of share buy-backs instead of dividends. If firms use earnings to buy back shares instead of paying out dividends, earnings and dividends will start departing.

Figure 5.5 shows share buybacks as a percentage of GDP in the US. The figure shows that share buybacks took off in the early 1980s. Firms have shifted from

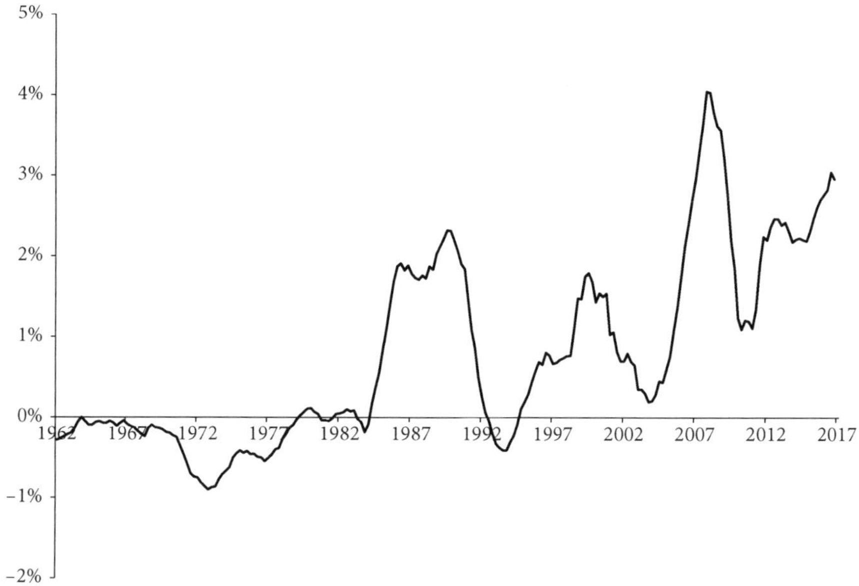

Figure 5.5 Total share buybacks in the US as a percentage of US GDP.
Data source: Gruber & Kamin (2017).

a strategy of returning money to shareholders via dividends to returning money via buying back shares. During the last couple of years, for instance over the 2012–2018 period, Standard & Poors report that the S&P 500 buyback yield (the amount S&P 500 firms use to buy back shares as a fraction of their stock-market value) has been close to 3% per year. Together with a dividend yield of slightly below 2% during the last couple of decades (see Chapter 4), this gives a total payout yield of around 4.5%. The dividend yield has historically been close to 4.5%, as shown in the previous chapter. This means that firms have not reduced shareholder compensation in recent decades, even when dividend yields have dropped, but have returned earnings to shareholders via share buybacks. Gruber & Kamin (2017) show that the increase in share buybacks is an international phenomenon, though more pronounced in the US.

When a company buys back its share, the number of outstanding shares drop. Theoretically, the share price should increase. Investors, as least in theory, receive the same return, but the channel through which they obtain this return is different; capital gains instead of dividends. We return to the question of how share buybacks influence expected stock returns in Part V when we judge the outlook for stocks.

5.2.3 Growth in earnings, dividends, and GNP

This chapter started out arguing that a reasonable hypothesis is that improvements in economic activity should lead to improvements in earnings. But should we measure improvements in economic activity as improvement in aggregate economic activity, as we have done until now, or improvements in GNP per capita? GNP per capita measures how much economic output each person on average produces. This is closely related to the concept of productivity.[3] If firms can produce more output with the same number of workers, i.e. productivity has increased, firms, all else equal, become more profitable.

Chapter 2 mentioned that growth in GNP per capita has been 2.0% per year on average. The average growth rate of GNP per capita appears from Table 5.1, too. Average growth in productivity (measured by growth in GNP per capita) has been close to average growth in earnings per share, and slightly above average growth in dividends per share for the full 1871–2018 period.

5.2.4 Growth in earnings/dividends/GNP and stock prices

Until now, we have established that total earnings and total economic activity follow each other in the long run. We have also established that total economic activity increases faster than earnings per share and dividends per share because of dilution, in particular before 1945. Dividends per share follow earnings per share reasonably well in the long run, even if dividends grow by slightly less than earnings. Finally, GNP per capita (that is closely related to productivity) lines up with earnings per share and dividends per share. The final part of the chain involves stock prices.

Figure 5.6 shows the stock-price earnings multiple, i.e. the ratio of stock prices to earnings per share, normalized to 1 in 1871, and its ten-year rolling average. 2000 and 2008 saw massive spikes in the stock-price earnings multiple, but apart from these one-time events, earnings and stock prices have followed each other reasonably well. Since the 1980s, however, stock prices have increased relative to earnings. In 2018, earnings per share were app. two times its value in 1871: USD 22 per one USD of earnings in 2018 versus USD 11 in 1871.

[3] Productivity measures how much a worker produces per unit of time (per hour, per day, per week, etc.) whereas GNP per capita is influenced by the fraction of the population that works and how many hours they work. In other words, there might be differences between GNP per capita and productivity. This being said, most economists view growth in GNP per capita as a good proxy for growth in productivity, in particular in the long run.

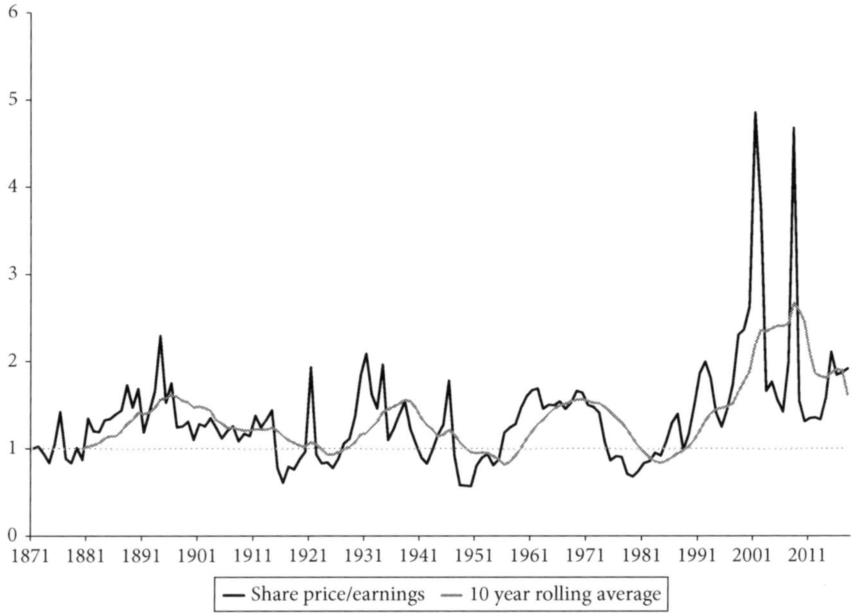

Figure 5.6 The stock-price earnings ratio normalized to 1 in 1871 and its ten-year rolling average. 1871–2018.
Data source: See Figure 3.1.

The growth rate of dividends is almost one percentage point lower than the growth rate of share prices (1.6% vs. 2.4%, see Table 5.1). We illustrate this in Figure 5.7, which shows the stock-price dividend multiple, i.e. the ratio of stock prices to dividends per share, normalized to 1 in 1871, and its ten-year rolling average.

Figure 5.7 reveals that until the 1980s, dividends per share and stock prices followed each other rather well. Since the 1980s, stock prices have soared in relation to dividends, though. Its value in year 2000, in particular, took the record with a price-dividend multiple exceeding 90, i.e. an investor had to pay USD 90 to get one dollar of dividends. This was 5–6 times higher than the stock-price dividend multiple of 17 in 1871. Clearly, the stock market was in bubble mode in year 2000. Valuations have come down somewhat since then but are still at an elevated level in a historical perspective.

Since the 1980s, stock prices have increased relative to dividends and earnings. The price-dividend ratio has increased by more than the price-earnings ratio, however, as seen by comparing Figures 5.6 and 5.7. The difference between the two is another way to illustrate the influence of share buybacks (and other factors that have lowered dividends relative to earnings). If firms pay out less in dividends

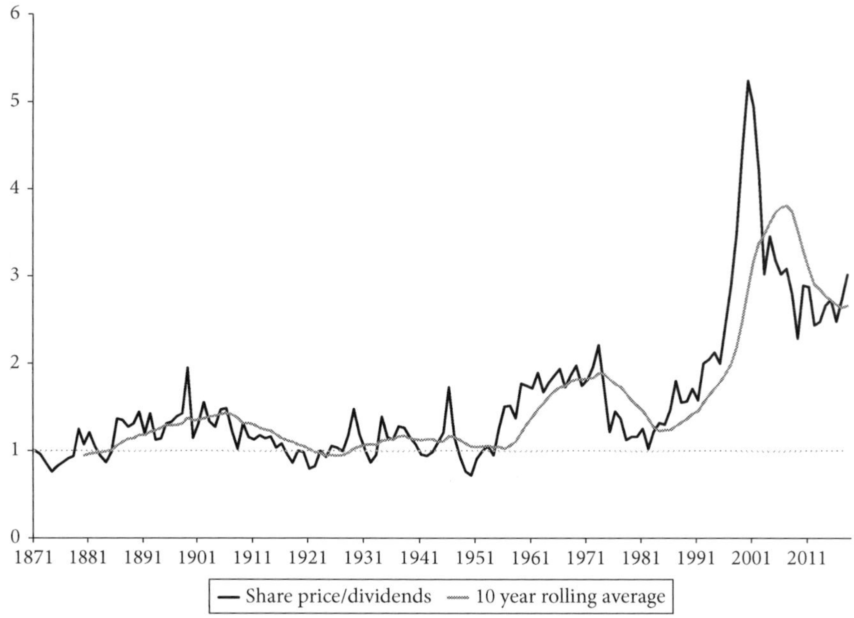

Figure 5.7 The stock-price dividend ratio normalized to 1 in 1871 and its ten-year rolling average. 1871–2018.
Data source: See Figure 3.1.

as a fraction of earnings, the price-dividend ratio increases relative to the price-earnings ratio.

The final relation we must consider is the one between stock prices and GNP. Let us start with what we have learned until now. Dividends per share, earnings per share, and stock prices have followed each other reasonably well until 1980 or so (Figures 5.6 and 5.7). Table 5.1 shows that GNP per capita has been growing at two percent per year in the long run, close to the rate of growth in share prices. Figure 5.8 illustrates this. The figure shows the stock-price GNP multiple (i.e. the S&P 500 divided by GNP per capita), normalized to 1 in 1871, and its ten-year rolling average. It fluctuates around a constant mean. Similar to the stock-price dividend multiple and the stock-price earnings multiple, there is a tendency for stock prices to increase relative to GNP per capita since the 1980s, though, even if not as dramatically as stock prices in relation to earnings (Figure 5.6) and, particularly, in relation to dividends (Figure 5.7). Rangvid (2006) points out that the stock-price GNP multiple might be a better predictor of stock returns, compared to the stock-price dividend and the stock-price earnings multiples, given that GNP has moved closer in harmony with stock prices than earnings and dividends since the 1980s. We return to this issue in Part V.

5.3 Aggregate GDP and the total value of the stock market

Growth in GNP per capita has lined up with growth in share prices (Figure 5.8). But what about the total value of the stock market? It turns out that the value of the aggregate stock market has outpaced aggregate economic activity during the last couple of decades. Figure 5.9 shows this. It depicts the total value of US corporate equities in relation to total GDP. Quarterly data are available from late 1951.

In the final quarter of 1951, the total value of US corporate equity was USD 151bn. The total value of production (GDP) was USD 360bn (at an annual rate), i.e. the value of the aggregate US stock market was around 40% of the value of total output in the US. In 2019, the value of the aggregate stock market had increased to USD 30,000bn whereas the value of total production had increased to 21,500bn. Growth in the aggregate value of the stock market has exceeded aggregate GDP growth, such that the value of the aggregate stock market has increased to 150% of the value of aggregate production in 2018. The aggregate stock market has significantly outpaced aggregate economic activity.

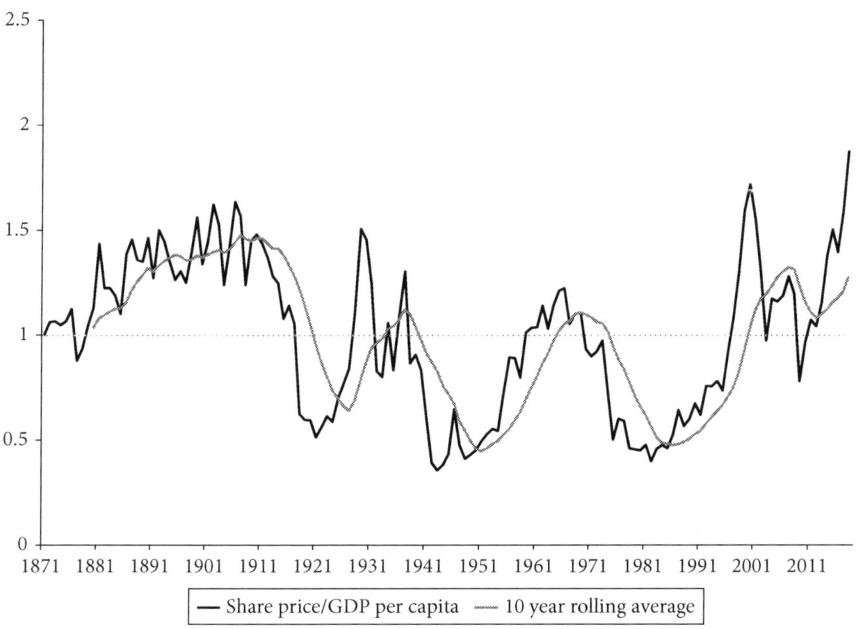

Figure 5.8 The stock-price GNP per capita ratio normalized to 1 in 1871 and its ten-year rolling average. 1871–2018.

Data source: See Figures 2.1 and 3.1.

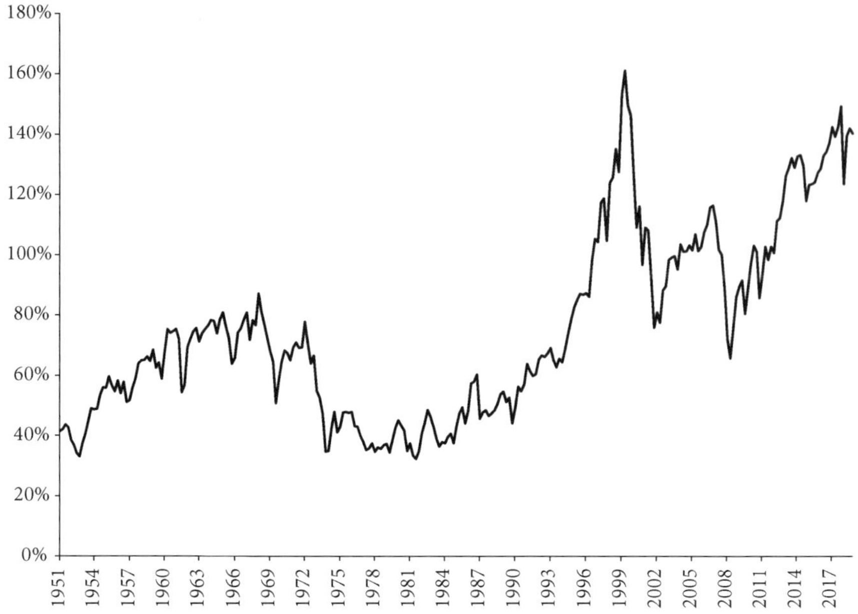

Figure 5.9 The value of the aggregate stock market relative to aggregate GDP.
Data source: FRED.

Greenwald, Lettau, and Ludvigson (GLL, 2019) study these dynamics in detail. They conclude that a reallocation of the rewards of production to equity owners at the expense of employees has driven this development. In other words, when economic growth and earnings have increased, a smaller fraction of earnings has gone to salaries, while owners have received a larger fraction. GLL also find that economic growth explains only a quarter of the growth in the aggregate value of the stock market over the 1981–2018 period. This is a shift from the preceding three decades. From 1952 to 1988, economic growth accounted for 92% of the rise in the stock market, GLL find.

If this whole chapter were be summarized, we conclude that US stock prices, GNP per capita, dividends per share, and earnings per share have been growing by around two percent in the very long run, with some important qualifications, however. For instance, stock prices have soared relative to fundamentals during recent decades, in particular in relation to dividends. This holds on a per-share basis but also for the total value of the stock market. On a per-share basis, share buybacks have been a contributing factor. On an aggregate level, research shows that the rewards from economic growth have benefitted equity owners in particular.

5.4 Checklist

This chapter has described how economic activity relates to underlying drivers of stock returns in the long run. The main conclusions to remember are:

- There are reasons to suspect that:
  a. Stock prices and dividends increase by more or less the same growth rate.
  b. Earnings and dividends increase by more or less the same growth rate.
  c. Economic activity and earnings increase by more or less the same growth rate.
- If these relations hold true, the stock-price earnings multiple, the stock-price dividend multiple, and the stock-price GNP multiple will fluctuate around a constant.
- Historically, growth in total earnings in the economy has closely followed growth in overall economic activity.
- Growth in overall economic activity has surpassed growth in earnings per share, in particular prior to 1945. The wedge between growth in total earnings in the economy and growth in earnings per share is sometimes called 'dilution'. Dilution refers to the part of growth in total earnings that shareholders do not reap. Dilution was more important historically than today, probably because the rate of creation of new firms has fallen.
- Growth in share prices relates to growth in dividends per share, earnings per share, and GNP per capita (productivity), implying that the stock-price earnings, stock-price dividends, and stock-price GNP per capita multiples have, overall, been reasonably stable. Since the 1980s, however, stock-price multiples have increased, though, in particular the stock-price dividend multiple, partly due to an increase in share buybacks.
- Aggregate growth in GNP has surpassed growth in the aggregate value of the stock market during the recent three decades, perhaps because equity owners have reaped a larger share of the benefits of economic growth.

6
Growth and returns across countries

The previous chapter examined the relation between long-run growth in economic activity and long-run growth in drivers of stock returns, i.e. share prices, dividends, and earnings, using US data. The chapter concluded that there is a fair amount of evidence indicating that growth in US economic activity has lined up with growth in US dividends, earnings, and share prices in the long run.

This chapter turns to the international evidence. It examines the relation between long-run economic growth and returns across countries. Have countries that have experienced high GDP growth historically also experienced high stock returns?

The chapter contains three main messages. First, there is no clear tendency that countries that have grown fast in the past are also countries that have delivered high stock returns in the past. Second, as in the US, stock prices have in many countries followed economic activity in the long run. Third, real interest rates relate to economic growth across countries in the long run, too.

Stock returns are:

$$\text{Stock returns} = \text{Dividend yield} + \text{capital gains}.$$

When stock returns and economic growth are not related across countries, as mentioned, but capital gains and economic growth are, it follows that dividend yields do not relate to economic growth across countries.

Stock returns are also:

$$\text{Stock returns} = \text{Risk-free rate} + \text{risk premium}.$$

When stock returns and economic growth are not related across countries, but interest rates (as proxies for risk-free rates) and economic growth are, it follows that risk premia do not relate to economic growth across countries. Stock returns and economic growth do not line up across countries because risk premia, dividend yields, and economic growth do not line up across countries.

One should not be too surprised that economic growth and stock returns do not line up across countries. We learned from the previous chapter that dilution might

From Main Street to Wall Street. Jesper Rangvid, Oxford University Press (2021). © Jesper Rangvid.
DOI: 10.1093/oso/9780198866404.003.0006

create a wedge between economic growth and growth in earnings of listed firms, and thus between economic growth and returns. We also learned that it matters whether firms pay out earnings as dividends. Buybacks cause a wedge here. Finally, the level of dividends yields and risk premia differ between countries in ways not related to the average long-run growth rate of economic activity.

Another conclusion emerging from this chapter is that long-run stock returns exceed long-run rates of economic growth by a wide margin. In the next chapter, we analyze further the stylized fact that stock returns exceed the risk-free rate and, hence, the rate of economic growth.

6.1 International data since 1900

An intuitive hypothesis is that differences in economic growth across countries relate to differences in returns across countries, i.e. that countries that have experienced high economic growth historically are also countries that have experienced high stock returns historically.

It turns out that this is not the case. In fact, the data tell us that there has been basically no relation between long-run average rates of economic growth in different countries and their long-run average stock returns.

Figure 6.1 shows this. The figure shows the average (geometric) real stock return obtained over more than a century, 1900–2016, for a large number of countries. The countries are ranked in descending order based on average real stock returns. The figure also shows the average (geometric) growth rate of real per capita GDP over the same period.

Figure 6.1 shows that the US stock market has returned 6.6% per year on average over the 1900–2016 period. No other stock market has performed as well. Next is the Australian stock market where returns have been 6.4% per year on average. Are the US and Australia also the countries where GDP per capita has grown the most? No. The country with the highest average growth rate in real per capita GDP is Japan at 2.6% per year. Growth in Australian GDP per capita has been 1.7% per year on average. This is one of the lowest growth rates. The US has experienced an average growth rate of 2.0%. This is one of the higher growth rates, but not the highest. The country with the lowest average real stock return is France (−0.5%). But the country with the lowest average rate of economic growth is Switzerland (1.4%). Basically, there is no strong relation between countries that have grown fast (slow) historically and countries that have delivered high (low) stock returns. The weak long-run relation between economic growth and stock returns was first reported by Ritter (2012).

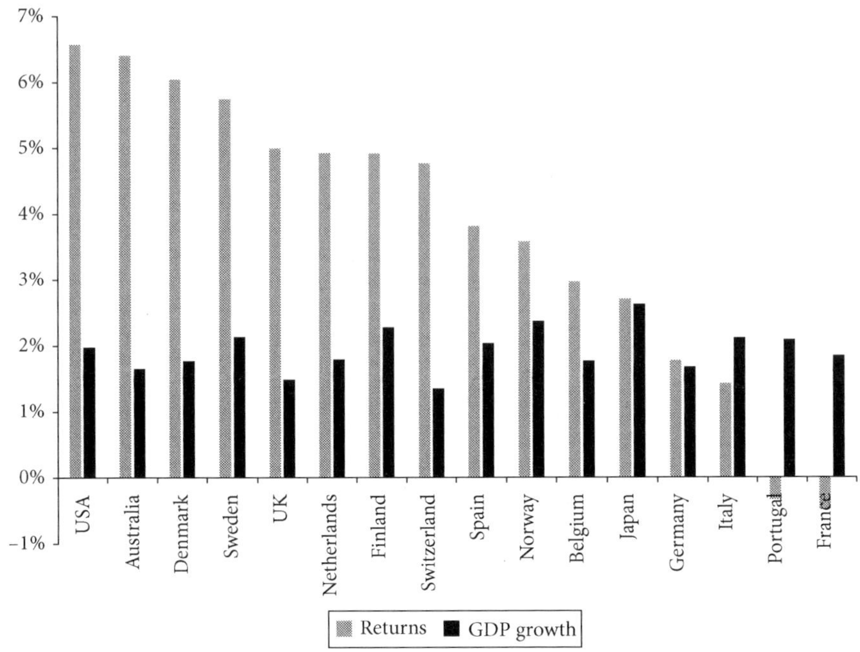

Figure 6.1 Real per capita GDP growth and real stock returns for selected countries. 1900–2016.

Data source: Jordà, Knoll, Kuvshinov, Schularick and Taylor (2019).

We also note from Figure 6.1 that average stock returns have been higher than average rates of economic growth in all countries, except Italy, Portugal, and France. In most countries, returns have been considerably higher.

We can also look at equity risk premiums and growth. We calculate the equity risk premium by subtracting real returns on long-term bonds (see next section) from real stock returns. Figure 6.2 shows that the conclusion is similar to the one we have just described for real stock returns: there is no simple relation between equity risk premia and economic growth across countries. In addition, we notice that the equity premium differs from country to country, from a high of close to 5% per annum in countries such as Finland, Japan, and the US to a low of around 0.5% in France and Germany. The average is 3.2% across countries.

We can split the sample period into subperiods, as we do in the next section. We can look at a subset of countries. We can look at aggregate GDP growth instead of per capita GDP growth. And, we can do other things. It does not help. There is no strong relation between economic growth and stock returns across countries.

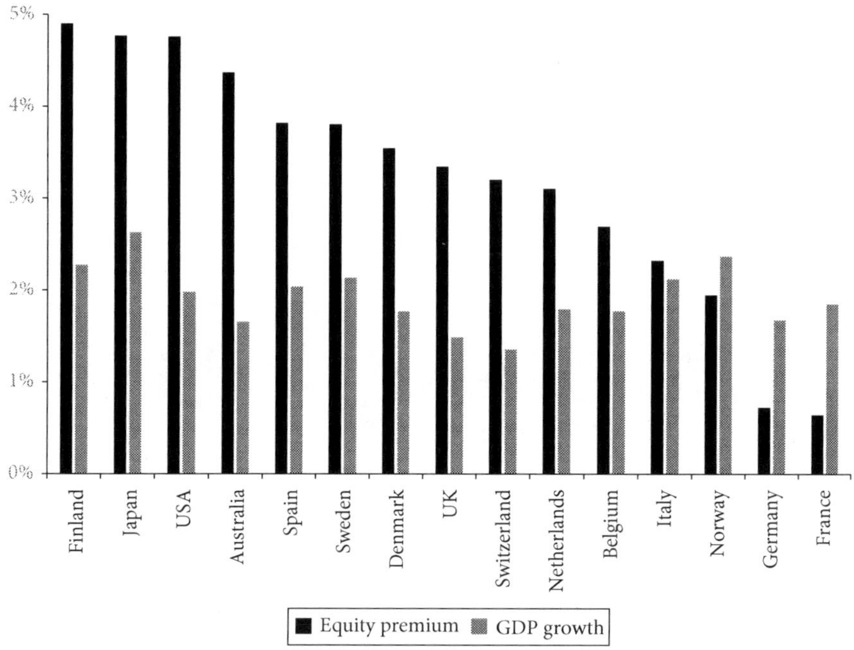

Figure 6.2 Real per capita GDP growth and equity risk premia for selected countries. 1900–2016.

Data source: Jordà, Knoll, Kuvshinov, Schularick and Taylor (2019).

6.2 International data since 1970

Countries were very different 100 years ago compared to today, as were stock markets and stock market indices. Even when researchers have put a lot of effort into verifying that data are of the highest quality, the concern remains that data in early subsamples in some countries are not on par with today's data or long-term data from the US. When making comparisons of international aggregate stock markets today, researchers and practitioners often look at Morgan Stanley International Capital market data; MSCI data. MSCI has collected stock market data since 1970 for a number of countries.

To further our understanding of the relation between economic growth, returns, and capital gains, Table 6.1 shows for each country the growth rate of real economic activity, average real capital gain, average real returns, and average dividend yields since 1970. On average across time and countries, real GDP per capita has been growing by 1.7% per year since 1970. Average annual real return across countries has been considerably higher, at 5.5%.

Table 6.1 Average growth rates of GDP per capita, real returns, real capital gains, dividend yields, and the fraction of returns coming from dividend yields. 1970–2016

	GDP per cap	Real returns	Capital gain	Dividend yield
Sweden	1.7%	9.3%	5.8%	3.5%
Denmark	1.5%	8.0%	5.1%	3.0%
Netherlands	1.7%	7.2%	2.7%	4.5%
Belgium	1.8%	6.6%	1.6%	5.0%
US	1.8%	6.0%	2.8%	3.2%
Norway	2.2%	5.9%	2.5%	3.4%
France	1.6%	5.6%	2.0%	3.5%
Canada	1.6%	5.5%	2.4%	3.1%
Switzerland	1.0%	5.5%	3.0%	2.5%
UK	1.8%	5.4%	1.2%	4.2%
Germany	1.9%	5.2%	2.3%	2.9%
Australia	1.6%	4.4%	0.1%	4.3%
Japan	2.0%	4.1%	2.4%	1.7%
Spain	1.9%	3.4%	−1.7%	5.1%
Italy	1.4%	1.2%	−1.9%	3.1%
Averages	1.7%	5.5%	2.0%	3.5%

Real capital gains and growth rates in real economic activity are of similar magnitudes. Across countries, real capital gains have been 2.0% per year, close to the average rate of growth in real per capita GDP (1.7%). Some countries have seen average capital gains far from 2%, particularly Sweden and Denmark, where capital gains have been very high, and Spain and Italy, where capital gains have been very low, i.e., there are outliers. The majority of countries have experienced capital gains in the interval from 0% to 3%, however, i.e. close to the average growth rate of per capita GDP.

It needs to be mentioned that this conclusion does not extend to the full 1900–2016 sample period. Over the full 1900–2016 sample, several countries have experienced even negative real capital gains on average but positive GDP growth rates. In other words, over the full 1900–2016 sample, the relation between capital gains and GDP growth is not strong across countries.

We conclude that economic growth is of the same magnitude as growth in stock prices in US data over the past 150 years (previous chapter) and in the majority of countries over the past 50 years.

Returns consists of two components, capital gains and dividend yields. The final column of Table 6.1 lists dividend yields. Dividend yields generally exceed the rate of economic growth. Only five countries have experienced dividend yields below three percent. The average dividend yield is 3.5%, twice the rate of economic growth. This means that per capita GDP growth rates and capital gains are typically around 2% per year on average in international data since 1970, whereas dividend yields exceed economic growth. Consequently, returns exceed rates of economic growth by a large margin.

6.3 Real interest rates and risk premiums

There is second way of looking at stock returns. Stock returns are also the risk-free interest rate plus a risk premium. Economic theory relates the real risk-free interest rate to the rate of growth in real per capita consumption. Consumption will in the long run be related to GDP. This means that economic theory relates the long-run real interest rate to long-run growth in per capita GDP.[1]

The intuition is as follows. We prefer a smooth consumption profile to one that sometimes provides us with very high consumption but at other times very low. If our current consumption is low but we expect future consumption to be high, we would like to move some of the otherwise high future consumption forward until today in order to smooth out consumption. To do so, we must borrow today to finance higher consumption today. When demand for credit goes up, the interest rate has to increase to balance demand for credit with supply of credit, i.e. balance consumption and savings. Conversely, if we expect lower growth in economic activity, and hence lower growth in consumption, the interest does not need to increase that must, as we do not want to move that much consumption forward. In this way, the level of the interest rate relates to the rate of growth in economic activity.

In the data, the average real risk-free interest rate on long-term government bonds is close to the average growth rate of real per capita GDP in a number of countries, in particular during the last 50 years or so. Figures 6.3 and 6.4 illustrate this. Figure 6.3 shows average annual growth rates of real GDP per capita together with the average real interest rate over the 1900–2016 period, country-by-country. Figure 6.4 shows the same for the 1970–2016 period.[2]

The long-run growth rate of real per capita GDP is close to 2%. For a large number of countries, the average real interest rate is close to 2%, too, over the full 1900–2016 period, as Figure 6.3 shows. This is the case for Australia, Canada, Switzerland, Denmark, the UK, the Netherlands, Norway, Sweden, and the USA.

[1] Macroeconomic textbooks derive this relationship, see for instance Blanchard & Fisher (1989) or Obstfeld & Rogoff (1996). There is not necessarily a one-to-one relation between economic growth and the real interest rate, as the relation depends on preference parameters, such as risk aversion. There is, however, a linear relation between the two, and in some special cases even a one-to-one (technically, if the utility function of the representative investor is logarithmic, see, e.g., Hamilton et al., 2015).

[2] The real interest rate is calculated as the nominal interest rate in a given year relative to inflation in that year, in logs. The interest rate is the interest rate on a long-term government bond.

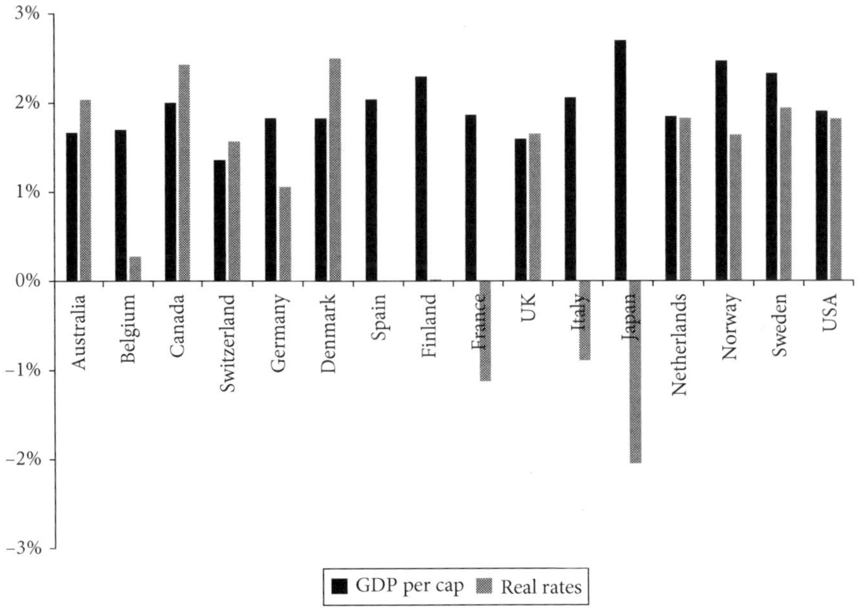

Figure 6.3 Real interest rates and growth rates of real per capita GDP. Yield on long-term govenment bond minus inflation. 1900–2016.
Data source: See Figures 6.1 and 6.2.

In the first half of the twentieth century, a number of countries experienced episodes of very high rates of inflation. Nominal interest rates did not react one-to-one to these short-lived but dramatic spikes in inflation rates, meaning that the average rate of inflation exceeded the average nominal interest rate in a number of countries, turning average real interest rates negative.

Focusing instead on the period since 1970, where no country has experienced episodes of dramatic short-term spikes in inflation rates, average real interest rates have been in the two-to-three percent interval for most countries, see Figure 6.4. The average real interest rate across countries is 2.6%. In a few countries, the difference between the average real interest rate and average growth in per capita real GDP exceeds several percentage points (e.g. Denmark), but for the majority of countries, average growth rates of GDP per capita have been reasonably close to average risk-free interest rates.[3]

[3] The correlation between average risk-free rates and average economic growth rates across countries is low. This is not strange. When all countries on average grow by close to 2% and average interest rates are close to 2%, too, the variation around these 2% become unsystematic. Low correlation should not distract from the fact that real growth and real interest rates are close to 2% in basically all countries. Academic studies have confirmed that real economic growth is positively related to real interest rates, see Harvey (1988).

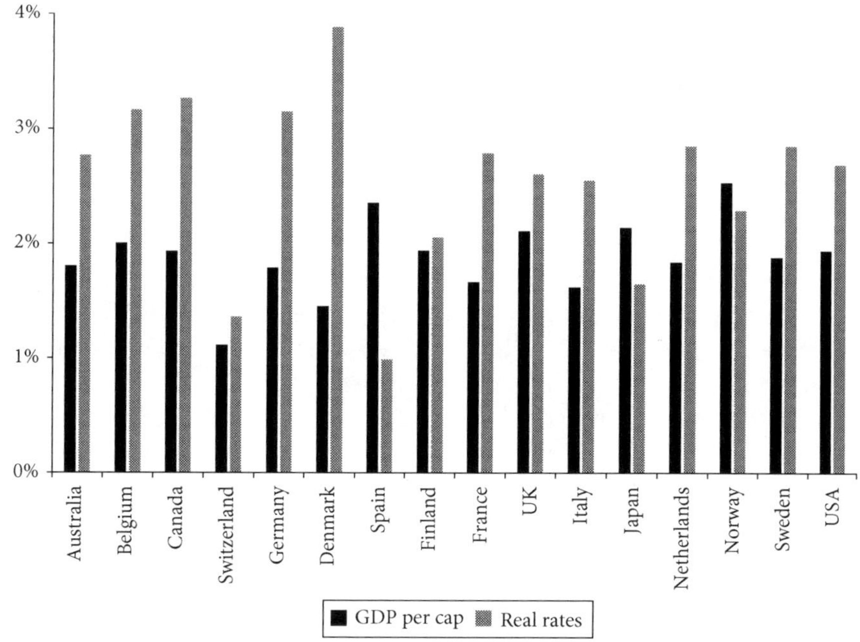

Figure 6.4 Real interest rates and growth rates of real per capita GDP. Yield on long-term govenment bond minus inflation. 1970–2016.
Data source: See Figures 6.1 and 6.2.

When real interest rates and economic growth rates are typically around 2% per year, but stock returns differ considerably country-by-country (Figure 6.1), then—logically—risk premia must also differ country-by-country. In light of the fact that theory does not predict a clear relation between economic growth and risk premia, this is not surprising. Rather, theory predicts that risk premia are related to the correlation between economic growth and stock returns, as further explained in Chapter 7.

6.4 $r > g$

There is overwhelming evidence that returns are generally considerably higher than rates of economic growth. In this chapter, this has been demonstrated for stock returns versus economic growth. Researchers have studied additional asset classes and conclude that returns to savings exceed rates of economic growth around the world.[4] Piketty (2014) and Piketty and Zucman (2014) promote the

[4] See Jorda, Knoll, Kuvshinov, Schularik, and Taylor (2019) for a comprehensive study.

hypothesis that when the return to savings exceeds the rate of economic growth, this will raise inequality. Piketty (2014) argues that when returns to savings are higher than rates of economic growth ($r > g$), wealth accumulation will primarily by driven by returns to savings and not by income growth. And, if capital is held by the already rich, wealth inequality will increase.

The arguments of Piketty (2014) have stirred controversy. For instance, wealth inequality can arise from other sources. If some groups of the population (the rich) hold more risky portfolios, these groups of the population will experience higher returns and thus higher wealth accumulation, but they also bear higher risk. A number of economists have also questioned the conclusions of Piketty from a theoretical point of view. When there is more wealth in the economy, as Piketty predicts there will be, it will be harder to earn a decent return on this wealth, as increased demand for savings will decrease returns to savings. In other words, the main mechanism that Piketty argues lies behind growing inequality should in itself reduce returns, thus reducing inequality. Also, if the increase in wealth is due to falling interest rates (falling interest rates imply higher bond prices and thus an increase in wealth tied up in bonds), then future consumption possibilities have not increased, even if wealth has increased. Current wealth increases but future returns from wealth fall when interest rates fall, leaving future consumption possibilities unaffected. In other words, if wealth goes up for the already wealthy as a result of falling interest rates, then they are in fact not necessarily better off.

We will not take this discussion further. We conclude that stock returns have been higher than rates of economic growth in most countries. Whether this contributes to inequality in itself and whether it implies unequal consumption possibilities across groups of the population is an important but different question.

6.5 Summing it up

Stock returns are given by:

$$\text{dividend yields} + \text{capital gains.}$$

Stock returns can also be written as:

$$\text{risk-free interest rate} + \text{risk premium.}$$

Economic theory relates the growth rate of GDP per capita to capital gains. Theory also relates the growth rate of GDP to the risk-free interest rate. In a large number of countries, capital gains are of the same magnitude as growth rates of GDP per capita. Similarly, long-run growth in GDP per capita is of the same magnitude as the risk-free rate in a number of countries. Economic growth relates to one component of stock returns.

Economic theory does not predict a simple linear relation between the level of economic growth and the level of dividend yields or risk premia. Not surprisingly, empirical evidence does not support such simple relations, either.

In the end, when average returns arise from two sources and economic growth relates to one them in a simple way but not the other, nothing secures a relation between economic growth and returns across countries. So, empirically, there is no such simple relation. In the next chapter, we will describe theory that will help us understand further why there is no simple linear relation between economic growth and stock returns across countries.

6.6 Checklist

This chapter has analyzed whether long-run average stock returns line up with long-run average growth rates of economic activity across countries. The main conclusions to remember are:

- There is no simple relation between long-run average growth in economic activity and long-run average stock market returns across countries. Countries that have grown fast in the past do not line up against countries that have experienced high stock returns in the past.
- Long-run economic growth influences part of long-run stock returns, however.
- Stock returns are given by capital gains plus dividend yields. Theory, as explained in the previous chapter, relates growth in per capita GDP to growth in real share prices (capital gains). Across countries, we see that long-run economic growth is of the same magnitude as one component of returns (capital gains) since 1970, but not the other.
- Stock returns can also be written as the sum of the risk-free interest rate and the risk premium. Theory relates growth in per capita GDP to the risk-free rate. In the data, long-run real economic growth rates are at levels close to long-run real interest rates across countries.

7
The equity premium

The returns that long-term stock-market investors have harvested are amazing. Average annual returns exceed average rates of annual economic growth by a factor of three to four, as Chapter 6 showed. Long-term stock-market returns also exceed the returns bond-market investors have obtained, again by a factor of three to four. How is this possible?

The difference between stock returns and a risk-free bond-market return is the equity premium. It is the compensation investors obtain from holding risky stocks instead of safe bonds. Economists face difficulties explaining its size. The equity premium is so large that economists call it an 'equity premium puzzle'.

The fact that average equity returns are considerably higher than the risk-free return is the same thing as saying that the risk-free return is low. So, voilà, economists encounter a 'risk-free rate puzzle' when they try to explain the large equity premium.

This chapter explains 'the equity premium puzzle' and 'the risk-free rate puzzle'. The chapter starts out comparing historical returns on stocks to historical returns on bonds, as well as the risks associated with these returns. The standard models economists use to explain the relative sizes of stock and bond returns, and hence the equity risk premium, are based on the exposure of stocks and bonds to economic growth. The chapter explains why these standard theories fail to explain the size of the equity premium. The chapter also explains how economists have changed their workhorse models to reconcile why returns on stocks are so high compared to bond returns.

The chapter yields an additional insight. Alongside its explanation of the equity premium puzzle, the chapter presents a framework for calculating the size of the equity premium. A key insight is that the equity premium does not depend linearly on economic growth in itself, but on the volatility of economic growth and its correlation with stock returns. Economic growth in itself affects the level of the risk-free rate, but not the risk premium. Two countries can experience the same level of economic growth, and thus the same level of the risk-free rate, but different volatilities of consumption growth and correlations between consumption growth and stock returns, causing stock returns to differ between countries. This is one more reason why Chapter 6 finds that economic growth does not line up with stock returns across countries.

From Main Street to Wall Street. Jesper Rangvid, Oxford University Press (2021). © Jesper Rangvid.
DOI: 10.1093/oso/9780198866404.003.0007

7.1 Return on stocks, bonds, and bills

Previous chapters have described the characteristics of long-run economic growth and returns. One main conclusion is that the average return on stocks exceeds the average growth rate in the economy by a large margin.

This chapter compares stock returns to bond returns and the risk-free rate. Figure 7.1 shows how USD 1 invested in 1871 accumulates over time in real terms, i.e. after inflation, if investing in stocks, treasury bonds, and treasury bills.[1]

Stocks have performed tremendously well relative to bills and bonds. One USD invested in short government bonds (Treasury Bills) in 1871, and proceeds continuously reinvested, has turned into around USD 33 in 2018 in real terms, i.e. after accounting for inflation. One dollar invested in long government bonds in 1871 has turned into around USD 40 in 2018. Stocks dominate this by a very large margin. As we have mentioned earlier, one USD invested in the stock market

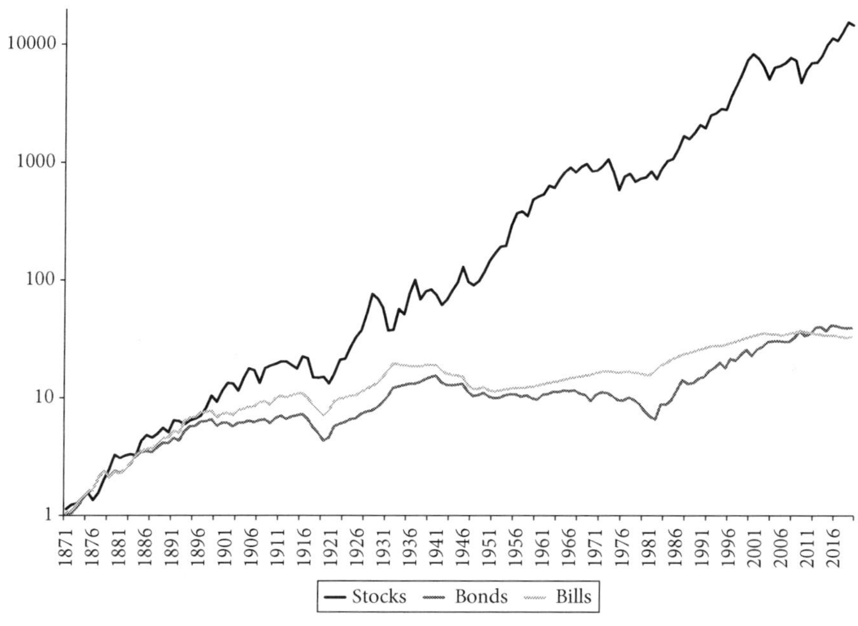

Figure 7.1 Cumulative real returns from US stocks, bonds, and bills. 1871–2018.
Data source: See Figure 3.1.

[1] The return from bonds comes from two sources: Interest payments and changes in the price of bonds. From Robert Shiller's webpage, e.g., we have data on bond yields going back far in time, but not data on bond returns. Campbell, Lo & Mackinley (1996), Equation 10.1.19, show how one can calculate approximate returns from bonds based on yields. In this calculation, one needs to assume a duration of the bonds. The calculations in this chapter are based on a ten-year duration.

Table 7.1 Average returns and risks from stocks, bonds, and bills

	Stocks	Bonds	Bills	Equity Premium	
				Wrt. bonds	Wrt. bills
Mean	6.7%	2.5%	2.4%	4.2%	4.3%
Mean. Post 1945	7.4%	1.9%	1.4%	5.5%	6.0%
Std.	16.9%	8.4%	6.2%	17.5%	17.3%
Std. Post 1945	15.6%	8.5%	2.6%	16.9%	15.6%
Mean/Std.	39.6%	29.7%	38.3%	23.3%	24.3%
Mean/Std. Post 1945	47.6%	22.4%	54.5%	32.1%	37.8%
Std. of average returns over T-year samples					
$T = 5$	7.6%	3.8%	2.8%	7.8%	7.7%
$T = 25$	3.4%	1.7%	1.2%	3.5%	3.5%
$T = 50$	2.4%	1.2%	0.9%	2.5%	2.4%
$T = 147$	1.4%	0.7%	0.5%	1.5%	1.4%
95% confidence intervals based on $T = 147$					
Lower	4.0%	1.1%	1.4%	1.2%	1.4%
Upper	9.5%	3.9%	3.4%	6.9%	7.0%

in 1871, and the proceeds continuously reinvested, has turned into almost USD 15,400.

We also know from earlier chapters that the average (geometric) annual US stock market return over the 1871–2018 period is around 6.8% per year. The average real return from bonds and bills have been around 2.5% per year, as Table 7.1 shows. The table also shows the averages for the post–1945 period. Stock returns have been a little higher after 1945 and returns from bills and bonds a little lower.[2]

Table 7.1 also shows the extra return that stocks provide on average over and above the returns from bonds and bills. This difference is the equity premium. The equity premium is around four percent (geometric average), when measured over the full sample period. For the post–1945 period, the equity premium is somewhat higher. The equity premium has been close to six percent since 1945.

The table also shows standard deviations of returns, i.e. how returns fluctuate around their means. Comparing average returns and standard deviations from stocks, bonds, and bills, an important lesson appears. Stocks returns are higher

[2] These are geometric averages. Chapter 3 showed that the arithmetic averages of stock returns are similar pre and post 1945. Table 3.1 also showed that the volatility of returns is lower after 1945. When arithmetic averages are identical, but volatility is lower after 1945, the geometric average is higher after 1945, as the geometric average approximately equals the arithmetic average minus volatility.

than bond and bill returns, but stock returns are also much more volatile. The standard deviation of stock returns is 17%, compared to 8% for bonds and 6% for bills. Bills provide the lowest return, but also the lowest risk. Stocks provide the highest return, but also the highest risk. Bonds are in between.

The fact that stocks are more risky than bonds that are then again more risky than bills, and that returns line up according to their risks, tells an important lesson: High stock returns come as a compensation for risk. Whether we can reconcile the magnitude of stock returns via investors' reluctance to take on risks is a different question – that is the question the equity-premium puzzle asks. But the sign is right. Stocks are riskier and command higher expected returns as a result.

This has another implication: high stock returns reflect not merely compensations to investors for postponing consumption, i.e. for saving. If this was the case, bond and bill returns should be as high as stock returns, as people can equally well save in bills and bonds. To reconcile the difference between stock and bond returns, we need to look for characteristics that differ between bonds and stocks. One such characteristic is risk.

The importance of understanding that stock returns are high because their risk is high cannot be overstated. You can increase your expected returns by taking on more risk, but taking on more risk also means exposing yourself to losses of, e.g., 30% or 40% during a year. If this happens the year you need to sell your stocks, it hurts.

An average is an estimated number. What is the uncertainty surrounding this average? Or, in other words, how certain are we that average stock returns really are larger than average bond and bill returns, taking into account the fact that averages are estimated? Statistical theory can guide us. If returns are statistically independent, the standard error of estimated average return is $\sigma/\sqrt{(T)}$ where σ is the standard deviation of annual returns and T is the sample size.

Table 7.1 presents standard deviations of average returns for different sample sizes, ranging from 5 years up to 147 years, assuming that the full-sample standard deviation (16.9%) is the true standard deviation, i.e. the relevant one for different sample sizes. 147 years correspond to the number of years between 1871–2018, i.e. our full sample period. With a 147-year sample, the standard deviation of average stock returns is 1.4% ($= 16.9\%/\sqrt{147}$). Statistical theory tells us that when the average annual stock return equals 6.8% and the standard deviation of this average is 1.4%, then the 95% confidence bound surrounding the estimate of average returns ranges from $6.8\% - 1.96 \cdot 1.4\% = 4.0\%$ to $6.8\% + 1.96 \cdot 1.4\% = 9.5\%$. If history repeats itself, there is a 2.5% probability that the average annual real return during the next 147 years will be larger than 9.4% and a 2.5% probability that it will be lower than 3.9%. Compare this to bond returns. There is a 95% chance that the true average annual return from bonds is between 1.1% and 3.9%. The bottom rows of Table 7.1 collect the confidence intervals for average returns. When the 95% confidence interval for average stock returns is [3.9%; 9.4%] and it is [1.1%; 3.9%] for average bond returns, i.e. the confidence bounds do not overlap, we can be on reasonably safe ground arguing that the average annual return from stocks is higher than the average annual return from bonds in the long run.

What about shorter periods, i.e. five years? If we assume that the true standard deviation over five-year periods is 16.9%, similar to the one estimated over the full sample period, the standard error surrounding the estimated average of annual stock returns is large at 7.6% ($= 16.9\%/\sqrt{5}$). This standard error is almost as big as the average itself. This implies that there is a 95% probability that the average annual stock return over a five-year period will be in the range [−8.1%; 21.5]. A lot of uncertainty surrounds our best guess of the average return over short periods. For bonds, the 95% range is [−4.9%; 9.9%].

We can do the same calculations for the average equity premium. The bottom row of Table 7.1 shows that we can be reasonably sure that stocks on average generate higher returns than bonds over long periods, as the confidence bounds for the average equity premiums are positive.

7.2 The equity premium puzzle

Two components determine the compensation investors require for taking on risk: how much risk they take on and how averse they are to take on that risk. If investors have no problem taking on risk, i.e. do not care about risk, the degree of risk compensation will be low. If investors are very risk averse, i.e. really want to avoid risk, the compensation will be large. The equity premium puzzle refers to the finding that investors must be implausibly risk averse to reconcile the size of the equity premium. But what are the risks investors are concerned about? What do we mean by 'implausibly risk averse'? And how do we quantify this?

The 'equity premium puzzle' was coined by Rajnish Mehra and Edward C. Prescott (a Nobel laureate in 2004) in a famous academic article published in 1985. The novelty of the Mehra and Prescott article lies in its demonstration that standard economic models cannot explain the size of equity premium. The ingredients in the standard model they used are as follows. At each point in time, investors make decisions about how much to consume and how much to save. Consumers prefer consumption today over consumption tomorrow: if a consumer should give up consumption today, he/she wants to be compensated by higher consumption tomorrow. The rate at which future consumption is discounted to the present is the consumer's discount factor, and consumers prefer more consumption to less. The rate at which the consumer's utility increases when consumption increases is diminishing.[3] Finally, consumers are risk averse, i.e. they want a compensation for taking on risk. These are the ingredients needed to demonstrate the equity premium puzzle.

In this framework, the relevant measure of risk is not volatility of returns per se. Instead, the relevant measure of risk relates to how stocks influence our future consumption possibilities. This makes sense. We save in order to postpone consumption from today until tomorrow, but when we invest in stocks we become uncertain about the exact size of our consumption possibilities tomorrow, because they then depend on uncertain stock market returns. If the stock market goes down, but this does not affect our consumption tomorrow, we will not require a risk premium if investing in stocks. But, if a drop in the stock market reduces our consumption possibilities tomorrow, we require a risk premium to be persuaded to buy stocks.

Economists specify these assumptions—consumers prefer early consumption to postponed consumption, consumers prefer more consumption to less but at a declining rate, consumers are risk averse, and consumers must decide how much to save—in mathematical terms. This allows them to calculate how risk averse investors need to be to reconcile the equity premium. In this economic model, the equity premium is given by the product of the aversion to take on risk and the amount of risk. The amount of risk in turn depends on the risk of consumption itself (the standard deviation of consumption growth), the risk of stocks (the standard deviation of stock returns), and the correlation between consumption growth and stock returns. In detail, in these models, the equity premium becomes:

$$\begin{aligned} \text{Equity premium} = {} & \text{Stock return} - \text{risk-free interest rate} = \\ & \text{Risk aversion} \cdot \\ & \text{Std.(consumption growth)} \cdot \\ & \text{Std.(stock returns)} \cdot \\ & \text{correlation(consumption growth, stock returns)}. \end{aligned} \tag{7.1}$$

It looks complicated at first sight, but it makes sense. It is also important for understanding the underlying determinants of stock returns.

Consumers dislike risk about their future consumption possibilities. You are more happy if you have one bicycle at your disposal every day than if you sometimes have two, but at other times none. When you save, you give up consumption today in exchange for consumption tomorrow. If you save in safe bills, you know how much you can increase your consumption tomorrow. If you reduce consumption today to buy stocks, you increase the uncertainty of your

[3] If you need a bicycle to go to work, but do not have one, you become happy when you get your first bike. When you have ten bicycles, you do not become much more happy if you get an additional one.

future consumption possibilities. The compensation for taking on stock-market risk depends upon:

1. **Risk aversion**: If you really do not like risk, i.e. if you are very risk averse, the excess return on stocks compared to bonds must be high to convince you to buy stocks. So, the higher is risk aversion, the higher is the equity premium.
2. **Volatility of consumption**: If your consumption stream is already quite volatile (standard deviation of consumption growth is high), you want to be compensated by higher stock returns if you give up consumption today in order to buy stocks and thereby add even more volatility to your already volatile consumption. So, the higher is the standard deviation of consumption growth, the higher is the quite premium.
3. **Volatility of stock returns**: The riskier are stocks, the more risk you add to your consumption by buying stocks. You want to be compensated. So, the higher is the standard deviation of stock returns, the higher is the equity premium.
4. **Correlation**: Finally, a high correlation between consumption growth and stock returns increases the equity premium. This is important to understand. Correlation can be positive and negative. If a financial asset helps you reduce consumption uncertainty, you value that asset dearly. If you can buy a stock that pays out a lot when your consumption is otherwise low, you are happy to buy that stock. It helps you keep up your consumption during periods where you would otherwise have seen your consumption fall. A stock that provides high stock returns when consumption growth is low has a negative correlation to consumption growth. This stock hedges your consumption risk. In fact, if a stock correlates negatively with consumption growth, you are willing to buy that stock even if the return it provides is lower than the risk-free rate (all else equal), i.e. if it has a negative equity premium. Alternatively, if stock returns are negative when your consumption is already low, it adds to the volatility of your consumption profile. This is the case of a positive correlation between stock return and consumption growth. You only want to invest in that stock if it provides you with high returns on average. So, the higher is the correlation between stock returns and consumption, and thereby the less consumption hedging stocks provide, the higher must the equity premium be to convince you to buy stocks instead of bonds.

From the data, we can calculate the equity premium, the volatility of stocks, the volatility of consumption growth, and the correlation between stock returns and consumption growth. We cannot directly observe the risk aversion coefficient, but we can use data to calculate the risk aversion coefficient needed to account for the historical equity premium. Table 7.2 shows the results of the calculations.

Table 7.2 Consumption growth (ΔC), stock returns (R), and risk aversion. Implications for the equity premium

	Consumption and returns			
	avg(ΔC)	std(ΔC)	std(R)	corr(ΔC, R)
1889–2019	2.1%	3.4%	18.4%	0.56
Post 1945	2.1%	1.7%	15.9%	0.45
		Implied equity premium		
Risk aversion:	1	10	20	50
1889–2019	0.4%	3.5%	7.0%	17.6%
Post 1945	0.1%	1.2%	2.5%	6.2%
		Implied risk-free rate		
Risk aversion:	1	10	20	50
1889–2019	1.9%	14.0%	16.0%	−49.1%
Post 1945	2.1%	19.4%	35.8%	66.8%

The relevant measure of consumption is per capita real consumption, as we evaluate the equity premium for a typical investor. Per capital real consumption has grown by app. 2% per year on average, exactly like GDP per capita. The standard deviation of consumption growth has been around 3.5% per year for the whole sample but less than 2% since 1945. The correlation between stock returns and per capital real consumption growth has been around 0.5.

We can calculate the resulting equity premium for different values of the risk aversion coefficient. Table 7.2 presents calculations for a risk aversion coefficient of 1, 10, 20, and 50. To reconcile an equity premium of around four percent, as for the full sample period, we need a risk aversion coefficient between 10 and 20 when relying on data spanning the entire 1889–2018 period.[4] Post 1945, the equity premium has been close to six percent (Table 7.1). To reconcile this, the risk aversion coefficient has to be close to 50, Table 7.2 shows.

Economists typically assume that a risk aversion coefficient of something like 'less than five' gives a reasonable description of peoples' attitudes towards taking on risk. A risk aversion coefficient of one generates an equity premium of 0.4%. A risk aversion coefficient of ten generates an equity premium of 3.5% for the full sample and 1.2% for the post WWII sample. Both are dramatically lower than the equity premium we observe in the data. The 'equity premium puzzle' thus refers to the fact that we need to assume that investors are very risk averse in order to understand the size of the equity premium.

[4] Robert Shiller provides per capita real consumption since 1889 on his webpage.

There are two reasons why economists believe that a risk aversion coefficient above five is too high. First, a risk aversion coefficient above five simply implies counter-intuitive reactions towards risk. Appendix 7.1 gives an example.

Second, if we nevertheless accept that risk aversion is high, we run into another problem, the so-called 'risk-free rate puzzle', as pointed out by Weil (1989). This refers to the fact that if we accept a high degree of risk aversion (in order to reconcile the equity risk premium), the implied risk-free interest rate becomes either way too high or way too low. The lower part of Table 7.2 illustrates.[5] If one assumes a risk aversion coefficient of 50, the model-implied risk-free rate becomes 67% for the post-1947 period. This is obviously way off. The risk-free rate has been around 2% in the data (Table 7.1). Furthermore, the risk-free interest rate becomes too sensitive to changes in consumption growth. If the risk aversion coefficient is 50, a one percentage point change in consumption grow implies a 50 percentage point increase in the risk-free interest rate. Obviously, this is grossly exaggerated, too.

So, we can match the empirical equity premium if we assume that investors are very risk averse. In this case, they must be compensated a lot if they should be convinced to buy risky stocks. This would explain the equity premium. However, assuming such a high degree of risk aversion leads to other problems. This is the reason economists label the high equity premium we observe in the data an 'equity premium puzzle'. It is difficult to understand why stocks have provided so much higher returns than bonds historically.

7.2.1 The equity premium puzzle around the world

Table 7.3 shows the historical equity premium for a number of countries, using data since 1900. In all countries, the equity premium is large, ranging from a low of 4.2% in Denmark to a high 10.8% in Italy and Japan. There is robust evidence that stocks yield higher returns than bonds over long periods of time, both in the US and around the world.

Table 7.3 shows the implied equity premium for different levels of risk aversion calculated, country by country, in the same way as for the US in Table 7.2. Even a risk aversion coefficient of 10 is not enough to account for the size of the equity premium in any country. The lowest risk aversion required in any country to explain the size of the equity premium in that country is twenty (Denmark). The equity premium puzzle is a global phenomena.

[5] For the very interested reader, the explicit expression for the risk-free interest rate is:

$$\text{Risk-free rate} = \delta + \text{Risk aversion} \cdot \text{avg}(\Delta C) - (\text{Risk aversion})^2 \cdot \text{std}(\Delta C)$$

where δ is the subjective discount factor. The calculations in Table 7.2 assume $\delta = 0$ for simplicity.

Table 7.3 The equity premium and equity premium puzzle internationally. Arithmetic averages

Risk aversion	EquityPremium	Implied equity premium			
		1	10	20	50
Australia	9.9%	0.2%	2.1%	4.2%	10.6%
Belgium	5.3%	−0.2%	−2.1%	−4.2%	−10.5%
Canada	7.1%	0.1%	1.5%	3.0%	7.5%
Denmark	4.2%	0.2%	2.1%	4.2%	10.4%
France	4.6%	−0.5%	−4.6%	−9.1%	−22.8%
Germany	6.1%	0.2%	1.6%	3.1%	7.8%
Italy	10.8%	0.0%	0.3%	0.5%	1.3%
Japan	10.8%	0.3%	2.5%	5.1%	12.7%
Netherlands	7.0%	−0.1%	−1.2%	−2.4%	−6.1%
Norway	6.7%	0.0%	−0.2%	−0.5%	−1.2%
Spain	6.1%	0.2%	2.5%	4.9%	12.3%
Sweden	8.7%	0.2%	1.9%	3.8%	9.5%
Switzerlands	5.1%	0.1%	1.5%	3.0%	7.4%
UK	6.1%	0.1%	1.4%	2.7%	6.8%
Avg.	7.0%	0.1%	0.7%	1.3%	3.3%

For those countries where the correlation between stock returns and consumption growth is negative, the theoretical implied equity premium is negative. This is because stock returns have been high when consumption has been low in these countries, i.e. stocks have helped investors in bad times. For this reason, investors should have been so happy to hold stocks that they would do so even at a negative equity premium. The historical equity premium is positive in these countries, too, however. The equity premium puzzle is even larger in countries where stocks hedge consumption risk.

7.3 What has been done to understand the puzzle?

Economists have been puzzled for years about the large equity premium. Considerable research has been devoted to understanding it. For instance, economists have found explanations that separate the equity-premium puzzle from the risk-free rate puzzle. Many of these explanations recognize that the level of consumption per se might not be the only thing that matters for how happy people are. Perhaps other things matter in combination with consumption today. Perhaps, for instance, a drop in consumption hurts more if it comes after a period of high consumption growth. Perhaps it hurts more if you today are forced to sell your big car (for instance because you have lost your job) and buy a smaller car, even when you were happy 20 years ago—when you had just finished your education—to buy your first small car. Getting a small car is great if you have no car, but not so great if you are used to driving a large Mercedes. You form consumption habits. In this situation, risk aversion becomes time-varying. It depends on the level of consumption we have gotten used to. We call it habit formation. Campbell & Cochrane (1999) made an important contribution building on these insights, showing how time-varying risk aversion caused by habit-formation could help understand the equity risk premium. Another possibility is that a change in consumption today might have long-lasting consequences. I.e., a drop in consumption today hurts, but if the drop in consumption today implies that consumption going forward will also be lower, it hurts even more. Models incorporating these features are sometimes called models with long-run risk. Bansal & Yaron (2005) is an important contribution. In this kind of model, it is not risk aversion that is time-varying, but risk itself. Economists have also studied models with disaster risk. Here, the idea is that investors are particularly concerned about very large crashes in stock markets, disasters. Sometimes stocks lose 50% or more. The mere possibility that disasters exist might imply that investors become overly concerned about their occurrence, even when the probability that disasters occur is small—disasters happen seldom. This can also help explain the high equity premium. Rietz (1988) and Barro (2006) made important contributions in this regard.

It will take us too far afield going into details with these explanations. The point is that progress has been made. Stock returns are a compensation for risk, but one has to think carefully about the types of risk that matter to investors when trying to explain the size of the equity premium.

A second insight follows from these discussions: There is no simple linear relation between consumption growth and the level of the risk premium. Consumption growth theoretically determines the risk-free rate but not the risk premium. As shown in Section 7.2, Eq. (7.1), the equity premium depends on risk aversion, the volatility of consumption growth and returns, and the correlation between the two. Consumption growth in itself does not influence the equity premium. For this reason also, it is understandable that we only see a weak relation between average rates of economic growth and average stock returns across countries, as demonstrated in Chapter 6. This chapter helps understanding this finding, too.

Before the chapter checklist, let us conclude with a couple of quotations. University of Rochester Professor Narayana Kocherlakota concluded in 1996, after a detailed study of attempts made to explain the equity premium puzzle that 'It seems that any resolution to the equity premium puzzle in the context of a representative agent model will have to assume that the agent is highly averse to consumption risk. Per capita consumption is very smooth, and therefore does not covary greatly with stock returns. Yet people continue to demand a high expected return for stocks relative to bonds. The only possible conclusion is that individuals are extremely averse to any marginal variation in consumption (either their own or societal).'

John Cochrane, who has been the President of the American Finance Association and Director of the NBER Asset Pricing Program, in Cochrane (2008b) concluded that 'No model has yet been able to account for the equity premium with low risk aversion. So, we may have to accept high risk aversion, at least for reconciling aggregate consumption with market returns in this style of model. At the same time, many economists' beliefs about the size of the equity premium are declining from the 8 percent postwar average, past the 6 percent average in longer samples, down to 2 or 3 percent or less. The U.S. economy and others with high sample equity premia may simply have been lucky. Did people in 1947 really think that the stock market would gain 8 percent per year more than bonds, and shy away from buying more stocks in the full knowledge of this mean, because the 16 percent annual standard deviation of stock returns seemed like too much risk? Or was the 8 percent mean return largely a surprise?' So, perhaps the equity premium puzzle will simply disappear because the equity premium will be lower in the future. We return to this in Chapter 19.

7.4 Checklist

This chapter has examined returns to stocks, bonds, and bills. The main conclusions to remember are:

- Historically, stocks have provided considerably higher returns than bonds and bills.
- In the US, the equity premium—the difference between average returns to stocks and bonds/bills—has averaged around 4%–5% if measured over the last app. 150 years. Since 1945, the equity premium has been even higher, at 5%–6%.
- There is one—and only one—reason why stocks return more than bonds on average: Stocks are riskier. The higher return to stocks is a compensation for taking on risks.
- It is not easy to pin down exactly what types of risks investors are concerned about.
- When economists try to reconcile the size of the equity premium, they face difficulties. The degree of risk aversion needed to explain the equity premium is implausibly high. For this reason, the large difference between average returns on stocks and bonds is labelled an 'equity premium puzzle'.
- Lots of academic research has been devoted to understanding the equity premium. Progress has been made.

- The equity premium depends on the risk aversion of the investor, the volatility of consumption growth and stock returns, and the correlation between the two. Consumption growth in itself does not influence the equity premium. When consumption growth does not influence the equity premium, it is no wonder that consumption growth and stock returns do not line up across countries, as Chapter 6 showed.
- The equity premium puzzle is an international phenomena.

Appendix 7.1. Implication of risk aversion for willingness to take on risk

An investor has USD 100,000 at his disposal. A bet, an investment, is presented to the investor. The bet specifies that there is a 50% chance of gaining a specific amount and a 50% chance of losing that amount. How much the investor is willing to pay to avoid the bet depends on the investor's reluctance to take on risk.

Economists model such choices by specifying the investor's preferences. These preferences are described by a so-called utility function. The utility function describes how happy the investor is with his/her level of consumption. The higher is consumption, the happier is the investor (the higher is utility), but happiness increases at a declining rate. A common specification with these characteristics is $U(C) = C^{(1-\gamma)}$, where γ is a parameter that measures the degree of risk aversion of the investor and C represents consumption. The calculations below are based on this utility function.

We can calculate the amount the investor would be willing to pay to avoid the bet and be as happy as with the bet. We do so by comparing the level of consumption with and without the bet that provides the investor with the same level of utility. As the bet makes consumption risky, we compare utility if not making the bet with the expected utility if making the bet. Table 7.4 contains examples of such calculations for different sizes of bets and different levels of risk aversion.

Let us assume that the bet specifies that there is a 50% chance of gaining USD 100 and a 50% chance of losing USD 100. When the investor has wealth of USD 100,000 and has a chance of gaining or willing a small amount, say USD 100, the investor is not willing to pay a lot to avoid the bet. Even if the investor is very risk averse, e.g. has a risk aversion coefficient of 50, the investor is willing to pay only USD 2 to avoid the bet. When wealth is high relative to the stakes at play, the investor is not very concerned.

When the stakes get high, high levels of risk aversion imply implausible attitudes towards risk. For instance, if the investor has an equal chance of losing USD 50,000, i.e. 50% of his wealth, or gaining USD 50,000, the investor is willing to pay almost the total amount involved in the bet up-front to avoid the bet when risk aversion is high. With a current wealth of USD 100,000, the calculations in Table 7.4 show that the investor is willing to pay USD 49,288 to avoid the chance of losing or gaining USD 50,000 when the risk aversion coefficient is fifty. This means that you are so afraid to take on risk that you rather pay

Table 7.4 Size of bet and willingness to avoid bet. Current wealth 100,000

	Size of risk aversion, γ			
Size of bet	1	10	20	50
100	0	0	1	2
1,000	5	50	99	241
10,000	506	4,424	6,763	8,718
50,000	13,528	45,997	48,142	49,288

basically the total amount you can at most lose up-front to avoid the bet. But doing so, you also avoid the opportunity to increase your wealth by 50%. It might be that you are not happy to take on the bet, but if you take on the bet, it cannot be that you are equally happy losing USD 49,288 for sure, compared to having the possibility of loosing, but also of gaining, USD 50,000. This is simply an implausible description of peoples' attitudes towards risk. People cannot be as risk averse as required to explain the equity premium puzzle.

PART III

ECONOMIC GROWTH AND STOCK RETURNS DURING THE BUSINESS CYCLE

8
Business-cycle fluctuations in economic activity

Two main points of Part II of this book were that (i) over long periods of time, economies activity expands and (ii) long-run economic growth relates to long-run growth in earnings, dividends, and stock prices. This part, Part II, deals with fluctuations in economic activity around the long-term growth trend, and their consequences for financial markets.

We call fluctuations in economic activity around the long-term growth trend 'the business cycle'. The business cycle consists of two phases. The first is a period of strong economic activity. The second, following the first, is a period of weak economic activity. We call the first phase of the business cycle an 'expansion' and the second phase a 'contraction' or 'recession'.

This chapter explains what the business cycle is and what causes business-cycle fluctuations. We first define a business cycle. Then, we turn to the empirical evidence on the lengths and strengths of the typical business cycle, i.e. how long does the typical business cycle last and how strong are movements in economic activity over the business cycle. As in previous chapters, we acknowledge that we have better data for the US. Thus, we start illustrating the business cycle using long-term US data. After this, we show how business cycles develop in other countries.

In the next chapter, we analyze how business-cycle fluctuations in economic activity line up with stock market fluctuations. We will see that stock-market movements are highly influenced by the business cycle. Generally, stocks do well when the economy expands but poorly when the economy contracts. Understanding the business cycle is of great value to investors.

8.1 What is the business cycle?

The classical text on business cycles is the path-breaking book from 1946 by economists Arthur F. Burns and Wesley C. Mitchell. Their book is empirical in nature, studying a large number of economic time series. The book provides what is today considered the original definition of a business cycle. They wrote (page 3):

From Main Street to Wall Street. Jesper Rangvid, Oxford University Press (2021). © Jesper Rangvid.
DOI: 10.1093/oso/9780198866404.003.0008

> Business cycles are a type of fluctuation found in the aggregate economic activity of nations that organize their work mainly in business enterprises: a cycle consists of expansions occurring at about the same time in many economic activities, followed by similarly general recessions, contractions, and revivals which merge into the expansion phase of the next cycle.

There are two points to highlight in this definition of the business cycle. First, business-cycle fluctuations relate to common fluctuations in a large number of different time series measuring business activities, such as production, output, income, prices, interest rates, monetary transactions, etc. This means that we will not call it a business-cycle turning point if only a few measures of business activities have changed. For the business cycle to change, widespread changes in business activity must happen. The second important point is that Burns & Mitchel (1946) divide the business cycle into different phases: expansions and contractions. Burns & Mitchel used statistical tools to analyze turning points in variables measuring business activities. Combining turning points in individual measures of business activities, they determined turning points in overall measures of the business cycle. Today, we say that turning points occur when business activity reaches its 'peak' and 'trough'. The peak measures the highest level of business activity before a contraction begins. A trough measures the lowest level of business activity before an expansion of business activity starts. Figure 8.1 illustrates the idea behind the Burns & Mitchell definition of business-cycle fluctuations.

Today, in the United States, the National Bureau of Economic Research (NBER) Business Cycle Dating Committee officially identifies turning points in the business cycle. The NBER was established in 1920, and published its first business-cycle dates in 1929. The Business Cycle Dating Committee was formally formed in 1978. The NBER definition of a business cycle follows the definition presented by Burns & Mitchell (1946). It divides economic activity into different phases and looks at several indicators of economic activity to evaluate when overall economic activity has changed. The NBER writes:

> The NBER's Business Cycle Dating Committee maintains a chronology of the U.S. business cycle. The chronology comprises alternating dates of peaks and troughs in economic activity. A recession is a period between a peak and a trough, and an expansion is a period between a trough and a peak. During a recession, a significant decline in economic activity spreads across the economy and can last from a few months to more than a year. Similarly, during an expansion, economic activity rises substantially, spreads across the economy, and usually lasts for several years.

Regarding the overall measure of economic activity, NBER writes:

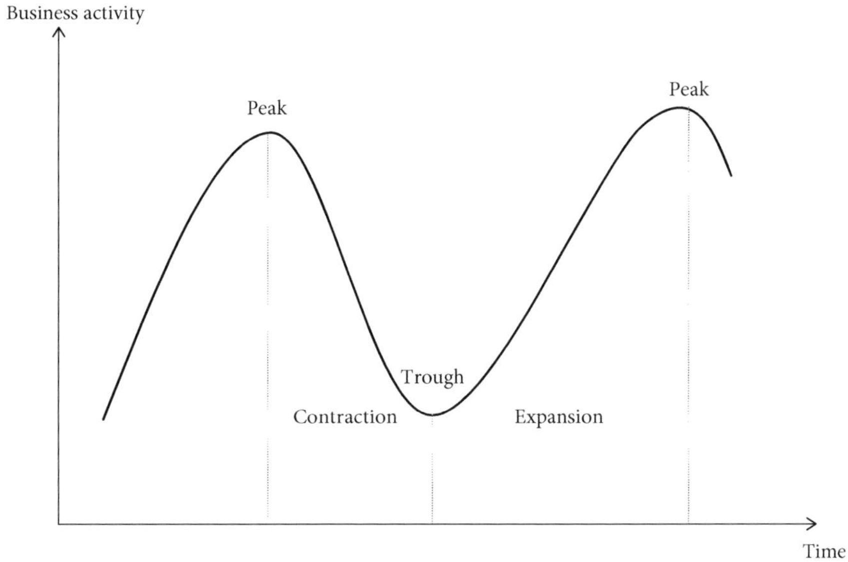

Figure 8.1 Illustrating the business cycle.

> The Committee does not have a fixed definition of economic activity. It examines and compares the behavior of various measures of broad activity: real GDP measured on the product and income sides, economy-wide employment, and real income. The Committee also may consider indicators that do not cover the entire economy, such as real sales and the Federal Reserve's index of industrial production.

The NBER committee determines turning points monthly. It looks at a range of broad quarterly economic indicators and a number of more 'narrow' monthly indicators. The broad quarterly indicators include most importantly GDP and GDI (Gross Domestic Income). The committee also looks at subcomponents of GDP, such as consumption, exports, etc. At the monthly level, the committee looks at industrial production, manufacturing sales, and different indicators of the strength of the labor market, such as hours worked and different surveys of employment. In addition, more recently, the committee has taken into account monthly GDP measures, though, it notices that these measures of monthly GDP are noisy.[1]

[1] The precise list of variables that the committee uses to determine peaks and troughs of the business cycle is available on the web page of the NBER Business Cycle Dating Committee.

Only a few countries have established agencies that formally determine peaks and troughs in economic activity.[2] When most countries do not have 'official' business-cycle dates, another definition is needed. A common rule-of-thump definition of a recession is when an economy experiences 'two consecutive quarters of negative GDP growth'. This is a straightforward definition. For a number of reasons, it is a second-best definition only, though. First, a quarter is a relatively long period of time. Given its importance, economists prefer a definition of a recession that operates at a finer interval, such as monthly. Typically, GDP is not available at the monthly frequency, however. Second, it is cumbersome to calculate GDP. There are frequent revisions to GDP figures. For this reason, it is preferable to base the dating of turning points on a range of indicators of economic activity, and not only GDP. Finally, as mentioned above, the NBER defines a recession as a 'significant decline in economic activity'. This means that if GDP drops for two quarters by, say, 0.01% per quarter, the 'two consecutive quarters' definition would call a recession, even when such a small decline is obviously not a 'significant drop in economic activity'. Nevertheless, because there is no business-cycle dating committee in most countries, the commonly-used international definition of a recession is two consecutive quarters of negative GDP growth. When dealing with the US, on the other hand, as we do in the next sections, we can rely on the official business-cycle dates.

8.2 Illustrating the US business cycle

To illustrate the US business cycle, Figure 8.2 shows how US industrial production has been developing over time (on a logarithmic scale).

There are several reasons why industrial production is useful when it comes to illustrating the business cycle. Industrial production is, as mentioned, one of the series that the NBER Business Cycle Dating Committee uses when it determines turning points in the US business cycle. Furthermore, it is a monthly series. It also extends back far in time. In fact, we have high-quality industrial production data at the monthly frequency extending back to January 1884.[3]

[2] In Europe, the Center for Economic Policy Research (CEPR) launched a Eurozone Business Cycle Dating Committee in 2003. Their definition of a recession follows that of the NBER. They define a recession as a '*significant decline in the level of economic activity, spread across the economy of the euro area, usually visible in two or more consecutive quarters of negative growth in GDP, employment and other measures of aggregate economic activity for the euro area as a whole*.'

[3] The Fed maintains and updates a time-series of industrial production on its webpage extending back to 1919. Data before 1919, i.e. from 1884–1919, are from Miron & Romer (1990) and Romer (1994), and the data series themselves are available on Christina Romer's homepage. This chapter uses the Adjusted Miron-Romer Index of Industrial Production, smoothed, damped, and seasonally

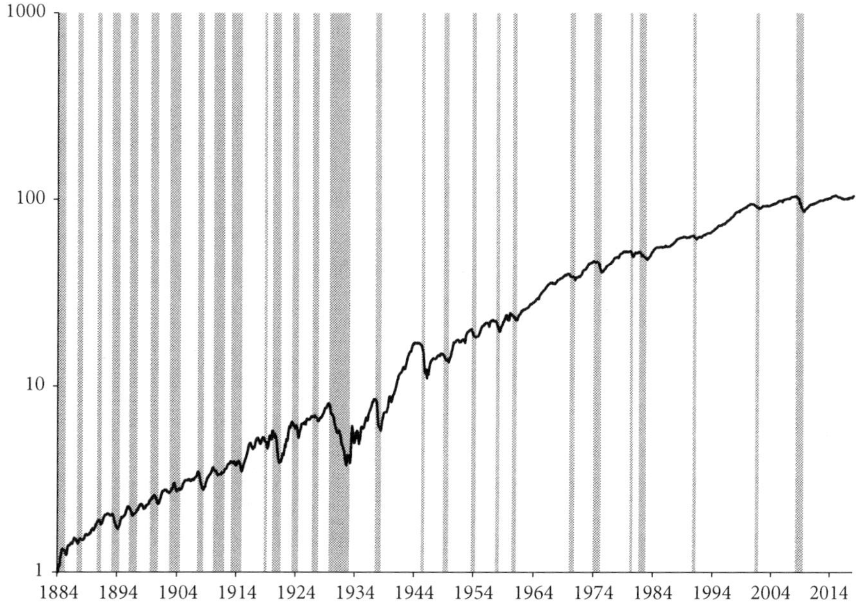

Figure 8.2 Index of US industrial production. 1884–2018. Logarithm scale. NBER-defined recessions indicated by shading.
Data source: FRED, Miron & Romer (1990), and Romer (1994).

Figure 8.2 shows that industrial production in 2018 was basically 100 times larger than it was in 1884. Industrial production is a real series; it measures the development in the total production in the industrial sector in the US. Given that Chapter 2 mentioned that real GDP has increased by a factor of 100+ over the last app. 150 years, and given that industrial production is related to overall economic activity, it is only natural that industrial production also has increased by a similar factor. Growth in industrial production has mirrored long-run growth in total economy activity.

Chapter 2 was devoted to a discussion of long-term growth. In this chapter, we are interested in the business cycle, i.e. fluctuations around the long-term growth trend. Figure 8.2 shows months where the US economy was in recession, according to the NBER recession definitions, as shaded areas.[4] Staring closely at the figure, one sees why such months are recession months. These are months where the

adjusted (Romer, 1994). The full series is thus a spliced series of the adjusted Miron-Romer data (before 1919) and the Fed data after 1919.

[4] Appendix 8.1 lists US recessions and expansions.

otherwise long-term growth in industrial production is interrupted by drops. One also sees that months with economic expansions (non-shaded areas in Figure 8.2) are followed by months of economic contractions (shaded areas) which are then again followed by a new cycle.

Recessions are not all equal. There are recessions where the fall in output is barely visible, such as the 1990–1991 recession. And, there are recessions where the fall in output is enormous. During the Great Depression from August 1929 to March 1933 industrial output fell by app. 50%. In other words, in less than four years, the industrial sector cut their production by more than half. Obviously, this had grave implications for the American economy. When firms in the industrial sector cut production by half, they also lower wages, cut investments, and reduce the number of employees, with devastating consequences for society.

Other grave recessions include the January 1920–July 1921 recession, where output fell by 32%, and the February 1945–October 1945 recession at the end of the Second World War. In the course of just 7 months, industrial production fell by 29%. As a comparison, industrial production fell by 17% during the more recent Great Recession from December 2007–June 2009.

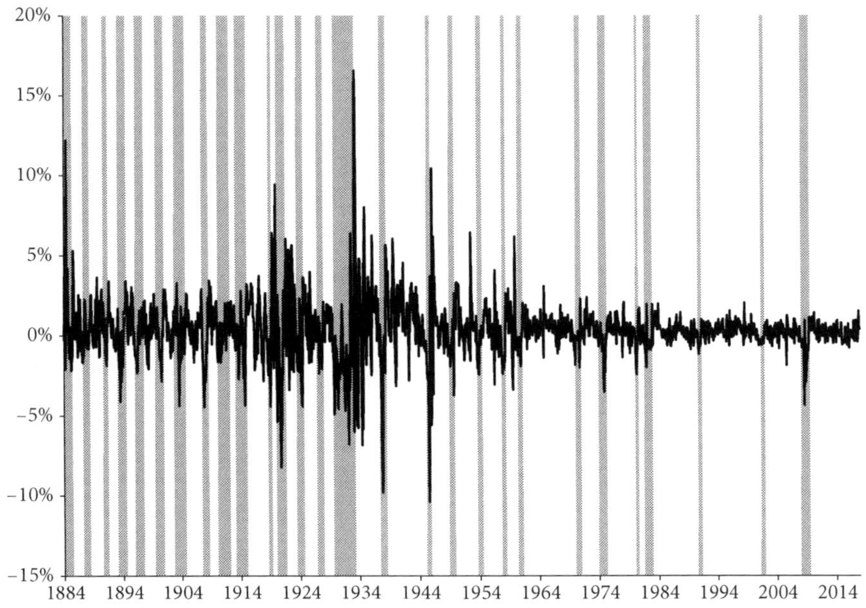

Figure 8.3 Monthly percentage changes in US industrial production. 1884–2018. NBER recessions indicated by shading.

Data source: See Figure 8.2.

Another way to illustrate fluctuations in economic activity is via the monthly (percentage) changes in industrial production. This is in Figure 8.3. Staring closely at Figure 8.3, it appears that growth is positive during most months. There are a number of periods where production falls, however. In some periods, production falls a lot. The largest single-month decline in industrial production was from July to August 1945 where production was cut by 10%. In just one month.

8.3 What causes business cycle fluctuations?

Business activity results from firms thinking about demand for their goods and what factors of production (and the costs associated with using these factors of production) are needed to satisfy demand. E.g., if a firm believes that, given how things look today, there is demand for 100 widgets at their current price, the firm will aim to supply this. When evaluating its production, the firm will recognize that if it changes the price at which it sells widgets, this will affect demand for widgets. The firm will also take into account that changes in the cost of production will affect the profit of the firm, all other things equal. Basically, the level of economic activity at any given point in time will depend on factors influencing demand and supply in the economy. This means that shocks to aggregate demand and supply can cause economic activity to deviate from trend temporarily, i.e. can cause business-cycle fluctuations.

It is important to have some understanding for what might cause business-cycle fluctuations as this can guide us towards the kind of indicators we should look for if we want to say something about the current and future stance of the business cycle. This section lays out reasons why aggregate demand might be temporarily affected by decisions of firms, households, or politicians. Afterwards, shocks to supply are described.

8.3.1 Shocks to aggregate demand

An aggregate demand shock is a shock that influences demand for goods and services in the economy. Aggregate demand consists of consumers' demand for goods and services, firms' demand for investments, the government's demand for government purchases, and how much foreign countries demand goods and services produced in the local economy, i.e. net exports.

Consumers might increase their demand for consumption goods and services if they suddenly became richer. For instance, an unexpected stock-market boom could cause consumption to increase unexpectedly. Similarly, if the central bank reduces the interest rate, consumers will find that it has become cheaper to borrow, and they might start borrowing, and increase consumption financed by borrowed funds. Another factor could be consumers' expectations of their future income streams. E.g., if consumers get worried about the global geopolitical political situation, they might fear that it will have an impact on their job. They lose confidence in the economy, and cut consumption today. Politicians also influence consumer behaviour. For instance, if politicians suddenly decide to make it more attractive to save for retirement, consumers might start saving more (and thus reduce consumption). Similarly, an unexpected tax cut provides consumers with higher income leading to more consumption.

Firms might suddenly increase their investments if they see costs of investments go down. This could be because the central bank lowers the interest rate. Hence, a change in the interest rate might influence both consumers and firms. Politicians might also affect firms' investments by changing tax rates associated with investments, for instance by allowing deductions for certain kinds of investments. Like consumers, if firms for some reason become more (less) optimistic about future economic conditions, they might start investing more (less) today.

The government can influence aggregate demand by changing government purchases and investments. The government can decide to build more roads and bridges, invest in new schools and hospitals, etc. The government can also influence aggregate demand by changing taxes.

Net exports could change if there is a change in economic conditions in foreign countries. If a large trading partner experiences an economic boom, consumers and firms in that country demand more from our country as well (some of the goods and investment equipment they use are produced in our country). The central bank can also influence net exports. If the central bank changes the interest rate, this usually affects the exchange rate. An interest rate reduction tends to depreciate the local currency, making locally produced goods and services relatively cheaper for foreigners, thereby increasing demand for our goods and services. In general, the central bank has strong power when it comes to influencing the business cycle. We devote Chapters 10 and 11 to central banks and how they affect the economy and the stock market.

8.3.2 Shocks to aggregate supply

The amount of goods and services firms are able to supply depends on the availability (and costs) of factors of production and how efficiently these factors can be used in the production process. The factors of production are primarily labor and capital, but might also include natural resources, such as land and raw materials. The efficiency with this these factors can be employed in the production process is called total factor productivity. Chapter 14 explains that one of the most important factors influencing productivity is research and technological progress. When thinking about aggregate supply shocks, we should think about factors that unexpectedly change the amount of labor, capital, natural resources, and technological progress, as well as their prices.

The **number of workers (labor)** in the economy might change for a number of reasons. Some of these could be politically determined. For instance, if the government decides to increase the retirement age, people will need to work longer, i.e. the labor supply increases. Similarly, if minimum wages are increased, i.e. workers are secured a higher minimum wage when working, more people might join the labor force. It is fair to argue that these policy-induced effects on labor supply are more likely to shift labor supply slowly, i.e. will typically not affect the economy at the business-cycle frequency. It could also be that more workers enter the country, i.e. immigration goes up. This could happen faster.

Capital could change if there is a disruption to the amount of capital in the economy. For instance, if a car producer has to call back huge numbers of trucks because a technical error has been discovered, available real capital is reduced. More dramatic, wars have historically destroyed large quantities of capital and thereby caused sudden declines in the supply of goods.

There might be sudden changes to the **amount of natural resources** available. A natural disaster can disrupt the production process and cause GDP to deviate temporarily from trend. For instance, a natural disaster might damage land and thus farming production, oil production at sea might be temporarily destroyed by hurricanes, and aircraft travelling might be temporarily shut down due to ash from a volcano eruption.

Technological innovations are probably more important for their impact on long-run trend growth than for causing business-cycle fluctuations. It cannot be completely disregarded at the business-cycle frequency, though. As an example, a sudden new technology that increases production on the short run might cause output to increase temporarily above its long-term growth trend.

Finally, sudden changes in **prices of factors of production** can cause changes to aggregate supply. Historically, oil-price changes have caused business-cycle fluctuations. A sudden increase in the price of oil will make production more expensive. If firms are reluctant to raise prices (they might be in doubt whether the oil-price increase is temporary or permanent), this hurts firms' profits and they cut production. Alternatively, firms can raise prices, but consumers will then reduce their demand. In any case, an oil-price increase can lead to a temporary fall in production. This seems like a good explanation of what caused the recession in the early 1970s. **Expectations to prices** also matter. For instance, if workers expect prices to increase in the future, they might demand higher wages already today. If wages increase today, but firms raise prices only later, the cost of production has increased (real wages have gone up), and firms might lay off workers. When prices then do rise in the future, real wages go down again, labor goes up, i.e. the effect was temporary, causing a business-cycle fluctuation.

8.4 Theories explaining business-cycle fluctuations

Economists debate how one should think about the propagation of shocks throughout the economy. One school of thought, typically labelled 'New Keynesian Economists', argue that prices and wages are sticky in the short run, i.e. prices and wages do not immediately react to shocks to demand and supply. For instance, wages might be sticky because they are determined by multi-year wage agreements, and prices might be sticky because there are costs associated with changing prices. If a negative shock to, e.g., aggregate demand hits the economy (for one of the reasons mentioned above), firms will cut production and thus cut demand for workers. Employment goes down. If real wages do not move much on the short run, workers will not reduce labor supply. Involuntary unemployment increases. Over time, prices and wages start falling. Wages fall by more than the price level, i.e. real wages go down, in order to clear the labor market. Output, employment, inflation, and wages are procyclical (move with the business cycle, i.e. fall during recessions and increase during expansions) whereas unemployment is countercyclical and involuntary.

Another school of thought, typically labeled 'Real Business Cycle Economists', believe that prices and wages are fully flexible. The main reason behind business-cycle fluctuations, they argue, is shocks to technology. They argue that the long-run growth trend itself is fluctuating. I.e., business-cycle fluctuations are not fluctuations around a long-term growth trend, but fluctuations in the trend itself. The story goes as follows. Imagine a negative shock to technology. Labor productivity falls, and, as a consequence, firms will not demand as many workers as previously. This leads to unemployment. Output also falls, as firms hire fewer workers. Output and employment move procyclically. In Real Business Cycle models, output falls more than demand, leading to a rise in prices. Inflation moves countercyclically, i.e. increases during recessions and falls during expansions. Nominal wages also adjust but not as much as prices, i.e. real wages fall during recessions (are procyclical). Importantly, unemployment in these models is typically not viewed as involuntary but as voluntary adjustments to technology shocks. Workers prefer to stay home when real wages are low during recessions.

It seems fair to argue that most economists today do not view all business-cycle fluctuations as mere reactions to technological shocks. How to interpret a severe recession as a severe shock to technology? Why can't firms and workers keep using existing technology? Second, and perhaps even more important, few economists today believe that all fluctuations in unemployment reflect voluntary reactions to technological shocks. It seems hard to believe that the 25% unemployment rate during the 1930s was due primarily to people staying voluntarily at home. Third, in Real Business Cycle Models there is no room for policy intervention. A recession is a natural response to a technology shock and unemployment is voluntary, so politicians better stay away from trying to influence it. Most economists today agree that situations might arise where policy initiatives (monetary and/or fiscal policy) that smooth out otherwise severe fluctuations in economic activity can be useful. All this said, most economists also recognize the important insight of the Real Business Cycle Theory that the long-term growth trend might not be deterministic, but in itself stochastic (fluctuating). The point is just that it is difficult to believe that all fluctuations in economic activity are due to fluctuations in technology and that all unemployment is voluntary.

8.5 The typical recession and expansion

Appendix 8.1 provides a complete list of all US recessions during our 1871–2018 sample. The shortest recession was the January 1980–July 1980 recession. Economic activity contracted six months. The longest lasted from October 1973 through March 1979, in total 65 months. The shortest expansion was the March 1919–January 1920 expansion, in total 10 months. The longest spans more than 120 months, from June 2009 and still ongoing at the time of writing.

These numbers indicate that expansions typically last longer than recessions. The average duration of a recession during the 1871–2018 period is slightly more than 1.5 years (19.2 months) whereas the average expansion lasts more than 3.5 years (40.1 months).

Figure 8.4 splits the full 1871–2018 period into subperiods before and after 1945, and show business-cycle characteristics for each subperiod. The figure highlights an important change in the characteristics of the business cycle: after World War II, expansions have lasted longer and recessions consequently shorter, compared to the period before 1945. Since World War II, the average recession has lasted less than one year and the average expansion close to five years. This implies that recessions have occurred with a lower frequency after WWII. During the 1871–1945 period, there were 18 recessions. During the equally long, but more recent, 1945–2018 period, there were 11 recessions. On average, the US economy was in recession in four out of ten months before WWII. After WWII, the economy has been in recession less than two out of ten months, on average. Figure 8.5 shows the duration of US expansions in numbers of months. It is clear from the figure how the duration of US expansions has increased since 1945. We return to possible explanations why expansions last longer after 1945 in Section 8.6.

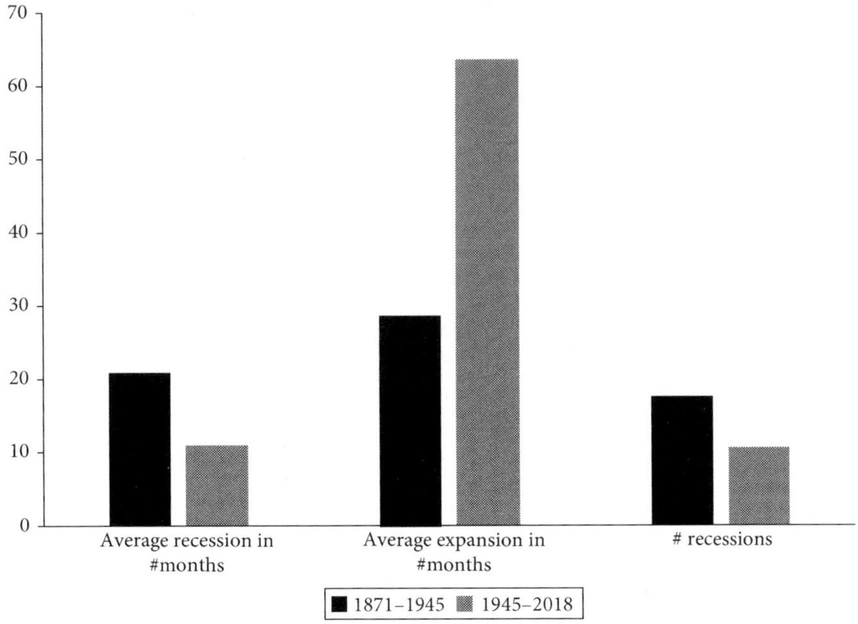

Figure 8.4 Average length of a recession and/or expansion and numbers of recessions. 1871–1945 versus 1946–2018.
Data source: NBER.

In contrast to their frequency, the severity of recessions has not changed. Table 8.1 shows that the average negative growth rate of industrial production has been around 8% during recessions (annualized), both before and after WWII.

An important conclusion, thus, is that recessions have become less frequent and of shorter duration, but output falls as much during recession months as before WWII. Romer (1989) investigated the characteristics of the US business cycles. She stated that (on page 33):

> What has not changed, at least not dramatically, between the prewar and postwar eras is the volatility of broad macroeconomic indicators and the average severity of recessions......... Expansions are noticeably longer after World War II than before World War I, indicating that recessions happen less often today than in the past.

Romer analysed US data until 1997. This chapter adds 20 years of data. The conclusions remain.

The average annualized growth rate during expansions has been lower after WWII, see Table 8.1. The average annualized growth rate of industrial production

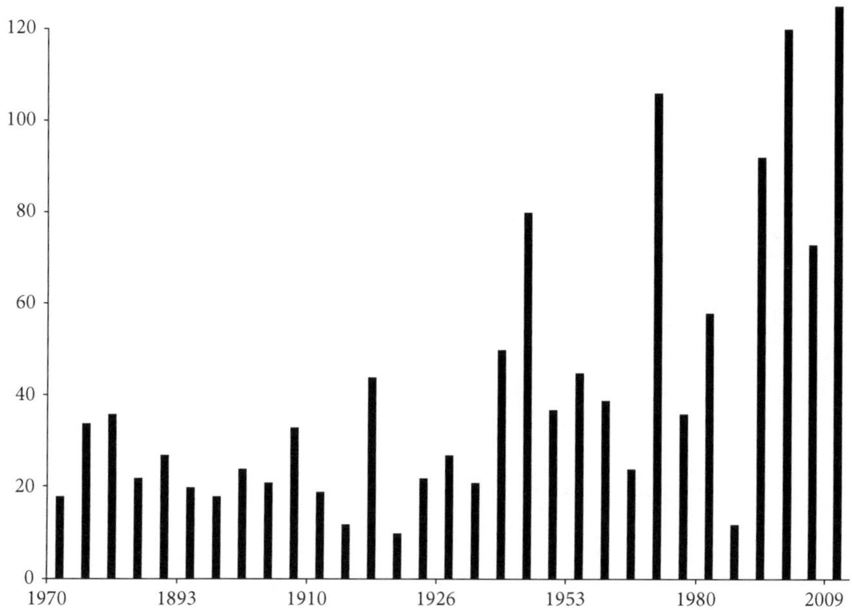

Figure 8.5 The duration of US expansions in number of months.
Data source: NBER.

during expansions was around 12% before WWII. After WWII, it has been less than half, at 5%. Table 8.1 includes data for both industrial production and GDP. Industrial production reacts stronger to expansions and recessions: during recessions, industrial production falls by around 8% annualized on average, whereas GDP falls by around 2% annualized. During expansions, industrial production grows by 5% on average whereas GDP grows with 4%. Industrial production fluctuates more over the business cycle than GDP. This is natural. GDP includes production of hospitals, schools, police activities, etc., i.e. public activities that need to continue also during recessions. Industrial firms, on the other hand, can cut production when demand is lacking.

Table 8.1 Average annualized growth rates of monthly industrial production and quarterly GDP during recessions and expansions

	Monthly IP growth			Quarterly GDP growth
	1884–2018	1884–1945	1946–2018	1947–2018
Average	3.8%	4.6%	3.0%	3.2%
Recession	−8.2%	−8.0%	−8.5%	−2.0%
Expansion	8.0%	12.5%	5.0%	4.1%

8.6 Why fewer and shorter recessions after 1945?

Why has the business cycle changed in some dimensions (frequency and duration) but not in others (severity per month). Most likely, politics play a major role.

Prior to the Great Depression in the early 1930s, government budgets were small, banks were left to their own devices, and monetary policy was not very effective.

Stress in the banking system contributed to the large contraction in economic activity during The Great Depression of the 1930s. Customers started withdrawing their deposits from banks as they feared they would lose their deposits in case their bank failed. The contraction in deposits caused banks to cut lending, as banks inter alia finance lending with deposits. This led to a credit crunch with severe implications for consumption and investments. As a reaction to this, in 1934, the Federal Deposit Insurance Mechanism (FDIC) was set up to avoid a repeat of the 1930s bank-run experience. A deposit insurance scheme helps stabilize the banking system and thereby the availability of credit. During the financial crisis of 2007–2009, as an example, few customers lined up to withdraw their deposits as in a classical bank run.[5]

Changes in the conduct of fiscal policy have affected the business cycle in two distinct ways. First, the size of government budgets has increased. Romer (1999) mentions that between 1901 and 1916, government expenditures accounted for around 1.4%–2.5% of GNP only. With such a small budget, it is difficult for governments to influence economic activity via fiscal policy. After WWII, government budgets have increased. In the Great Depression of 2007–2009, for instance, the deficit on the US government budget amounted to almost 10% of GDP. By increasing public consumption and investments during recessions, workers are employed and aggregate demand is increased. This helps with shortening a recession as well as reducing its impact on economic activity.

Automatic stabilizers have also been introduced. Automatic stabilizers refer to those parts of fiscal policy that work 'automatically'. For instance, progressive taxes (higher taxes on higher incomes) make the fraction of income that goes to taxes increase in a boom, thereby dampening the expansion, and lowers that fraction in a contraction, helping to support demand during a recession. Similarly, unemployment benefits increase when the economy is contracting, supporting aggregate demand. These policies were not available, or considerably less so, before WWII.

As described in more detail in Chapter 10, monetary policy also plays a role in reducing the impact of recessions.

[5] Instead, another kind of 'bank run' occurred where institutional investors did not renew funding to banks. Chapter 12 describes the financial crisis of 2008.

In total, monetary, fiscal, and financial-sector policies have served to reduce the impact of negative shocks to the economy. Similarly, automatic stabilizers and discrete changes in monetary policy have cooled down potential booms.

Why are recessions, on the other hand, as severe today as they have 'always been'? Again, we might look at politics. Policy can also cause recessions. For instance, the dramatic hike in interest rates in the early 1980s seem to have contributed, and potentially even caused, the 1981 recession. The 1981 recession was one of the longest post-WWII recessions. Romer (1999, page 40) writes:

> Average severity of recessions has declined only slightly because the average size of the recessions we have created is not much smaller than the average of the wide range of small, medium, and large prewar recessions.

So, fiscal and monetary policy, together with financial-sector stabilization policies, have helped to eliminate some shocks. This has eliminated some types of recessions. In addition, it has supported aggregate demand during recessions, which has shortened the duration of recessions. On the other hand, some recessions appear to be policy-induced, implying that the severity of the typical recession has, in the end, not been significantly impacted.

8.7 The international evidence

As mentioned, there is no international body that—like the NBER Business Cycle Dating Committee in the US—determines when different countries are in recessions. Likewise, official recession-dating committees do not exist in most countries. When looking at international data, one needs to resort to alternative measures of recessions that can be applied across different countries. As mentioned, the 'two consecutive quarters of negative GDP growth' is a reasonable, if imperfect, straightforward definition.

Figures 8.6 through 8.11 plot the quarterly GDP growth rates for six of the seven G-7 countries since 1960, i.e. all G-7 countries except the US, as we have already paid close attention to the US in the preceding parts of this chapter. The data have been sourced from the OECD Main Economic Indicators. Shaded areas indicate recessions, as determined by the 'two consecutive quarters of negative GDP growth' criteria.

A first lesson is that all countries experience recessions. A second lesson is that countries differ in terms of the frequency and duration of recessions. During 1960–2018, Canada and France experienced four recessions whereas Italy experienced twelve and Germany ten. Japan stands out in terms of how recessions are distributed across time. From 1960 to 1992, i.e. for 32 years, Japan did not experience

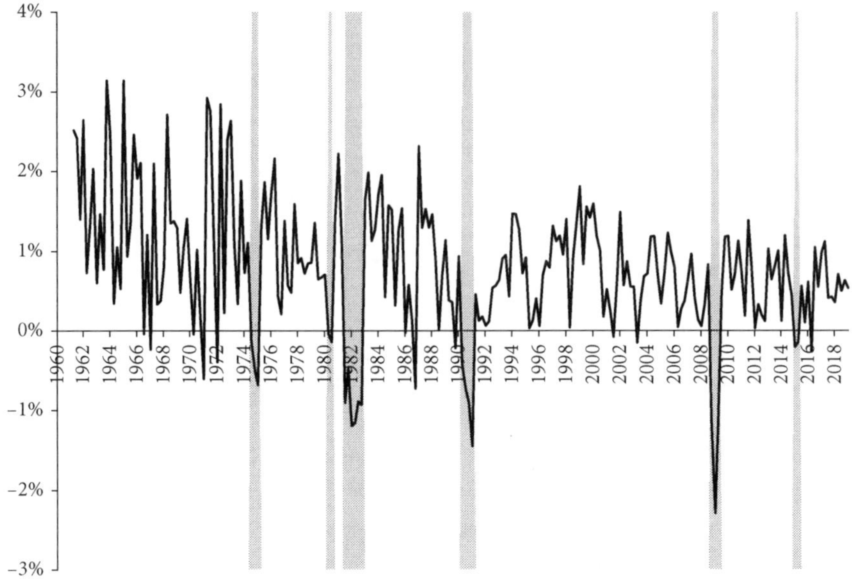

Figure 8.6 Canadian GDP growth.

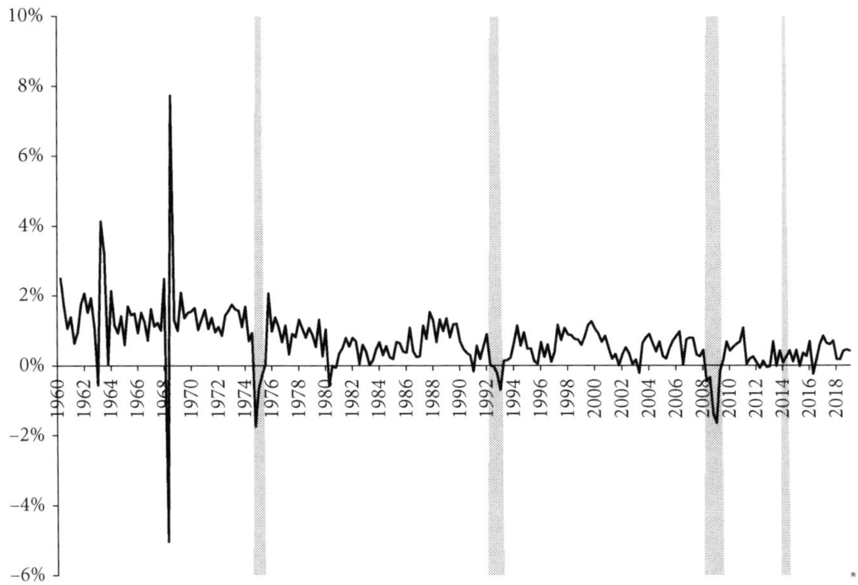

Figure 8.7 French GDP growth.

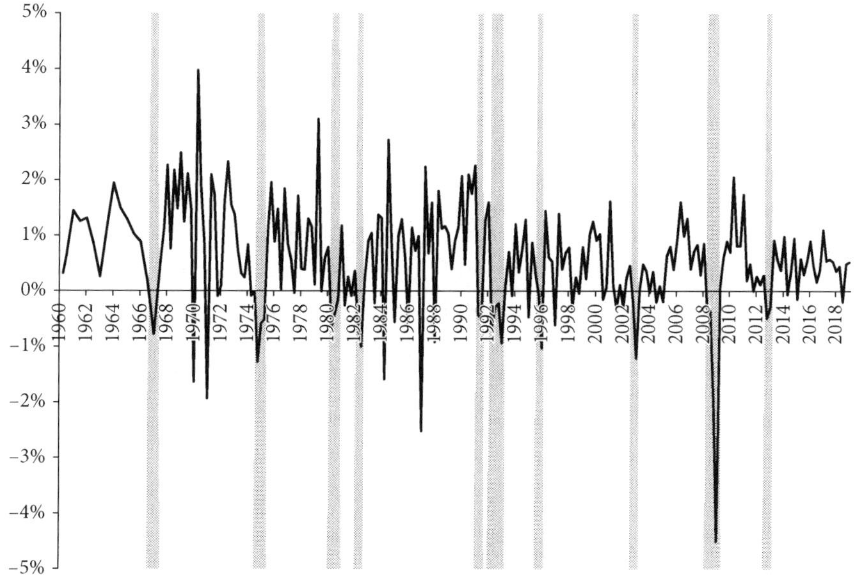

Figure 8.8 German GDP growth.

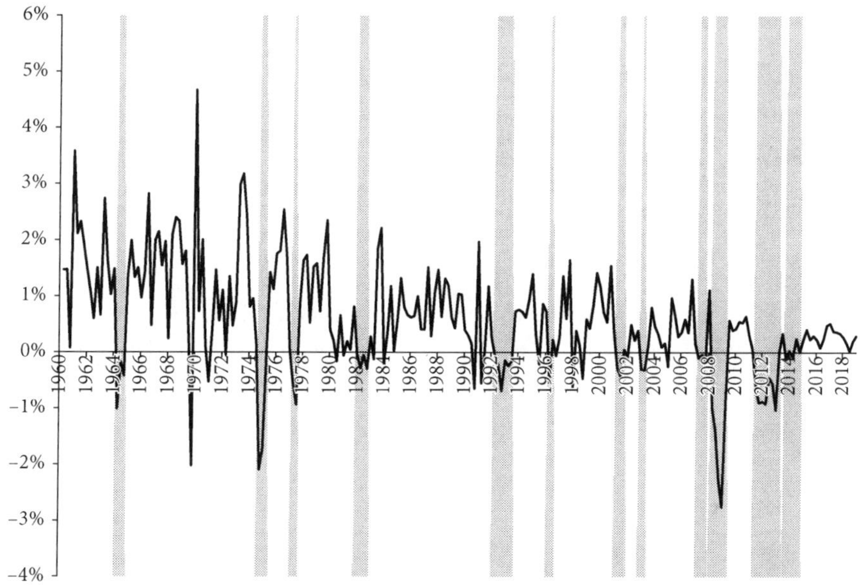

Figure 8.9 Italian GDP growth.

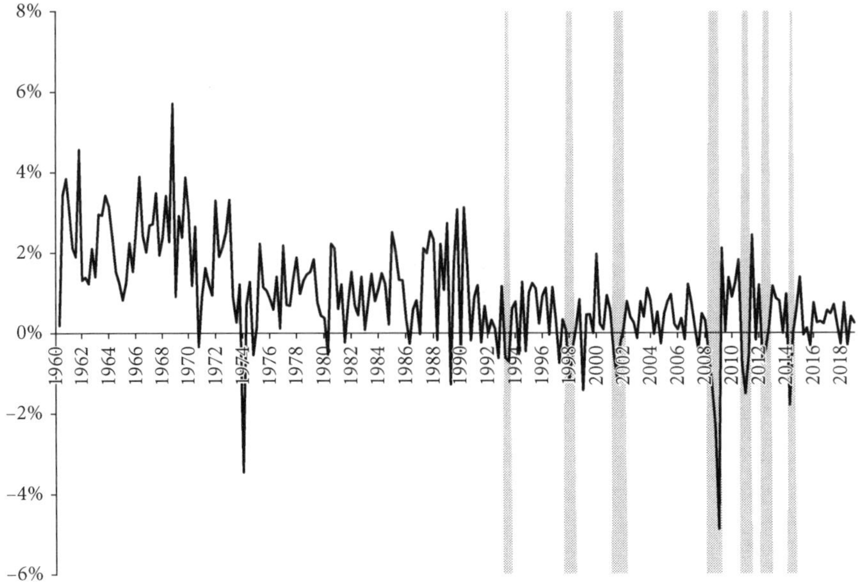

Figure 8.10 Japanese GDP growth.

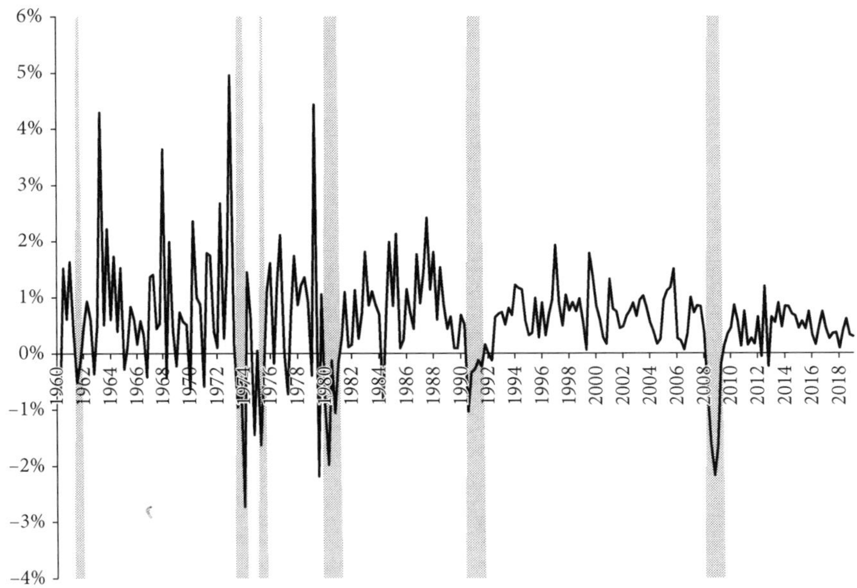

Figure 8.11 UK GDP growth.

Table 8.2 Growth rates (annualized) of quarterly GDP during expansions and recessions, and numbers of quarters where the economies have been in recession. 1960–2018

	Canada	France	Germany	Italy	Japan	UK
Growth rates						
Average	3.2%	2.8%	2.4%	2.4%	3.8%	2.4%
Recession	−3.5%	−2.3%	−2.8%	−2.1%	−4.1%	−3.6%
Expansion	3.7%	3.2%	2.8%	3.6%	4.7%	3.0%
Number						
Total	236	236	236	236	236	236
Recession	20	14	27	46	21	22
Fraction	8.5%	5.9%	11.4%	19.5%	8.9%	9.2%

a single recession. It is remarkable for a country to grow uninterrupted for more than 30 years. On the other hand, since the early 1990s, it has been difficult for Japan to create economic growth.

Some recessions are common to all countries, i.e. are global recessions, and some recessions are individual. For instance, most countries were in recession during the early-to-mid 1970s. The first oil crisis—a global hike in oil prices—is to blame. Similarly, most countries were in recession during the early 1980s and during the Great Recession of 2007–2009. On the other hand, the high number of recessions in Italy in itself indicates that many of these recessions were caused by domestic events.

Table 8.2 collects average (annualized) growth rates of real GDP during recessions and expansions for the six countries appearing in Figures 8.6 through 8.11. On average, annualized growth in real GDP has been between 2% in Germany and close to 4% in Japan. During recessions, the average fall in GDP has been between 2% and 4% (annualized). During expansions, the average growth rates has been between 3% and 4.7%. These numbers are not very different from the numbers for the US based on quarterly growth in GDP (Table 8.1). The countries in Table 8.2 have been in recession between 6% and 20% of the time. The average is 11%. This is also not very different from the US either, which has been in recession 14.6% of the time after WWII on average (Table 8.1).

8.8 Checklist

This chapter has described business-cycle fluctuations in economic activity. The main conclusions to remember are:

- The business cycle refers to alternations between economic expansions and contractions. A cycle consists of one expansion followed by one contraction. Contractions are also called recessions.
- Peaks and troughs are turning points of the business cycle, i.e. business activity reaches its peak the month before the economy enters a phase of contraction.
- All countries experience business cycles.
- In the US, the NBER Business Cycle Dating Committee determines the beginning and the end of a business cycle. Internationally, the 'two consecutive quarters of negative GDP growth' definition is often used.
- Business cycles vary in duration, frequency, and severity.
- Some recessions are severe while others are relatively mild. During the Great Depression from August 1929 to March 1933, for instance, US industrial output fell by 50%. On the other hand, during the July 1990 to March 1991 recession, industrial output fell by only 4%. On average, GDP falls by 0.5% per quarter during recessions.
- The duration and frequency of recessions (in the US) has decreased after the Second World War.
  - Before WWII, the average recession lasted 21 months and the average expansion 29.
  - After WWII, the average recession lasts 11 months and the average expansion 58.
- The increased use of fiscal, monetary, and financial-sector stabilization policies after WWII has contributed to the reduction in the frequency and duration of recessions.
- In some cases, macroeconomic policies have initiated recessions.

Appendix 8.1. US recessions and expansions as defined by the NBER. Number of months during recessions and expansions.

Peak month	Trough month	Peak to trough Recessions	Trough to peak Expansions
	December 1854		
June 1857	December 1858	18	30
October 1860	June 1861	8	22
April 1865	December 1867	32	46
June 1869	December 1870	18	18
October 1873	March 1879	65	34
March 1882	May 1885	38	36
March 1887	April 1888	13	22
July 1890	May 1891	10	27
January 1893	June 1894	17	20
December 1895	June 1897	18	18
June 1899	December 1900	18	24
September 1902	August 1904	23	21
May 1907	June 1908	13	33
January 1910	January 1912	24	19
January 1913	December 1914	23	12
August 1918	March 1919	7	44
January 1920	July 1921	18	10
May 1923	July 1924	14	22
October 1926	November 1927	13	27
August 1929	March 1933	43	21
May 1937	June 1938	13	50
February 1945	October 1945	8	80
November 1948	October 1949	11	37
July 1953	May 1954	10	45
August 1957	April 1958	8	39
April 1960	February 1961	10	24
December 1969	November 1970	11	106
November 1973	March 1975	16	36
January 1980	July 1980	6	58
July 1981	November 1982	16	12
July 1990	March 1991	8	92
March 2001	November 2001	8	120
December 2007	June 2009	18	73

9
The stock market over the business cycle

Part II of this book described how stock-market movements relate to economic growth in the long run. This part describes how the stock market relates to the business cycle, i.e. to fluctuations in economic activity around the long-term growth trend.

We start out by documenting the stylized facts: stocks do badly during recessions and excellently during expansions. On average, US real stock-market returns have been almost eleven(!) percentage points higher during expansions on an annualized basis. Stock returns will have already turned negative during the late phase of an expansion, i.e. before the arrival of a recession. Right after the recession, on the other hand, the stock market performs fantastically well. Across the business cycle, therefore, stock returns are low during late stages of expansions (i.e. when a recession is approaching) as well as during recessions, but turn positive during early phases of expansions, i.e. right after the end of recessions. Returns stay positive during the early and medium phases of expansions. Late in the expansion, it all starts all over, and stock returns start shrinking before the arrival of the next recession.

Bonds do better than stocks during recessions. This has not least to do with the fact that central banks lower the monetary policy rate during recessions (as we will see in the next chapter). Lower interest rates lead to higher bond prices, causing bonds to perform well during recessions.

Earnings of firms drop during recessions. Quite a lot in fact. Stock prices drop as well, whereas dividends do not. Or, at least, not as much as stock prices. This means that the stock-price dividend multiple contracts during recessions. If stock prices drop by more than dividends, it must be because investors have increased their expectations of future discount rates and/or lowered their expectations to future dividend/earnings growth. The chapter discusses the academic research on this issue. This research concludes that stock returns are low during recessions because risk aversion, and thus risk premia and discount rates, goes up, at least in the US. Internationally, there is evidence indicating that stock returns are low during bad times because investors expect future growth to be low.

From Main Street to Wall Street. Jesper Rangvid, Oxford University Press (2021). © Jesper Rangvid.
DOI: 10.1093/oso/9780198866404.003.0009

9.1 The US stock market during recessions and expansions

Figure 9.1 shows the cumulated real return from the US stock market since 1871 on a logarithmic scale, based on continuous reinvestment of dividends. The main impression Figure 9.1 leaves behind is that the stock market grows. This is what Part II of the book dealt with. Long-term multidecade growth and returns are fascinating and intriguing, as Part II discussed, but many investors have shorter investment horizons. Over shorter horizons, i.e. over the business cycle, fluctuations in economic activity around the long-term growth trend are of first-order importance for stock returns.

Shading indicate recessions in Figure 9.1. Recessions are typically periods with low or negative returns on the stock market. The most extreme example is the Great Depression of 1929–1933. From the beginning of the recession in September 1929 to its end in March 1933, the stock market fell by a mind-blowing 80%! In other words, if you made an investment of USD 100 in the stock market in September 1929, and kept on with this investment until March 1933, you would have seen the value of your investment cut to 20 dollar in March 1933. Investors did collect

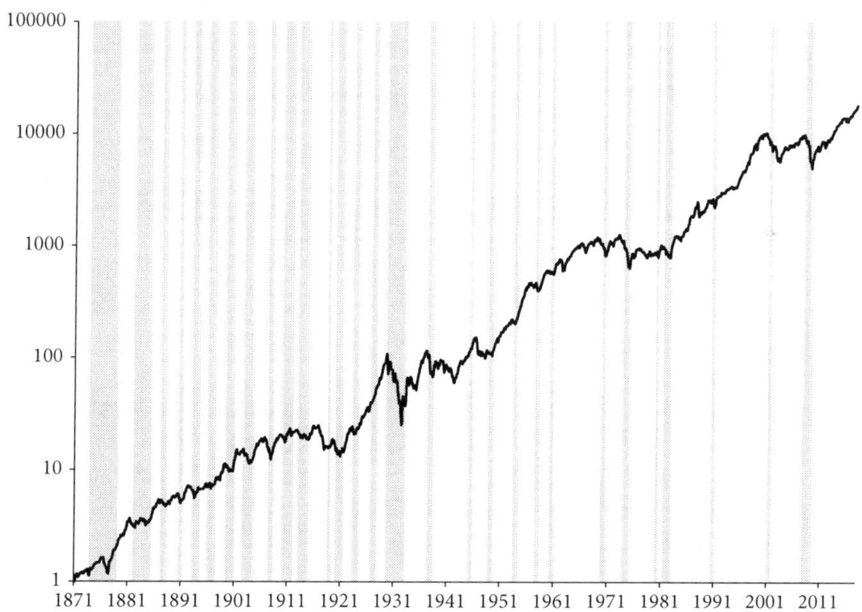

Figure 9.1 Real cumulative return from the US stock market. NBER recessions indicated by shading.

Data source: See Figure 3.1.

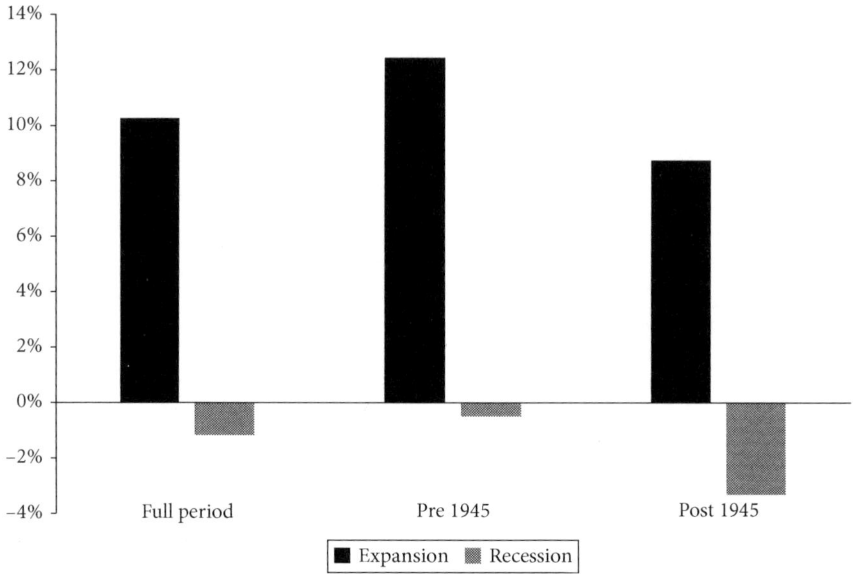

Figure 9.2 Real average annualized monthly US stock returns during recessions and expansions. 1871–2018 and subperiods before and after 1945.
Data source: See Figure 3.1.

some dividends, but the average annual real return during the Great Depression was still a negative 20.1% per year. The cumulative loss was 65% in real terms.

How much larger are returns during expansions? Figure 9.2 shows average real stock returns during recessions and expansions. We know from previous chapters that the average long-term (geometric) annual real stock return is close to seven percent per annum. Splitting returns into recessions and expansions, Figure 9.2 shows that average (geometric) stock returns across expansions is app. 10% on an annualized basis over the full 1871–2018 period. Across expansions, investors are handsomely rewarded for being in the stock market. Across recessions, however, returns are negative on average, at −1.2% at an annualized rate. During recessions, investors have lost money on average in real terms. When the average real return during expansions is around 10% and the average return during recessions is a negative 1.2%, expansions on average deliver around 11 percentage points higher returns.

When the average monthly return is higher during expansions, and expansions usually last longer than recessions, the cumulative return from the stock market is on average much higher during expansions. Table 9.1 shows that the average

Table 9.1 Cumulative US real returns during recessions and expansions

	1871–2018	1871–1945	1946–2018
Expansions	50.5%	32.1%	78.2%
Recessions	3.5%	4.8%	1.7%

cumulative real return across all expansions from 1871 through 2018 is 50.5%. During recessions, it is only 3.5%.[1]

Recessions have been worse for stock-market investors after 1945, as Figure 9.2 also shows. Before 1945, the monthly (annualized) real return from the stock market was basically zero during recessions. After 1945, i.e. in more modern times, recessions have generally been associated with even lower returns. This implies that even when recessions have been rarer and shorter since 1945, as the previous chapter showed, investors have generally been hit harder during recessions, and have gained even higher returns during expansions. Cumulative returns reveal this, too. Table 9.1 shows that cumulative returns during expansions have been considerably higher post–1945.

9.2 Variation across recessions and expansions

Figure 9.2 and Table 9.1 show averages across recessions and expansions. Not all recessions are associated with falling stock markets, though, and not all expansions have delivered positive returns. Figures 9.3 and 9.4 collect cumulative real returns during each recession and expansion, respectively, in the US since 1871.

The recession with the largest cumulative loss in the stock market was the Great Depression of 1929–1933. The Great Depression was also the longest recession in history, lasting 3.5 years, as the previous chapter showed. Stocks on average returned less than −2.4% per months. When real returns are negative by 2.4% per month, and this lasts for 36 months, investors loose a large fraction of their wealth. The cumulative loss during the Great Depression was 65%.

Not all recessions lead to negative cumulative returns, though. For instance, at the most extreme, the stock market returned (in real terms) 87% during the November 1873 through March 1879 recession. Individual recessions can

[1] Average cumulative returns are small but positive during recessions, whereas average monthly returns are negative. How can this be? As the next section shows, there are some recessions that have delivered high cumulative returns. When averaging across the cumulative returns during recessions, the long-lasting recessions with positive cumulative returns generated so much higher cumulative returns than the ones with negative cumulative returns that the average becomes positive.

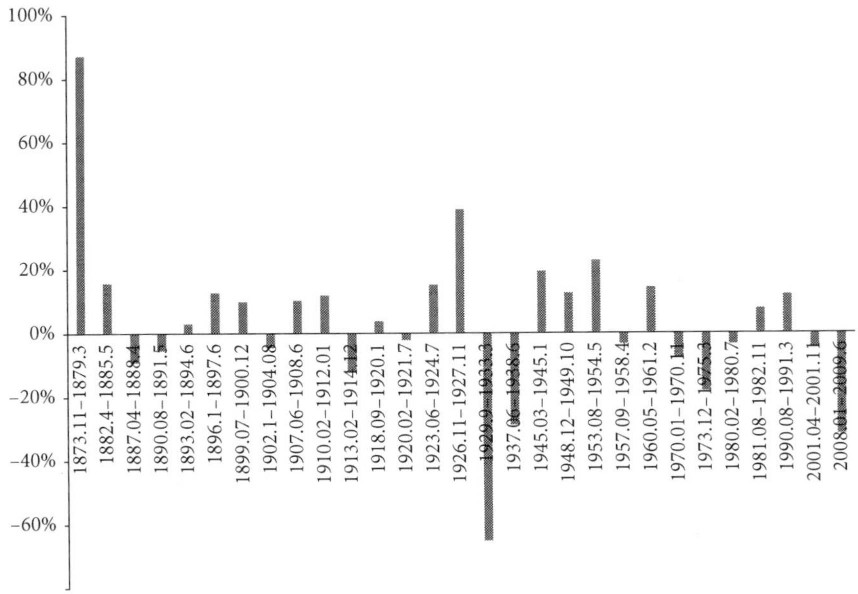

Figure 9.3 Cumulative US real returns during individual recessions.
Data source: See Figure 3.1.

thus differ substantially from the average recession, some delivering much lower returns than the average and some even delivering positive returns. Across all recession months, however, the stock market has returned −1.2% (in annualized terms) on average. This is the number plotted in Figure 9.2. Also, out of the 29 recessions from 1871 through 2018, 13 delivered a negative cumulative real return. Compare this to expansions. Out of the 30 expansions, only three delivered negative cumulative real return.

Why are some recessions so much worse than others? Muir (2017) provides an interesting result. He shows that recessions associated with financial crisis tend to be much worse for stock markets. Prime examples are the 1929–1933 and 2008–2009 recessions. These were recessions caused by financial crises, i.e. problems in the banking sector. Stock markets fell dramatically. Figure 9.4 shows that the 2008 recession delivered the second-lowest return during any recessions (the 1929–1933 Great Depression the lowest, as mentioned). Chapter 12 describes the 2008–2009 financial crisis and recession in more detail.

On average, expansions have returned 50.5% (Table 9.1). As for recessions, there is dispersion across the average expansion. The expansion after the financial crisis of 2008, which has also been the longest expansion on record, has basically been one long boom. It is the mother of all stock-market expansions. Cumulative real returns have been 350%. Next, the dot.com period during the 1990s delivered a cumulative return of 200%. The November 1945 through November 1948

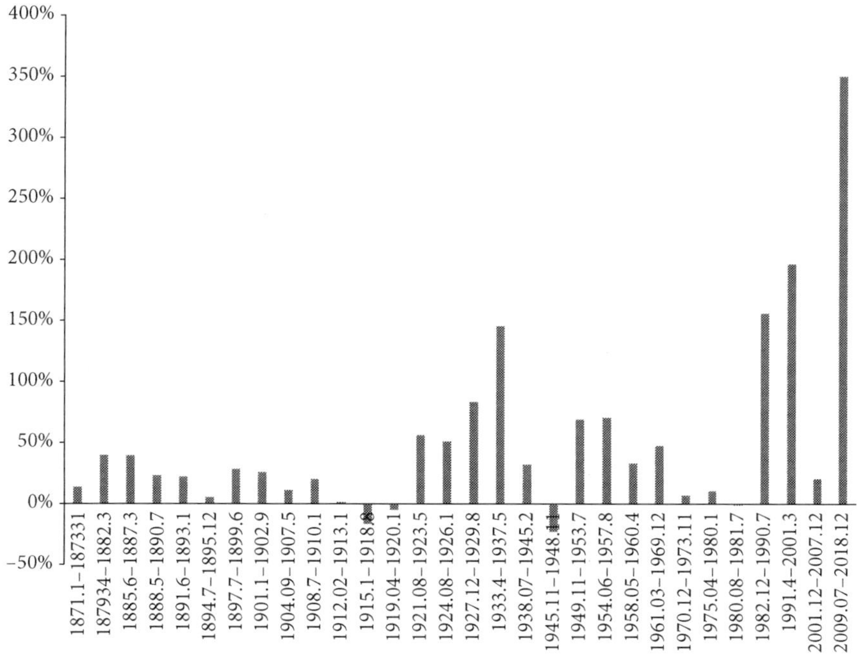

Figure 9.4 Cumulative US real returns during individual expansions.
Data source: See Figure 3.1.

recession, at the other extreme, delivered a negative cumulative return of 22%. Despite variation around the average expansion and recession, the main conclusion is that returns have generally been much higher during expansions.

What about risk? The standard deviation of real stock returns across recession months is 5.3%. Across expansions, it is 3.4%. In other words, not only have returns typically been considerably higher during expansions, the certainty with which returns are achieved has also been higher. This also means that when returns have been so much higher during expansions (10% vs. −1% annualized monthly returns) and risks lower, the reward-risk relationship has been considerably higher during expansions. All in all, taking into account both average returns and risks, the stock market is a much nicer place to be during expansions.

9.3 Bonds over the business cycle

Central banks have a tendency to hike interest rates during expansions and lower them during recessions, as we will see in the next chapter that deals with monetary policy. This indicates that there might a relation between bond returns and the

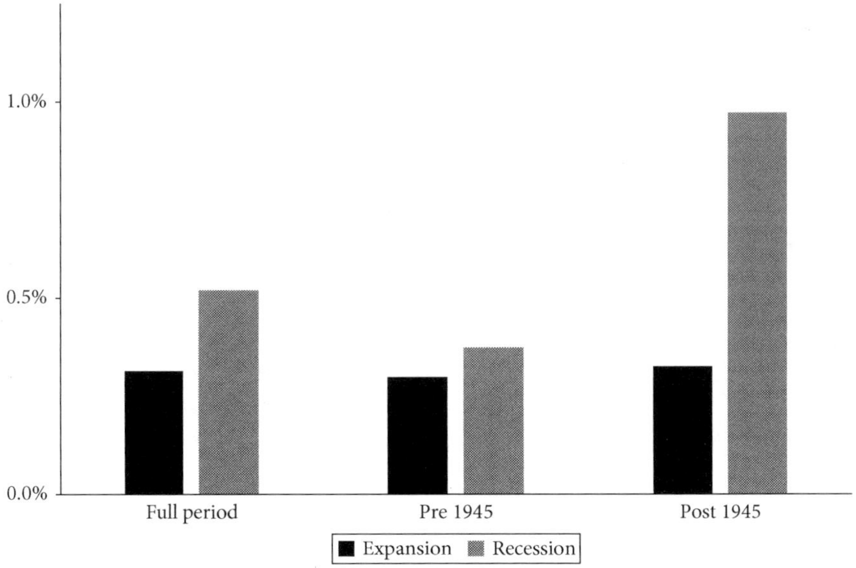

Figure 9.5 Real average annualized monthly bond returns during recessions and expansions. 1871–2018 and subperiods before and after 1945.
Data source: See Figure 3.1.

business cycle. And indeed there is. Over the business cycle, the returns to long-term bonds behave opposite to the returns on stocks, as Figure 9.5 illustrates. The figure is similar to Figure 9.2, but contains average real returns from long-term government bonds. Even when bond returns do not differ as much as stock returns between recessions and expansions, the conclusion that bonds perform relatively better during recessions is clear. This has been particularly true since 1945. Since 1945, bond returns have been almost twice as large during recessions as they have been during expansions. The fact that stocks perform relatively badly, and bonds relatively well, during recessions indicates that investors can improve performance if switching between bonds and stocks over the business cycle.

9.4 Should you avoid stocks during recessions?

When it is so much nicer to be invested in the stock market during expansions, should you then completely avoid the stock market during recessions? If you can exactly time the market and avoid the big drops, you would do better, but it is difficult to predict recessions and time the market, as we return to in Part IV. Furthermore, as we have seen, not all recessions are associated with big drops.

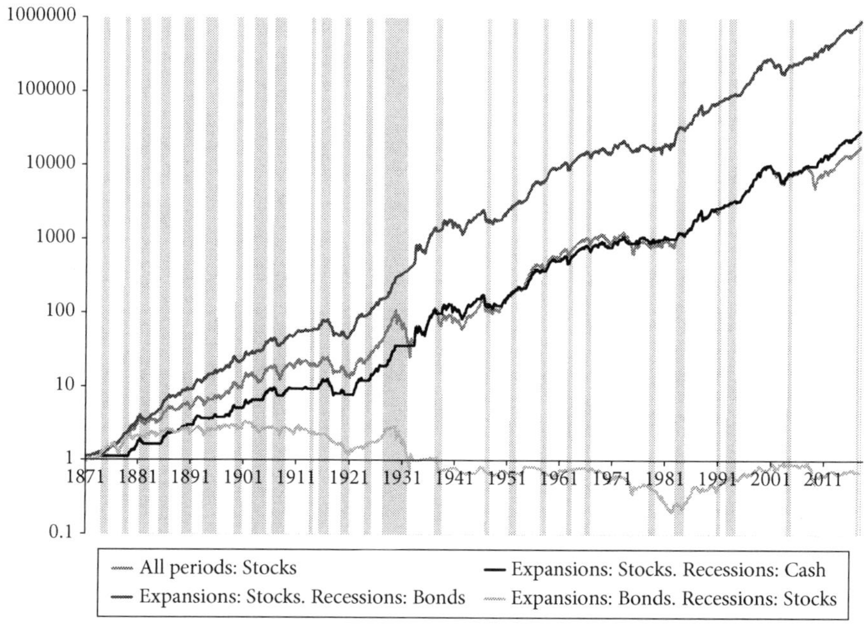

Figure 9.6 Real cumulative returns. Different asset allocations across the business cycle. NBER recessions indicated by shading.
Data source: See Figure 3.1.

Nevertheless, it is useful to know what the potential gains to market timing around recessions are.

We need to take a stand on what to do with our funds during recessions if not being invested in the stock market. Figure 9.6 shows the cumulative real returns from four investment strategies: (i) being in the stock market all the time, (ii) being in the stock market during expansions and staying on the sideline, i.e. being in cash, during recessions, (iii) being in the stock market during expansions and bonds during recessions, and, to illustrate a very unfortunate strategy, (iv) being in the stock market during recessions and bonds during expansions.

Being in stocks during all months is the strategy also depicted in Figure 9.1. It is included in Figure 9.6 to compare with the alternatives. Compare it, first, to the cumulative return one would have received if staying out of the stock market during recessions and keeping your money in cash, i.e. not investing it anywhere. Figure 9.2 showed that returns are close to zero, though negative (−1.2%), during recessions. When average returns are close to zero during recessions, average returns from being investing in stocks in all periods, and only being invested in stocks during expansions, is small. Recessions are volatile months, however. Across all months, the standard deviation of returns is 14% (annualized). Leaving

Table 9.2 Returns and risks of market-timing strategies

	All periods: Stocks	**Exp.: Stocks Rec.: Cash**	**Exp.: Stocks Rec.: Bonds**	**Exp.: Bonds Rec.: Stocks**
		Full period: 1871–2018		
Annualized Return	6.9%	7.3%	9.8%	−0.2%
STD	14.1%	10.2%	10.9%	11.0%
Reward/risk	49.0%	71.3%	89.7%	−2.1%
		Before 1945: 1871–1945		
Annualized Return	6.8%	7.1%	10.9%	−0.3%
STD	15.6%	10.2%	10.6%	12.3%
Reward/risk	43.8%	69.0%	102.7%	−2.2%
		After 1945: 1946–2018		
Annualized Return	7.0%	7.5%	8.7%	−0.2%
STD	12.3%	10.1%	11.2%	9.5%
Reward/risk	56.7%	73.7%	77.1%	−2.0%

out recession months, standard deviation drops to 10%. The overall risk-return ratio is improved from 49% to 71%. You get almost the same return but less risk if you keep your money out of the stock market and in cash during recessions. Table 9.2 collects these numbers. The table also splits into subperiods before and after 1945. The conclusion that returns are not much affected if you stay on the sideline during recessions, but risk is reduced, also appears during subperiods.

Consider now the third strategy, the one where you switch out of stocks and into bonds during recessions. Bonds have generated positive returns during recessions (Figure 9.5). This would have been a fantastic (hypothetical) strategy. Instead of ending up with USD 15,400 in 2018 (after investing USD 1 in 1871 and reinvesting all dividends; the number mentioned earlier), such a perfect market timer would end up with app. USD 900,000! This corresponds to an average annual (geometric) return of something like 9.8% over a 147-year period. At the same time, risk is low in this strategy, so the risk-reward ratio is 90% (Table 9.2).

Finally, to complete the picture of how important the business cycle is for the stock market, consider the opposite investment strategy, i.e. being in bonds during expansions and stocks during recessions. This would have been a disaster. The investor would see his/her USD 1 in 1871 accumulate to only USD 0.72 in 2018. I.e., after being invested for almost 150 years, you end up with less than you started out with (in real terms). This corresponds to an average annual return of −0.2%. Table 9.2 shows that this strategy is a disaster both before and after 1945.

It is important to interpret these figures with caution. They suggest a perfect market timing strategy where investors move in and out of the different assets exactly at those points in time where the business cycle turns. Part IV will demonstrate that it is very difficult (read impossible) to predict turning points in the business cycle with perfection. No investor is able to time the market perfectly. Nevertheless, Figure 9.6 and Table 9.2 illustrate the importance of the business cycle for the stock market.

9.5 Stock prices and dividends during recessions

So, stock returns are typically low during recessions and high during expansions. But what gives? Is it stock prices or dividends that drop?

Table 9.3 shows annualized changes in real monthly stock prices (i.e. real capital gains), real dividends, real earnings, and consumer prices. Focus on capital gains and dividend growth first.

Over the full 1871–2018 period, real share prices fell by close to 3% in annualized terms during recessions whereas the annualized growth rate in real dividends is close to zero (−0.1%). During recessions, investors lower the price they want to pay for stocks even when firms leave dividends basically unadjusted (in real terms). During expansions, this is turned upside-down. Real share prices grow strongly, by more than 4% in annualized terms, and real dividends increase as well, by a little more than 2%. When investors cut stock prices during recessions, but firms keep dividends constant, stock prices fall by more than dividends and the stock-price dividend multiple contracts. During expansions, investors are willing to pay more for stocks and firms increase dividends, but stock prices rise more than dividends, implying that the stock-price dividend

Table 9.3 Annualized real monthly capital gains, dividends, earnings growth, and consumer-price inflation

	Capital gains	Dividends	Earnings	Inflation
		Full period: 1871–2018		
All months	2.3%	1.5%	1.8%	2.0%
Recession	−2.9%	−0.1%	−15.2%	−2.0%
Expansion	4.4%	2.2%	8.6%	3.6%
		1871–1945		
All months	1.4%	0.8%	0.6%	0.5%
Recession	−3.1%	0.2%	−9.5%	−3.9%
Expansion	4.6%	1.2%	8.0%	3.7%
		1946–2018		
All months	3.3%	2.4%	3.0%	3.6%
Recession	−2.4%	−0.8%	−32.7	3.9%
Expansion	4.3%	2.9%	9.0%	3.6%

multiple expands. This means that stock prices are more volatile than dividends over the business cycle: stock prices increase more than dividends during expansions but fall more than dividends during recessions. We conclude that the main reason why returns are low during recessions is that stock prices fall and the stock-price multiple contracts. This also lines up well with the conclusion from Chapter 4 that valuation change is important for stock returns in the short run.

Notice from Table 9.3 that the average dividend growth rate during recessions differs somewhat depending on whether one looks at the period before 1945 or after. Before 1945, firms kept dividends basically constant in real terms during recessions, if anything the average growth rate is slightly positive (0.2%), whereas the growth rate of dividends has been negative since 1945 (−0.8%). Hence, since 1945, both stock prices and dividends have been falling during recession. Regardless of what subperiod one looks at, however, stock prices have been reacting stronger to the business cycle than dividends. Both before and after 1945, stock prices have fallen more than dividends during recessions, but increased more than dividends during expansions.

9.5.1 Inflation

Table 9.3 also summarizes the behaviour of inflation over the business cycle. Before 1945, consumer prices fell markedly during recessions. The average rate of deflation was close to 4% p.a. During expansions, prices increased by close to 4% p.a.. I.e., the rate of inflation during expansions was almost equal to the rate of deflation during recessions. Before 1945, expansions were shorter, as the previous chapter showed, implying that the overall rate of inflation, across expansions and recessions, was barely positive, at 0.5% p.a. Adding inflation to real capital gains and real dividend growth, gives nominal capital gains and dividend growth. Real capital gains are negative during recessions. When consumer prices fall during recessions, as they did before 1945, nominal share prices dropped by even more than real.

Since 1945, inflation has been higher. The overall rate of inflation has been app. 3.6% p.a., and has not differed much between recessions and expansions. The reason inflation has been higher during recessions after 1945 has a lot to do with the high rates of inflation that followed the oil-price shocks in the early 1970s and 1980s. These oil-price shocks contributed significantly to the 1974–1975 and 1980 recessions. Oil prices more than doubled in January 1974. This caused firms to raise prices, i.e. caused inflation to rise. With higher prices, consumers cut consumption and firms cut investment. The stock market tanked.

9.5.2 Earnings

The final numbers in Table 9.3 relate to the behaviour of earnings over the business cycle. On average during all months, real earnings of firms grow by slightly less than two percent per year, as demonstrated in earlier chapters. Earnings are very volatile over the business cycle, however. They fall dramatically during recessions only to increase as dramatic during expansions. On average, real earnings fall by around 15% in annualized terms during recessions only to gain almost nine percent during expansions. The volatility of earnings has increased since 1945. To a large extent, the 2008 Great Recession is responsible. Earnings per share were around USD 80 in 2007. During the fourth quarter of 2008, earnings per share were negative at minus USD 23, according to Standard & Poors. It has been discussed whether the earnings figures for the Great Recession, as reported by Standard & Poors for the S&P 500 firms, are somewhat exaggerated (Siegel, 2016). It is beyond discussion, however, that the Great Recession caused a large drop in profitability, as Chapter 5 also illustrated. Chapter 5 showed that aggregate profits of US firms, as appearing in the National Income and Products Statistics (NIPA), fell dramatically during the Great Recession. At the end 2007, i.e. right before the Great Recession, aggregate profits amounted to app. USD 1,400bn. During the last quarter of 2008, profits had taken a hit of around 50%, to app. USD 700bn.

9.6 Before, during, and after recessions

Table 9.4 shows the behaviour of real stock returns, real capital gains, and changes in real dividends and earnings for each recession after 1945 one year before a recession starts ($T-1$) and the year following a recession ($T+1$). For instance, one year prior to the November 1948–October 1949 recession, stocks returned 3.8% in real terms, stock prices fell by 1.9%, dividends increased by 7.5%, and earnings increased by 38.5%. Similarly, from October 1949 through October 1950, i.e. one year after the end of the recession, stocks returned 28.9%, share prices increased by 20.5%, dividends grew by 23.6%, and earnings by 12.4%, all in real terms, i.e. after inflation.

Stock prices tend to drop in anticipation of recessions, only to rebound strongly after the end of the recessions. Given that dividend growth does not vary markedly between the period before and after recession, but capital gains behave differently, stock returns are low before recessions, but very high right after the end of a recession. Earnings are volatile, but tend to fall before recessions and increase afterwards.

Taken together, this means that stock prices fall before and during recessions, but rebound strongly right after the end of a recession. So, during the late stage

Table 9.4 Real stock returns, capital gains, dividend growth, and earnings growth during the year before the beginning of a recession ($T-1$) and the year right after the end of a recession ($T+1$)

		Returns		Capital gains		Dividend growth		Earnings growth	
		$T-1$	$T+1$	$T-1$	$T+1$	$T-1$	$T+1$	$T-1$	$T+1$
November 1948	October 1949	3.8%	28.9%	−1.9%	20.5%	7.5%	23.6%	38.1%	12.4%
July 1953	May 1954	1.7%	37.9%	−3.9%	31.9%	−2.8%	8.4%	7.0%	21.6%
August 1957	April 1958	−5.6%	39.1%	−9.1%	34.4%	−7.4%	0.8%	−2.9%	4.1%
April 1960	February 1961	−3.3%	15.1%	−6.3%	11.8%	7.3%	3.6%	−1.7%	4.0%
December 1969	November 1970	10.0%	10.0%	6.7%	6.6%	0.4%	−5.6%	3.2%	4.3%
November 1973	March 1975	−23.5%	18.5%	−25.8%	13.8%	−1.3%	−5.2%	16.9%	−3.4%
January 1980	July 1980	8.3%	2.0%	2.8%	−2.7%	−2.3%	−2.9%	2.2%	−8.2%
July 1981	November 1982	−0.7%	21.0%	−5.3%	15.8%	−3.0%	−0.4%	−7.0%	3.1%
July 1990	March 1991	−6.6%	9.4%	−9.6%	6.0%	5.8%	−1.5%	−15.6%	−24.8%
March 2001	November 2001	−20.1%	−19.9%	−21.2%	−21.2%	−8.2%	−0.7%	−19.6%	7.7%
December 2007	June 2009	−5.5%	18.2%	−7.2%	15.8%	6.7%	−14.8%	−24.9%	784.2%
Average		−4.5%	15.1%	−7.9%	11.2%	−0.5%	−1.8%	−4.2%	79.3%

of the business cycle—before the recession, but still during the expansion—stocks take a big hit. Share prices fall and stock returns are low. This continues during the recession. Right after the end of a recession, i.e. during the early phase of an expansion, share prices rebound spectacularly and returns are very high. It is important to be invested in the stock market when the recession ends. We can summarize it as follows:

	Expansion	Late expansion	Recession	Early expansion	Expansion
Stocks perform:	Great	Bad	Bad	Fantastic	Great

9.7 Why do stock returns drop so much during recessions?

How come stock prices drop so much during recessions, causing stock price multiples and in the end stock returns to drop dramatically, too? And how come that they drop so much more than dividends? Chapter 3 showed that the ratio of stock price to dividends is related to the difference between expected returns and growth:

$$\frac{\text{Stock price}}{\text{Current dividends}} = \frac{1}{\text{Expected stock returns} - \text{Expected dividend growth}}. \tag{9.1}$$

Chapter 3 also showed that stock returns can be expressed as the risk-free rate plus the expected risk premium. This means that the ratio of stock prices to dividends can also be written as:

$$\frac{\text{Stock price}}{\text{Current dividends}} = \frac{1}{\text{Risk-free rate} + \text{Expected risk premium} - \text{Expected dividend growth}}. \tag{9.2}$$

Eq. (9.2) tells us that when stock prices drop faster than dividends, this can only happen if the risk-free rate increases, risk premia go up, or expected growth falls.

If anything, the risk-free rate tends to drop during recessions, as central banks lower the interest rate during recessions (next chapter). All else equal, a lower risk-free rate pushes up stock prices in Eq. (9.2). Stock prices drop during recessions, however. This means that we must turn our attention to expected risk premia and growth when trying to understand why stock prices drop during recessions. But what gives? Do expected risk premia go up or growth expectations down during recessions?[2]

One might be tempted to say 'both'. It seems intuitive that risk aversion, and thus required risk premia, go up during recessions. Times are bad, people get nervous, and people increase their risk aversion. At the same time, it seems natural that people expect growth to be lower during recessions.

A large body of academic research analyses the question of whether the stock-price dividend ratio (or the dividend yield) moves because the expected risk premium moves or because expected dividend growth moves. In the US, most of the variation in dividend yields come from variation in expected risk premiums, at least when looking at data since 1929. Campbell and Shiller (1988a, 1988b), Fama & French (1988, 1989), Cochrane (1992, 2008a), and others all show that in the US expected risk premia increases in bad times, pushing down stock prices in relation to dividends. Kroencke (2019) has an interesting recent analysis where he looks specifically at US recessions since 1950. He finds that stock prices fall more than dividends during US recessions because risk aversion increases.

One may then asks why risk aversion increases during recessions. Campbell & Cochrane (1999) developed an influential way of thinking about this, as also mentioned in Chapter 7. They assumed that when consumption of an individual is low in relation to the level of consumption the individual is used to, risk aversion is high. They call it 'habit-formation'. If you should invest in the risky stock market during these points in time, you require a hefty compensation. Your risk aversion has gone up, pushing up required stock returns. Campbell & Cochrane (1999) show that it fits the US data.

What if you look at other countries, or US data going back very far in time? Rangvid, Schmeling & Schrimpf (2014) study international data. They find that, internationally, most of the variation in dividend yields comes from movements in growth rates. The same is true for US data extending back further in time, as Chen (2008) and Golez & Koudijs (2018) find.

To conclude, for stock prices to fall more than dividends during recessions, as we see in the data, either risk premia must increase or expected growth must fall. For recent US data, the evidence is clear. Risk aversion, and thus risk premia, move. For international data, and historical US data, there is evidence that expected growth moves, too.

[2] Note, by the way, another important implication here. To explain the large drops in stock prices around recessions, logically either expected risk premia or expected growth has to move. We cannot have it that expected return and expected growth are both constant. If they were, there would be no movements in the ratio of stock prices to dividends. This is important because we sometimes hear that it is impossible to predict returns and economic growth. But if this were true, the stock-price dividend ratio should be constant. But it is not. We just cannot have it all at the same time. If we see variation in the stock-price dividend ratio—which we do—then, either expected risk premia or expected growth, or both, vary. We return to this in Chapter 16.

9.8 Checklist

This chapter has described how the stock market behaves over the business cycle, detailing how returns and the different components of returns differ between recessions and expansions. The main conclusions to remember are:

- Stocks perform well during expansions. Stocks have returned around 10% in annualized terms during expansions (after taking account of inflation). On average, across expansions, cumulative stock returns have been around 50%.
- Stocks perform badly during recessions. Real stocks returns have been negative at around minus one percent in annualized terms during recessions.
- There is variation across the average recession. Some recessions resulted in very large negative returns and some even in slightly positive. Similarly, there is variation around the average expansion. The main conclusion is, though, that generally the stock market is a nicer place to be during expansions.
- There are potentially large gains to be made if one is able to time the market, i.e. switch out of stocks and into bonds during recessions and vice versa during expansions. Unfortunately, as we will see later in the book, it is difficult to time recessions and expansions precisely, but knowing the potential gains is useful.
- During recessions, earnings drop and real share prices fall. Firms smooth dividends, though, i.e. even when earnings drop considerably during recessions, firms do not adjust dividends as much.
- Real share prices, dividends, and earnings increase during expansions.
- Share prices fall by more than dividends during recessions. Vice versa for expansions.
- For stock prices to fall more than dividends, risk premia must increase and/or investors must lower their expectations to future growth. Empirically, research has shown that changes in risk premia account for the larger fraction of fluctuations in stock prices relative to dividends in US data since 1929. For international data, and US data extending very far back in time, there is evidence that stock-price drops relative to dividends are caused by drops in expected growth rates, too.
- Stock prices start falling before the recession arrives, i.e. during the late phase of an expansion.
- Stocks perform strongly during the early phase of an expansion, i.e. right after the end of the recession.

10

Monetary policy and the business cycle

The previous chapter showed how stock returns depend on the business cycle. Stocks do well during expansions but poorly during recessions. Central banks influence and react to the business cycle. Thereby, central banks influence the stock market.

Monetary policy aims at keeping consumer prices stable and the financial system well-functioning. Monetary policy is conducted by central banks, in most countries a politically independent public authority. To achieve their goals, central banks use their monetary policy instruments, the most important of which is the monetary policy rate, a short nominal interest rate. By changing the short interest rate, the central bank influences financial markets, first via its influence over other interest rates (longer interest rates on government bonds, interest rates on commercial debt, mortgage rates, etc.) and then via spill-overs to other asset prices, such as stock prices, exchange rates, house prices, etc.

The stance of monetary policy, i.e. whether monetary policy is tight or loose, depends on the business cycle. At the same time, changes in monetary policy influence the business cycle and its future path. When monetary policy influences the business cycle, and the business cycle influences the stock market, as we learned in the previous chapter, there are good reasons to believe that monetary policy also influences the stock market.

This chapter describes what monetary policy is. It also analyzes what causes monetary policy to change. The next chapter examines how changes in the monetary policy rate affect the stock market.

10.1 What is monetary policy?

Monetary policy is conducted by the central bank in a country: the Fed in the US, the ECB (the European Central Bank) in the euro area, the Bank of England in the UK, Danmarks Nationalbank in Denmark, etc.

Central banks use monetary policy instruments to achieve their goals. This process is called the transmission mechanism. It goes as follows:

From Main Street to Wall Street. Jesper Rangvid, Oxford University Press (2021). © Jesper Rangvid.
DOI: 10.1093/oso/9780198866404.003.0010

The central bank decides on the appropriate stance of its *monetary policy instruments.*

⇓

Changes in monetary policy instruments affect outcome variables via the *transmission mechanism.*

⇓

Monetary policy aims to achieve certain *monetary policy goals.*

Let us describe the three parts—instruments, transmission mechanism, and goals—one by one.

10.1.1 Monetary policy instruments

The most important monetary policy instrument is the monetary policy rate. The policy interest rate is a short nominal interest rate. It determines the rate of interest private commercial banks pay when they are in need of short-term funding from the central bank or receive when they have excess short-term funding that they park at the central bank. As an example, imagine that a private commercial bank needs to deposit money somewhere for one week. If only one bank needs a place to park excess liquidity, it can probably deposit it at another private bank (at a bank in need of short-term funding). However, if many private banks, the banking system, have excess funds in aggregate, the banking system in aggregate will turn to the central bank.[1] The private banks can thus deposit money in or borrow money from the central bank. Furthermore, only private commercial banks (and the government) have accounts at the central bank. Non-financial corporations and households cannot deposit at or borrow from the central bank. In this way, the central bank is the 'bank of the banks'.

The policy rate is the interest rate that private commercial banks pay, or receive, when they deal with the central bank. In some countries, the policy rate is a deposit rate, in others the borrowing rate. This depends on the specific set-up, and the specifics vary from country to country. The policy rate may also be a rate that the central wants the private banks to charge when they do businesses with each other. In fact, this is how it works in the US. The Fed determines the Fed Funds Target Rate. This is a target for the rate the Fed wants private banks to borrow from and lend to each other on a short-term basis. The key point to remember is that the policy rate is an interest rate set by the central bank that affects the rate commercial

[1] Individual banks might also turn to the central bank even when they can deposit funds at other commercial banks. Many factors influence whether banks decide to deposit funds at the central bank or other private banks. The main point is that private commercial banks can deposit and borrow in the central bank.

banks charge when they do businesses with each other or with the central bank on a short-term basis. The policy rate is a short-term interest rate. As examples, the Fed Funds Rate is the rate on overnight loans, i.e. day-to-day loans, between US commercial banks. In the Eurozone, the Deposit Facility rate of the ECB is the rate Eurozone banks receive when they deposit money in ECB overnight, i.e. one-day deposits. The rate on Certificates of Deposit of the Danish central bank is the rate commercial banks receive when they make one-week deposits at the Danish central bank.

When the central bank determines the interest rate commercial banks are charged when exchanging liquidity with the central bank on a short-term basis, the central bank targets 'prices' on financial markets. This is a shift from earlier in history where central banks targeted 'quantities', most importantly the quantity of money, or the money supply. The main reason central banks today focus on the short-term interest rate as their main policy instrument is that the link between the interest rate and the variables that the central bank is ultimately interested in influencing (inflation, economic activity, and financial stability) is simply stronger than the link between the money supply and those outcome variables. This view on monetary policy gained momentum during the 1980s (Bernanke, 2006) when experiences of high inflation during the 1970s were analysed and interpreted.

In additional to their main instrument, the short interest rate, central banks have a number of additional instruments at their disposal, such as the amount of money banks can deposit at or lend from the central bank, foreign currency interventions, and, since the financial crisis of 2008–09, 'unconventional money policy' that we will return to in Chapter 12.

10.1.2 Monetary policy goals

Most central banks today are independent. Independence means that central bankers independently make decisions about the policy instruments, i.e. it is not elected politicians who decide on the use of the instruments, but appointed public employees (central bank governors). The belief that the goals of monetary policy are best achieved when central banks are independent in their use of monetary policy instruments resulted from an active research agenda during the 1980s and 1990s that found that independent central banks are more effective in keeping inflation under control, see, e.g., Alesina & Summers (1993), Crowe & Meade, (2007), and Cukierman (2008).

Central bank governors are typically appointed for a fixed term, such as five years, for instance. During that period governors typically cannot be dismissed, unless in extreme situations. Central bank governors have to be reappointed, or new governors have to be appointed, at fixed intervals, though. At these instances, policy might play a role, as it is the government who appoints the central bank governor. But when appointed, the governor should be independent when it comes to choosing how monetary policy is conducted.

Politicians determine the goals the central bank should pursue, however. The main goal for most central banks is to keep inflation stable and relatively low. Typically, this is expressed as a rate of inflation that the central bank should achieve over the medium term. Such a policy is referred to as an 'inflation target'. For instance, since 2012 the 'The FOMC (Federal Open Market Committee) implements monetary policy to help maintain an inflation rate of 2 percent over the medium term',[2] while the ECB 'aims at maintaining inflation rates below, but close to, 2% over the medium term.' Monetary policy does not aim for zero percent inflation. The reason is that there is a risk of undershooting the inflation target from time to time, i.e. if the goal is zero percent, undershooting the goal would mean deflation. Deflation is generally viewed as harmful to the overall goal of a stable and prosperous economy. If inflation is negative, i.e. prices are falling, consumers have an incentive to postpone consumption and firms an incentive to postpone investments, both of which would cause economic progress to slow. Monetary policy also does not aim for a rate of inflation around two percent always and at any point in time. Instead, monetary policy allows inflation to deviate temporarily from target. There is no clear definition what 'medium term' refers to, but think of it as 'a couple of years'.

Central banks have a role in securing financial stability, too.[3] The weight attached to this goal has increased since the 2008 financial crisis. The main goal, however, remains the rate of inflation.

Why is the goal of central banks inflation, and not economic growth, unemployment, or something similar that in the end determines economic prosperity? It is broadly understood that long-run movements in real economic variables, such as real economic growth and unemployment, are determined by factors others than those the central bank can influence. In the long-run, economic growth is determined by productivity, savings rates, population growth, ability to allocate capital to finance risky projects, etc. In the long run, monetary policy can

[2] In the US, the broad long-run monetary policy objectives are maximum employment, stable prices, and moderate long-term interest rates. However, as of 2012, the FOMC has emphasized that it views an inflation rate of two percent as 'most consistent over the longer run with the Federal Reserve's statutory mandate.'

[3] In many countries, though not all, central banks are also financial supervisors, i.e. are responsible for the oversight of whether financial institutions fulfill regulatory requirements, such as capital and liquidity requirements.

influence the rate of inflation, but not the path of these real economic variables. Therefore, the goal of monetary policy is to keep a stable, low, but not too low, rate of inflation. This is the best way monetary policy can contribute to long-run economic prosperity. By keeping inflation low and stable, consumers and firms are better able to make long-term real decisions regarding consumption, savings, and investments.

When changing the short interest rate, the central bank influences real economic variables in the short run. For instance, a low interest rate might temporarily boost consumption and investment. Over time, such monetary stimulus will vanish. As an example, imagine that the economy is doing badly and the central bank fears inflation will undershoot its target of 2%. The central bank lowers its policy rate, say from 4% to 3%. This will lower the real short term interest rate, as inflation has a tendency to move slowly. Imagine, for the sake of illustration, that inflation remains at 1% in the short horizon. In that case, the real interest rate is reduced from 3% (= 4% − 1%) to 2% (= 3% − 1%). At lower real rates, firms have stronger incentives to borrow to finance investments and consumers to borrow to finance consumption. This gives a temporary boost to economic activity, pushing up consumer prices and in the end inflation. If inflation increases to, e.g., 3%, it has now become too high, compared to the goal of 2% inflation. The central bank will need to increase interest rates to a level where the real interest rate does not fuel nor dampen inflation. So, in the short run, central banks change the interest rate to influence inflation, and thereby possibly economic activity, but, in the long run, it cannot affect economic activity. If the central bank keeps pursuing an ever more expansionary monetary policy, in order to keep on boosting economic activity, it can end up creating a too high rate of inflation which hurts economic activity, as Box 10.1 explains.

Box 10.1. Hyperinflation

From history, we know that very high rates of inflation are very bad for economic activity. They cause the payment system to stop functioning. When the payment system does not work, market economies have difficulties flourishing. Extreme examples are the German hyperinflation in the 1920s, or more recent experiences of Zimbabwe and Venezuela. Hanke & Kwok (2009) estimate that Zimbabwe saw its annual inflation rate rise from 24,411 percent in 2007 to an estimated 89.7 sextillion percent in mid-November 2008. 89.7 sextillion is 89.7 and 20 zeros, i.e. 89,700,000,000,000,000,000,000 percent. The economy collapsed. In the end, a small dose of stable inflation seems to be the right goal for monetary policy.

10.1.3 The transmission mechanism

Monetary policy uses a nominal short interest rate (the instrument) to achieve a certain path of inflation (the goal). Inflation is the rate at which prices on goods and services change. Prices on goods and services are set by firms based on the intersection of demand and supply, i.e. the intersection of how much buyers are willing to pay for goods and services and what firms charge for these goods and services. In other words, the central bank directly controls a short interest rate, but it does not control inflation directly. The central bank believes, though, that changes in the short interest rate will affect changes in consumer prices (inflation) via its effect on demand and supply.

There are several channels through which the short interest rate affects inflation. To illustrate, imagine that the central bank fears inflation pressures are building up. It increases the short interest rate. This will increase other interest rates in the economy, such as borrowing rates in banks, mortgage rates, rates on commercial loans (in banks or via the bond market), rates on student loans, etc. When interest rates go up, demand for credit contracts, and consumption and investments decline. Also, increases in the interest rate, all else equal, dampen asset prices, such as stock prices, causing wealth to decline.[4] When wealth declines, savers cut back on consumption. In total, hikes in the short interest rate reduce total demand in the economy. When demand is reduced, firms lower the rate at which they would otherwise increase prices. This leads to lower inflation. Increases in the interest rate also strengthens the domestic currency. This causes prices on imported goods to fall (measured in domestic currency), i.e. also reduces inflation.

The transmission from changes in the short interest rate to inflation is complicated and uncertain, both with respect to magnitude (how much asset markets, firms, and consumers react to changes in monetary policy instruments) and timing (how long it takes for the channels to play out). Central banks use economic and statistical models to make qualified estimates of the impact of changes in monetary policy on inflation, but nothing is certain. Sometimes firms, consumers, and financial markets react in unexpected ways. To make things even more complicated, all these variables (asset prices, other interest rates, the investment, savings, and consumption decisions of firms and consumers, etc.) are influenced by shocks to the economy. On their webpage, the ECB provides a nice illustration of how it views the transmission mechanism. It is reprinted in Figure 10.1. It is not easy to be a central banker.

[4] Remember from Chapter 3 that stock prices are given by discounted dividends. All else equal, when the central bank raises the interest rate, it increases the discount rate. This lowers the present value of future dividends, causing stock prices to fall.

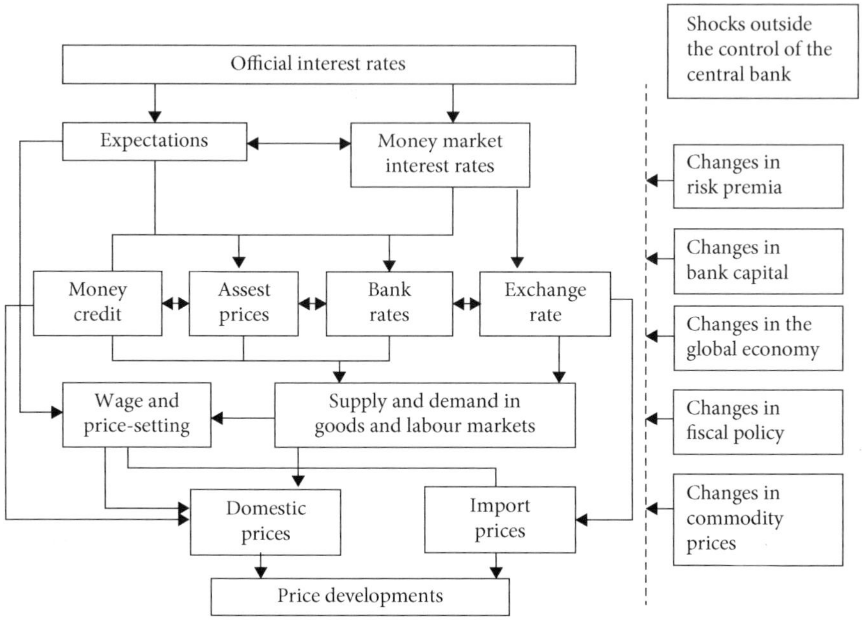

Figure 10.1 The transmission mechanism of monetary policy.
Data source: ECB. Reprinted with permission from the ECB.

10.2 When do central banks change the policy instrument?

At the overall level, central banks change their policy instruments when they judge future inflation will miss its target. At the more detailed level, a number of complication arise. First, it takes time before a change in the policy instrument affects inflation. A rule of thumb is that it takes six to nine month. When it takes time to influence inflation, central banks should react before inflation moves away from target. Central banks therefore need to assess how current economic and financial conditions affect future rates of inflation. This involves the use of many indicators, variables, models, and methods. It is a complicated task.

Demand pressure is closely linked to movements in the business cycle. When the economic starts to lose speed, i.e. when consumption and investments are low, price pressure in the economy is low. Central banks react to this. They make monetary policy more expansionary, i.e. lower the policy rate. Hence, we should see the policy rate drop during recessions. In the best of all worlds, central banks manage to lower the policy rate before the recession kicks in. Similarly, we

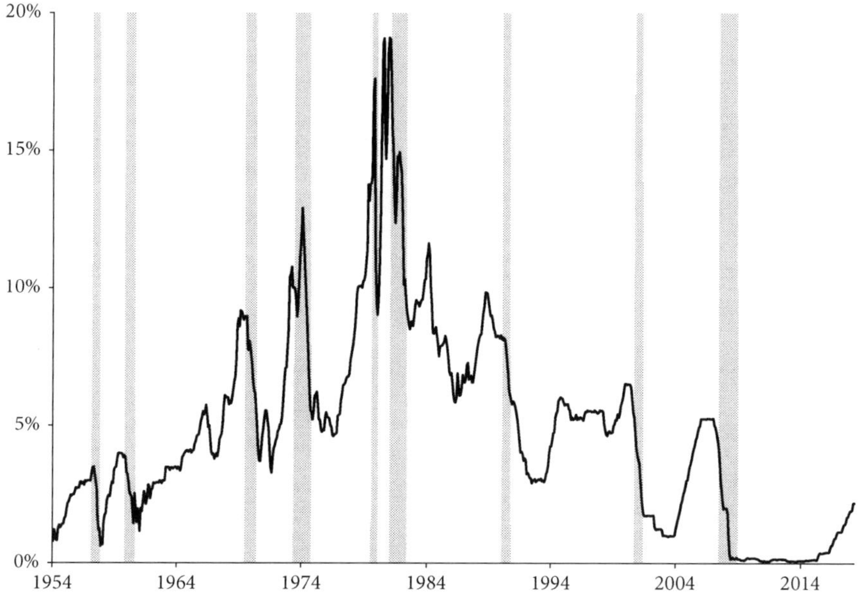

Figure 10.2 The Effective Fed Funds Rate. NBER-defined recessions indicated by shading.
Data source: FRED.

should see the policy rate increase during expansions, in order to take the heat out of the economy and secure that inflation does not run loose. Overall, there should be a clear link between the business cycle and the stance of monetary policy.

Figure 10.2 shows the path of the Effective Fed Funds Rate since its inception in July 1954, together with indications of recessions. There is a clear relation between movements in the Fed Funds Rate and recessions: during recessions, the Fed Funds Rate is lowered considerably. Just as an example, the Fed Funds Rate was app. 4% in January 2008. What later became the Great Recession had just started. The Fed quickly recognized that this would be an unusually severe recession. It dramatically lowered the Fed Funds Rate, to close to zero percent within a year. Similar dramatic drops in the policy rate can be seen during other recessions.

After a recession, the Fed is typically in no hurry to raise rates. The Fed wants to be reassured that the economy is out of the recession before it starts hiking rates. The Fed fears that if it increases interest rates prematurely, it could choke off the rebound. This means that central bankers drastically cut interest rates during recessions but increase them slowly when the recession has come to an end. One way to illustrate the more dramatic actions taken during recessions is to compare the average monthly changes in interest rates during recessions to those during expansions. The average monthly rate of reduction in the Fed Funds Rate during recessions is 0.35 percentage points, whereas the average monthly increase during expansions is only 0.05 percentage points. Central bankers react decisively during recessions.

10.2.1 Taylor-rule

With hindsight, we know when a recession took place. In real time, the central bank does not. As explained in Chapter 8, the NBER Business Cycle Dating Committee dates peaks and troughs with a lag of several months. How does the central bank react in real time?

As mentioned, central banks use a lot of information when they determine monetary policy. They look at economic data, financial market data, expectations of consumers, firms, and market participants, etc. They incorporate all this information into forecasts for economic activity and inflation, using a variety of complicated methods and models.

But can't we somehow, in more simple terms, get a feeling for how the central bank thinks and what it relies upon when it changes the policy rate? In 1993, Stanford University Professor John B. Taylor suggested a simple way to describe how the Fed reacts.

Taylor's idea was to formulate a model – a rule – for how monetary policy should be conducted. He wanted the rule to be simple so that everybody can follow and replicate it. He argued that the Fed should change the Fed Funds Rate when inflation and economic activity (GDP) move away from their respective targets. He assumed that the inflation target is 2% (which, in fact, it has been since 2012, but remember that Taylor wrote his article in 1993) and that the equilibrium level of the real interest rate is also 2%. Taylor assumed that the target for economic activity is the level of economic activity associated with 'full employment'. Under these assumptions, the rule implies that 'If both the inflation rate and real GDP are on target then the federal funds rate would equal 4 percent or 2 percent in real terms' (Taylor, 1993, page 202). On the other hand, when inflation and/or real GDP differ from their respective targets, the Fed Funds Rate should be changed. In particular, if inflation is above target (2%), the Fed Funds Rate should be increased. Similarly, if GDP is above its level associated with 'full employment', the Fed Funds Rate should be increased. The Taylor rule is explained in Box 10.2.

Box 10.2. Taylor rule

Taylor (1993) proposed the following rule:

$$i_t = \pi_t + 2\% + 0.5\,(\pi_t - 2\%) + 0.5\,\left(y_t - \bar{y}_t\right). \tag{10.1}$$

where i_t is the level of the Fed Funds Rate in period t, π_t is the rate of inflation measured over the previous four quarters, π^* is the inflation target, r^* is the equilibrium real interest rate, y_t is real GDP, and $\bar{y}_t$ is the level of real GDP associated with full employment. The rule implies that if $y_t = \bar{y}_t$ and $\pi_t = \pi^*$, the Fed Funds Rate should be 4% when the inflation target π^* is 2%. The associated real interest rate is then 2% (4% − 2%).

The Taylor rule implies that if inflation increases by, say, one percentage point, the Fed Funds Rate should be increased by 1.5 percentage points, thereby increasing the real Fed Funds Rate by half a percentage point. The increase in the real Fed Funds Rate should cause economic activity and, in the end, inflation pressures to fall. Similarly, if output is one percentage point above potential, the Fed Funds Rate should be increased by half a percentage point, again increasing the real Fed Funds Rate (for a given inflation rate).

The Fed itself provides time series of the Taylor rule on its webpage. Figure 10.3 shows the Taylor rule and the Fed Funds Rate.

Given the simplicity of the Taylor rule—in particular in contrast to the complicated way monetary policy is implemented in practice—it is eye-opening how well the rule describes monetary policy in practice: the rate implied by the rule follows the Fed Funds Rate rather well. One may argue that it is not very surprising that the long-term movements in the Fed Funds Rate and the Taylor rule relate, as they are both affected by long-run movements in inflation, as shown in the next section. The more interesting fact, thus, is that the business-cycle fluctuations in the Fed Funds Rate relate to the Taylor rule.

The Taylor rule prescribes that the policy rate should be lowered during recessions (due to GDP being low relatively to target and inflation typically being low as well). This is in fact what happens: the policy rate is lowered during recessions, as described in the previous section. Conversely, the rule prescribes that the policy rate should be hiked during expansions in order to take the heat out of the economy, and this is what the Fed does. The Taylor rule, and variants thereof, has been used to describe monetary policy in other countries, too (see, e.g., Clarida, Gali, & Gertler, 1998).

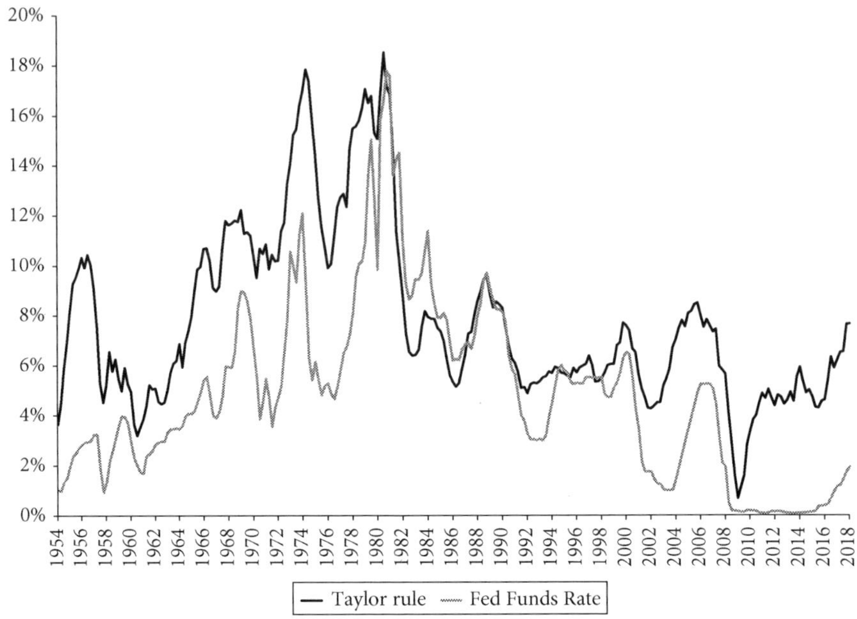

Figure 10.3 The Taylor rule and the Fed Funds Rate.
Data source: FRED.

The relation between the Fed funds rate and the Taylor rule is not perfect, though. For instance, prior to the financial crisis of 2008, the Fed reduced the policy rate more than the Taylor rule implied. Some have argued that this 'loose' monetary policy helped fuel the housing bubble that eventually caused the financial crisis, as also discussed in Chapter 12. Since the financial crisis, the policy rate has been kept at a lower rate than the Taylor rule implies.

Taylor proposed the rule also for a political reason. John B. Taylor is a fierce proponent of 'rule-based monetary policy'. In 1983, economists Robert Barro and Robert Gordon wrote a famous academic article entitled "Rules, discretion and reputation in a model of monetary policy". They argued that if a central bank follows a rule, inflation expectations will be better anchored. Taylor, too, believes that the hands of central banks should be tied. On the other hand, the Fed argues that it needs room for discretion. As an example, the Fed calculates that if it had followed a Taylor rule between 2010–2015 '2.5 million more Americans would be out of work today'.

The strength of the Taylor rule rests with its simplicity. On the other hand, this simplicity is then also what makes the rule less suitable in real life where flexibility is sometimes required.

10.3 Long-run movements in the Fed Funds Rate

In the short run, the Fed changes its policy rate according to its assessment of the stance of the business cycle. On top of this, there are long-term persistent movements in policy rates. Figures 10.2 and 10.3 show that the Fed Funds Rate was on an upward-sloping trend until the early 1980s, interrupted by short-run movements due to the business cycle. Since then, the Fed Funds Rate has been decreasing, interrupted by short-term movements. Since 2008, the Fed Funds Rate has been basically zero. Long-run movements in the rate of inflation influence long-term movements in the policy rate. The rate of inflation basically followed the same long-term path, as Figure 10.4 shows.

Nominal interest rates are determined by three components: the real rate of interest, the rate of inflation, and the inflation risk premium. The inflation risk premium is the compensation investors require if they are to hold assets that are safe in nominal terms but risky in real terms due to future inflation rates being unknown. When the rate of inflation increased during the 1960s and 1970s, this, all else equal, pushed up nominal interest rates. The policy rate followed. Since 1990, inflation has been on a downward trending path, and the Fed Funds Rate has

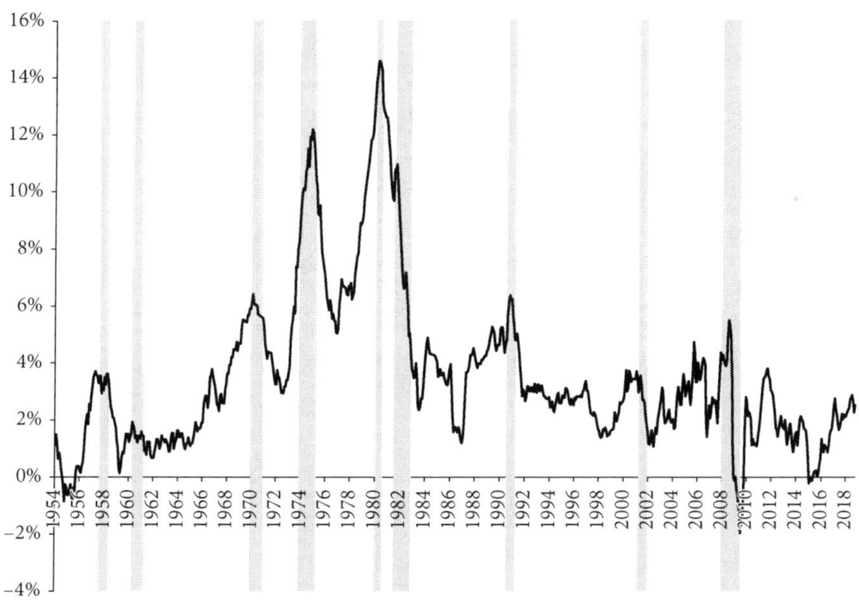

Figure 10.4 US inflation: Annual percentage change in the CPI (Consumer Price Index). NBER recessions indicated by shading.

Data source: FRED.

followed. The fact that inflation has been low and stable—in particular compared to the 1970s and 1980s—also means that investors have lowered their assessment of the uncertainty surrounding future rates of inflation. This has brought down inflation risk premia, too. So, the Fed Funds Rate has fallen since the early 1980s, not least due to a persistent fall in the rate of inflation and consequently a fall in the inflation risk premium.

10.4 Checklist

This chapter has described how monetary policy is conducted. Monetary policy influences, and is influenced by, the business cycle. The business cycle, in turn, influences stock markets, as we learned in the previous chapter. For this reason, it is important to understand monetary policy. The main conclusions to remember are:

- The main goal of most central banks is to keep inflation stable and not too high. In many countries, around 2% per year.
- A stable and not too high rate of inflation secures a stable nominal environment within which firms, households, investors etc. can make economic decisions. This fosters real economic growth.
- Central banks use a short interest rate to achieve their goals.
- The short interest rate affects interest rates on fixed income assets of longer maturities, the exchange rate, and other assets prices. Central banks change the monetary policy rate to affect these variables in order to, in the end, affect demand and supply pressures in the economy and thus inflation.
- Central banks raise (lower) the interest rate when there is a pressure for inflation to exceed (fall below) the inflation goal. This generally happens when economic activity is relatively high (low).
- The Taylor rule is a simple specification of a reaction function of the Fed. It links changes in the monetary policy rate to inflation deviations from target and to deviations of economic activity from target. The Taylor rule gives a reasonable description of the Fed Funds Rate in the US. The rule has been examined for other countries, too.
- Inflation rates were high during the 1970s and early 1980s, but have come down since then. Central bank policy rates were similarly high during the 1970s and 1980s, but have come down since then.

11
Monetary policy, interest rates and stock markets

The previous chapter showed that central banks react to the business cycle, lowering the policy rate in bad times and increasing it in good. The central bank does so in order to achieve certain policy goals, most prominently low and stable inflation.

In this chapter, we are interested in understanding how monetary policy, in itself and through its dependence on the business cycle, affects prices on financial assets. We start out describing how changes in the monetary policy rate affect other interest rates in the economy. We will see that changes in the policy rate affect yields on government bonds with longer maturity as well as corporate bonds. At the same time, these interest rates also depend on the business cycle. For instance, the credit risk premia, the compensation investors require for holding corporate bonds instead of government bonds, increases during recessions.

We then turn to the relationship between monetary policy and the stock market. Changes in monetary policy typically have a negative impact on the stock market, i.e., when the central bank increases the policy rate, the stock market suffers. There are some subtle issues that one needs to be aware of, however. We saw in the previous chapter that monetary policy is tightened when economic activity is booming, but turns accommodating during recessions. At the same time, we know from Chapter 9 that the stock market does well during expansions, and vice versa during recessions. When economic activity affects both monetary policy and the stock market, we need to evaluate whether monetary policy in itself affects the stock market or whether it works via its effect on the business cycle. In other words, we must tease out the independent effect of monetary policy on the stock market, isolating it from the effect of economic activity. Academic research has done so. The conclusion is that economic activity in itself, and monetary policy in itself, both affect the stock market. They (monetary policy and economic activity) are related, but they also separately affect the stock market. For this reason, sometimes stocks might do fine even during a period where the central bank raises the policy rate. This can happen if economic activity is booming, supporting stocks but also forcing the central bank to raise rates. It is important to be aware of both channels, i.e. how economic activity affects the stock market and how monetary policy affects stock market.

From Main Street to Wall Street. Jesper Rangvid, Oxford University Press (2021). © Jesper Rangvid.
DOI: 10.1093/oso/9780198866404.003.0011

11.1 Effect on interest rates

We first study how changes in the policy rate affect other interest rates in the economy. As mentioned in the previous chapter, the monetary policy rate is a short interest rate, often a day-to-day interest rate. What really matters for real economic activity is the interest rate you pay when borrowing to buy a house, the interest rate you pay on car loans, student loans, etc., as well as the interest rate firms pay when borrowing to make investments. These are typically multi-year loans. Yields on long-term loans are usually higher than yields on short-term loans. We need to figure out the relation between yields on loans with different maturities, monetary policy, and the business cycle. Borrowers also have to compensate investors for the risk that the borrower cannot repay the loan. This is the credit risk premium. This means that yields can be split into different components:

1. The yield on a short risk-free loan.
2. The premium you have to pay on top of the short-term yield when borrowing for a longer period of time.
3. The premium you have to pay to compensate the lender for the perceived risk that you might not pay back your loan.

Per definition, changes in the policy rate affect the first component, the yield on a short risk-free investment. The question is whether monetary policy also affects the premium you pay for borrowing longer and the credit risk premium.

11.1.1 Long versus short interest rates

When you borrow for a longer period, the interest rate on your loan is a long-term interest rate. There is no definition of 'long', other that it is longer than short. A one-year interest rate is a long interest rate when compared to a day-to-day interest rate. But a one-year interest rate is a short interest rate compared to a thirty-year interest rate. Long and short are relative concepts. This being said, an often-used measure of a long interest rate is a ten-year interest rate. And, an often-used measure of a short interest rate is a one- or three-months interest rate.

How are long and short interest rates related? The long interest rate is the sum of the current short interest rate, expected future short interest rates, and a risk premium to compensate for the uncertainty involved in estimating future short interest rates and other risks, e.g. credit risks.

Imagine you consider buying a one-year bond. This will provide you with a certain return/yield over one year. Imagine now that you also consider buying a two-year bond. You will obviously only buy this two-year bond if its return corresponds at least to the return on the one-year bond and the expected one-year return on a one-year bond bought after the first year:[1]

Return on two-year bond at least equal to:
Return on one-year bond
+
expected return on one-year bond one year from now.

Today, we do not know what the one-year return is in one year. To compensate the investor for this uncertainty, a risk premium is added so that the return on a two-year bond becomes:

Return on two-year bond
= Return on one-year bond
+
expected return on one-year bond one year from now
+
risk premium.

The same logic applies to bonds with even longer maturities. This means that the return on a long-term bond is the sum of the current short-term return, expected future short-term returns, and a risk premium. Expressed in annualized yields (as we typically do), yields on long-term bonds are approximately equal to the average of current and future short-term yields and a risk premium.

As mentioned, we expect yields on longer-maturity bonds to be higher than yields on short-maturity bonds. We call the relation between yields and time to maturity the yield curve or the term structure. The yield curve is typically upward sloping. Figure 11.1 shows the yield curve of US government bonds on a random day, the first day in 2020. Yields on long-maturity bonds are higher than yields on short-maturity bonds.[2]

[1] There is an alternative way to express this. Yields are typically quoted in per annum terms. This means that the yield on a two-year bond ($i_{0,2}$) is typically quoted as $(1 + i_{0,2})^2 = (1 + i_{0,1})(1 + i_{1,2})$, where $i_{0,1}$ is the yield on a one-year bond today and $i_{1,2}$ is the yield on a one-year bond in one year. This is approximately equal to $i_{0,2} = (i_{0,1} + i_{1,2})/2$. The yield on a three-year bond is at least $i_{0,3} = (i_{0,1} + i_{1,2} + i_{2,3})/3$, and so on. In other words, the yield on a long-term bond is approximately equal to the average of future short-term yields.

[2] The figure interpolates linearly between yields. Models and estimation procedures exist that provide smooth yield curves.

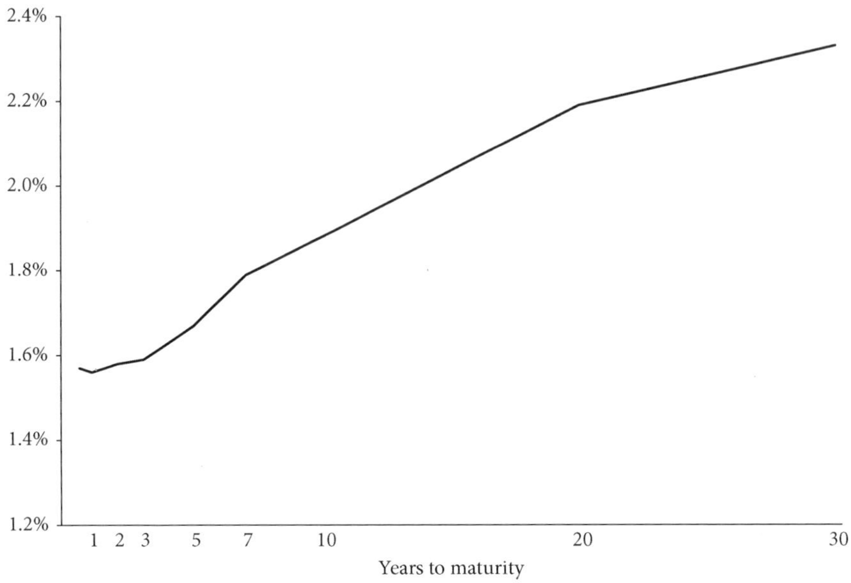

Figure 11.1 The yield curve. US government bonds. Primo 2020.
Data source: FRED.

11.1.2 Monetary policy and the yield curve

The monetary policy rate is a very short interest rate (the day-to-day rate). A change in the policy rate today thus changes one component of long-term yields (the current short-term yield). However, a change in the policy rate today might also tell us something about future short-term interest rates. If the Fed hikes interest rates today, this might tell us something about its intentions at its next meetings. As the yield on long-term bonds is the average of current and expected future short-term yields, changes to expectations of future monetary policy rates affect yields on long-term bonds today. At the same time we would probably expect that the effect from changes in the current policy rate gets weaker when we consider yields on loans of longer and longer maturities. We might learn something about the stance of monetary policy over the next couple of years if the Fed changes its policy rate today, but it probably does not materially impact our expectations to what the Fed will do in ten years. In summary, we expect a strong relation between the monetary policy rate and yields on short-term government bonds. We expect the effect to be less pronounced when we consider yields on bonds of long maturities.

Figure 11.2 shows developments over time in yields on US Treasury bills and bonds of different maturities, ranging from three-month Treasury bills to ten-year

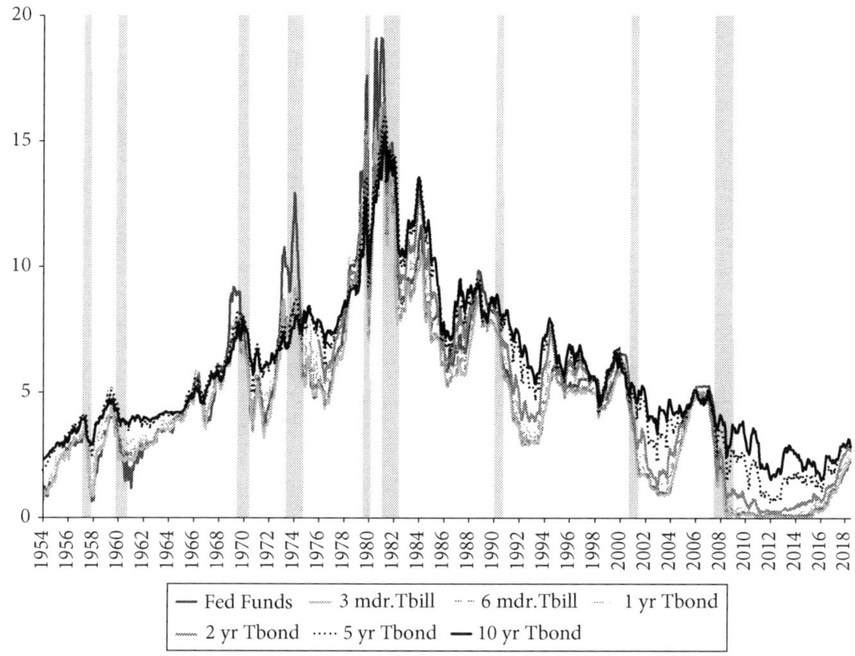

Figure 11.2 The Fed Funds Rate and yields on US Treasury securities of different maturities. NBER recessions indicated by shading.
Data source: FRED.

Treasury bonds, together with the Effective Fed Funds Rate. The series are highly correlated. Yields fall during recessions, where the Fed lowers the Fed Funds Rate. This is the transmission of monetary policy to financial market conditions.

Figure 11.2 also shows that yields on short-maturity debt securities follow the Fed Funds Rate closer that yields on longer-term securities. This appear even clearer from Figure 11.3 that shows the differences, one-by-one, between yields on the different government debt securities and the Fed Funds Rate. Figure 11.3 shows that the spreads between yields on Treasury bonds of different maturities follow a clear business-cycle pattern. During recessions, the policy rate is reduced to stimulate economic activity, as discussed in the previous chapter. The monetary policy rate is thus low at the end of a recession. Long rates fall during recessions but not as much as short rates. When short rates fall more than long rates during recessions, long rates are considerably higher than short rates at the end of recessions, i.e. when expansions begin. When the economy has been expanding for some time, the Fed starts raising rates again, thereby narrowing the difference between long and short yields. At the end of an expansion, the Fed has raised

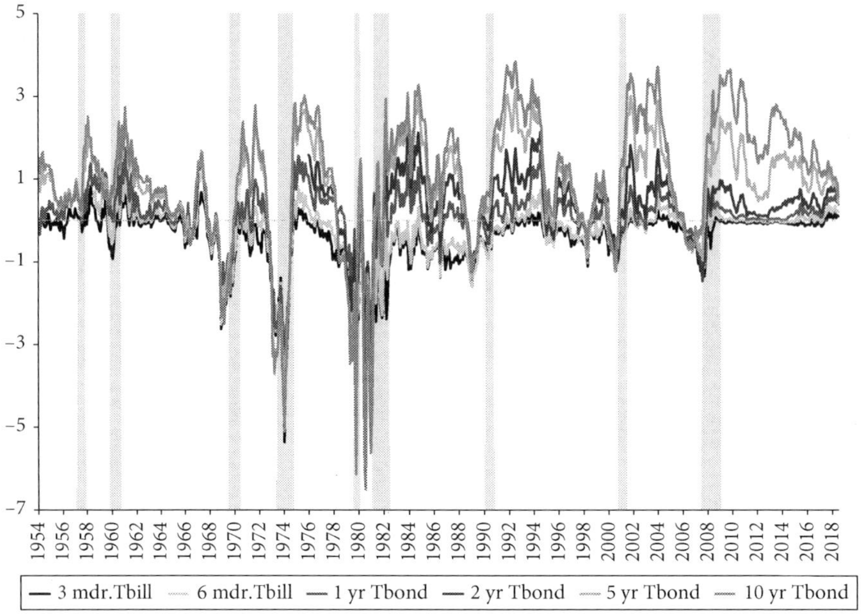

Figure 11.3 The differences between the Fed Funds Rate and yields on Treasury securities of different maturities. NBER recessions indicated by shading.
Data source: FRED.

short rates so much that there is almost no difference between short and long yields. Then the recession hits, and it all starts over again with the Fed lowering rates, increasing the spread between long and short yields during the recession, etc. Figure 11.4 illustrates these stylized movements.

When yields on long-term bonds are less volatile than yields on short-term bonds, and the Fed moves short rates in response to recessions, the spread between long- and short-term yields says something about the likelihood that a recession is approaching: When the spread is high, i.e. long yields are considerably higher than short yields, history tells us that the likelihood that the economy will start contracting is low. When the spread tightens, i.e. short yields approach long yields, the probability that a recessions occurs increases. This is a good rule of thumb. The yield curve is one of the most reliable indicators of recessions. Chapter 15 discusses this in more detail.

We can draw a number of conclusions. The business cycle affects the monetary policy rate, as described in the previous chapter. Changes in the monetary policy rate affect the whole term structure of yields, but affect yields on relatively short bonds more than yields on relatively long bonds. The difference between yields

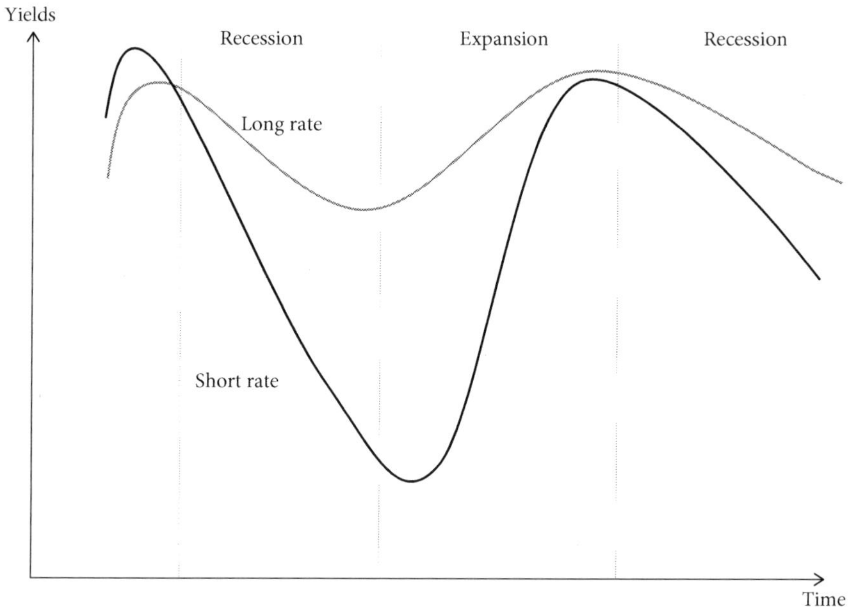

Figure 11.4 Movements in long and short yields during the business cycle.

on short and long bonds tell us something about the likelihood that a recession is approaching.

11.1.3 The risk premium. Corporate bonds

Figures 11.2 and 11.3 showed yields on government bonds. When corporations borrow in the bond market, they issue corporate bonds. Corporate bonds are more risky than government bonds, as companies typically have a higher probability of defaulting.[3] For this reason, investors require a compensation when buying a corporate bond over and above the compensation they require if buying an otherwise similar government bond. This compensation is called a credit risk premium. The size of the credit risk premium matters. The larger the credit risk premium, the more expensive it is for firms to finance their activities and investments. If the credit risk premium increases, firms will cut investments, with negative consequences for economic activity.

[3] Sovereigns can also default, but default risk of sovereigns in advanced economies is generally lower than the default risk of corporations. We leave default risks of sovereigns aside here.

When the business cycle, via its impact on monetary policy, affects yields on government bonds of different maturities, one may wonder whether the business cycle also affects the credit risk premium. In order to say something here, we must first rank firms according to their creditworthiness. Rating agencies, such as Moody's, Standard & Poors, and Fitch are paid by issuing corporations to assess the credit quality of the bonds they issue, i.e. estimate the likelihood that the corporation will face difficulties honoring the obligations of its issued bonds. Corporate bonds are split between investment grade and speculative grade, where the credit risk in investment grade bonds is lower than in speculative grade bonds. Each grade class is split into finer rating categories. At Moody's, for instance, Aaa-rated bonds are investment grade bonds with the lowest credit risk, whereas Baa-rated bonds are those with the highest credit risk within the Investment grade class. When Baa bonds are riskier than Aaa bonds, the yield on Baa-rated bonds is higher than the yield on Aaa rated bonds, all else equal. Investors buying Baa bonds require a compensation to buy these riskier bonds.

Figure 11.5 shows the development in yields on Aaa- and Baa-rated bonds since 1919. Yields on corporate bonds follow the same overall pattern as yields on government securities. Yields increase during the 1950s, 1960s, and 1970s, and

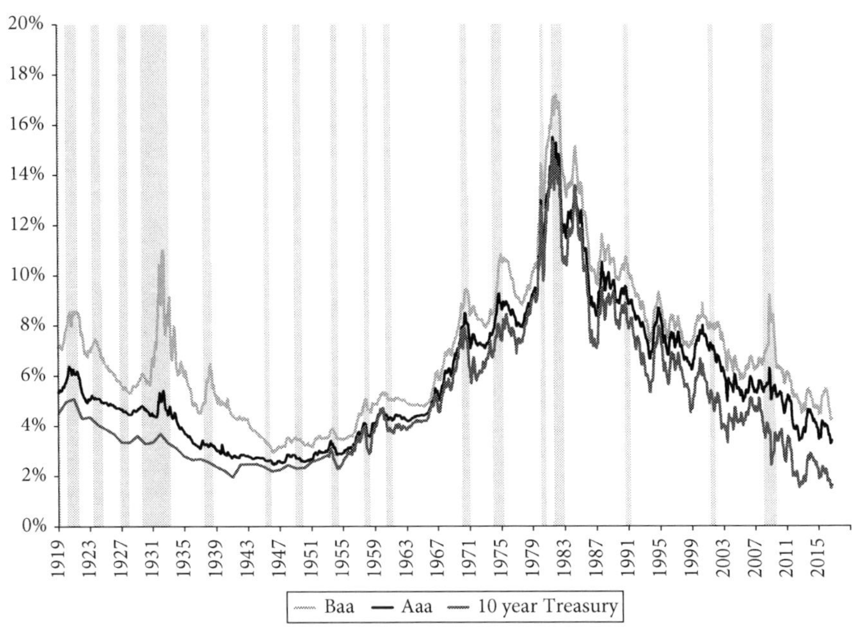

Figure 11.5 Yields on corporate bonds rated Baa and Aaa by Moody's as well as yields on ten-year Treasuries. NBER recessions indicated by shading.
Data source: FRED.

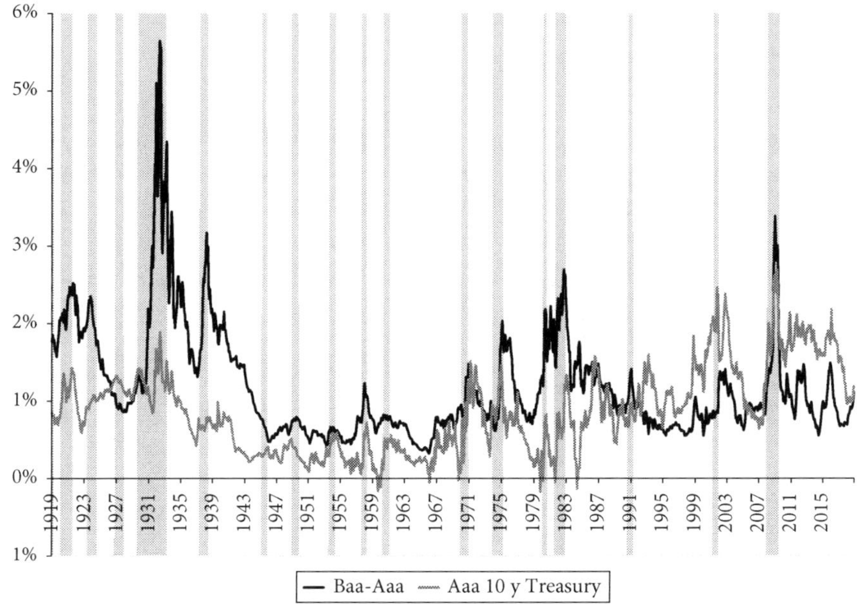

Figure 11.6 Spread between yields on corporate bonds rated Baa and Aaa by Moody's and spread between yields on Aaa corporates and ten-year Treasuries. NBER recessions indicated by shading.

Data source: FRED.

have been falling since the early 1980s, just like government bonds (Figure 11.2). Furthermore, yields on bonds with higher credit risk are naturally higher than yields on bonds with lower credit risk. Assuming the same maturity:

Yields on Baa-rated bonds > Yields on Aaa-rated bonds > Yields on government bonds.

The credit risk premium follows a business cycle pattern (Figure 11.6). Yields on corporate bonds, even Aaa rated, increase relative to yields on Treasuries during recessions. And yields on lower-rated bonds (Baa) increase even more than yields on Aaa rated bonds during recessions. This is natural. During recessions, economic activity suffers and firms struggle. Some firms struggle so much that they cannot honor their obligations. Default rates consequently follow a business-cycle pattern, i.e. default rates are higher during recessions; see Moody's (2009). Yields on Baa-rated bonds increase even more than yields on Aaa rated bonds, as Baa-rated firms are more likely to default. The risk compensation investors require to buy corporate bonds increases during recessions.

11.2 Effect on stock prices

We know from Chapter 9 that the stock market suffers during recessions and blossoms during expansions. In the previous chapter, we learned that central banks increase the policy rate when the economy is doing well and lower it during recessions. When stock markets react to the economy, and central banks react to the economy, it seems reasonable to hypothesize that the stock market reacts to changes in monetary policy. As an example, if the central bank increases the policy rate to cool down the economy, stock market investors should notice and lower their forecasts for economic activity. This influences the assessment of stocks. Also, stock prices are discounted dividends. When the central bank raises the policy rate, this, all else equal, increases the discount rate, and, hence, reduces stock prices. Stock market investors follow every word from central bankers.

11.2.1 Short-run relation

Figure 11.7 shows the relation between monthly changes in the Effective Fed Funds Rate (along the horizontal axis) and monthly changes in stock prices (along the vertical axis).[4]

The relation in Figure 11.7 is noisy. Lots of changes in the stock market are unrelated to changes in the Fed Funds Rate. In fact, variation in the Fed Funds Rate accounts for less than one percent of the variation in stock-price changes. This does not mean that there is no relation at all, though. A trend line has been added to the figure. The trend line shows the average relationship between monetary policy changes and stock price changes. It has a negative slope, indicating that the stock market reacts negatively to changes in the Effective Fed Funds Rate on average. The relation between changes in monetary policy and stock prices is—what economists call—marginally statistically significant. This means that the relation is not random. The size of the average relation is such that when the Effective Fed Funds Rate increases (falls) by one percentage point, stock prices fall (increase) by half a percent during the same month.

In Figure 11.7, changes in the Effective Fed Funds rate are related to changes in nominal stock prices. One could also look at the relation between the level of the Fed Funds Rate and changes in stock prices, or look at real stock prices. The conclusion is the same. There is a small, though very noisy, negative relation

[4] The Effective Fed Funds rate dropped from almost 18% in April 1980 to 11% in May 1980, i.e. a drop of seven percentage points in one month. Figure 11.7 leaves out this single observation in order to keep the figure readable. Adding this single observation does not change any conclusions.

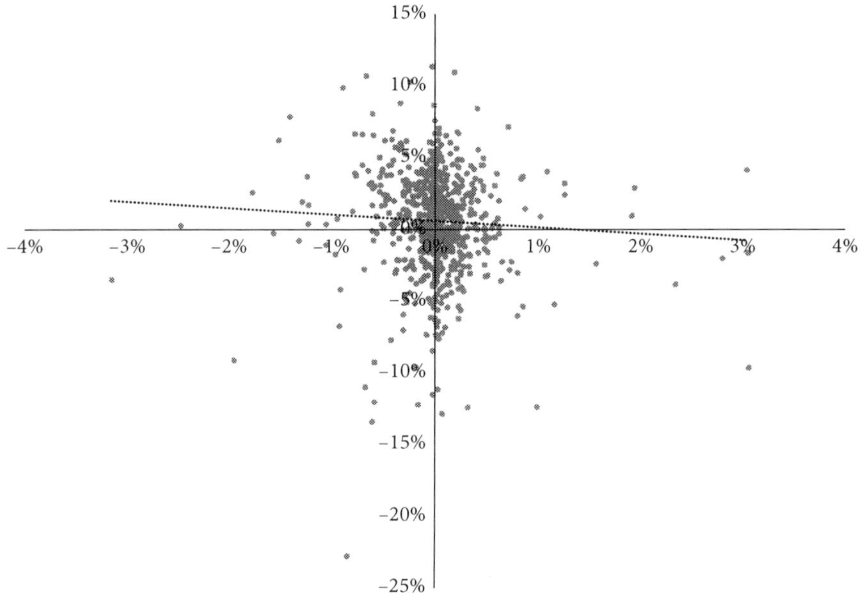

Figure 11.7 Monthly changes in the Effective Fed Funds Rate (horizontal axis) against monthly percentage changes in stock prices (vertical axis). July 1954–December 2016.

Data source: FRED and webpage of Robert J. Shiller.

between the Effective Fed Funds Rate and the stock market in the short run, i.e. within a month.

11.2.2 Long-run relation

The previous section illustrated the relation between the policy rate and stock prices in the short run, from month to month. Often, periods of contractional monetary policy last several years, only to be followed by long periods where the Fed loosens monetary policy. How does the stock market react to a significant change in the stance of monetary policy, i.e. to a change from contractional to expansionary monetary policy?

With the benefit of hindsight, we can select dates with clear changes to the path of the policy rate, i.e. dates when the Fed shifted from lowering rates to increasing rates and vice versa. This is a backward looking exercise. Nobody knows in real time whether the Fed changes course significantly, i.e. embarks on a rate-hiking cycle, or whether a rate hike is a one-time event. But we can use this exercise to

Figure 11.8 Reduction cycle initiated.
Data source: FRED.

see whether significant changes in monetary policy have been followed by clear changes in the stock market.

The Fed started targeting the Effective Fed Funds Rate in September 1982. Figure 11.8 shows the Fed Funds Target from September 1982 together with indications of months where the Fed started a rate-reduction cycle. Figure 11.9 shows initiations of rate-hiking cycles.[5]

Figure 11.7 revealed a short-run negative relation between changes in the policy rate and stock prices. Figure 11.10 shows longer-term developments in real stock prices (nominal stock prices behave similarly), i.e. developments twelve months before to twelve months after the initiation of a rate-hiking, respectively, rate-reduction, cycle. The figure is constructed such that it identifies each turning point indicated in Figures 11.8 and 11.9 and then looks at how the stock market behaves twelve months before, respectively after, each turning point. Figure 11.10 shows the average behaviour of stock-market movements around those turning points.

Figure 11.10 shows that hiking cycles have generally been accompanied by increasing stock prices, in particular the first six-to-eight months after the

[5] Notice that in December 2008, the Fed changed policy framework and now indicates a target, i.e. an upper and a lower limit, for the Effective Fed Funds Rate and not an explicit number.

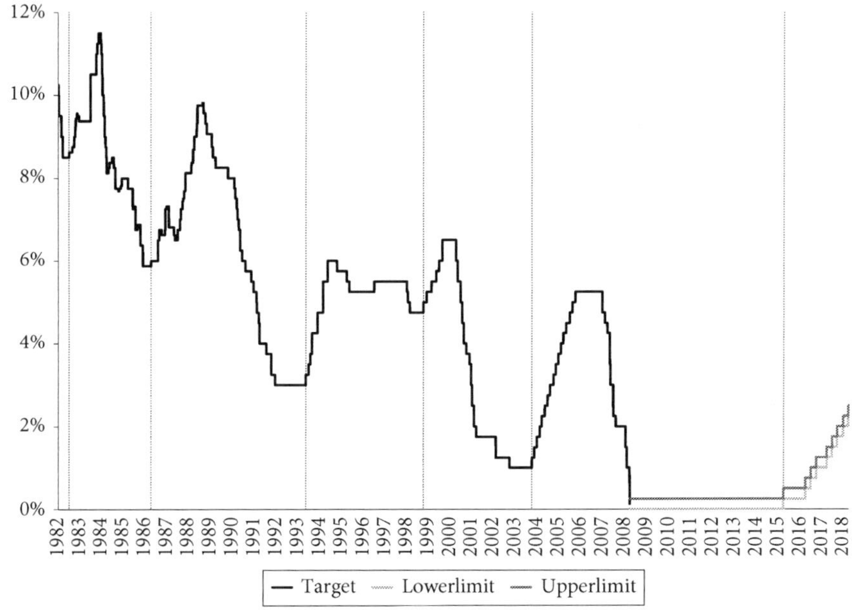

Figure 11.9 Hike cycle initiated.
Data source: FRED.

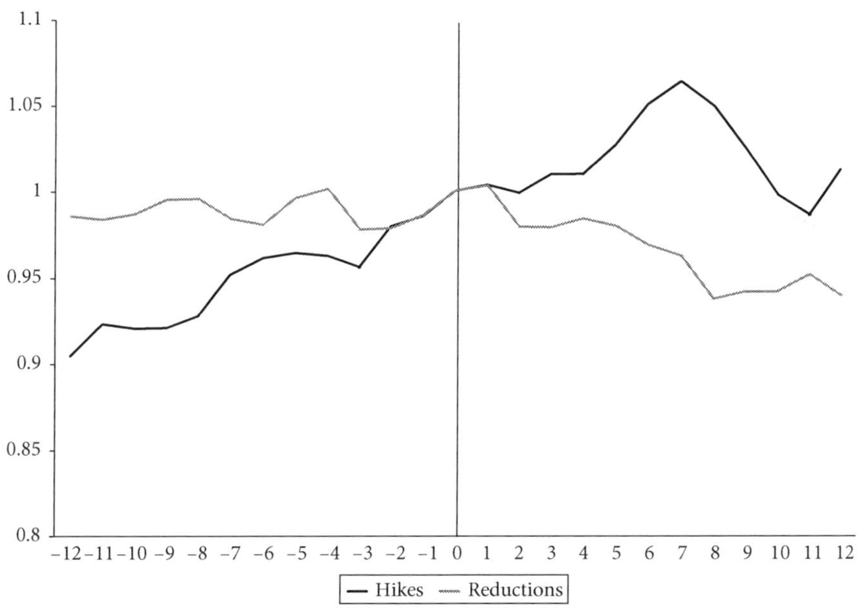

Figure 11.10 Cumulative changes in real stock prices surrounding changes in the direction of the path of monetary policy rates. Stock prices are shown from 12 months before the change in the monetary policy rate up to 12 month after.
Data source: FRED and webpage of Robert J. Shiller.

initiation of a rate-hiking cycle. Stock-market investors should not necessarily be afraid when the Fed embarks on a longer rate-hiking cycle.

Now you might feel a little confused. When simply correlating all monetary policy changes with stock price changes, there is a negative relation (Figure 11.7). Tightening monetary policy (increases in the policy rate) hurts the stock market on the short run. On the other hand, when the Fed embarks on a longer period of rate hikes, the stock market performs well for the first six months or so after the change in policy (Figure 11.10). And vice versa for a period of rate reduction.

Perhaps you should not be too confused. Monetary policy is influenced by underlying economic activity. When the Fed embarks on a rate-hiking cycle, it is typically because the economy is performing well. And, a well-performing economy is good for stock markets (Chapter 9). On the other hand, when the Fed initiates a rate-reduction cycle, it is usually because the economy suffers. And, the stock market suffers during bad economic times. In this sense, the short-run month-to-month relation (Figure 11.7) probably reflects better the influence of monetary policy in itself on the stock market. What this also tells us, however, is that if we want to understand the impact of monetary policy on the stock market in itself, i.e. isolated from the impact of the business cycle, we somehow have to disentangle the effect of the business cycle from the effect of monetary policy itself. Academic research has done so.

11.2.3 Disentangling shocks to monetary policy from the business cycle

It is no easy task to isolate the effect of changes in monetary policy from changes in underlying economic activity. First, changes in monetary policy are to some extent expected by market participants. If the economy is doing well, investors expect the Fed to increase interest rates. There is uncertainty surrounding the timing and magnitude of the policy change, but central bankers wish to avoid turbulence on financial markets, i.e. wish to avoid surprising financial markets too much. They try to prepare markets for policy changes (via speeches, statements, publications, etc.). When a change in policy is expected, it has already been incorporated into stock prices implying that when the change in fact occurs, it should have no or only little effect on the stock market. Second, there is uncertainty with respect to the timing and magnitude of the transmission mechanism. How long will it take before a change in the policy rate affects economic activity and how large will the effect be? Finally, many different types of new information influence the stock market. New information about monetary policy is one of them. This implies that the stock market might move in a different way than the change in monetary policy in itself implies, if other types of new information about the economy arrived at more or less the same time as news about monetary policy was revealed.

There is a large academic literature dealing with the relationship between monetary policy and the stock market.[6] This literature tries to separate the effect of monetary policy in itself from other factors influencing the stock market. Bernanke & Kuttner (2005) is an important and classic study. They extrapolated 'surprise' monetary policy changes, i.e. changes in the Fed Funds Rate not expected by market participants. Bernanke & Kuttner (2005) looked at days with monetary policy announcements. They then compared the expected Fed Funds Rate (expectations were extracted from futures prices) to the actual Fed Funds Rate on those days. They found that the US stock market has a tendency to increase by around 1% in response to a surprise (i.e. unexpected) 25 basis-point lowering of the policy rate whereas the stock market basically does not react when the change in policy is expected. This holds both for day-to-day changes in the monetary policy rate and for monthly changes. In other words, Bernanke & Kuttner (2005) isolated the effect of monetary policy on the stock market and found it to be negative. Lueven & Tong (2012) follow the same approach as Bernanke & Kuttner (2005) but relate changes in US monetary policy to global stock markets. They find that a 25 basis-point unexpected increase in the US monetary policy rate reduces global stock markets by around 1%. Rigobon & Sachs (2004) refine the statistical procedures used to relate day-to-day surprise changes in the policy rate to the stock market and find slightly smaller, but still negative, effects. It seems a robust conclusion that an unexpected tightening in monetary policy affects the stock market negatively on the short run. This appears from simple correlations as in Figure 11.7 and from more detailed academic studies.

It is important to know the contemporaneous short-run relation between changes in monetary policy and the stock market, but one would also like to know whether the effect persists. Patelis (1997) looked at long-run effects from changes in monetary policy. He found that monetary policy predicts stock returns over a longer horizon. He also found that the relation between monetary policy shocks and expected returns changes sign over the horizon: an increase in the Fed Funds Rate predicts excess stock returns negatively on the short horizon, but positively on longer horizons (several quarters or years).

There has also been research studying how changes in the assessed probability of future monetary policy actions affects the stock market. For instance, imagine market participants expect the central bank to change the policy rate by, e.g., one percent over the coming year. Then, for some reason, market participants revise their assessment and now expect the central bank to change the policy rate by

[6] There is also literature looking at the relation between monetary policy and bond markets. An overview of this research is provided by Burachi & Whelan (2016).

two percent over the coming year. This change in expectations might actually have an effect on stock prices today, even if no actual change in the monetary policy rate happens today. But how to measure changes in the expected path of future monetary policy actions? Schmeling & Wagner (2019) use a clever technique. They scan monetary policy statements from the ECB for negative and positive words in order to assess whether the ECB has become more or less pessimistic with respect to the economic outlook. They find that the stock market reacts negatively when the ECB becomes more concerned about the outlook for the economy. Neuhierl & Weber (2019) use information from financial instruments (implied rates from Fed Funds futures) to extrapolate changes to future monetary policy. They find that when market participants increase their expectations for the future path of the policy rate, the stock market reacts negatively.

11.3 Checklist

This chapter has described the relation between monetary policy, interest rates, and stock prices. The main conclusions to remember are:

- The monetary policy rate affects other interest rates in the economy. The shorter the maturity of a bond, the more its yield reacts to changes in the policy rate.
- The difference between yields on bonds of different maturities follow a business cycle pattern. Chapter 10 showed that the monetary policy rate is reduced during recessions. Yields on long-maturity bonds fall during recessions, too, but not as much as the monetary policy rate. The difference between the policy rate (and, more generally, yields on short-maturity bonds) and yields on longer-maturity fixed-income assets, thus, tells us something about business-cycle turning points. In particular, when short-term yields approach the level of long-term yields, i.e. the yield curve flattens, a recession often arrives shortly after. We return to this in Chapter 15.
- Corporate bonds contain a credit risk premia. Credit risk rises during recessions.
- The stock market reacts negatively to changes in monetary policy on the short run; day-to-day or month-to-month. When the monetary policy rate is increased, the stock market falls. A rule of thumb is that the stock market falls by one percentage point when the monetary policy rate is hiked unexpectedly by 25 basis points.
- Typically, rates are hiked when the economy is doing well (and lowered when the economy suffers), as described in Chapter 10, making it difficult to disentangle the longer-term effects of monetary policy on the stock market

from the effect of the business cycle. With this caveat in mind, stocks have done well over rate-hiking cycles, and badly during rate-reduction cycles. The reason is that the economy has done well (poorly) over rate-hiking (rate-reduction) cycles.

- The stock market reacts when there is a change in the expected path of future policy rates. If there is a change in expectations, and monetary policy is expected to be tightened in the future, the stock market suffers today.

12

The 2008–2009 financial crisis and its aftermath

We now know that the stock market generally performs well during expansions, and vice versa during contractions. We also know that the central bank increases the interest rate during expansions and lowers it during recessions. And, we know that there are spill-overs between the stock market, the business cycle, and how the central bank sets interest rates.

Low interest rates spur investment and consumption. When the economy is doing well, earnings of firms are high and stock prices rise. Higher stock prices increase wealth of households, and they consume more. Higher stock prices also lower firms' cost-of-capital. Firms increase investments. At some point, when the economy grows so fast that inflation starts to rise, the central bank starts a rate-hiking cycle, and all processes reverse. This is the nature of the business cycle.

It is crucial that investors understand these processes. To further this understanding, this chapter moves from insights based on many years of data to a specific example of a business cycle. The chapter examines how the expansion gets going, and what makes it end. The chapter will also describe how the central bank influences these developments. Finally, it looks at the consequences for the stock market.

The specific example is the 2008–2009 financial crisis and the years surrounding it. The chapter starts out describing the situation prevailing before the crisis (the expansion), then moves on to the crisis itself (the contraction), and finally its aftermath. The purpose is to move from an overall understanding of the business cycle that we have dealt with in the previous chapters to a specific case. This specific case is, on top of it, a fascinating one. One from which we learn a lot.

Allow me to add a personal note here. During 2012–2013, I chaired a committee appointed by the then Danish government. The purpose of the committee was to investigate the causes and the consequences of the financial crisis in Denmark. The government wanted to learn what happened prior to and during the financial crisis, but also what could be done to improve the resilience of the financial sector going forward. It was a high-profile committee. The report from the committee, published in September 2013, was comprehensive, analysing both the international situation affecting Denmark, as well as the Danish situation itself. It is fair to

From Main Street to Wall Street. Jesper Rangvid, Oxford University Press (2021). © Jesper Rangvid.
DOI: 10.1093/oso/9780198866404.003.0012

say that there was a lot—as in really a lot—of public and political attention devoted to the work of the committee. The committee is today known as the 'Rangvid-committee'. Many of the conclusions in this chapter originate from the conclusions of the report from the Rangvid-committee.[1]

12.1 The period leading up to the financial crisis

The period leading up to the financial crisis, the mid-2000s, was a period with stable and reasonably high economic growth, low unemployment, high optimism, low interest rates, easy access to credit, and financial innovation. Times were good. The economy was expanding, and risk taking was high, both in financial institutions and among households. Credit expanded, and asset prices, in particular house prices, soared.

The crisis originated in the US. Start at the end of the previous recession, the March 2001 through November 2001 recession. This was a mild recession. Chapter 8 showed that the average drop in industrial production during recessions since 1947 has been 8% on an annualized basis. During the 2001 recession, the annualized drop in industrial production was around 5%. Similarly, real GDP was higher during the fourth quarter of 2001, when the recession ended, than when entering it in early 2001. Unemployment did increase, from 4.3% in March 2001 to 5.5% in November 2001. An increase in the unemployment rate of around one percentage point is a fairly modest increase during a recession. During the 2008 recession, for instance, unemployment increased from 5% to 9.5%, i.e. almost a doubling. In spite of the fact that the 2001 recession was mild, the Fed reacted aggressively cutting the Fed Funds Target from 5.5% in March 2001 to 2% in November 2001. The Fed even continued lowering the target for the Fed Funds Rate after the end of the recession to, back then, a historically low level of 1% in 2003. The Fed kept the policy rate at 1% until 2004 where it started a hiking cycle.

There is discussion whether the Fed kept rates too low for too long after the 2001 recession. Figure 12.1 shows that the Fed kept the policy rate at a lower level than that implied by the Taylor rule. Bernanke (2010), then Chairman of the Board of Governors of the Fed, defends the Fed. He argues that the Fed—given the data it had available at the time—did as it should, i.e. monetary policy was not too expansionary before the crisis, given the way things looked when decisions were made. Bernanke (2010) argues that the Fed followed the Taylor rule if calculated on the basis of data available in real time. The main reason for the discrepancy

[1] Unfortunately, the report of the committee is only available in Danish. An English summary exits, though.

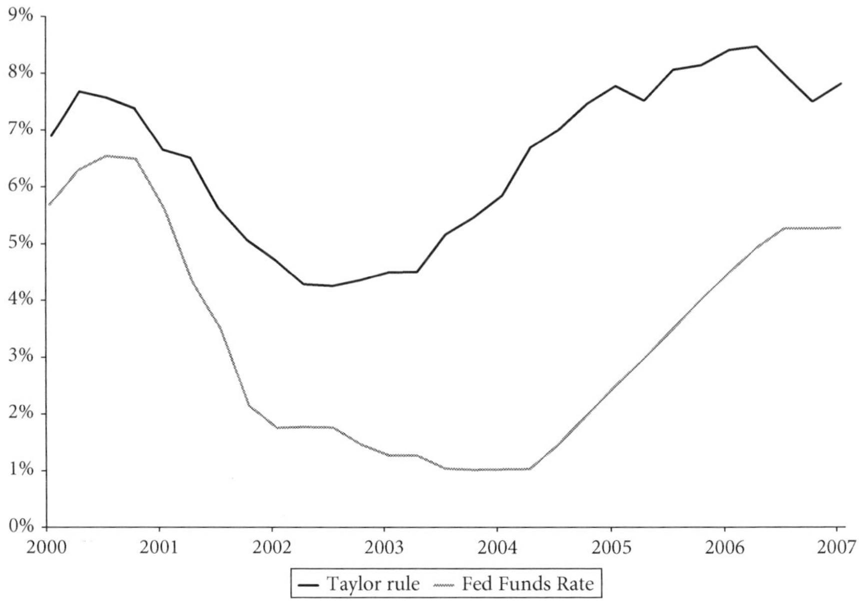

Figure 12.1 The Fed Funds Rate and the Taylor rule. 2000–2007.
Data source: FRED.

between what the Fed observed in real time and what we observe today was a misjudgment of the output gap. Back then, economic activity was estimated to be close to its potential level. Today, with revised data at our disposal, we know that output was above potential during the mid-2000s. One should be cautious blaming the Fed for keeping the policy rate too low during the mid-2000s, given what the Fed knew back then. In hindsight, however, monetary policy was too expansionary.

Low interest rates, together with a stronger economy, increased demand for housing. House prices soared. Figure 12.2 shows the development in real house prices in the US since 1970, normalized to one in 1970. The unusual behaviour of US house prices before the financial crisis is clear. Historically, real house prices have been reasonably stable. During the early- and mid-2000s, this changed dramatically. From 1970–2000, i.e. in the course of thirty years, house prices increased by 40%. From 2000–2007, real house prices also increased by 40%, but this time in the course of seven years only.

The stock market boomed, too. Figure 12.3 shows the impact of the 2001 recession on the stock market and the upswing during the mid-2000s. The 2001 recession was a stock-market induced recession. Stock markets soared during the late 1990s. The stock market started falling in the middle of 2000, and the recession started in 2001. From its peak in July 2000 to its low in February 2003, the stock

Figure 12.2 Real house prices in the US. 1970–2010.
Data source: OECD.

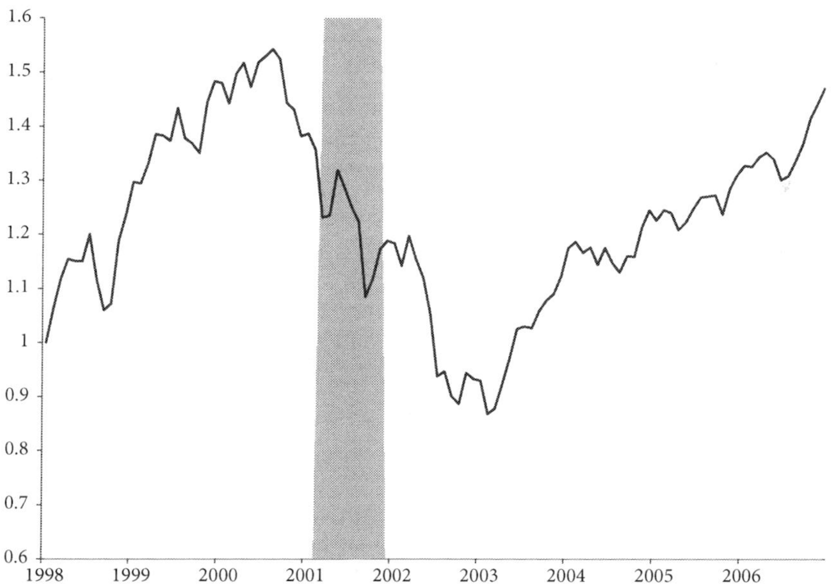

Figure 12.3 Stock price movements before, during, and after the 2001 recession. NBER recessions indicated by shading.
Data source: Webpage of Robert J. Shiller.

market lost more than 40%. During the boom of the mid-2000s, the stock market then gained around 70%. The strong economy during the mid-2000s led to strong growth in house prices and stock prices.

12.1.1 Developments in the financial sector

When house prices increase, households buying houses need to borrow even more. Demand for credit increased rapidly. The prelude to the financial crisis of 2008–2009 can be found in the way credit was extended. Two features are worth paying special attention to: lending to less creditworthy groups of the population increased significantly and borrowing shifted from traditional banks to shadow banks who financed their lending via complicated financial products.

In the US, mortgage borrowers can be prime borrowers or subprime borrowers. The difference between the two is that the probability of default is higher for subprime borrowers. During the mid-2000s, lending to subprime borrowers expanded rapidly, from less than 5% of total mortgages to more than 10%, within a few years (Fed, 2009).

Why did subprime lending expand so rapidly before the crisis? One reason was the generally good economic situation, explained above. Low interest rates and a healthy economy in general increased demand for housing. Another reason can be traced to developments in financial markets and institutions.

The mid-2000s saw a massive expansion in structured credit obligations. In structured credit products, pools of loans are sliced and diced into different tranches that are then sold to investors. A structured credit obligation is an asset-backed security, i.e. a security backed by underlying assets, for instance subprime loans. The different tranches are supposed to differ by their credit quality. Rating agencies rate the different tranches, and investors buy them based on their ratings. A tranche rated AAA is more expensive, i.e. its expected return is lower, but also supposed to be less risky than a lower-rated tranche. Sometimes, additional assets are included in the tranches to secure higher ratings, i.e. subprime loans are pooled with other assets (e.g., car loans or student loans) to supposedly make them safer. Furthermore, one type of structured credit product can be sliced and diced with other structured credit products, to create what became known as Collateralized Debt Obligations (CDO). And these can then again be mixed with other CDOs to create so-called 'squared CDOs'. This seems complicated, and it is.

In general, there are good things to be said about securitization, i.e. the bundling of loans into securities that can be traded. Securitization makes loans liquid. This increases investor demand to the benefit of the borrower (lowers borrowing costs). Securitization also allows for diversification of risks, as a pool of loans is more diversified than a single loan. The splitting of loans into securities of different credit quality furthermore has the potential to make risk sharing more efficient, as investors looking for riskier credit products can buy the more risky tranches, and others the less risky.

The problem during the mid-2000s was that securitization spiraled out of control. Investors buying CDOs simply did not know what the risk embedded in the CDOs was. The original mortgage loan had been mixed with other mortgage loans, and slides and diced, and then mixed with other types of loans, and sliced and diced, and so forth. Rating agencies were supposed to be the ones making sure that investors got the risk they wanted. Rating agencies only discovered the inherent risk in the mortgage system late in the crisis, however. They kept on rating mortgage product as 'safe' for too long. In addition, there were conflicts of interest. Rating agencies are paid by the issuer of a security. If a security is rated as relatively safe, the price of the security increases. Hence, issuers have an interest in a high rating, and rating agencies are paid by issuers, so rating agencies might have a bias towards rating products too optimistically. In 2006, 44% of Moody's earnings came from the rating of structured products.[2]

The issuance of structured credit products expanded rapidly in the years leading up to the crisis. In 2000, issuance in Europe and the US amounted to app. USD 500bn. In 2006, it amounted to app. USD 3000bn, i.e. an six-fold increase.

Financial intermediation refers to the channeling of funds from savers/investors to borrowers. In the run-up to the financial crisis, financial intermediation increased in complexity as well. So, both the financial products and the structure of financial institutions changed.

The change in the structure of financial intermediation is revealed by the increase in 'shadow banking'. 'Shadow banks' are financial entities that share similarities with traditional banks, such as maturity transformation (funding themselves short term but lending long term), liquidity transformation (turning liquid funds into illiquid, such as long-term loans), and credit transformation (moving credit risk from one investor to another), but operate outside the regulated banking system. The consequence of the increase in shadow banking was that many financial products (loans) that traditionally would have been included on the balance sheets of traditional regulated banks ended up outside these banks' balance sheets. As an example, a regulated bank might set up an investment company, often called a Special Purpose Vehicle (SPV) or Asset-Backed Commercial Paper (ABCP) Conduit. These companies bought the loans from the originating regulated banks (via structured credit products). The

[2] Coval, Jurek, Stafford (2009) write: 'According to Fitch Ratings (2007), roughly 60 percent of all global structured products were AAA-rated, in contrast to less than 1 percent of the corporate issues..... For example, 27 of the 30 tranches of asset-backed collateralized debt obligations underwritten by Merrill Lynch in 2007, saw their triple-A ratings downgraded to "junk".'

loans were long-term—they were mortgage loans. The companies financed the purchase of the loans via short-term funding, for instance via the Commercial Paper market. The end-result was that loans moved from the balance sheet of regulated banks to the balance sheet of the investment vehicle, i.e. a 'shadow bank'.

By transferring the loan from the originating bank to the unregulated shadow bank, the originating regulated bank reduces its capital requirement. The problem was that the originating banks sometimes extended different kinds of guarantees towards their sponsored/associated shadow bank. When the crisis unfolded, the losses on the original loans and the liquidity risks inherent in the shadow banks ended up on the balance sheets of the originating banks. This was not supposed to happen, but it did.

So, in the end, low interest rates fuelled demand for housing. Banks extended many loans. In particular, loans to less creditworthy borrowers (subprime loans) increased. Banks sold off these loans, i.e. the loans were removed from their balance sheets. This happened in complicated ways, both in terms of complicated financial securities and a more complicated financial system. In the end, a lot of risks had been build up in the housing market and the financial system. The risks were hidden in financial products (e.g., via high ratings of products) and in financial institutions (in the less transparent shadow banking system). It was only waiting to implode.

12.2 The crisis

The Fed started raising interest rates in 2004 (Figure 12.1). For borrowers who had borrowed at adjustable mortgage rates, mortgage payments increased. Some of the borrowers, in particular subprime borrowers, could not afford paying these higher mortgage payments. Default rates starting increasing in 2005, i.e. shortly after interest rates started increasing. Default rates of subprime borrowers are generally higher than default rates of prime borrowers, but the increase in default rates of subprime borrowers was dramatic.

Even when lending to subprime borrowers had expanded rapidly during the early 2000s, subprime lending nevertheless constituted a small fraction of total mortgage lending. The increase in losses on subprime loans thus—in itself—cannot explain the magnitude of the financial crisis. The real problem was that nobody knew where those loses were concentrated. The spreading of risk in the financial system via complicated products and institutions, described in the previous section, implied that risks had been sliced and diced such that it was difficult for financial markets and regulators to disentangle which financial institutions were exposed to losses and which were not.

During 2007 and 2008, financial institutions exposed to subprime losses started getting into trouble. Given that nobody knew what financial institution would be next on the list, trust between institutions suffered. There is nothing as damaging for financial institutions as a loss of trust. Financial institutions depend upon being able to raise short-term funding to finance long-term loans. When trust evaporates, the key functions of financial institutions are hampered.

Lack of trust skyrocketed, and the crisis turned into a full-blown global financial crisis. It peaked during the week surrounding September 15, 2008. On that day, the investment bank Lehman Brothers filed for bankruptcy. Negotiations had been intense during the weekend preceding Monday September 15, 2008. Potential acquires of Lehman Brothers wanted some form of Fed/government help if they should take over Lehman. The US government declined, and Lehman failed. Given that the government just a few days earlier had taken over the government-sponsored, but private, mortgage enterprises Fannie May and Freddie Mac, it was clear to everybody that even very large financial institutions could get in trouble. Everybody ran for the exit, and lending between financial institutions came to a complete stop. The breakdown of trust between banks is clear from Figure 12.4. Figure 12.4 shows one measure of the cost of raising funds in the interbank market relative to the risk-free rate, the so-called TED spread. This is the

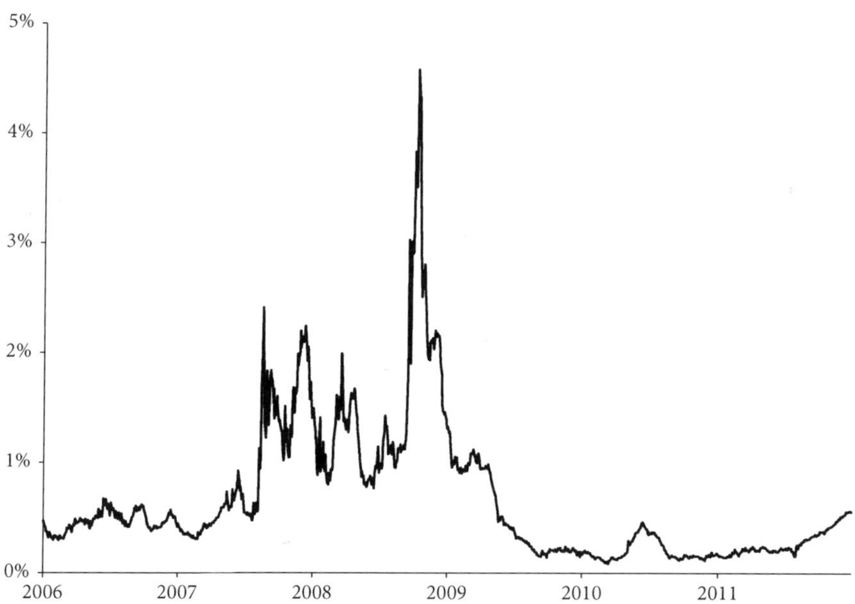

Figure 12.4 TED spread. Spread between 3-month USD LIBOR and 3-month Treasury Bill. Daily data.

Data source: FRED.

difference between a three-months LIBOR yield and the three-months Treasury Bill yield.[3] Before the crisis, a bank paid around fifty basis points above the risk-free rate when borrowing from another bank on an unsecured basis. This spread between secured and unsecured lending was stable before the crisis. Lack of trust between banks started increasing in 2007, and spiked dramatically in the weeks following September 15, 2008.

When banks get in trouble, trouble spreads to the rest of the economy. Banks stop lending, with consequences for consumption and investments. Firms and households get nervous. They increase savings and cut investments. House prices fall. Unemployment increases, which make firms and households even more nervous. Government finances weaken. What started as a financial crisis turned into a full-blown economic crisis. GDP suffered dramatically, as Figure 12.5 shows, not only in the US and other advanced economies, but all around the world. The figure shows how global output and global industrial production developed before and after the financial crisis. Before the crisis, growth was steady. As a

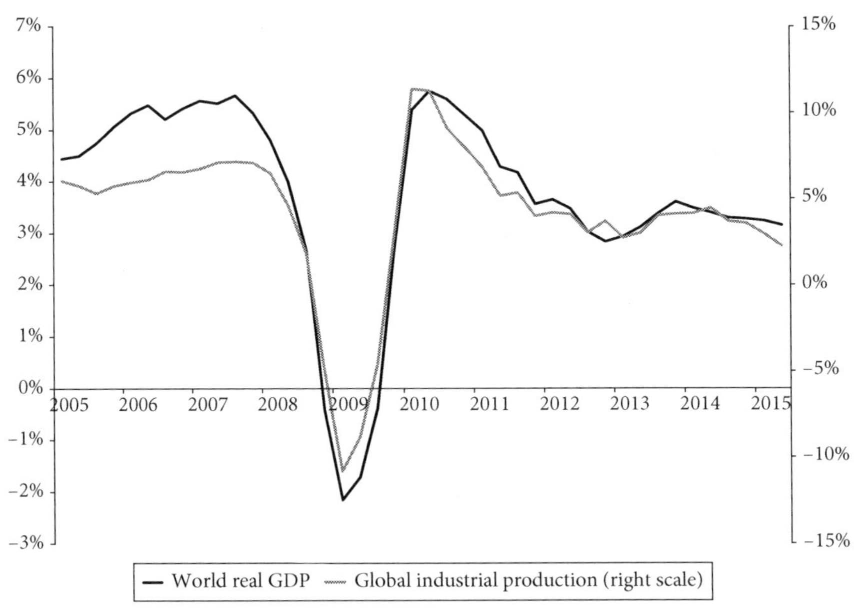

Figure 12.5 Year-on-year change in global real GDP and global industrial production.
Data source: IMF.

[3] The LIBOR (London InterBank Offered Rate) measures the costs for a bank of borrowing funds from another bank. When LIBOR increases, banks charge more to lend to other banks. When trust between banks evaporates, LIBOR increases.

result of the crisis, economic activity suffered dramatically. The crisis had dramatic consequences for economic prosperity.

12.3 The aftermath of the crisis

Seeing economies in free-fall, governments and central banks around the world reacted to soften the blow. In most countries, governments had to provide guarantees to banks. In many cases, banks were bailed out. Central banks acted as lenders of last resort, providing liquidity to banks. The Fed and other central banks lowered interest rates dramatically. The Fed lowered rates to a historically low 0%–0.25%.

The Fed kept rates at zero percent until 2016 where it started a new rate-hiking cycle, as Figure 12.6 reveals. Even a policy rate of zero percent did not provide enough monetary stimulus to the economy, however, given the severity of the recession. Central banks started using other tools, today known as 'quantitative easing', or QE. Quantitative easing means that the central bank directly buys securities, such as government bonds, mortgage bonds, and sometimes corporate bonds, on financial markets. The purpose is to increase demand for those securi-

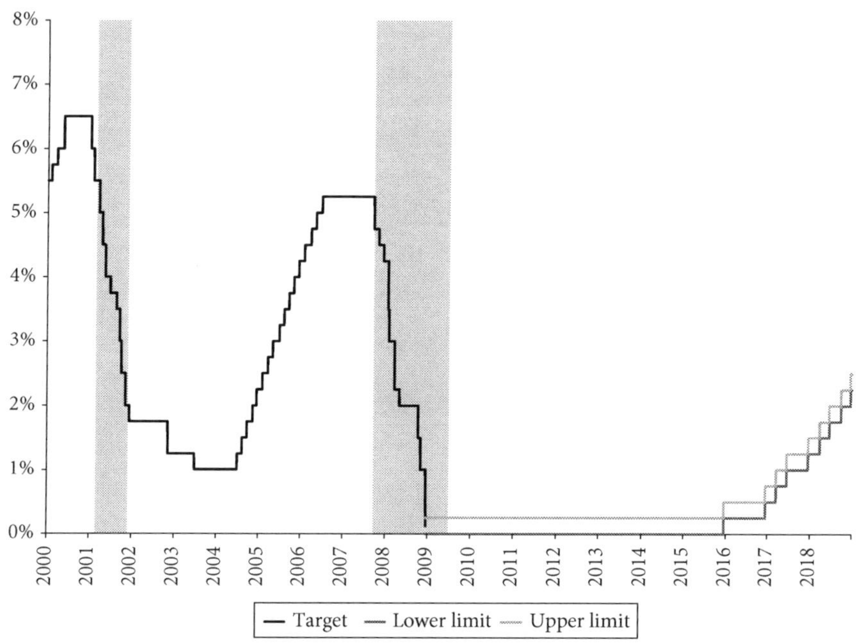

Figure 12.6 The Fed Funds Rate Target before, during, and after the 2008 financial crisis. NBER recessions indicated by shading.

Data source: FRED.

ties, thereby pushing yields further down. This makes borrowing cheaper for firms and households and helps stimulate investments and consumption. QE implied that the balance sheet of central banks increased (when central banks buys bonds from the market, their balance sheets increase). The balance sheet of the Fed was stable and amounted to something like 5% of US GDP before the crisis. It increased to more than 20% of GDP after the crisis. Similarly, the balance sheet of the ECB increased from around 10% of Eurozone GDP before the crisis to more than a third of GDP after the crisis. Research has analyzed whether QE helped; see, e.g., Krishnamurthy & Vissing-Jorgensen (2011) and Krishnamurthy, Nagel & Vissing-Jorgensen (2015). A balanced conclusion seems to be that QE brought down yields, as intended.

In addition to monetary policy, fiscal policy turned expansionary in many countries. As unemployment increased, costs of unemployment schemes increased. Governments also took discretionary action by increasing government investments and discretionary spending in order to stimulate demand and thereby keep the economy going. Deficits on government budgets ballooned. Figure 12.7 shows that the US government deficit in 2009 was the largest since 1947. Fiscal policy was indeed very expansionary. In some countries, the deficit increased so

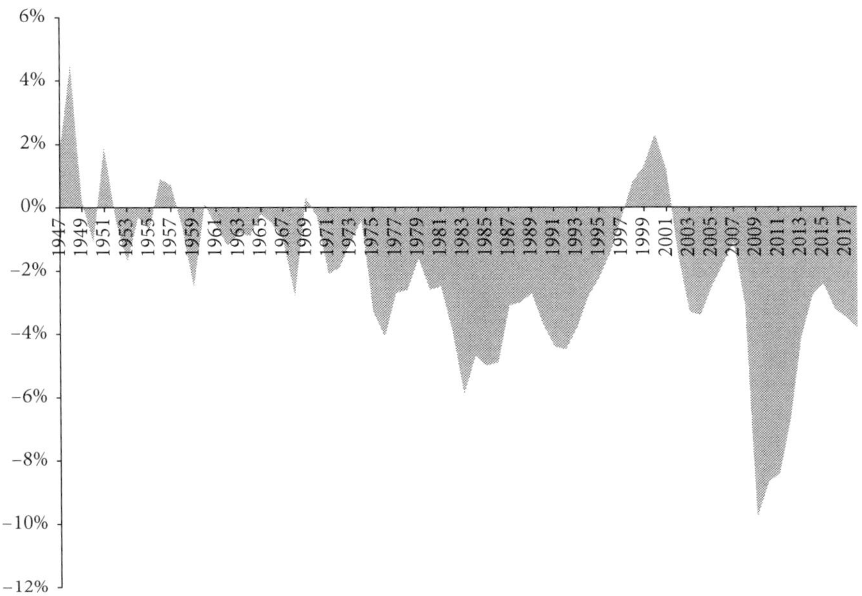

Figure 12.7 Deficit on US federal government budget in percentage of US GDP. 1947–2018.

Data source: Office of Management and Budget, The White House.

much that investors started doubting the creditworthiness of governments, such as in Ireland, Italy, and Greece.

In the end, the many policy initiatives from governments and central banks around the world helped soften the blow. Compare with the Great Depression of the early 1930a. During the 1930 recession, US GDP fell by 25% and unemployment increased by as much. During the 2008 Great Recession, GDP fell by something like 5% and unemployment reached 10%. The financial crisis of 2008 turned into a Great Recession, though luckily not a Great Depression. Policy intervention helped avoiding this.

The costs of the financial crisis are nevertheless inconceivably high. Figure 12.8 provides one illustration. It shows the level of global real GDP (in USD) before and after the financial crisis together with a hypothetical path of GDP. The hypothetical path of global real GDP is calculated by extrapolating global GDP by its average growth rate over the past 15 years (3% p.a.) as of 2007. The figure thus illustrates what could have been the path of real global GDP had there been no crisis together with the actual path of real global GDP.

The figure reveals the drop in global GDP following the crisis. The figure also reveals how world GDP continues to be lower than it potentially could have been in the absence of the crisis. The difference between hypothetical world GDP without

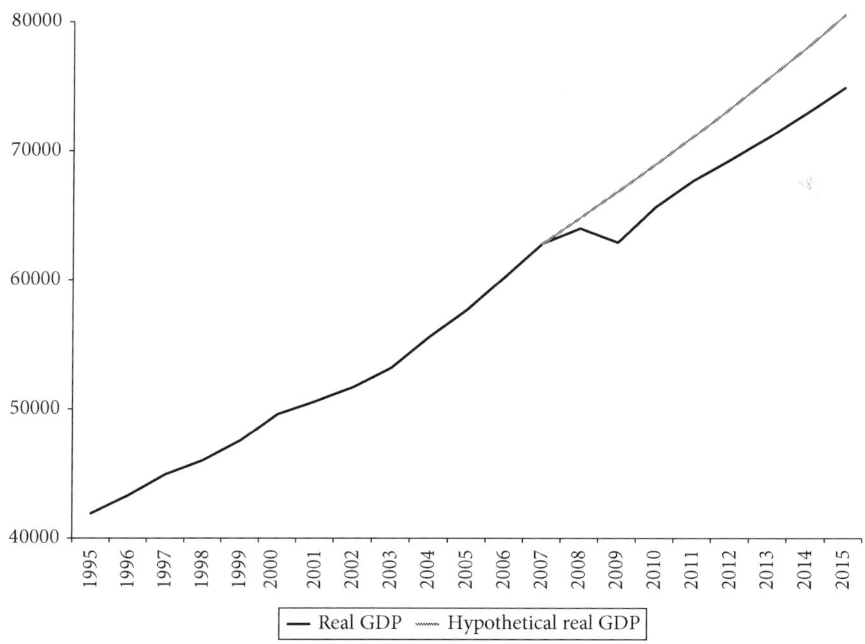

Figure 12.8 Global real GDP in billions of USD.
Data source: The World Bank.

the crisis and actual world GDP is in the neighborhood of 4,000–5,000 billion USD—per year. There is nothing that seems to suggest that world production will catch up. There seems to have been a permanent downward shift in the level of global production.

The Fed (2013) made an assessment of the cost of the crisis in the US. The Fed judges that 'There are few estimates of what society gave up due to the crisis: Our conservative estimate is $50,000 to $120,000 for every U.S. household.'

12.3.1 The stock market during and after the crisis

The crisis was severe, but expansionary fiscal and monetary policy prevented the crisis from becoming as deep as The Great Depression of the 1930s. Economic activity dropped significantly during the crisis, but growth returned in 2009–2010. How did the stock market react? It reacted as we would expect, given what has been discussed in previous chapters. During the crisis, economic activity suffered. Stock markets tanked, as Figure 12.9 shows. From its pre-crisis peak in January 2007 to its through in March 2009, stock prices were almost cut in half.

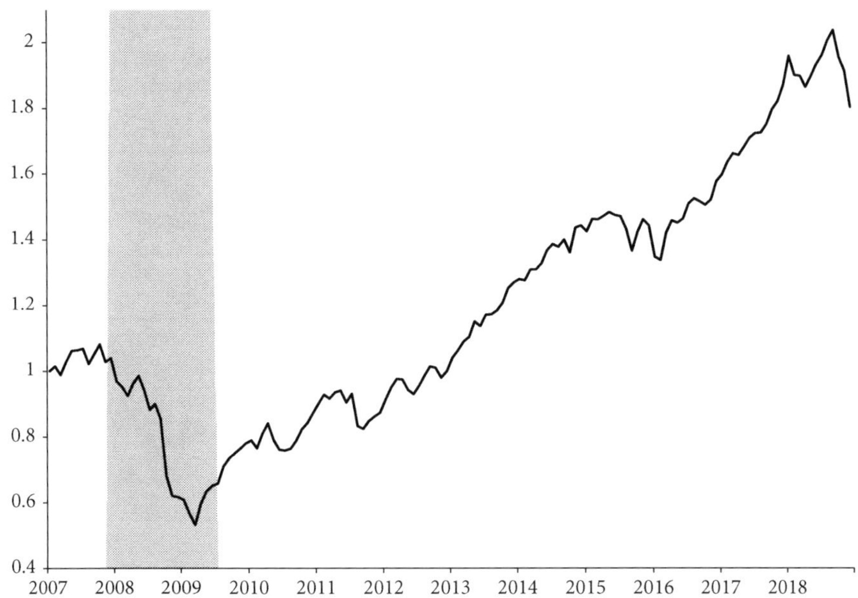

Figure 12.9 US stock market during and after the 2008–09 financial crisis. Normalized to 1 in January 2007. NBER recessions indicated by shading.
Data source: Webpage of Robert J. Shiller.

After the crisis, interest rates were kept very low, monetary policy added even further stimulus via quantitative easing, and fiscal policy was expansionary. The economy recovered, and the stock market soared. But it took four years before the stock market reached its pre-crisis level.

12.4 Checklist

This chapter has provided an overview of the prelude to the financial crisis of 2008, its consequences for the real economy, and the developments in the stock market before, during, and after the crisis. The point of the chapter is to illustrate how a recession plays out using a specific example. The main conclusions to remember are:

- After the 2001 recession, the Fed lowered its policy rate dramatically, from around 6% to around 1–2% within a year or so. The Fed kept rates low until 2004. There is discussion whether the Fed kept rates too low for too long.
- Low interest rates, together with a strong economy, sparked demand for housing. Lending increased and house prices soared.
- Lending to subprime borrowers increased in particular. Lenders did not bear the risk of the loans directly, however, as risks were shifted around the global financial system via complicated financial products, shadow banks, bad incentives, and inadequate risk assessments.
- Structured credit products were in fashion. Risks were concentrated in off-balance sheet institutions, so-called Special Purpose Vehicles (SPVs).
- The Fed started raising rates in 2004. Borrowers, initially primarily subprime borrowers, started facing difficulties paying their mortgages.
- Losses ended up on banks' balance sheets, as banks had provided guarantees and other credit enhancements to SPVs. This was not supposed to happen, but it did.
- The crisis intensified after the fall of the investment bank Lehman Brothers on September 15, 2008. The fall of Lehman Brothers made the severity of the crisis clear to everybody. The financial crisis turned into a global economic crisis.
- House prices fell, firms suffered, unemployment increased, government deficits increased. All around the world. The recession that erupted became the worst since the Great Depression of the 1930s.
- The Fed, and other central banks around the world, reacted by lowering rates. Fiscal policy turned expansionary. The actions of governments and central banks prevented as severe a crisis as the one in the early 1930s. It turned into the Great Recession instead.

- The economic loses from the Great Recessions are enormous. They appear to be permanent.
- The Fed kept its policy rate at zero percent until 2016. After losing around 50% during the 2007–2009 financial crisis, stock markets rebounded after the crisis. Between 2009 and 2018, the stock market tripled.

13
Value, size, sector, and momentum stocks

The stock market has provided amazing returns over the long run. Aggregate stock market returns are per definition the weighted, i.e. average, return of the individual stocks on the stock market. When it is an average, some stocks have performed better and some have performed worse. This is not interesting information. What is interesting, on the other hand, is that some types of stock systematically seem to deliver higher average returns than the overall stock market.

Portfolios of these types of stocks are also called factors. Alternatively, some of them are called 'anomalies', as it is hard to explain why their returns are higher than the return on the overall stock market. In this chapter, we will study the characteristics of the most important and well-known factors. We will see that factors that perform better than the overall stock market tend to suffer more during recessions. Conversely, those factors that provide lower average returns than the overall stock market do so because they perform relatively better during recessions. The business cycle again plays an important role for understanding stock-market patterns.

13.1 Value and growth, small and big

Value stocks and small-cap stocks have historically performed better than the overall stock market. Their counterparts are growth and large-cap stocks.

13.1.1 Value stocks

Value stocks are stocks bought at a 'good value'. This means that the price of the stock is low compared to some indicator that measures the 'fundamental' value of the stock/company.

Value investing has a long history in finance. Professors Benjamin Graham and David Dodd published their path-breaking monograph Security Analysis in 1934. Graham and Dodd developed the idea that stocks whose current price is below its fundamental value are attractive. Graham and Dodd argued that one should take a close look at the company and judge the soundness of its underlying business. They also argued that some stocks, for irrational reasons, get out of

From Main Street to Wall Street. Jesper Rangvid, Oxford University Press (2021). © Jesper Rangvid.
DOI: 10.1093/oso/9780198866404.003.0013

favour. When this happens their market price falls below its fundamental value. These stocks, Graham and Dodd argued, provide good investment opportunities. The fundamental idea of Graham and Dodd has been refined and tested in many different ways, but the basic principle is the same: buy stocks whose price is low relative to an indicator of the fundamental value of the stock/company.

One can imagine several indicators of the 'fundamental' value of a company. This could be the earnings of the company, the accounting (or book) value of the equity in the company, the level of debt of the company (market value to debt is leverage), the dividends paid out by the company (dividends to market value is the dividend yield), etc. Graham and Dodd called the difference between the current stock price and the fundamental, or intrinsic, value of the stock the 'margin of safety'.

Fundamentally, there can be two reasons why a company trades at a low price relative to its fundamental or intrinsic value: a rational and an irrational/behavioural reason. If value stocks are particularly risky, there are rational reasons why their expected returns are high. Investors will only buy these particularly risky stocks if investors are compensated by higher expected returns. In this case, the stock is not a particularly good bargain. Its expected return is high because the risk is high.

On the other hand—and this is the hypothesis of many value investors—it might be that the stock has fallen out of fashion, the stock market is too pessimistic about the outlook for the company, a new management might turn the company around, etc. In this case, the stock might be a bargain.

The famous value investor Warren Buffet has expressed this nicely: 'it's far better to buy a wonderful company at a fair price, than to buy a fair company at a wonderful price.' The challenge is of course to distinguish the wonderful company from the fair company. And, to distinguish the fair price from the wonderful price. One might think that it is always better to buy at a low price (relative to the fundamental), but if the low price is in fact the right price, this is no bargain. In other words, one does not a priori know whether the current low price (in relation to the intrinsic or fundamental value) is rational or not, i.e. whether buying into value stocks is a particularly good investment or not. The only way to judge this is to look at the data.

13.1.2 Small-cap stocks

Small cap stocks are easy to explain: These are stocks with low market value (market capitalization) relative to other companies.

The idea of investing in small-cap stocks goes back at least to an article published by Rolf Banz in 1981. Banz showed that small-cap stocks provide higher average returns than large-cap stocks. His result has been confirmed in numerous subsequent academic studies.

Why should small-cap stocks be associated with higher average returns? Again, there are rational and irrational reasons. Rational reasons would say that small-cap stocks are riskier. Small firms are perhaps not as well-established as large-cap firms and thus face difficulties generating sustainable revenues. They might be new firms that need to demonstrate a viable business model. On the other hand, small firms might also 'go under the radar'. This is the irrational reason. Investors might not pay sufficient attention to small companies causing demand for their stocks to be relatively low. In this case, small-cap stocks might trade at a discount, pushing up their expected returns.

13.2 Returns on value and small-cap stocks

The famous Chicago economist and Nobel prize winner Gene F. Fama developed with his former student, now Dartmouth College Professor, Kenneth R. French important research on value and small cap stocks. Professor French updates an impressive freely-available database with monthly and annual returns on stocks classified according to different characteristics. The US data start in 1927.

The classification of a stock as a value stock or a growth stock (or a small-cap or large-cap stock) is done once a year. The classification works as follows. Data on the book value (accounting value) of equity are collected. Company-by-company, the end-of-the-year book value of equity is compared to the market value of the stock (stock price times the number of outstanding stocks) on June 30 the following year. I.e. for each stock, a book-to-market value is calculated, based on June 30 stock-price data and December 31 accounting data.[1] All stocks are ranked according to their book-to-market value. Stocks are sorted into quintiles, from those stocks with the lowest book-to-market value to those stocks with the highest. Growth stocks are those twenty percent of stocks that have the lowest book-to-market ratio, i.e. stocks where the market value is high relative to the book-value of equity. Value stocks are the twenty percent of stocks with the highest book-to-market values, i.e. stocks where investors pay relatively little to get ownership of the equity of the

[1] A book-to-market value larger than one means that the market value of equity is lower than the accounting value of equity. Investors will not pay the recorded book value for the company's equity. And, vice versa for a book-to-market value smaller than one.

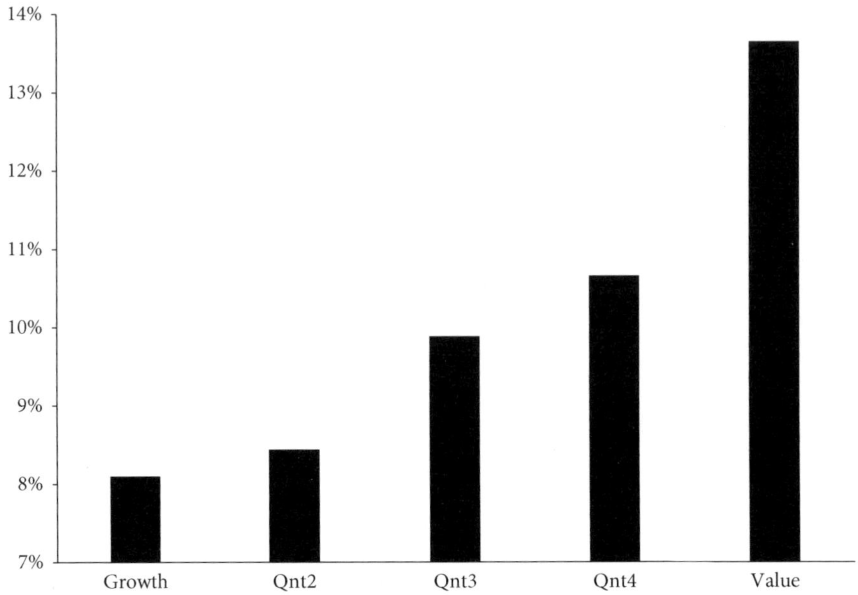

Figure 13.1 Average real return on stocks sorted on book-to-market value. 1927–2017.

Data source: Webpage of Kenneth R. French.

firm. The ranking of the stocks is done once a year. A stock that one year is a growth stock might be reclassified as a value stock next year.

Sorting according to size works in a similar fashion. The market values of all stocks are calculated once a year. Stocks are ranked according to their market value. Stocks are sorted into quintiles. The twenty percent of stocks with the lowest market capitalization are small-cap stocks. The twenty percent of stocks with the highest capitalizations are large-cap stocks. As practically anywhere in this book, we deflate nominal returns by inflation, i.e. all returns are real.

Figure 13.1 shows average real returns on the book-to-market sorted portfolios and Figure 13.2 shows returns on portfolios of firms sorted according to size. Figure 13.1 reveals that value stocks (those with high book-to-market values) have performed considerably better than growth stocks. The annual real return to value firms over the period from 1927–2017 has been close to 14% on average, whereas the average annual return to growth firms has been 8%.

The story is similar for small-cap firms versus large-cap firms. Figure 13.2 shows that small-cap firms have returned around 14% per year on average in real terms whereas large-cap firms have returned around 8% per year on average. Small-cap stocks have performed impressively.

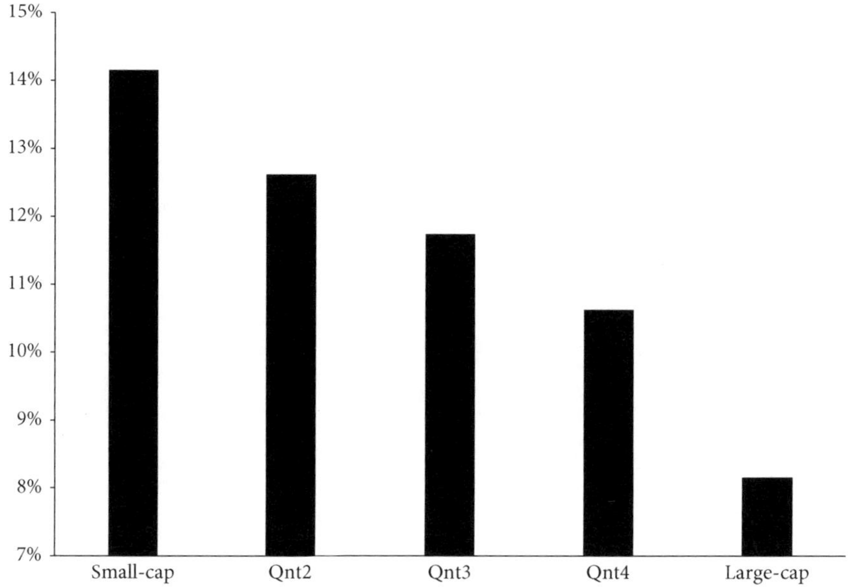

Figure 13.2 Average real return on stocks sorted by on size (market capitalization). 1927–2017.

Data source: See Figure 13.1.

13.2.1 Why do value stocks and small-cap stocks provide higher returns on average? Remember the business cycle

During the 1960s and 1970s, economists developed a framework for understanding why some stocks deliver higher expected returns than other. The fundamental insight was that stocks co-moving positively with the overall stock market should provide higher returns on average. This is the famous Capital Asset Pricing Model (or CAPM). The CAPM was, and for many still is, the workhorse model of finance. The idea in the CAPM is that a stock is particularly attractive if its value increases when the overall stock market falls. If you hold a well-diversified portfolio and think about adding a stock to your portfolio, you would be particularly happy to include a stock that pays out a lot when the rest of the market falls (the stock commoves negatively with the aggregate stock market). Its expected return will be low. On the other hand, if a stock co-moves positively with the overall stock market, you are not willing to pay a high price for this stock, and its expected return will be high.

During the 1980s, economists discovered that high average returns on small-cap stocks and value stocks cannot be rationalized by the CAPM. Value stocks do not commove positively with the aggregate stock market. The same is the case for small-cap stocks.

What, then, might explain the high average return on value and small-cap stocks? Recent research argues that perhaps it has to do with their exposure to the business cycle.[2] I.e., that value and small-cap stocks offer high average returns to compensate investors for the risk that these stocks perform worse than growth stocks and large-cap stocks during recessions. The reason is as follows. Imagine you consider buying two different stocks. One of them performs well during recessions while the other does not. Recessions are periods in time where unemployment increases, wage growth is poor, and, overall, the economic situation is terrible. Stocks on average perform badly during recessions, as we have seen many times in this book. But some stocks might perform a little better than the overall stock market. You would probably be willing to pay more for the stock that performs relatively well when times are otherwise bad. Higher price means lower expected returns. If small-cap stocks and value stocks perform worse than growth stocks and large-cap stocks during recessions, it makes sense that their average returns are higher.

Figure 13.3 shows the cumulative returns from value and growth stocks. The overall better performance of value appears clearly. One dollar invested in value stocks in 1927, and all dividends continuously reinvested in value stocks, would have turned into almost USD 6,000 in 2017 in real terms. One dollar invested in growth stocks would have turned into USD 237. More important for the message of this section, however, Figure 13.3 also shows that value stocks tend to take larger hits during recessions. For instance, during the Great Depression in the early 1930s, value stocks lost a wobbling 85% from September 1929 to June 1932. Almost all wealth invested in value stocks were lost. The aggregate stock market crashed, i.e. all stocks lost in value, including growth stocks. Growth stocks lost 77%. Growth stocks certainly took a huge hit, but value stocks performed even worse. The same happened for small-cap stocks versus large-cap stocks, though the difference is a little smaller. Small-cap stocks lost 85% and large-cap stocks 82%. During the Great Recession from October 2007 through March 2009, value stocks lost 57%. Growth stocks lost a lot as well, but less than value stocks: 44%. Small-cap stocks lost 59% whereas large-cap stocks lost 49%. The Great Recession and the Great Depression are just two, though significant, episodes. Table 13.1

[2] Fama & French (1992, 1993) proceeded in the following way to understand the differences in returns across value/growth and size portfolios. They formed 'high minus low' portfolios, subtracting the return on the growth portfolio from the return on the value portfolio, month by month, and subtracting the return on the large-cap portfolio from the return on the small-cap portfolio. They called the resulting portfolios 'HML' (high minus low) and 'SMB' (small minus big). They added these two zero-cost portfolios to the market portfolio in a so-called 'three-factor model'. They showed that the three-factor model performs considerably better than the CAPM when it comes to pricing the cross section of stock returns.

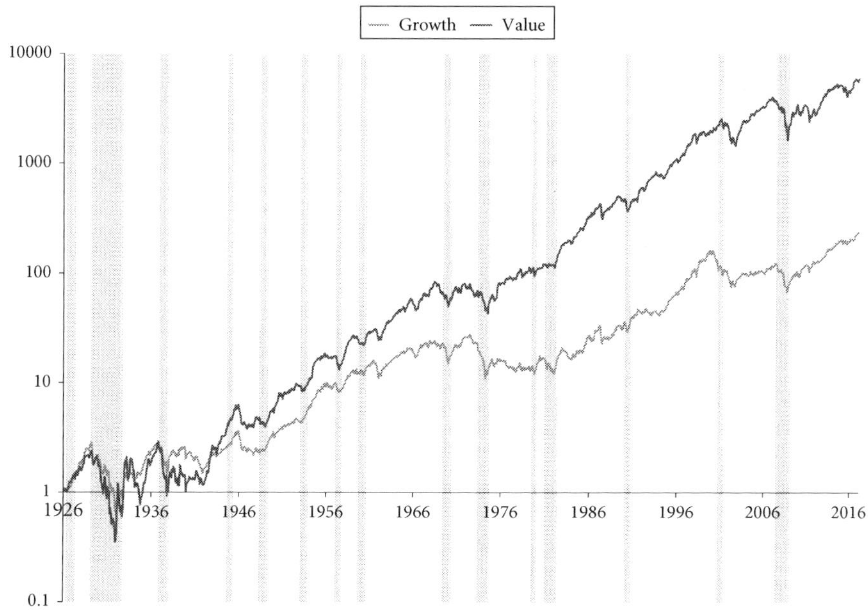

Figure 13.3 Cumulative real return on value and growth stocks. NBER recessions indicated by shading. 1927–2017.

Data source: See Figure 13.1.

Table 13.1 Average monthly real returns during recessions and expansions for value and growth stocks

	Recessions			Expansions		
	Growth	Value	Diff.	Growth	Value	Diff.
1927–2017	−1.0%	−2.2%	**−1.2%**	0.6%	0.9%	**0.3%**
Since 1945	−0.5%	−0.9%	**−0.4%**	0.5%	0.9%	**0.4%**

collects the overall performance across all recessions and expansions for growth and value stocks.

Table 13.1 reveals that regardless of whether we look at the full sample since 1927 or the post-1945 sample, value stocks have performed worse than growth stocks during recessions. This underperformance during recessions is compensated by higher returns during expansions. Value stocks have lost 2.2% per month on average during recessions. Growth stocks have lost as well, but less: 1% per month. During expansions, value stocks have gained 0.9% per month versus growth stocks' 0.6%. In other words, during recessions, value stocks have underperformed growth stocks by 1.2% per month. During expansions, on the

Table 13.2 Average monthly real returns during recessions and expansions of stocks from small and large corporations

	Recessions			Expansions		
	Large	Small	Diff.	Large	Small	Diff.
1927–2017	−0.2%	−0.3%	**-0.1%**	0.8%	1.5%	**0.7%**
Since 1947	0.0%	−0.1%	**-0.1%**	0.7%	1.0%	**0.3%**

other hand, value stocks have outperformed growth stocks by 0.3% per month. Given there are more expansion months in the total sample, value stocks beat growth stocks over the full sample (Figure 13.3). The conclusion is that if you buy value stocks to get access to this average outperformance, you should know that when times are bad, these stocks perform even worse than growth stocks.

Table 13.2 shows that the same patterns characterize small-cap versus large-cap stocks. Small-cap stocks loose 0.3% per month during recessions versus 0.2% per month for large-cap stocks. Small-cap stocks compensate for this underperformance during recessions by delivering better performance during expansions: 1.5% per month versus 0.8% for large-cap stocks, i.e. overperforms by 0.7% per month during expansions.

The conclusion is that over long periods of time, several decades, there is evidence that value stocks and small-cap stocks perform better than growth stocks and large-cap stocks. One reason is that value and small-cap stocks both deliver lower returns than growth and large-cap stocks during recessions. Growth stocks and large-cap stocks also perform badly during recessions, but value stocks and small-cap stocks perform even worse. Investors do not like this, as recessions are rough times. If they should buy value and small-cap stocks—knowing that these stocks take larger hits when times are generally bad—they want to be compensated by higher returns during expansions and thus on average higher returns across the business cycle.

13.3 Returns on stocks from firms in different sectors

One can sort stocks according to other criteria, for instance sectors. Figure 13.4 shows the average return to firms in different sectors. Car-industry stocks have on average returned more than 12% per year. Utility-sector stocks have on average returned around 8% per year.

Similar to the investigation of value, growth, small-cap, and large-cap firms, we can investigate how firms in the car industry and firms in the utility industry have performed during recessions and expansions. Table 13.3 shows the results.

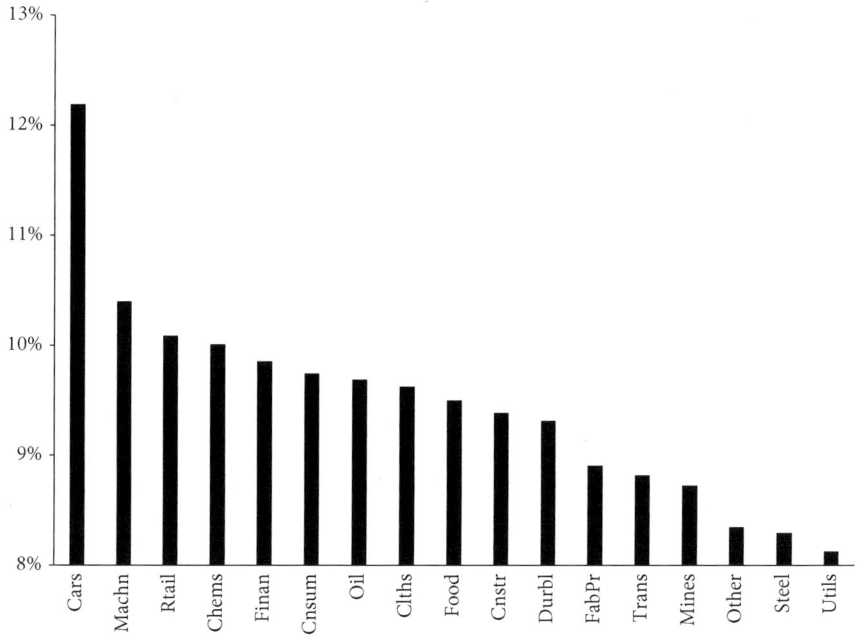

Figure 13.4 Average return on stocks from firms in different sectors. 1927–2017.
Data source: See Figure 13.1.

Table 13.3 Average returns during recessions and expansions of stocks from firms in the car industry and the utilities industry

	Recessions			Expansions		
	Utilities	Cars	Diff.	Utilities	Cars	Diff.
1927–2017	0.2%	−0.2%	**−0.4%**	0.8%	1.1%	**0.3%**
Since 1945	0.5%	−0.0%	**−0.5%**	0.6%	0.9%	**0.3%**

Car-industry stocks perform worse than utilities-industry stocks during recessions. The average return on firms in the car sector during recessions has been a negative 0.2%. Firms in the utility sectors have delivered positive returns during recessions, at 0.2% per month on average. Firms in the car industry have underperformed by 0.4% per month during recessions. The relatively low return on car-industry stocks during recessions is compensated by higher returns during expansions. Outperformance is 0.3% per month during expansions. Sectors that deliver high returns on average across several business cycles do so because these sectors suffer more during recessions.

13.4 An anomaly: Momentum return

Value stocks, small-cap stocks, and cyclical stocks (such as stocks issued by firms in the car industry) provide higher returns on average than growth stocks, large-cap stocks, and defensive stocks (such as stocks issued by firms in the utilities industry). One reason is that these stocks fall more during recessions. This all makes sense.

Stocks that provide high average return but perform well during recessions are hard to find. There is one particular kind of stock where this is the case, though: momentum stocks. The fact that momentum stocks perform well, even during recessions, makes the high average return to momentum stocks puzzling.

Momentum strategies buy stocks that have performed well in the past in the hope that they will continue to perform well. Already this should ring an alarm. Any investment house states that past performance is no guarantee for future performance. What has happened in the past cannot be taken as proof that it will happen again in the future. Momentum strategies seem to go against this view.

Figure 13.5 shows one-year ahead returns from stocks ranked in quintiles according to their return over the preceding year, i.e. past returns. The 20% of stocks with the lowest return during the preceding year have had average

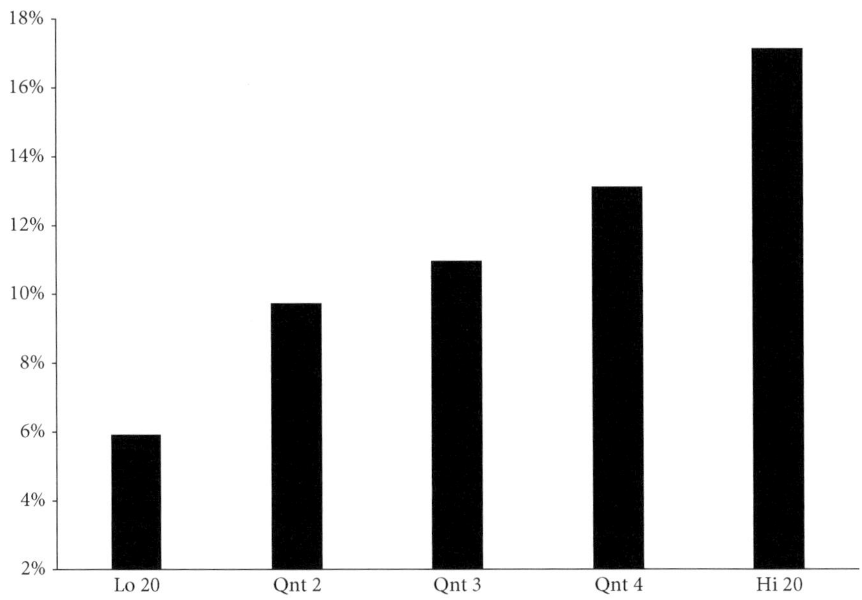

Figure 13.5 Average returns on low and high momentum stocks. 1927–2017.
Data source: See Figure 13.1.

Table 13.4 Average returns during recessions and expansions for low and high momentum stocks

	Recessions			Expansions		
	Low	High	Diff.	Low	High	Diff.
1927–2017	−0.6%	−0.1%	**0.5%**	0.5%	1.4%	**0.9%**
Since 1947	−0.2%	0.3%	**0.5%**	0.3%	1.2%	**0.9%**

annual return of around 6% per year going forward. Contrast this with the twenty percent of stocks with the highest return during the previous year. They have delivered returns around 17% over the next year. This is a huge difference. There is momentum in stocks with high past performance.

Given what we have learned so far in this chapter, one would be tempted to hypothesize that the reason why momentum stocks deliver such high returns probably has to do with their exposure to recessions. As Table 13.4 shows, this is not the case.

Table 13.4 reveals that returns to momentum stocks are higher than returns to low-momentum stocks, during expansions and during recessions. I.e. whether the economy has performed well or not, momentum stocks have performed well. Momentum stocks, thus, behave differently from other types of stocks that have generated relatively high returns historically. For this reason, the return to momentum stocks is often described as an anomaly.

Researchers have tried to explain why momentum stocks provide such high returns. The rational explanation is that it is a compensation for some risks. The behavioural explanation is that investors are naïve and make predictions and trades in naïve ways. It seems fair to say that the rational explanations have a hard time explaining momentum returns. Perhaps investors naively project that if a stock has done well in the past, they expect it to continue. They bid up the price of the stock over the short horizon. Only later, when investors learn that the stock will not continue to perform, overperformance disappears. This might sound reasonable. In all fairness, though, the sensible conclusion is that researchers have not found the full explanation why momentum stocks perform so well.

13.5 Checklist

This chapter has demonstrated that some types of stocks, on average over long periods of time, tend to provide higher returns than other types of stocks. The main conclusions to remember are:

- Stocks that trade at a low price relatively to a fundamental indicator of the value of the company provide higher returns on average than stocks that trade at a high price. The variable most frequently used to represent the 'fundamental value' is the book value of equity. Value stocks are high book-to-market stocks. They provide higher average return than growth stocks in the long run.
- Stocks with low book-to-market ratios, i.e. a high market value in relation to book value of equity provide low average returns over long periods of time. These are growth stocks.
- Stocks with low market value, i.e. small-cap stocks, provide high returns on average over long periods of time compared to large-cap stocks.
- Value stocks and small-cap stocks perform worse than growth stocks and large-cap stocks during recessions. Investors do not like assets that perform exceptionally bad when times are already bad. Investors thus require an additional expected return if they should hold value and small-cap stocks. Value and small-cap stocks perform so much better during expansions that it compensates for their relative underperformance during recessions. The overall superior performance of value and growth stocks thus comes at the cost of underperformance during recessions.
- Cyclical stocks are stocks that fluctuate with the business cycle. For instance, the return on stocks issued by firms in the car industry fluctuates with the business cycle. When the economy is doing poorly, consumers cut back on car purchases, hurting performance of these stocks. Consequently, to hold these stocks, investors require an additional return during expansions. So, cyclical stocks provide higher average return over long periods of time than defensive stocks (such as utility stocks), to compensate for the underperformance of cyclical stocks during recessions.
- Momentum stocks are stocks that have seen rapid stock price increases recently. Momentum stocks tend to continue to perform well over the next year or so. Stocks that have recently underperformed continue to underperform over the short horizon. In contrast to value stocks, small-cap stocks, and cyclical stocks, high-momentum stocks do not underperform during recessions. It is remains puzzling what explains the superior performance of momentum stocks.

PART IV

THE PROSPECTS FOR ECONOMIC GROWTH

14
The outlook for long-run economic growth

Chapter 5 studied the relation between long-run economic growth and stock markets. We saw that earnings of firms, and thus the dividends that firms are able pay out, are related to economic activity in the long run. Growth in share prices consequently relates to economic growth, too. Growth in earnings, dividends, and share prices might temporarily deviate from underlying economic growth, but, eventually, growth in earnings, dividends, and share prices relate to growth in economic activity. Furthermore real interest rates relate to real economic growth in the long run.

When stock markets and interest rates relate to economic growth in the long run, we must evaluate the prospects for long-run economic growth if we want to say something about future long-run growth in earnings and share prices. Long-run will in this chapter be several decades, i.e. very long. Obviously, when dealing with multi-decade forecasts, lots of uncertainty prevails. Nevertheless, given their importance, we need estimates of long-run growth, even if they are uncertain.

The chapter will start out discussing the theory of long-run economic growth. After this, the chapter evaluates whether we can expect historical growth to be repeated. We then move on to discuss likely scenarios for long-run growth. Finally, we present the arguments in a heated discussion where one side argues that growth will be tremendously high going forward, but the other argues future growth will be low. We conclude that it does not seem likely that growth will be superhigh going forward. Will it be very low, then? Not necessarily. In many parts of the world, growth will most likely be just fine.

14.1 What causes economic growth?

Economic growth refers to growth in the amount of goods and services produced. Loosely stated, two factors contribute to long-run growth in economic activity:

1. Growth in the number of workers participating in production.
2. Growth in the number of machines available for production and growth in the number of goods and services a given number of workers and machines can produce. Together this is called productivity growth.

From Main Street to Wall Street. Jesper Rangvid, Oxford University Press (2021). © Jesper Rangvid.
DOI: 10.1093/oso/9780198866404.003.0014

At the risk of too much simplicity, imagine one man (or woman) can dig one hole a day. If the number of people participating in production increases, aggregate economic activity goes up. More men dig more holes. If one man gets a tractor (better machine), he can dig more holes. Finally, if one man is able to improve his use of the tractor, he will be able to produce more holes. Improvements in how much a worker can produce per hour (getting more and better machines, and improving the use of machines) are improvements in productivity.

14.1.1 The labour force

We measure the number of people contributing to production by the number of people participating in the labour market. Population growth is not a sufficient condition for growth in the labour force. If the size of the population increases because people live longer and spend more time in retirement, this does not necessarily mean that the number of people participating in production increases. Nevertheless, in the long run, population growth approximates growth in the labour force.

What matters for the economic well-being of individuals is growth in per capita GDP. Increasing the labour force increases total production, but does not necessarily increase GDP per capita. If one man digs one hole, two men will dig two holes, but per capita income has not increased. Increasing capital per se will not necessarily deliver sustainable growth either. It might help giving one man one extra spade (good to have if the first is broken), but giving him four or five spades will not improve production much. There are diminishing returns to scale. We need growth in productivity to get growth in GDP per capita.

14.1.2 Productivity

Productivity is the amount of goods and services each member of the labor force produces within a unit of time (the number of holes a worker can dig per day). Understanding productivity is key to understanding long-run economic growth. There is a limit to how much the labor force can grow, but in principle no limit to productivity growth.

Newer academic literature promotes the idea that idea-generation is key to promoting productivity growth. In 1990, Paul Romer carefully explained how idea-generation can lead to sustainable long-run economic growth. In 2018, he received the Nobel Prize in Economics for his insights. His main argument is that growth is possible if we find better ways to utilize finite resources. And this, he showed, is possible when ideas, in contrast to labor and capital, are nonrival economic goods. What does this mean? A spade is a rivalrous good. If used by one worker, it cannot be used by another worker at the same time. A spade is also a tool with decreasing returns. Productivity increases a lot if one man gets one spade, but does not increase much more if one man gets ten spades. There is constant or decreasing returns to capital and labour.

Ideas, on the other hand, are nonrivalrous. An idea can be used by everybody. Also, the importance of an idea is not diminished if used by many. The idea of using a tractor to dig a hole instead of a spade can be applied by all hole-producers. There is increasing returns to ideas. This fundamental insight—that there is constant or diminishing returns to labour and capital, but increasing returns to ideas—was crucial for understanding what drives sustainable growth.

If new ideas generate productivity, what then generates new ideas? This is a difficult question. It is also one that is important for our judgement of the prospects for long-run future growth. We thus wait a little with this. Let us first see how we can evaluate whether growth actually comes from growth in labour, capital, or productivity.

14.1.3 Growth accounting

Economists calculate the fractions of growth in economic activity due to growth in the number of people participating in production, growth in capital, and growth in 'the rest' (often called 'Total Factor Productivity'). When economic growth has been higher than growth in the number of people and machines, productivity has increased. Total factor productivity has gone up. Economists measure the impact of labour, capital, and productivity on economic growth via 'growth accounting'. Growth accounting is explained in Box 14.1.

Growth-accounting calculations lead to a clear conclusion: productivity growth is what matters for growth in output per worker. As an example, in his survey of the literature, Jones (2016) finds that 80% of growth comes from growth in productivity. Many other studies confirm this finding. Productivity growth is the underlying source of economic growth. This does not mean that growth in labour and capital are unimportant for economic growth, but it means that productivity growth is needed if per capita GDP should increase in the long run.

Box 14.1. Growth accounting

Imagine that total production has increased by 3%. Imagine also that the amount of machines has increased by 1.5% and the number of workers by 0.5%. Imagine finally that 40% of production is due to machines and 60% to workers. Growth accounting would imply that growth in machines and workers on their own account for 40% · 1.5% + 60% · 0.5% = 0.4 · 0.015 + 0.6 · 0.005 = 0.009 = 0.9% growth. Economic growth is 3%, i.e. productivity has in this example increased by 2.1%. Growth in productivity has accounted for 70% (= 2.1%/3.0%) of total economic growth, while growth in factors of production (machines and labour) has accounted for the remaining 30%.

Economists often prefer to express growth accounting in terms of growth in output per worker (labour productivity) instead of growth in total economic activity. The growth-accounting formula now asks how important growth in capital per worker (how many machines does each worker have at his/her disposal) and how important growth in productivity is for growth in output per worker.

14.1.4 Converge, catching up, and the frontier

In addition to the amount of productive inputs (labour, capital, land, etc.) and the rate at which new ideas are developed (leading to productivity growth), another factor is important for determining potential future growth rates: the current level of economic activity. Everything else constant, it is more likely that a less-developed economy will grow faster than a developed economy. This is called 'catching up' or 'convergence'.[1] There are two reasons why it is reasonable to expect less developed countries to grow faster than richer countries, i.e. to 'catch up'. First, less developed countries can adapt ideas already developed in richer countries at lower costs. Second, because less developed countries use less capital, the rate at which returns to capital decreases (when more capital is added to the production process returns to capital decrease) is lower than in richer countries.

Throughout the last couple of decades, many Asian countries have experienced growth rates considerably higher than the growth rates of advanced economies. Think of China, Vietnam, and India. They have embarked on a process of conver-

[1] Economists talk about different kinds of convergence. Sigma-convergence refers to a reduction in the distance between the *levels* of economic activity between countries. Beta-convergence refers to a reduction in the distance between the *growth rates* of economic activity between countries.

gence. Why did they start converging during the 1980s or so, but not earlier? And why have African countries only started converging recently (if they have)? Basically, what starts a process of converging? There is no universal explanation, but some ingredients are necessary. The economy must be in a position to understand and use new ideas, attract capital in order to invest in new ideas, and be open to global markets, such that capital and ideas can be imported and goods and services exported. Institutions, juridical standards, and the level of education need to be in place before growth kicks off.

When growth kicks off, the process can be long and sustained. Benefits can be enormous. Figure 14.1 provides one way of illustrating this. It shows the number of people on planet earth living below the poverty line of USD 1.9 per day. In 1990, more than one in every three persons, i.e. more than 1.8 billion individuals, had to get by on less than USD 1.9 (in 2013 prices) a day. Almost two billion people lived below the poverty line. Fast forward 25 years, and less than 10% of the global population live below the poverty line. The number of people living in poverty has been reduced by around one billion. In light of the fact that the global population has increased by around two billion during the same period, from around 5.5bn in

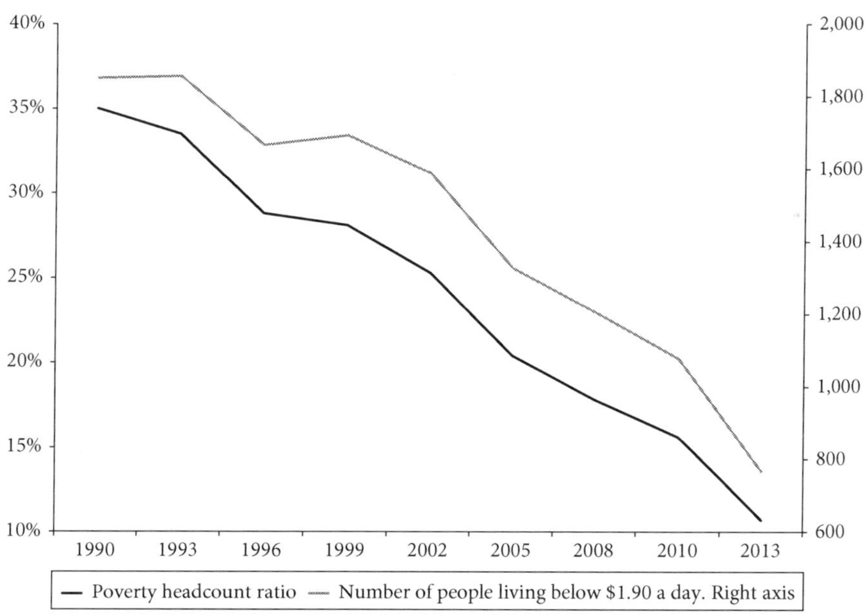

Figure 14.1 The number (in millions) and fraction of the global population (the poverty headcount ratio) living in poverty.

Data source: The World Bank.

1990 to slightly below 7.5bn in 2013, the reduction in poverty becomes even more impressive.

Developments in East Asia and the Pacific, where poverty has been almost eliminated, are primarily responsible. This, in the end, is the result of economic growth. And, this is why economic growth and its underlying determinants are so important to understand. It improves peoples' life.

14.2 2% economic growth forever?

Equipped with insights from theories of long-run economic growth, let us turn to data. A first hypothesis could be that historical growth rates are good guesses of future growth rates.

Chapter 2 noted that the average growth rate of US real per capital GDP from 1870 to today was 2% per year. The same held true for a number of other advanced countries. Figure 14.2 repeats this message but adds a trend line that deterministically increases by 2% every year. Figure 14.2 shows how stable growth seems to have been when measured over very long periods. Even the worst

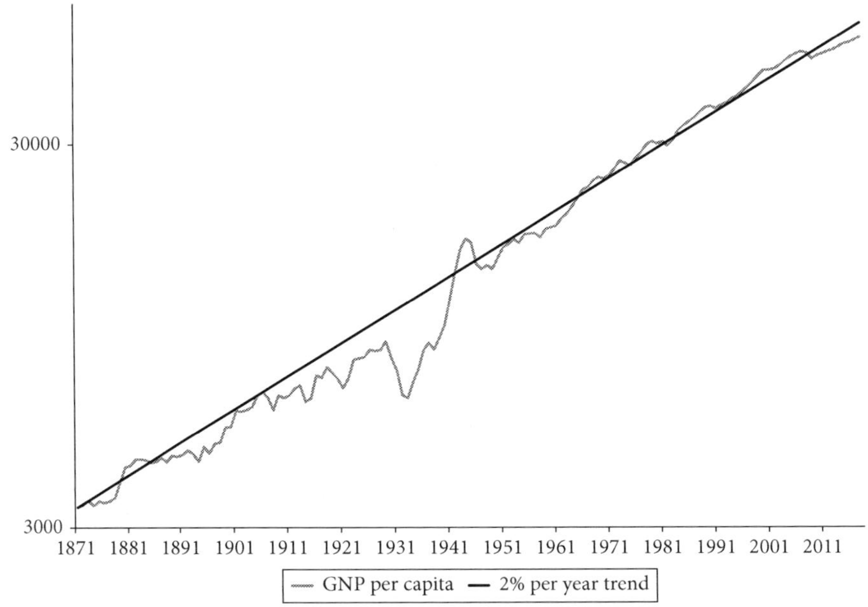

Figure 14.2 Growth in US real per capita GDP together with trend growth of 2% per year. 1871–2018. Logarithmic scale.

Data source: See Figure 2.1.

recession in history, the Great Depression of 1929–1930, seems like a temporary disturbance. The period since the Second World War has been remarkable stable. The Great Recession of 2008–2009 is almost not visible in Figure 14.2. Chapter 8 discussed why there are fewer recessions, and thus more stable growth, since 1945.

Given Figure 14.2, one might be tempted to hypothesize that annual growth in real per capita GDP will be 2% 'forever and always'. And, consequently, that the best forecast of long-run annual growth is 'forever and always' 2%.

Perhaps 2% per year is a reasonable forecast. But how do we know that the last 150 years are representative for the next many decades? In this book, we analyse the last 150 years because this is the period for which we have good data on stocks and bonds. Perhaps, however, the last 150 years were unusual. Figure 14.3 shows GDP per capita for the UK during the last 2,000 years.[2]

Figure 14.3 reveals a fascinating stylized fact: economic growth was basically non-existent prior to the late nineteenth century. In fact, before 1850, average annual growth of real per capita GDP was a miniscule 0.08% per year. This is 25 times smaller than 2% per year. In year AD 1, per capita GDP was 600 USD (in

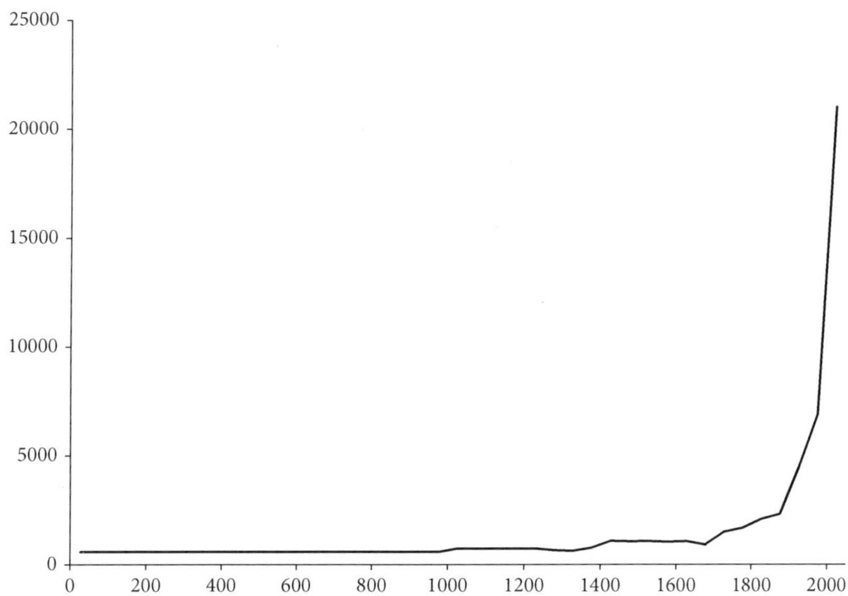

Figure 14.3 Real GDP per capital in the U.K. since year 0. Measured in 1990 prices.
Data source: Maddisson database: www.ggdc.net/maddisson.

[2] Figure 14.3 illustrates developments for the UK, as the UK is the country with the most comprehensive time series available on The Maddison-Project webpage.

1990 prices). In year 1500, it was USD 1086. Over the course of 1,500 years, per capita GDP had not even doubled. In 1850, it was USD 2,330. This means that real GDP per capita had increased from USD 600 to USD 2330, i.e. by a factor of three, during a period spanning 1,850 years. During the next 150 years, it increased by a factor of ten.

So, economic activity has grown by app. 2% per year during the last 150 years or so. Average growth has not always been 2%, though. We cannot simply assume that historical growth will repeat itself.

14.3 What should we expect?

As mentioned, there are two main ingredients when it comes to predicting future long-run economic growth: the number of people working and growth in productivity. Let us take them one by one.

14.3.1 Population forecasts

The Swedish physician and statistician Hans Rosling once coined the numbers 1114 and 1125 the 'zip codes of the world'. In 2010, the populations of the Americas, Europe, and Africa were close to one billion each. The first three numbers of the first zip code. The population in Asia was around four billion, the last number of the first zip code. In 2050, the population of the Americas and Europe will still be around one billion each, whereas the population in Africa will have doubled to approximately two billion, and the population in Asia will have grown to five billion. This is an easy way to remember how the global population will develop in the years to come. Populations in Europe and the Americas will not grow whereas population growth will be high in Africa and modest in Asia.

The zip codes numbers are easy to remember. We want to be more precise, though. A solid source of data with projections of the number of people in different parts of the world is the World Population Prospects published by the United Nations. The world population equaled 7.5 billion in 2017. The U.N. expects that the world will contain around 10 billion people in 2060. This is an increase of around 33%. Or, an annual increase of 0.7%. Even if global productivity remained constant over the next 40 years, population growth implies that aggregate global GDP will increase by 0.7% per year on average over the next 40 years.

Figures 14.4 and 14.5 split the overall population growth rate from 2020 to 2060 into ten-year periods. Figure 14.4 shows how the number of people develops whereas Figure 14.5 shows the average growth rate during different decades. The global population will most likely continue to increase over the coming decades

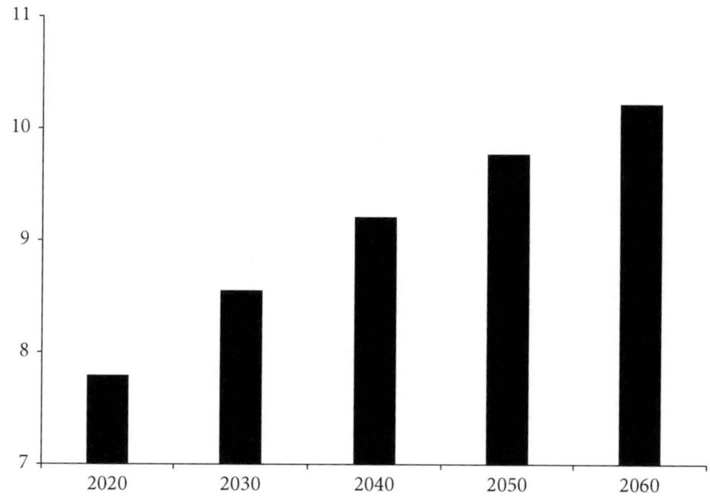

Figure 14.4 Global population in billions.

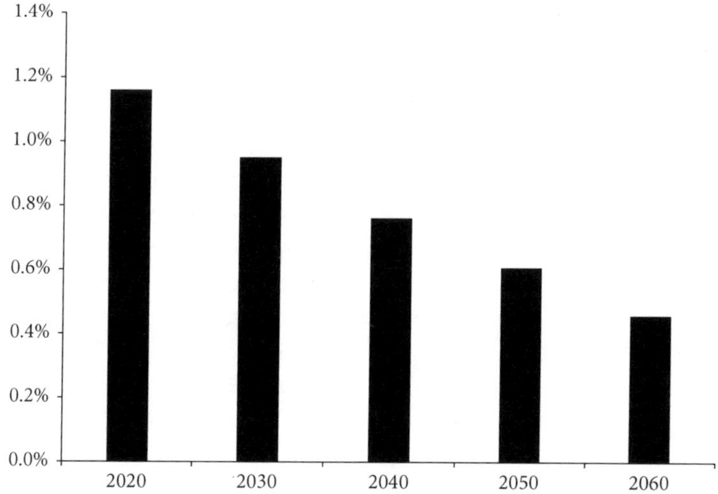

Figure 14.5 Global population growth. Percentage average annual increase during decades.

Data source: World Population Prospects, The United Nations.

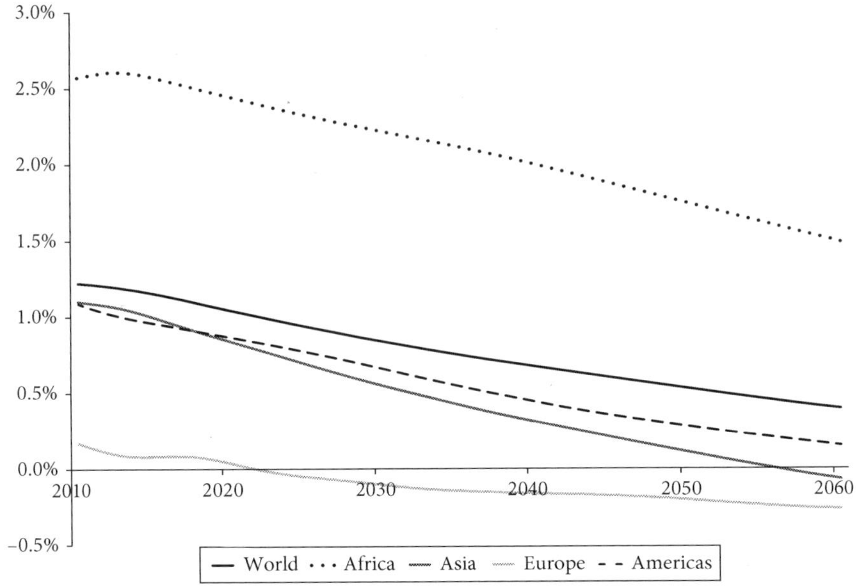

Figure 14.6 Annual growth in world population, and populations in different regions of the world.

Data source: World Population Prospects, The United Nations.

(Figure 14.4), but at a decreasing rate (Figure 14.5). In itself, population grow will continue to cause global growth, but at a decreasing rate.

There are regional differences, as Figure 14.6 shows. Starting in the early 2020s, Europe will see negative population growth rates, i.e. a shrinking population. 740 million inhabitants in 2015 versus less than 700 million in 2060. The average growth rate is a negative 0.1% per year. On the other hand, there will be more Africans. 3bn in 2060 versus 1.2bn in 2015. The average growth rate is 2%.

All regions will face falling population growth rates. It turns negative in Asia when we get close to 2060. Even in Africa, annual population growth will fall from around 2.6% in 2015 to 1.5% in 2060. If a population grows by 2.6% per year, the size of the population will double in 28 years (remember the 'Rule of 72' from Chapter 3). When it grows by 1.5% per year, it takes 47 years.

Life expectancies are also increasing. In many countries, retirement age is not increasing to the same extent. In other words, more people will be in retirement. This means that the number of people participating in production will increase by less than the total population. In Europe, the working population will decline by more than the total population. This exerts, in itself, a dampening effect on economic growth in Europe.

The overall conclusion is that the global population will be increasing for the next 40 years or so. Everything else constant, this spurs aggregate economic growth. The global population will be increasing at a slowing rate, though. And there will be regional differences. Many more people will be living in Africa, but fewer will be living in Europe.

14.3.2 GDP per capita forecasts

Total growth is growth in the number of people times how much each of them produces. In 2012, OECD embarked on a path-breaking journey and started publishing long-term projections for GDP per capita growth rates and growth rates of total GDP (next section). OECD predicts per capital growth until 2060.

OECD expects global economic activity per capita to increase by 2.4% per year on average over the 50-years period from 2010–2060. This is an important number to remember.

As with population forecasts, there will be large regional differences. One important factor here is the catching-up effect mentioned earlier, i.e. the hypothesis that relatively poor countries will grow relatively fast—catch up. It requires less-developed countries to improve their regulatory framework, human capital, and open up. A second factor contributing to higher growth in less developed countries is their relatively larger possibilities for increasing education levels and thereby the quality of human capital in the workforce. For instance, there is a significant potential to increase years of schooling in many less-developed countries.

For these reasons, per capita growth is expected to be higher in non-OECD countries until 2060, as Figure 14.7 shows. At the same time, catching up means that the difference between growth rates of OECD and non-OECD countries will shrink. Figure 14.7 shows that growth rates in Non-OECD countries are expected to fall from around 4% per annum in 2020 to around 2.3% per annum in 2060, whereas growth rates in OECD countries are expected to fall from around 1.7% per annum to around 1.4%. The difference between annual growth rates in Non-OECD and OECD countries thus shrinks from 1.7%-points in year 2020 to only 0.3%-points in year 2060. Growth rates will be more similar around the world.

Figure 14.8 shows average annual growth rates for different countries. OECD expects US per capita real GDP to grow by 1.4% going forward. This is considerably below the historical growth rate of 2%.

Other countries can expect higher growth. Indian real per capita GDP is expected to grow by more than 4% per year, as an example. Something growing by 4% per year over 50 years will cumulatively increase by a factor of seven. On average, each person in India will increase his/her annual output from around 3,000 USD (on a Purchasing Power Parity, PPP, basis) in 2010 to almost 24,000

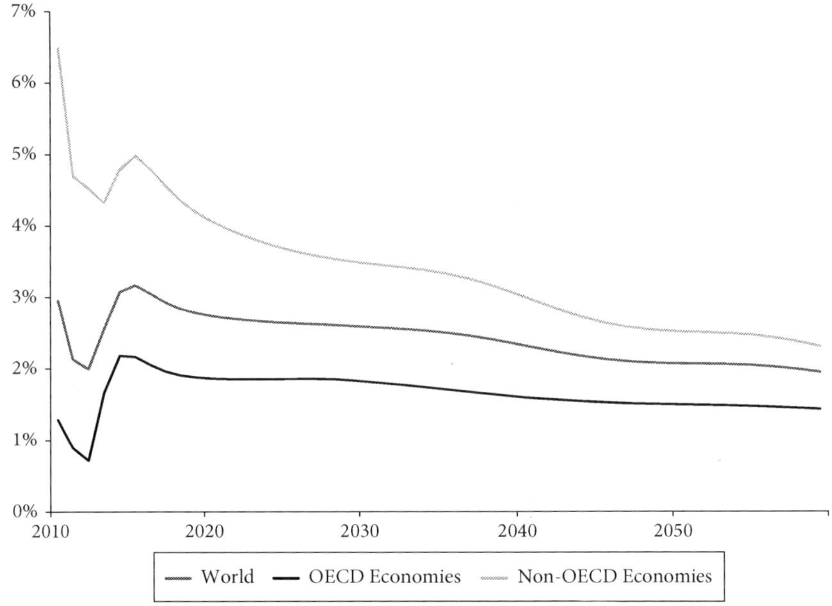

Figure 14.7 Growth in real per capita GDP in different regions.
Data source: OECD.

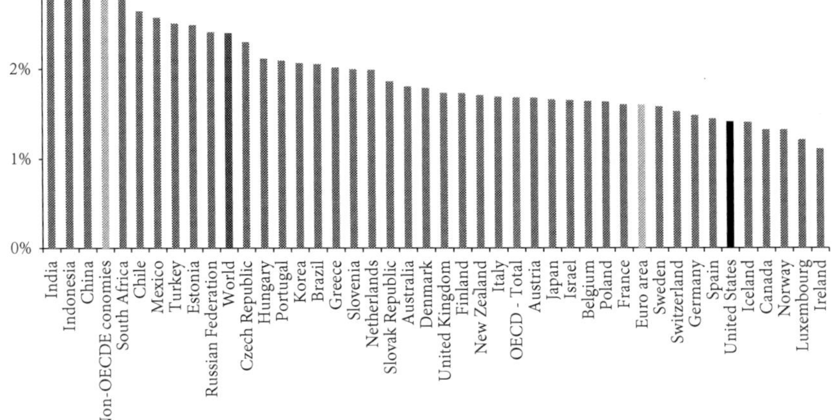

Figure 14.8 Average expected growth rates of real per capita GDP from 2010 through 2060 in different countries.
Data source: OECD.

USD in 2060.[3] Taking into account the fact that the population in India is already at 1.3bn (in 2015) and expected to increase to almost 1.7bn in 2060, this is a massive improvement in living standard for a very large number of people.

Many advanced countries will see GDP per capita increase by less than 1.5% per year. Taking into account that their populations will remain more or less constant, as Section 14.3.1 explained, there will be large changes to the relative sizes of economies going forward. This becomes clear when studying the expected long-term growth path of total GDP.

14.3.3 Aggregate GDP forecasts

Let us jump right to the conclusion. Over the next 40 years, it would be no surprise if global economic output increases by a factor of three. In 2016, the total value of everything produced globally amounts to app. USD 70 trillion (on a real PPP basis). The expectation is that it will be app. 220 trillion in 2060. A massive increase in economic activity. Given the point of this book—understanding and scrutinizing the relation between economic activity and the behaviour of financial assets—it is of first-order importance to recognize that our best forecast is that global economic activity will increase significantly going forward. The average expected growth rate of global real GDP is 2.7% per year.[4]

Due to differences in population growth and growth in GDP per capita between regions and countries, there will be massive differences between growth rates of total GDP across countries and regions. Non-OECD countries are expected to grow considerably faster than OECD countries. Growth is expected to be on a declining path in all regions, however. The reason is that population growth and growth in GDP per capita will both fall, as previous sections concluded. There will be growth, but at a slower pace.

Figure 14.9 shows expected growth rates of aggregate real GDP in selected developed (US, Germany, and Japan) and emerging (Brazil, China, and India) economies. For most of the period, emerging economies will grow faster than developed, but the differences shrink.

China and India are large. Populations exceed 1.3bn in both countries. When non-OECD countries grow faster than OECD countries, economic powers will shift. China will take over as the largest economy in the world. The size of the

[3] Purchasing Power Parity (PPP) basis means that it adjusts for differences in price levels across countries. In this way, the purchasing power of incomes can be better compared across countries.

[4] Notice that this is different from the 2.4% expected growth in global GDP per capita and the 0.7% increase in the global population mentioned earlier. The reason is that 2.4% and 0.7% are unweighted averages, i.e. each country weighting the same when calculating such a global average. When calculating total GDP growth, each country is weighted by its share in the world economy in every single year.

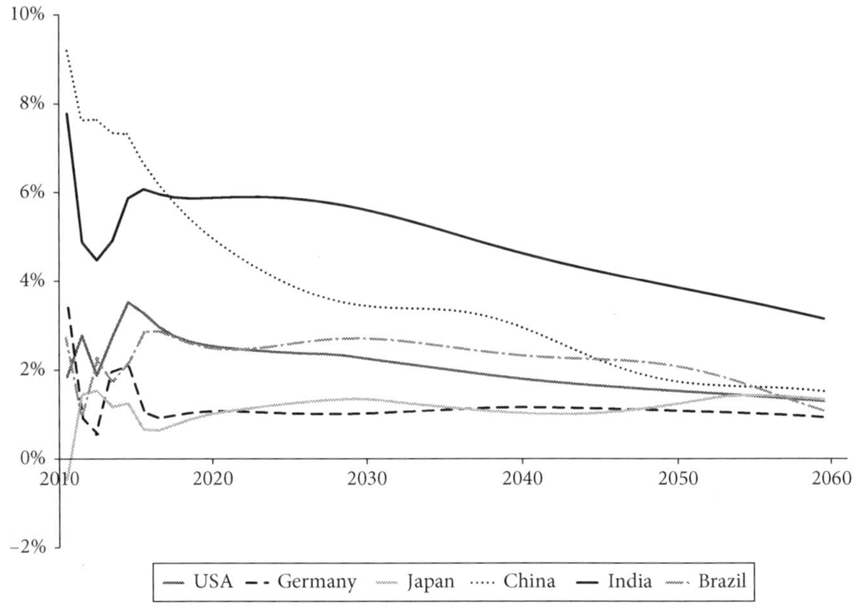

Figure 14.9 Growth in total real GDP in different countries. 2010–2060.
Data source: OECD.

Indian economy is expected to exceed that of the US in 2060. After 2060, the US will only be the third-largest economy in the world. This is a significant change. For instance, as a fraction of the global economy, the Indian economy increases from around 7% today to around 15% in 2060. The fraction of global output produced in the US will continuously fall during the period. China will see its peak around 2045 when a quarter of total output in the world will be Chinese.

These are important changes in world economic powers. Interestingly, perhaps we are just returning to how things were some hundreds years ago. Figure 14.10 shows the fractions of global GDP produced in China going back to 1700 and Figure 14.11 shows the US fraction. Before the industrial revolution in the late 19th century, around a third of global economic output was produced in China. Less than five percent in the US. China was the economic superpower and the US was inhabited by small farmers producing goods for themselves and their families. Then came the industrial revolution. China took no part in this, but the US benefitted tremendously. The next 100 years saw a massive shift in global economic powers. The US economy replaced the Chinese economy in terms of its importance for global economic output. In the 1950s, the US economy accounted for almost 30% of global economic output, and China for less than five percent. Roles had been reversed. Throughout the last couple of decades, we have witnessed

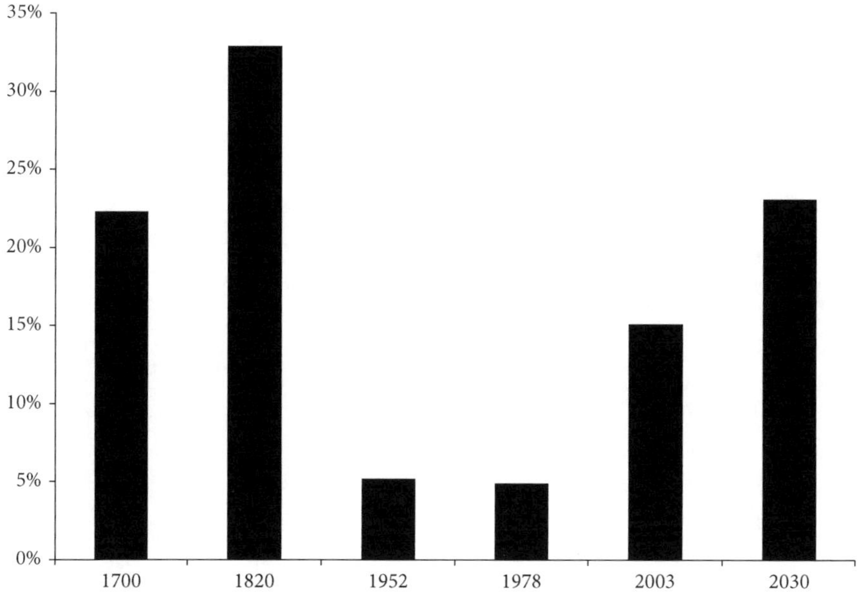

Figure 14.10 Chinese fraction of global GDP.

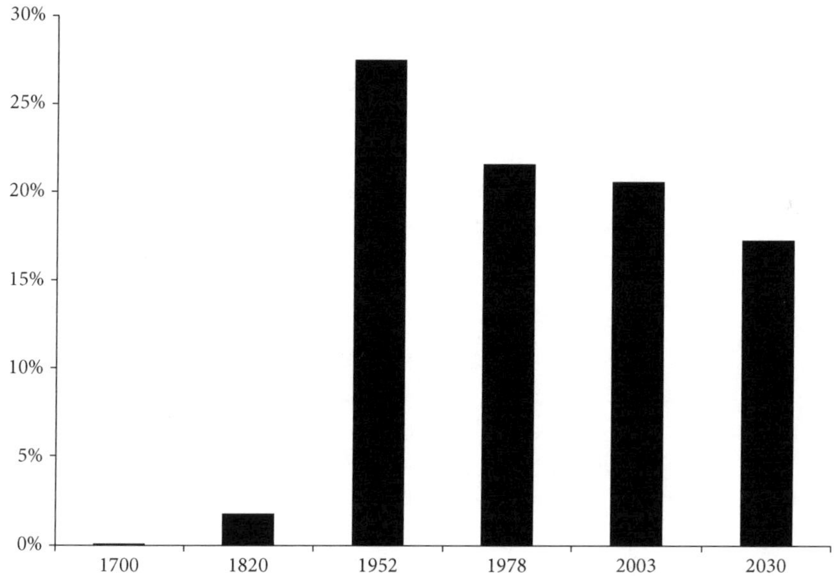

Figure 14.11 US fraction of global GDP.

Data source: Maddisson database: www.ggdc.net/maddisson.

a shift again. The importance of China for global economic activity has increased, and that of the US has declined, similarly to that of Europe and other traditionally advanced economies. Going forward, countries such as China, India, Indonesia, Mexico, and Brazil will continue to increase their share of global economic output. As PWC (2017) puts it: 'Twenty years ago (in 1995), the E7 countries (seven large emerging markets: China, India, Indonesia, Brazil, Russia, Mexico, and Turkey) were half the size of the G7 countries (US, UK, France, Germany, Japan, Canada, and Italy). In 2015, E7 and G7 were roughly of the same size. In 2040, in just 25 years, E7 countries could double the size of the G7 countries.'

14.3.3.1 An important caveat

A well-heeded warning is warranted before concluding this section. Forecasts such as those presented in this section are based on a number of underlying assumptions, in particular that no major disruptions to economic activity take place. Such major disruptions could be wars that destroy significant parts of capital (and humans), global warming getting out of control, major impediments to trade between countries, levels of education not going up, and so on. The forecasts are best guesses, but if major disruptions to our civilizations occur, this will influence the path of economic activity. It is impossible to predict such major disruptions, however. Hopefully, they will not occur. For this reason, they can and should not be incorporated into forecasts such as those presented here. But if the expected path is influenced by major shocks, the future will be different from what is predicted. We should think of these scenarios as likely outcomes if no major disruptions occur, and economies behave as theory, experience, and past and current developments in the data predict. But, probably, something that we cannot foresee today will happen over the next 50 years. We just do not know what it is. Therefore, we stick to our best forecasts, but keep caveats in mind when interpreting forecasts.

14.4 A heated debate

The previous section showed OECD's estimates of long-run economic growth. These estimates are probably the best we have. They present a well-balanced view. Recently, however, the prospects for US long-run future growth have been heavily debated. Two polar views clash. One group of economists, spearheaded by Robert J. Gordon from Northwestern University, thinks that productivity growth will be lower going forward. Another group of economists, led by Erik Brynjolfsson from MIT, believes productivity growth will be very high going forward. The last section of this chapter summarizes the main views.

14.4.1 Lower productivity growth going forward

Robert G. Gordon is one of the leading scholars on economic growth. He is, for instance, a member of the NBER Business Cycle Dating Committee. In 2012, he presented an important research paper that essentially argued that growth in the US will be considerably lower going forward. Subsequently, he has written a number of research papers on the topic, and, in 2016, published a book. Several economists have expressed sympathy with Gordon's overall point that growth will be lower going forward, see for instance Fernald and Jones (2014).

Gordon starts out examining why growth in the US has been so high during the period since 1870. According to Gordon, three major breakthroughs were crucial. The first industrial revolution (1750–1830) led to steam engines, railroads, etc. The second (1870–1900) led to electricity, cars, and other major innovations. It took app. 100 years (1870–1960) to percolate through the economy before its full effects were harvested. The third major breakthrough is the internet revolution that, Gordon argues, started in the 1960s and climaxed in the mid-1990s.

Gordon believes it is unlikely that new major innovations that really push productivity forward will be discovered. Humankind has already made the most obvious innovations, he argues. In addition, he sees four headwinds facing future US productivity and economic growth:[5]

1. Demographics: There will be more people retiring than entering the labour market. The labour force will shrink. Gordon estimates that this reduces growth by 0.3%-points per year compared to what we have been used to during the last 150 years.
2. Education: During the twentieth century, average levels of education increased. Going forward, Gordon believes that it will be impossible to sustain the same rate of educational improvement. He subtracts 0.2%-points from annual growth.
3. Inequality: We noted already in Chapter 2 that inequality has increased dramatically during recent decades in the US. This means that the large majority of people in the US will not benefit from increases in income. He subtracts 0.5%-point growth for the bottom 99% of the income distribution.
4. Debt: Both government and household debt has increased. At some point, debt has to be paid back. Gordon subtracts 0.2%-point growth per year.

[5] The four headwinds are from Gordon (2014). In Gordon (2012), there were two more, globalization and the environment.

In total, from a historical 2% annual growth rate of US GDP per capita, Gordon subtracts 0.3%-point, 0.2%-point, 0.5%-point, and 0.2%-point, respectively, yielding an annual per capita growth rate of 0.8% for the bottom 99% of the income distribution. For the economy as a whole, Gordon adds back the 0.5% growth that inequality subtracts. Growth in productivity will be 0.8% plus 0.5%, i.e. 1.3%. 1.3% growth in GDP per capita is only two thirds of the historical 2% annual growth. And 99% of the population will only see incomes increase by 0.8%. Growth, in Gordon's opinion, will be low going forward.

Fernald and Jones (2014) argue, like Gordon, that improvements in educational achievement were strong from 1870 through 1950, but have levelled off since. They, too, expect that improvements will be modest going forward. They also note the changes in demographics that Gordon notices. Similarly, resources devoted to research have been increasing, but there is a limit to this as well, putting a damper on the extent to which new ideas are generated. So, while Fernald and Jones might not be as pessimistic as Gordon, they share several of his concerns.

14.4.2 Higher productivity growth going forward

Erik Brynjolfsson from MIT sees things very differently. Brynjolfsson believes that economic growth will be very high, and much higher than we have been used to, going forward. His book from 2011, written together with Andrew McAfee, presents the main arguments. Brynjolfsson and McAfee expect IT to change the way production happens. They predict an enormous increase in computer power that will cause a massive technological change. Think machine learning, artificial intelligence, etc. Think also about robots replacing humans in production, improvements in medicine, driverless cars, big data, etc. These innovations will increase productivity for the economy as a whole. Brynjolfsson and McAfee believe the economy is at an inflection point, i.e. a point where there will be a dramatic shift in the way production takes place. From here, they expect growth to increase exponentially, i.e. growth rates will increase at an ever-faster rate. The reason is automatization of many productive activities. Driverless cars will make chauffeurs redundant. Artificial intelligence and speech recognition will make some service workers redundant. These automatic production processes produce goods and services much faster than humans, without making the mistakes human make. Inequality will also increase, as many people will see their jobs disappear. Brynjolfsson and McAfee believe it will be difficult for these people to rejoin the labour force as they do not have the skills needed in this new world. Groups of the population will be left behind, but, overall, the economy will benefit from dramatic productivity improvements, Brynjolfsson and McAfee argue.

14.4.3 What should we conclude? Will productivity growth at the frontier (e.g., in the US) be high or low going forward?

Consider Brynjolfsson arguments first. Will innovations in IT occur at such a pace that economic growth will increase exponentially? In 2015, Yale professor Nordhaus surveyed the arguments for and against this idea of 'singularity', i.e. the idea that 'rapid growth in computation and artificial intelligence will cross some boundary or Singularity, after which economic growth will accelerate sharply as an ever-increasing pace of improvements cascade through the economy' (Nordhaus, 2015, page 2). Together with Paul Romer, Nordhaus shared the 2018 Nobel Prize in Economics for his contributions to theories of long-run growth, i.e. Nordhaus is an authority on the theories of long-run growth.

The main argument in the singularity hypothesis is that computer power has and will grow tremendously. From 2007 to 2015, computer power has grown by 82% per year. Singularity proponents argue that, one day, computers will be able to do computations faster than the human brain. Artificial intelligence will take over, reaching singularity.

Nordhaus presents several empirical facts indicating that singularity is not near. For instance, when productivity of the IT sector increases so fast, the price of IT goods and services should decline fast relative to the prices of other goods and services. This should cause an increase in the consumption of IT products and services. Nordhaus finds no such tendency in the US data. There are other indications that singularity is far away. Overall productivity improvements do not occur at the rate one would expect if productivity of one sector increases very fast. In the singularity world, productivity of capital increases very fast. This should cause the price of capital to decline, and the capital to income ratio to increase. This has not happened. What about IT capital itself? Again, the evidence falls to the negative side. If anything, there is some evidence that capital constitutes a rising share of labour income, but it is weak. Nordhaus draws the conclusion, which seems like a reasonable one, that 'growth Singularity is not near'.

What about Gordon's argumentation? Gordon thinks the US faces low growth going forward. This is bad news—if it holds true—for the US. Gordon makes sensible points. OECD also expects per capita GDP in the US to increase by 1.4% per year, as Figure 14.8 showed.

This negative projection does not necessarily apply to other countries, however. Many countries face fewer headwinds than the US. For instance, levels of education will improve in many emerging and developing countries, keeping up economic growth. The demographic headwinds are also less of a challenge in many countries. Furthermore, even when inequality is increasing in many countries, the extent to which this is happening in the US is exceptional. Furthermore, remember that ideas cause growth. Research can help foster ideas. Countries like China and other big emerging countries invest heavily in research. US benefits from ideas generated in these countries. According to Freeman (2009), as of 2010, China produces more Ph.D.s in science and engineering than the United States does. Twenty years earlier, China produced almost none. New ideas generated outside the US might help the US grow. At the moment, the balance of evidence points towards lower growth going forward in the US and other advanced economies, but there are many other countries, where growth will be fine, even if at a declining rate, as mentioned.

14.5 Summing it up

The Western world has grown tremendously during the last 150 years or so, i.e. since the industrial revolution. This was due to increases in populations, but, even more important, to increases in productivity, and thus GDP per capita.

Going forward, we will most likely see changes to the picture we have become used to. Populations will stay flat in the Western world, and even fall in some parts (Europe and Japan). In many parts of the emerging and developing world, populations will increase. Emerging economies also have the potential to catch up and improve education and regulatory environments, thereby continuing (for some countries) or initiating (for other countries) a period of high economic growth.

Aggregate global output will continue to expand. Perhaps by a factor of two to three over the next 40 years. This is an important projection to keep in mind. At the same time, keep also in mind that growth rates are projected to fall over time for all regions in the world, due to lower population and productivity growth. There will be lots of growth, but the rate at which economies grow will shrink.

Growth will be different across regions. Countries that grew strongly during the last 150 years, such as the US, Europe, and later Japan, will see growth below 2% per year over the next many years. Many emerging market countries will see growth above 3% per year. Large emerging countries will be the dominant forces in the global economy in the future.

14.6 Checklist

This chapter has demonstrated that:

- In a very long-run perspective, economic growth is a recent phenomenon. Up until the nineteenth century, economic activity almost did not expand. The last 150 years have been remarkable.

- During the last 150 years or so, average growth in real per capita GDP in the US and many other currently advanced economies has been around 2% per year.
- It is useful to break total economic growth into growth in the size of populations and how much each individual produces. The chapter has dealt with projections until 2060.
- Our best estimate is that the global population will increase going forward. From around 7.5bn today to around 10bn in 2060. This corresponds to an unweighted average (across countries and years) annual growth rate of 0.7%.
- Populations will not grow in the Western world (the US, Australia, Europe, and Japan), and might even fall in some regions. Population growth will happen in the rest of the world. Particularly in Africa, but also in some Asian countries, such as India and Indonesia.
- Our best estimate is that global real GDP per capita will increase going forward, by around 2.5% per year. Western economies will see lower growth rates in per capita GDP, however, typically around 1.5% per year on average. Emerging and developing economies will see faster growth.
- When both population and GDP per capita grow, total GDP will obviously also grow. A good guess is that global aggregate output will be around two to three times larger in 2060 than it is today. The average annual growth rate of aggregate global GDP is close to three percent.
- Growth will be higher in emerging and developing economies than in advanced economies. Across economies, growth rates are expected to fall over time, however, due to lower population growth and lower growth in per capita GDP.
- Emerging economies will become increasingly important for global economic activity. China's fraction of global output, for example, is expected to increase to around 30%. Fifty years ago, it was below 5%. Total output of large emerging economies will be considerable larger than total output of large advanced economies. Economic powers will shift from advanced economies to emerging economies.
- There is heated debate whether the US, the still largest economy in the world, will see significantly lower growth rates going forward or whether growth rates will increase exponentially, reaching a point of singularity. Singularity refers to a point where economic growth basically explodes, leading to unimaginable changes to civilization.
- Singularity arises from massive improvements in computerpower that facilitate artificial intelligence, super intelligence, etc. This should lead to an explosion of new ideas and productivity improvements. It sounds fascinating. The question is whether it is detectable in the data. Most economists cannot detect it. Singularity seems far away.

15

Judging the stance of the business cycle

The business cycle refers to fluctuations in economic activity around the long-term growth trend. Chapter 8 described the business cycle, i.e. the recurrent alternations between expansions and contractions. Chapter 8 also discussed stylized facts about business cycles. Expansions are usually longer than contractions. In the post-1945 US economy, contractions have on average lasted 15 months while expansions have lasted 60 months. Contractions (recessions) have occurred with lower frequency since 1945. Recessions are characterized by large drops in economic activity. Typically, industrial output falls by 8% (annualized) during recessions while real GDP contracts by 2% annualized. On the other hand, GDP expands by 4% per year on average during expansions. These business-cycles patterns describe both the US and other countries.

This chapter starts out discussing if and how we can detect business-cycle turning points. What variables should we study if we want to say something about the likelihood that the business cycle will change? Economists talk about business-cycle 'indicators'. We distinguish between lagging, coincident, and leading indicators. Lagging indicators refer to economic variables that react to a change in the business cycle, i.e. variables that react after a business-cycle turning point. Coincident indicators tell us something about where we are right now in the business cycle. Leading indicators, which are probably the most important ones, tell us about the near-term outlook for the business cycle, i.e. forecast the business cycle.

It is important to sound a warning before taking off: business-cycle turning points are hard to predict. Life would be so much easier if they were easy to forecast. Alas, they are not. Often, some indicators point to a change in the business cycle, whereas other do not. At other instances, some indicators point to a mild recession whereas others indicate a severe recession. There is uncertainty.

It is not an option for investors to neglect the business cycle, however. It has first-order impact on your returns, as Chapter 9 demonstrated. So, we need indicators. Just remember that there is uncertainty out there.

From Main Street to Wall Street. Jesper Rangvid, Oxford University Press (2021). © Jesper Rangvid.
DOI: 10.1093/oso/9780198866404.003.0015

15.1 Indicators and the business cycle

We call variables that tell us something about the current and future stance of the business cycle 'indicators'. They do not tell the exact truth, but they indicate it. We are primarily interested in knowing:

- What is the current stance of the business cycle? Are we right now in a recession or expansion? At the outset, it might seem like a trivial question, but it is not. For instance, as mentioned in Chapter 8, it is only several months after the fact that the NBER Business Cycle Dating Committee decides that a recession has begun. The reason is that there is uncertainty about the current stance of the business cycle. Different indicators might point to different conclusions. Which of the indicators are reliable and which ones are noisy?
- What is the likely path of the future business cycle? When we have identified the current stance of the business cycle, e.g., we have concluded that the economy expands, we would like to know how long the expansion lasts. When does the next recession arrive? The identification of the future path of the business cycle is even more important to investors than knowing where we are right now. The reason is that asset prices are forward looking, i.e. react to expected changes in future economic conditions. If we believe a recession is approaching, we should start thinking about lowering our exposure to risky assets.

To help us determine the current and future stance of the business cycle, economists distinguish between different types of indicators.

15.1.1 Lagging, coincident, and leading indicators

It was as long ago as in 1938 that business-cycle pioneers Arthur Burns and Wesley Michell proposed to distinguish between lagging, coincident, and leading indicators. Their idea was that some variables might be more informative about the current stance of the business cycle whereas others might contain more information about its future stance. By focusing on those variables that contain relatively more information about different phases of the business cycle, one reduces noise in the signals.

Coincident indicators are variables that define the business cycle. Where is the economy right now? Are we in a recession or an expansion? These are variables measuring aggregate economic activity itself, such as production, income, employment, sales, etc.

Leading indicators are variables that signal an upcoming change in the business cycle. These typically include expectations of consumers and firms, asset prices (interest rates, or interest rate spreads, stocks prices, etc.), new orders, etc. Leading indicators get the lion's share of attention and are the most important ones for investors.

Lagging indicators change direction after the business cycle has changed, e.g., after a recession has started. For instance, unemployment, and particularly the duration of unemployment, tends to increase after the start of a recession. Cost and amount of borrowing, and certain consumer prices, also tend to change after a change in the business cycle. These indicators are useful for confirming where the economy is positioned in the business cycle, late or early, and for policy responses to the business cycle. They are, however, probably relatively less important for investors.

15.1.2 Individual and composite indicators

The economy is composed of a multitude of economic agents (firms, households, consumers, financial markets, public authorities, etc.) making a multitude of economic decisions (buying, selling, producing, investing, saving, etc.). There are many individual economic variables out there. In order to reduce noise in signals from individual time series, they are sometimes aggregated into composite indicators. Composite indicators reveal turning points common to a number of underlying individual series.

15.1.3 Recession indicators/probabilities

Recessions are harmful to the economic well-being of a large number of agents in the economy. Recessions are also bad for investors. So, we are interested in knowing when the next recession is about to arrive. Economists have developed models that assess/estimate the probability of a recession arriving soon. The models are often based on the same variables that enter the composite index of leading indicators, but represent another useful way of summarizing information.

15.2 Composite indicators. Evidence from the US

Many composite indicators are available. Large banks, public authorities, and private firms publish their own composite indicator of the business cycle. It is not possible, nor necessary, to cover all of them. Instead, we highlight the most important ones.

15.2.1 Lagging, coincident, and leading composite indicators

One of the most important business-cycle indicators is the one maintained by the Conference Board.[1] The Bureau of Economic Analysis (BEA) initially constructed it. In 1995, the BEA chose The Conference Board to maintain and update its leading indicator for the US. It is in some sense the 'official' composite leading indicator for the US economy. The index is displayed in Figure 15.1.

The composite leading indicator is increasing over time. This is natural as the index consists of variables such as new orders, stock prices, and other variables that are growing over time.[2] The main thing to notice, though, is that the index

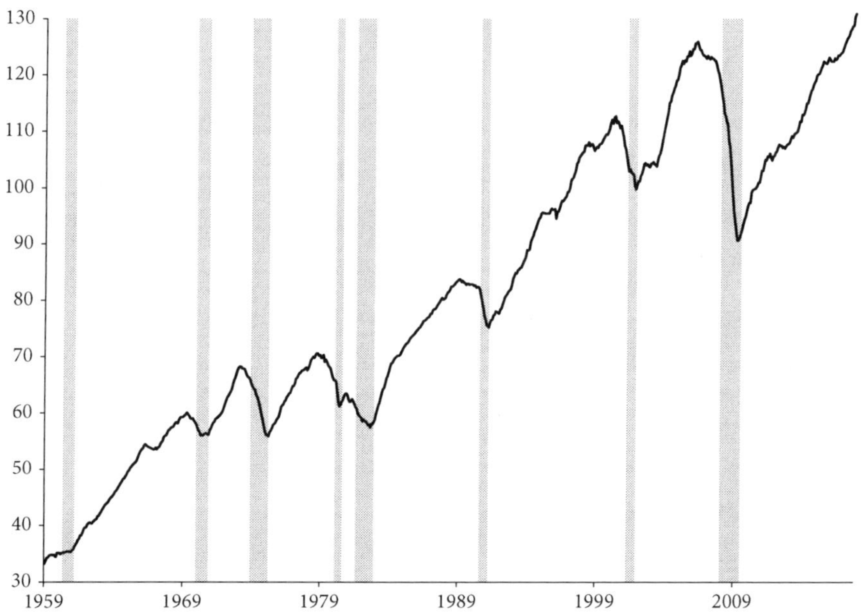

Figure 15.1 Composite leading indicator for the US economy. NBER-defined recessions indicated by shading.
Data source: Datastream.

[1] The Conference Board is a membership-based think tank. Members are corporations and organizations.

[2] The choice of underlying variables in the index changes from time to time. At the time of writing, the index includes ten variables: average weekly hours (manufacturing), average weekly initial claims for unemployment insurance, manufacturers' new orders (consumer goods; materials), ISM® Index of

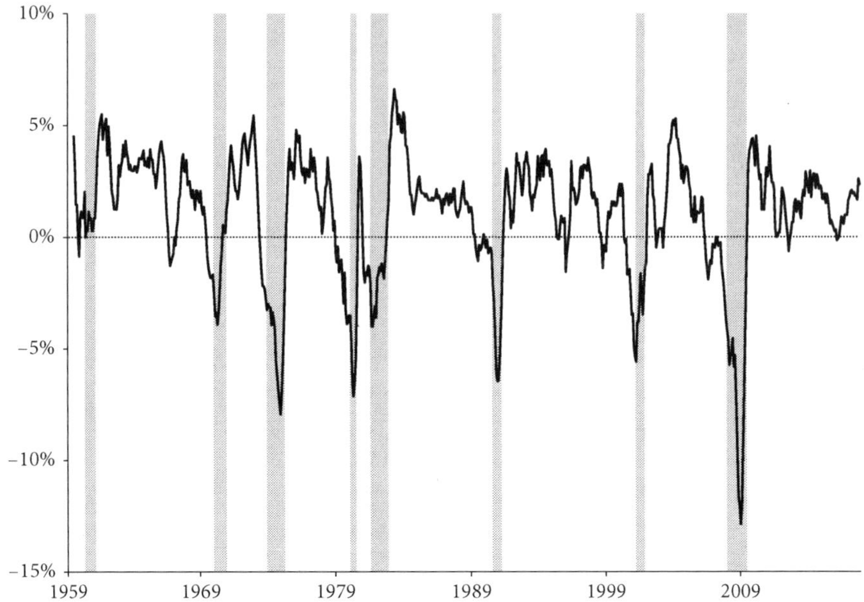

Figure 15.2 Six-month percentage difference in the Composite Leading Indicator for the US economy. NBER-defined recessions indicated by shading.
Data source: Datastream.

generally tends to peak before a recession starts. This means that a change of direction in the index tends to indicate that a recession is under way. Figure 15.2 shows percentage changes in the index over subsequent six-month periods. Often, when a recession starts, the index has been falling for the past six months. When the index has fallen by a couple of percentage points over the past six months, there is a fair chance that a recession is about to arrive.

The leading indicator predicts recessions. The coincident indicator, on the other hand, overlaps with recessions whereas the lagging indicator changes direction during a recession. Figure 15.3 shows the three indicators for the years surrounding the 2007–2009 recession.

For the 2007–2009 recession, the indicators behaved as expected. The leading indicator changed direction in 2006. In late 2007, it was down by two to three percent over a six-month period, indicating a worsening of economic conditions. It predicted the arrival of the recession. Similarly, the leading indicator changed

New Orders, manufacturers' new orders (nondefense capital goods excluding aircraft orders), building permits (new private housing units), stock prices (500 common stocks), Leading Credit Index™, interest rate spread (10-year Treasury bonds less federal funds), and average consumer expectations for business conditions.

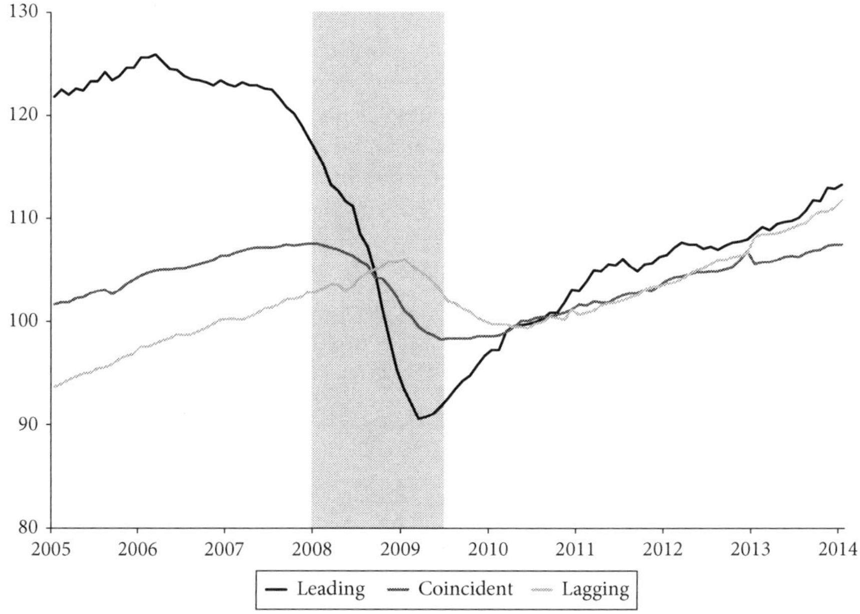

Figure 15.3 Composite leading, coincident, and lagging indicator of the US economy. The 2007–2009 recession. NBER-defined recession indicated by shading.
Data source: Datastream.

direction prior to the end of the recession. It thus gave early indications when the recession was about to end. The turning points in the coincident indicator overlap exactly with the recession. Its growth rate turned negative when the recession started and positive when it ended in 2009. Finally, the lagging indicator changed direction only late in the recession, as it is supposed to do. All indicators fulfilled their tasks.

15.3 Selected individual leading indicators

There are many variables out there. In fact, so many that one can easily loose track of the big picture. That is why we have composite indicators, based on the studies of smart people who have searched for variables one can rely upon and combine in efficient ways. Nevertheless, it is sometimes useful to study a few selected individual variables. The advantage of studying individual variables is that they have not been subject to statistical procedures that combine them into composite indices. Some of the individual variables economists pay most attention to are mentioned in this section.

15.3.1 The yield curve

The yield curve, or the term spread, is the difference between yields on a long-term and a short-term government bond. When used for recession forecasts, typically, the yield on the three-month Treasury bill is subtracted from the yield on the ten-year Treasury bond. Many economists view the yield curve as the variable that contains the most reliable information about the arrival of the next recession, see for instance Fed (2019). Let us first see the term spread in action and then let us discuss it.

Figure 15.4 shows the term spread. From the figure, it is clear why economists place emphasis on the term spread when judging the likelihood that a recession will arrive: The term spread has a tendency to fall when a recession is approaching.[3]

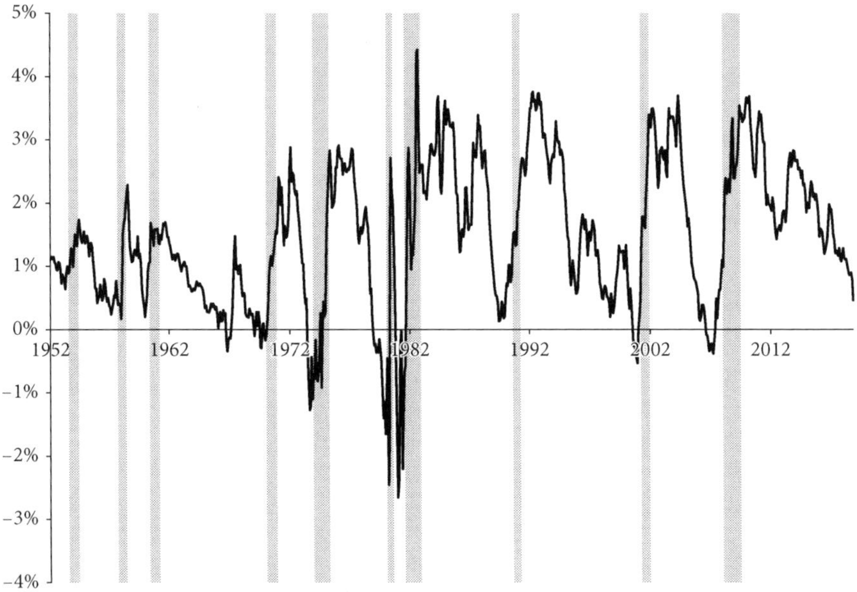

Figure 15.4 The term spread: The difference between the yields on the ten-year government bond and the three-month Treasury Bill. NBER-defined recessions indicated by shading.

Data source: FRED.

[3] Before 1952, the interest rate of the Fed was pegged, implying that interest rates were unrelated to underlying economic activity or inflation pressure. The 1951 Treasury Accord restored the independence of the Fed, and the Fed could start using the interest rate in its conduct of monetary policy. This is why Figure 15.4 starts in 1952.

Most of the time, during most parts of expansions, the yield curve is upward sloping: long rates are usually higher short rates, and the term spread consequently positive. There are two reasons. First, long rates contain a maturity risk premium. The risk premium compensates investors for bearing the higher risk inherent in long-maturity bonds (compared to short-maturity bonds), as described in Chapter 11. Second, during expansions, the expectation is that future monetary policy rates will rise because inflation tends to rise in late phases of expansions. When long rates summarize expectations for future short rates, as also shown in Chapter 11, expected increases in future short rates will increase the long rate today.

When the recession approaches, the yield curve flattens. This means that either the long interest rate goes down, the short rate goes up, or a combination of the two. When the term spread is negative, short-term yields have risen above long-term yields. Looking carefully at Figure 15.4, the yield spread reaches its trough right before a recession, i.e. a flattening of the yield curve indicates that a recession is approaching.

Why does the term spread fall prior to a recession? When the economy is doing well, the Fed hikes the short interest rate to cool down the economy and dampen future inflation. The faster the economy sprints ahead, i.e. the more mature the expansion is, the more rates will be hiked by the Fed. Hikes in the short interest rate drag down the term spread. What about the long rate? When the economy is doing well, expected inflation increases, pushing up the long interest rate, but it also leads the Fed to increase the short rate to dampen inflation expectation, as just mentioned. This restrains the rise in long rates. The long rate rises but by less than the short, as Chapter 11 showed. Eventually, the yield spread turns negative, as the Fed at late stages of expansions increases short rates aggressively and long rates do not follow.

The flattening of the yield curve also has direct implications for economic growth. If long rates fall relative to short rates, it becomes less attractive for banks to make maturity transformation (converting short-term liabilities to long-term assets). This might reduce credit extension by banks, restraining future economic growth. Also for this reason, a flattening of the yield curve forecasts recessions. Conversely, a steeper yield curve provides banks with higher incentives to provide credit, boosting economic activity.

Figure 15.4 also reveals that just prior to the recession, one or two months before, the yield spread starts increasing again. The reason is that, at this point in time, the Fed judges that the recession is just about to arrive. The Fed thus reduces the policy rate dramatically to restrain the severity of the recession. This increases the term spread, as long rates do not move as much as short rates.

The Fed goes further in interpreting the yield spread as a forecaster of recessions. It calculates a recession probability based the term spread. The NY Fed estimates the probability of a recession occurring twelve months ahead (Estrella & Trubin,

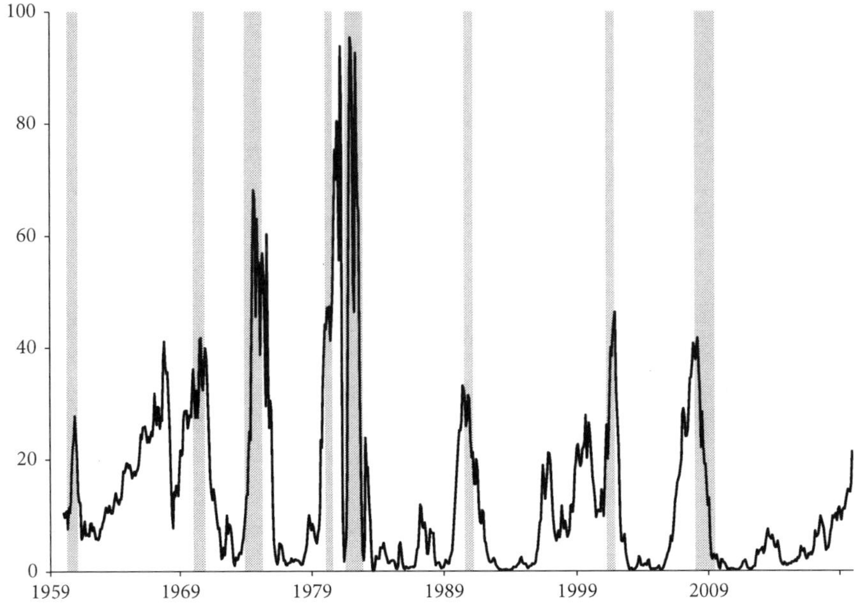

Figure 15.5 Recession probabilities implied by the term spread, as calculated by the New York Fed. NBER-defined recessions indicated by shading.
Data source: New York Fed.

2006). Observing a term spread in, e.g., July in a given year, the model calculates the probability that the economy will be in recession in July the following year. Figure 15.5 shows these recession probabilities.[4] It works well. It indicates increasing probabilities of recessions before they in fact arrive. This is no surprise given what we have just discussed. Why translate the term spread into probabilities, then? Simply because it is easier to communicate probabilities. It is easier to understand that the probability of a recession in 12 months is, e.g., 30% than understanding the implication of a flattening yield curve.

15.3.2 Purchasing Managers' Index (PMI)

A recession is a period in time when economic conditions are bad. Firms observe when consumers stop buying their goods and suppliers start struggling. What

[4] The way to interpret the graph is as follows. Consider the last data point in the graph. Based on the yield spread in December 2018, the model predicts that there is a 21% probability that the US economy is in recession in December 2019.

about asking firms how they view the economy? This is what the Institute for Supply Management (a non-profit organization) started doing in 1948, and has done every month since then. The ISM asks purchasing managers in several hundred manufacturing firms whether they see an improvement, no change, or deterioration of a number of metrics, such as the number of new orders, employment levels, delivery times by suppliers, etc. The index is constructed such that it is centered around 50, implying that a reading of the index of more than 50 indicates that more than half of respondents find that economic conditions are better during the current period compared to the previous. When the number is above 50, the manufacturing sector expands. The resulting index is the Purchasing Managers' Index (PMI).[5] It is shown in Figure 15.6.

The PMI drops significantly during recessions. There is also a tendency for it to start falling before recessions kick in. The PMI, however, is not as strong a recession indicator as the term spread. It is more noisy. We are talking small differences here, i.e. the term spread and the PMI are correlated, but it seems from

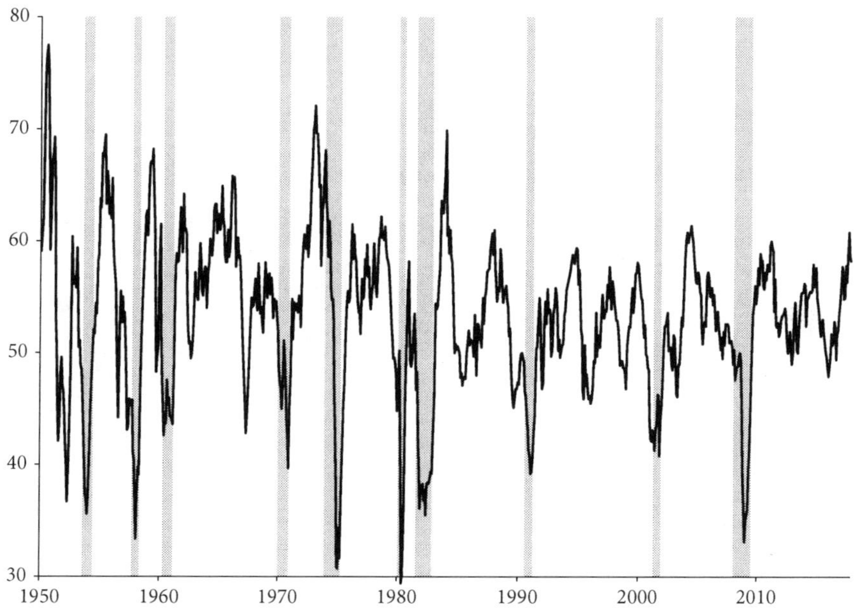

Figure 15.6 Purchasing Managers' Index (PMI).
Data source: Datastream.

[5] Some refer to the index as the ISM index, as the Institute for Supply Management compiles it.

the graphs that the term spread historically has been a more reliable recession indicator. This has also been documented in research, see also Fed (2019).

15.3.3 Consumer Sentiment indexes

The PMI is based on asking purchasing managers what has actually happened: have they received more or less new orders? We could also ask firms (and consumers) how they feel about the economy. Do they view the economy as strong or weak? This is what Professor George Katona of the University of Michigan started working on in 1946. Since 1978, new figures for the consumer sentiment index have been published on a monthly basis by the Survey Research Center at the University of Michigan. Each month at least 500 consumers report their views on current and future economic conditions. The overall index is shown in Figure 15.7.

Consumers clearly become more pessimistic during recessions. Consumer Sentiments thus tracks the business cycle. Consumer sentiments are volatile, though, i.e., sentiments reach their troughs during recessions, but signal recessions

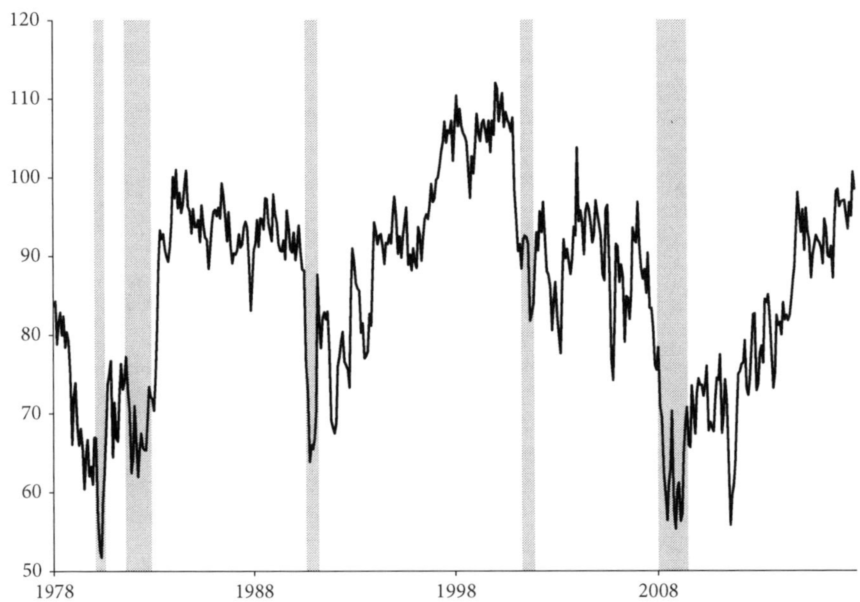

Figure 15.7 Consumer sentiment index from the University of Michigan. NBER-defined recessions indicated by shading.
Data source: FRED.

more often than they occur. For this reason, sometimes consumer sentiments are smoothed, for instance by reporting the six-month average monthly change. It is still rather volatile, though.

15.3.4 Professional and non-professional forecasters

PMIs and consumer confidence measures ask firms and consumers how they view different aspects of economic activity. But, with all respect, perhaps consumers and firms are not the best forecasters out there. So, what about asking professional forecasters, i.e. professionals paid to watch and interpret the daily flow of economic data? The Federal Reserve Bank of Philadelphia maintains a Survey of Professional Forecasters, going back to 1968. A number of professional forecasters submit each quarter their forecasts for several economic variables over the next year. The Philadelphia Fed combines the forecasts in different ways (mean, median, range, etc.) and publishes the results once a quarter.

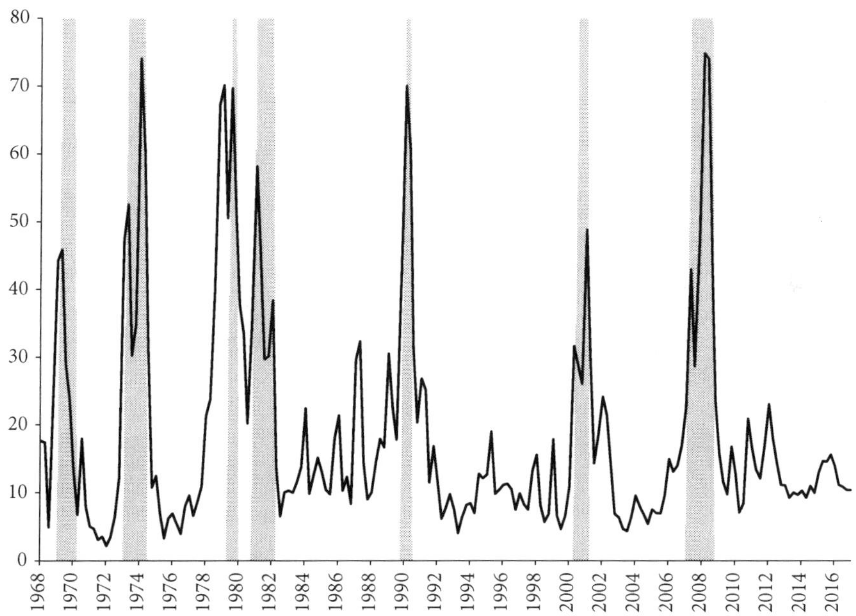

Figure 15.8 Probability of next-quarter GDP growth being negative. From the Survey of Professional Forecasters. NBER-defined recessions indicated by shading.
Data source: Philadelphia Fed.

There are forecasts for nominal and real GDP, inflation, employment, industrial production, different interest rates, housing starts, etc. There is no explicit forecast for a recession occurring, but there are forecasts of the probability of negative growth in real GDP. Figure 15.8 shows the time series of professional forecasters' assessment that GDP growth will be negative the following quarter. Professional forecasters do a pretty good job. Leading up to a number of recessions, the mean probability of negative GDP growth next quarter is increasing. The more the economy approaches a recession, the more professional forecasters view it as likely that growth will be negative. In other words, professional forecasters have some success in predicting the arrival of a recession.

15.3.5 Indices of higher frequency

With the exception of the term spread that can be calculated at high frequency, all of the indicators mentioned above are collected once a month or once a quarter, and often published several weeks after the end of a month or quarter. This is not strange as macroeconomic variables are generally available at a monthly (or quarterly) frequency, and available with some lag only. Are there ways investors can track the outlook for the economy at a higher frequency?

Some economic variables are published weekly (e.g., initial jobless claims), many are published monthly (industrial production, employment, etc.) and those tracking the whole economy (GDP and its subcomponents) quarterly. They are published on different days. During the last decade or so, economists have worked on combining different variables published at different intervals on different days into so-called real-time indicators of economic activity. Many of these are updated daily.

The Atlanta Fed publishes a Nowcast for GDP growth, i.e. an estimate (based on a number of underlying variables released at different frequencies that are turned into a single best estimate of GDP growth in the current quarter). These NowCasts give real-time assessments of the eventual GDP growth rate in a given quarter. Every day it provides an estimate of GDP growth during the current quarter. This helps assess the current stage of the business cycle. The Atlanta Fed GDPNow cast (in its current version) has been available since 2014. It is shown in Figure 15.9. It seems fair to argue that the index is rather volatile. Within a quarter, the best estimate for GDP growth during the current quarter can easily jump by a full percentage point, or even more. One might pay attention to these high frequency indicators of economic activity, but one must also take care not to pay too much attention, as they are very noisy.

Figure 15.9 The GDPNow cast from The Federal Reserve Bank of Atlanta.
Data source: Atlanta Fed.

15.4 Evidence from other countries

15.4.1 Leading indicators

OECD computes Composite Leading Indicators (CLI) for all OECD countries as well as aggregate CLIs for economic regions or groups of countries (Europe, G7, OECD countries, etc.). Figures 15.10–15.15 show for the 1970–2018 period the CLIs for Canada, France, Germany, Italy, Japan, and the UK, i.e. the G7 countries minus the US, as the US has been covered in the previous parts of this chapter. The figures show the monthly CLI for each country together with the change in industrial production over the following six months. Recessions are indicated in each graph, based on the two-quarters-with-negative-GDP-growth definition also employed in Chapter 8.

The CLIs generally capture recessions rather well. The CLIs tend to be low during recessions. The CLIs do not, however, to the same extent as the CLI for the US, drop before recessions. In some cases they do, but not always. For instance, CLIs tended to drop in the middle of 2008. At that point, the 2008 Great Recessions was already happening in many countries.

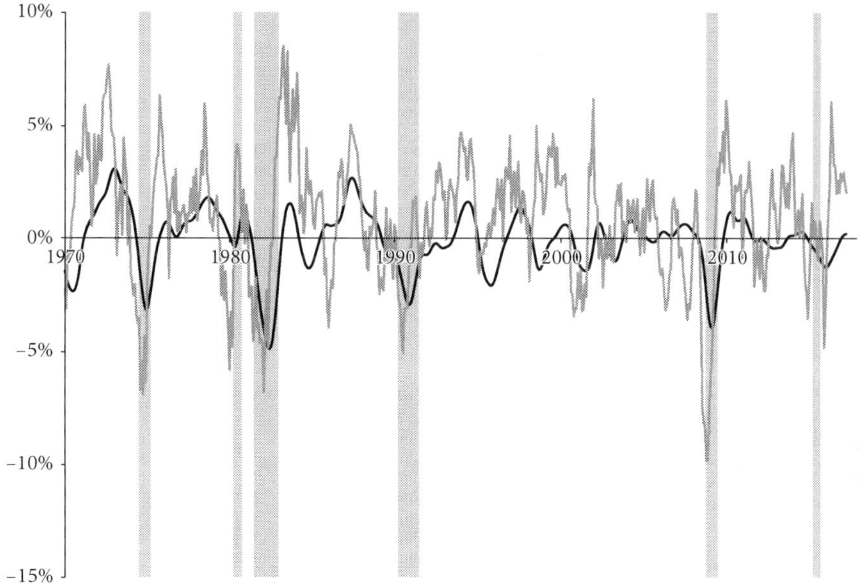

Figure 15.10 Canada CLI.

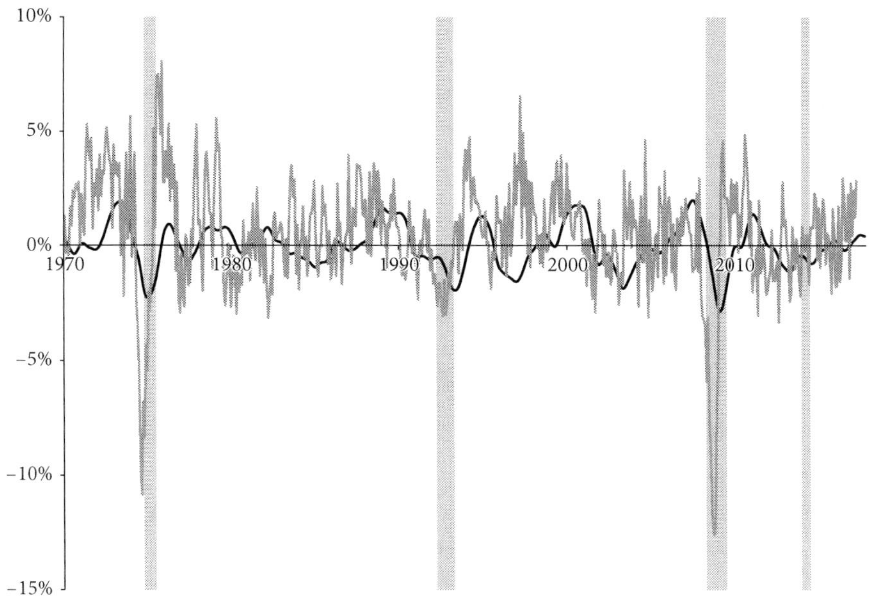

Figure 15.11 France CLI.

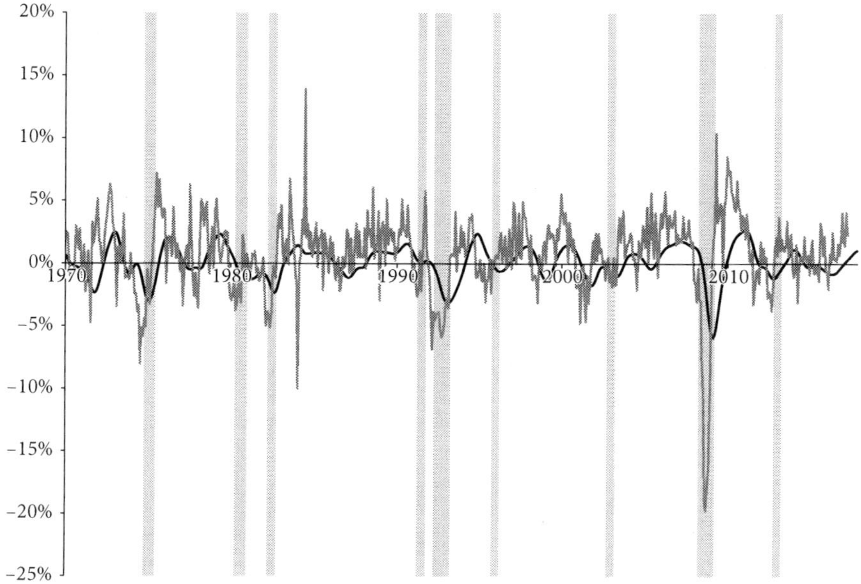

Figure 15.12 Germany CLI.

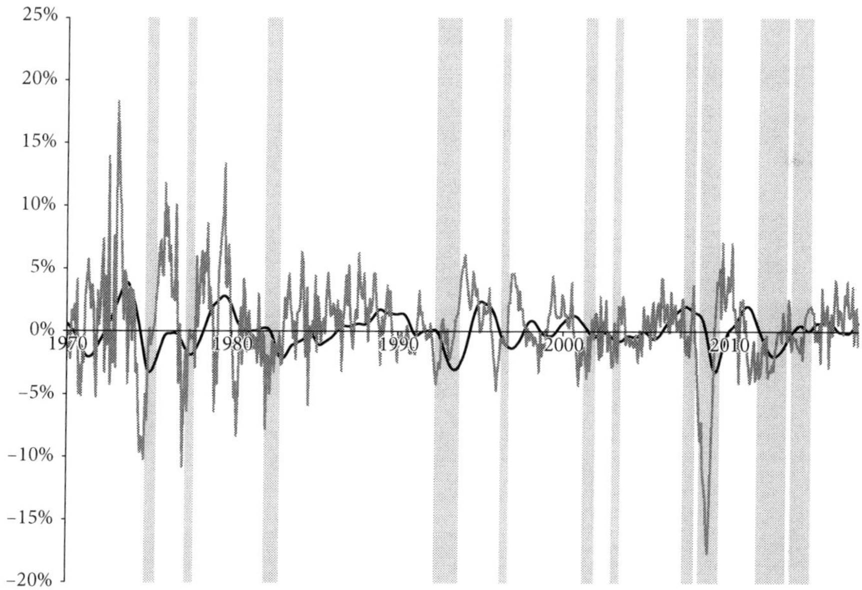

Figure 15.13 Italy CLI.

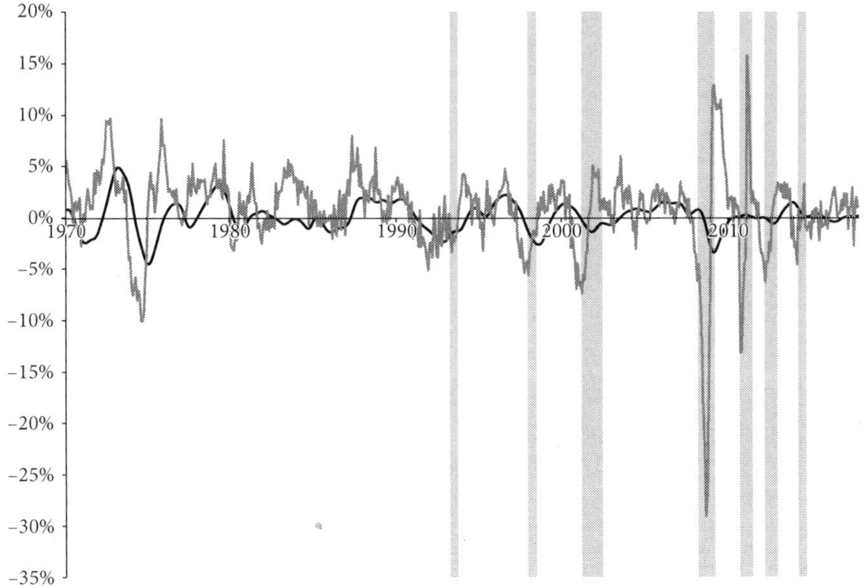

Figure 15.14 Japan CLI.

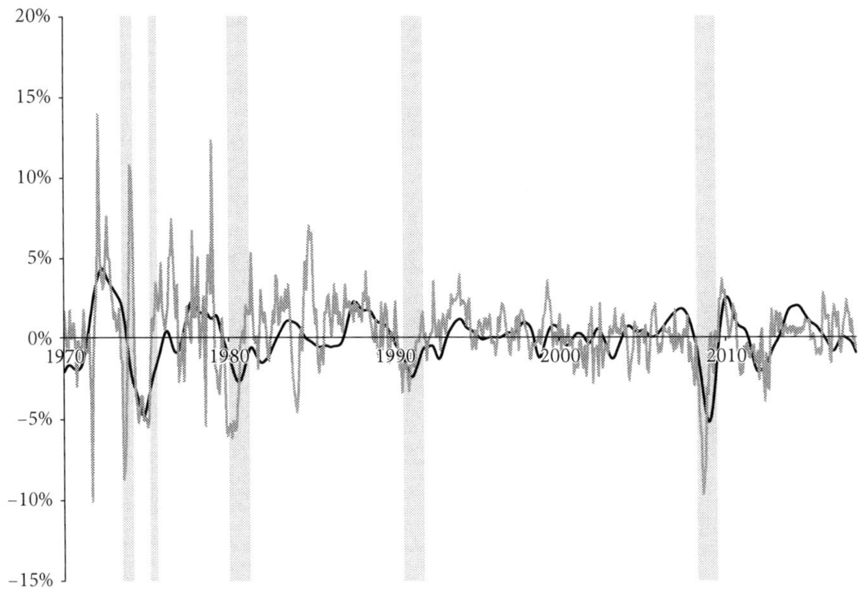

Figure 15.15 United Kingdom CLI.

If analysing international yield-spread data, the conclusion is somewhat similar to the conclusion for CLIs. There is information about the future business cycle in international yield spreads, but it is not as strong as for the US. In Japan, for instance, interest rates of all maturities have been very low for many years. This implies that there has been basically no variation in the yield spread. When there is no variation in the yield spread, there is no relation between recessions and yield spreads, either. The yield spread in Japan has not been a useful predictor of economic downturns. For other countries, the yield curve tends to flatten prior to recessions. We conclude that CLIs and yield spreads are relevant variables to follow and contain useful information in the US, but the precision of their signals differs from country to country.

15.5 Checklist

This chapter has demonstrated that:

- The yield curve—the difference between yields on long and short maturity government bonds—is probably the most successful and famous recession indicator. The yield curve tends to flatten before recessions. With some success, the US yield curve has been able to foretell whether a US recession is approaching.
- Sentiments of consumers and firms also seem to capture the arrival of recessions, though not as well as the yield curve.
- High-frequency, i.e. daily, indicators of the stance of the business cycle have been constructed. These are noisy, though.
- Economists collect groups of variables that tell something about the future path of economic activity into composite indicators. Composite leading indicators have some success in capturing turning points in economic activity.
- Yield spreads and composite indicators can be constructed for many economies. They help in saying something about future developments in economic activity but their precision differs from country to country.
- The overall conclusion is that variables exist that contain information about the future business cycle, but—at the same time and important to remember—there is noise in short-run changes in economic activity. Hence, there is noise surrounding forecasts of business-cycle turning points.

PART V
THE PROSPECTS FOR RETURNS

16
Predicting returns: Theory

This part of the book deals with the outlook for stocks. Based on insights gained in the previous parts on the joint dynamics of the stock market and the economy in the short and the long run, we now turn to the question of how we can use those insights to judge the outlook for the stock market? In particular, can we use our knowledge of the business cycle and long-term growth prospects to forecast stock-market returns?

Fifty years or so ago, the answer to the question of whether the stock market contains a predictable component would have been a resounding no. Economists believed that movements in the stock market were random. Changes in stock prices cannot be predicted, it was believed, so the best guess of future stock returns is past stock returns. The theoretical underpinnings of this—for investors—somewhat pessimistic view was the 'efficient market hypothesis' in its original form. This states that stock prices incorporate all relevant information, and stock prices are determined as future dividends discounted by a constant, time-invariant discount rate. If stock prices change, it is because new, i.e. unforeseen, information has been revealed to the market.

This all changed in the early 1980s, not least following the publication of an academic article in 1981 by Yale University Professor Robert J. Shiller. Shiller (1981) demonstrated that stock prices are far too volatile to be solely determined by future dividends discounted by a constant discount rate. Belief in the old version of efficient markets vanished. The hypothesis that the discount rate is not constant but time-varying emerged. Eventually, Shiller received the Nobel Prize in Economics for his insights on these matters

A large academic literature followed. Today, it is well-accepted that returns (not only stock returns, but returns on most asset classes) contain a predictable component. This does not mean that we can easily say how stocks will develop in the future, but it does not mean either that we cannot say anything at all. Theory has also been developed that reconciles return predictability with efficient capital markets.

This chapter provides a brief description of the history of academic thinking on the subject of return predictability, such that we in subsequent chapters can be more specific about what kind of variables tell us something about the outlook for stocks. The chapter starts by describing the initial formulations of the efficient market hypothesis in the 1970s, with its view that returns are unpredictable,

From Main Street to Wall Street. Jesper Rangvid, Oxford University Press (2021). © Jesper Rangvid.
DOI: 10.1093/oso/9780198866404.003.0016

moving on to Shiller (1981). Finally, it describes the current view on return predictability.

16.1 Efficient markets and return predictability

During the 1960s and 1970s, most financial economists believed that expected stock returns are constant. If investors now expect the stock market to return 6%, investors will also tomorrow expect the stock market to return 6%. Predictability means that changes in expected returns are correlated with changes in subsequent realized returns. So, when people in the 1960s and 1970s believed that expected returns were constant, people also believed that returns cannot be predicted.

The academic foundation for the belief in constant expected returns (= no stock return predictability) was not least due to the phenomenally influential article of Fama (1970) on Efficient Capital Markets. In this article, Fama advocates a definition of efficient capital markets: 'A market in which prices always 'fully reflect' available information is called 'efficient'.' Asset prices, and hence asset returns, only change when new unforeseen information hits the market.

If we expect firms to do well, this is incorporated into the price today, according to the theory. If we expect the Fed to lower rates, this is incorporated into the price today. If we expect the business cycle to turn, this is incorporated into the price today. Etc. Only if new information is released, asset prices will be affected. Stock prices are assumed to follow a so-called 'random walk'.[1] This means that it is not possible to earn return over and above the market return without taking on additional risk. For instance, according to the efficient market hypothesis, investors should not be able to earn higher returns by picking certain stocks, unless these stocks are more risky. If some stocks trade at low prices, there are good reasons. Investors cannot systematically find cheap stocks. To be clear, the theory does not imply that expected returns on all assets are the same at any given point in time. On the contrary. Assets that are more risky (have higher systematic risk) should deliver higher expected returns. The CAPM was the workhorse model.[2] But, over time, asset returns change in unpredictable ways only.

[1] A random walk is a process describing how (in this case) stock prices behave over time. When stock prices follow a random walk, stock prices today are equal to stock prices tomorrow plus a random news component: $p_{t+1} = p_t + \varepsilon_{t+1}$, where p_t (p_{t+1}) is the stock price today (tomorrow) and ε_{t+1} is the random news component realized tomorrow. The random news component is assumed to be unpredictable. For this reason, our best guess of the stock price tomorrow is the stock price today.

[2] The Capital Asset Pricing Model (CAPM) states that investors are compensated for baring systematic risk, i.e. more risky stocks deliver higher expected returns.

16.1.1 Shiller (1981)

All this changed with Shiller (1981). Shiller's observations were as follows. The price of a stock today is the expected future dividends paid by the company issuing the stock discounted back until today, as described in Chapter 3. When the discount rate is constant, we find the price by discounting future dividends with this constant discount rate. To make this operational, Shiller used the insight that if one assumes a terminal value for the stock price, i.e. assumes some value of the stock far out in the future, then one can work backwards to find the theoretical price at any point in time based on actually observed future dividends.

Shiller's clue was that he examined what happens if we impose the assumption of efficient markets: any difference between the theoretical 'correct' stock price and the observed actual stock price should be due to the release of random new unforeseen information only. If the market is efficient, the theoretical stock price, i.e. the discounted value of future dividends, should equal the observed stock price plus a random forecast error. A forecast error is obviously uncorrelated with the forecast—if not, it would be incorporated into the forecast. Using basic insights from statistics, Shiller (1981) showed that this implies that the variance of the theoretical stock price is equal to the sum of the variance of the actual stock price and the variance of the forecast error:

$$var(\text{theoretical price}) = var(\text{actual price}) + var(\text{forecast error}).$$

As variances are positive numbers, i.e. the variance of the forecast error is positive, the efficient market hypothesis implies that the variance of the actual stock price must be lower than the variance of the theoretical stock price:

$$var(\text{theoretical price}) > var(\text{actual price}).$$

The second key point of Shiller (1981) was that he found a way to empirically back out the theoretical stock price. He used this to show that the variance of the actual stock price is far greater than the variance of the theoretical stock price, in contrast to the implications of efficient markets. Figure 16.1 is an updated version of the central figure in Shiller (1981). It contains the actual real stock price and the theoretical rational real stock price based on realized real dividends discounted by a constant discount rate, both plotted on a logarithmic scale. The discount rate is assumed to be a constant 1/1.065, reflecting historic annual real stock returns of app. 6.5%.

The theoretical stock price develops smoothly over time. The actual stock price, however, is wildly fluctuating around the theoretical stock price. Stock prices are 'excessively volatile'; too volatile to be accounted for by the volatility of underlying

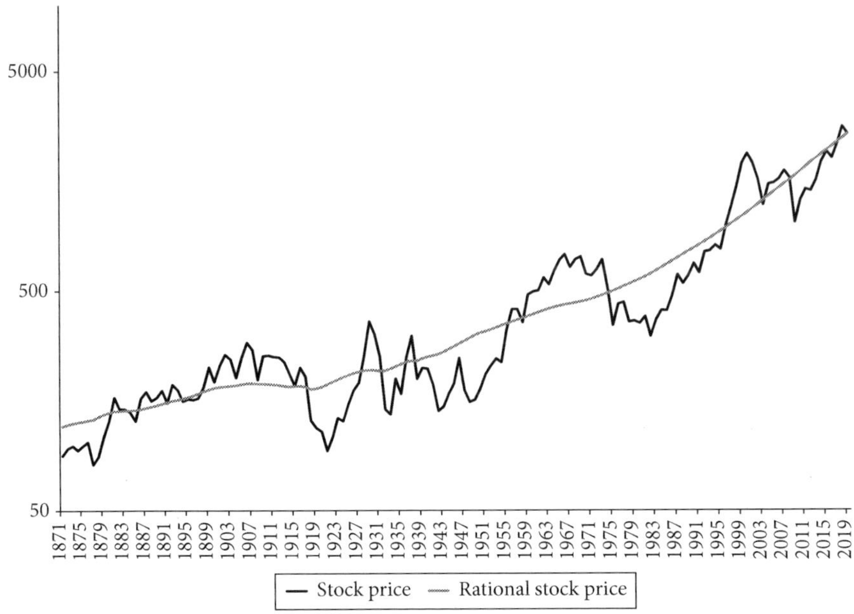

Figure 16.1 Actual real stock price and rational (theoretical) real stock price based on discounted dividends. Logarithmic scale.
Data source: Webpage of Robert J. Shiller.

dividends.[3] The volatility of the percentage annual change in the actual stock price is twelve times larger than the volatility of the percentage annual change in the theoretical stock price. This is too large a difference for it to be explained by mismeasurement, data challenges, or the like.

It is difficult to exaggerate the importance of this finding. First, it questioned the basic assumption of market efficiency, i.e. that the price is always right and investors form beliefs by discounting future cash-flows and use these as their best guess of the price.[4] Second, it questioned whether discount rates are constant. If discount rates are not constant but time-varying, returns might be predictable. It is this second implication that we are particular interested in here.

[3] To produce Figure 16.1, one needs to assume a value for the terminal price. In calculating this graph, I have assumed that the actual price at the last observation—in 2019—equals the theoretically correct value in 2019. This is a simplification, but it is not crucial. Lots, as in lots(!), of empirical research has shown that the main insight of Shiller (1981) is robust. This has been done by using alternative assumptions about the terminal value, and by using completely different test procedures, not requiring an assumption about the terminal stock price. In the end, the 'excess volatility' of stock prices is one of the truly important, and robust, findings in empirical asset pricing.

[4] The idea that markets are not always efficient has lead to the development of 'behavioural finance'. For a comprehensive survey, see Beshears, Choi, Laibson, and Madrian (2018).

The pattern observed in Figure 16.1 is one where actual stock prices fluctuate around the fundamental theoretical value. If the stock price is above its fundamental value, there is a tendency for it to come down again, and vice versa. This indicates mean reversion, and thus predictability, in stock prices. In other words, establishing that stock prices are 'too volatile' to be accounted for by underlying fundamentals is the same thing as saying that stock returns are predictable.

As shown earlier in the book, e.g. in Chapter 3, if discount rates are constant and if dividends grow by a constant factor, the stock price today will be given by the so-called Gordon formula:

$$\frac{\text{Stock price}}{\text{Current dividends}} = \frac{1}{\text{Expected stock returns} - \text{Expected dividend growth}}. \tag{16.1}$$

There is a lot of volatility in the left-hand-side of this equation, as Figure 16.1 reveals (remember that the theoretical stock price is based on actual dividends). Stock prices fluctuate much more than underlying dividends. This means that the right-hand-side must be volatile, too. When the theoretical stock price is not volatile enough to account for the volatility of the actual stock price, dividend growth is also not volatile enough to account for the volatility of the left-hand-side of Eq. (16.1). In other words, fluctuations in the stock-price to dividend ratio must be due primarily to changes in future stock returns. Notice also that the stock price-dividend ratio is inversely related to expected stock returns. This means that when the left-hand-side increases, i.e. stock prices raise in relation to dividends, the right-hand-side must increase, too. And, when dividend growth does not move that much, the adjustment must primarily happen via a reduction in returns. In other words, high stock prices in relation to dividends should predict low future returns.

The Gordon model underlying Eq. (16.1) is derived under the assumption of constant discount rates and constant dividend growth. The whole point here is that discount rates are time-varying, i.e. predictable over time. We can use the intuition from the Gordon model, but to incorporate what we are actually after, we must resort to more complicated models. And here comes Shiller again, this time in collaboration with his then Ph.D. student, and today one of the leading researchers in asset pricing, Professor John H. Campbell from Harvard University. In the 1980s, Campbell & Shiller (1988a, 1988b) developed a model where they allow both expected returns (discount rates) and dividend growth rates to be time-varying. The model Campbell & Shiller derived is a dynamic version of Eq. (16.1). Hence, it is sometimes called the 'dynamic Gordon model'. Instead of relating the price-dividend ratio to constant expected returns and constant dividend growth rates as in Eq. (16.1), the 'dynamic Gordon model' relates the price-dividend ratio to the expectation of all future dividend growth rates and returns, and allow these to potentially vary through time. In this way, variation in the price-dividend ratio predicts returns and dividend growth. Their model, like Eq. (16.1), implies a negative relation between the price-dividend ratio today and expected returns: a high price-dividend ratio today predicts lower future returns. Campbell & Shiller, and subsequently many others, tested whether movements in the price-dividend ratio predict returns. It does, as we will see in subsequent chapters.

16.2 Can returns be predictable in efficient markets?

The previous section explained how the empirical evidence changed the perception of return predictability. Stock prices are just too volatile to be the discounted (constant discount rates) sum of future dividends. But what about the concept of efficient markets? Can markets be efficient and returns predictable at the same time?

Today, it is recognized that returns can be predictable in efficient capital markets. Many economic models have been formulated that allow for some degree of return predictability in efficient markets. Even Eugene Fama himself changed his views on 'efficient capital markets' in light of the evidence on return predictability. In 1991, Fama published a paper called 'Efficient Markets: II', i.e. a second version of efficient markets, taking into account these new results. In this paper, Fama interpreted findings on return predictability in the late 1980s as rational events. Basically, today, it is well-understood that a rejection of the hypothesis that stock prices are future dividends discounted by a constant discount rate is not the same as rejecting the hypothesis that markets are efficient. Markets can be efficient, also when discount rates are time-varying.

What can cause rational return predictability? The current price of an asset, like all prices, is determined by demand and supply. Shifts in demand and supply thus cause shifts in asset prices. Consider the arrival of a recession. The value of risky assets will drop in recessions as expected earnings and dividends drop. Also, investors are afraid of losing their jobs. When you are afraid of losing your job and stocks perform badly during recessions, you do not want to be hit twice. You would like to get out of stocks. We say that the risk aversion of investors increases during recessions. When risk aversion increases, and investors do not want to hold risky assets, demand for risky assets drop. When demand drops, prices of risky assets drop, and expected returns go up (for a given cash-flow, a lower stock price means higher returns). So, when we expect a recession, risk aversion goes up, stock prices fall, and expected returns increase. This is rational and efficient.

Economists have formulated models that more explicitly detail these effects. One famous model is the habit-persistence model of John Campbell of Harvard University and John Cochrane of University of Chicago, published in 1999. Their idea, also mentioned in Chapter 7, is that people do not like to see consumption dropping below the level of consumption they are used to. When a recession hits, your consumption falls compared to what you have been used to. Your risk aversion goes up during these periods. This forecasts returns. Campbell and Cochrane show that such behaviour can account for many features of asset markets, including return predictability. Habit formation is not the only channel that can give rise to time-varying expected returns, i.e. return predictability. Other types of explanations rely on 'time-varying disaster risk' (Barro, 2006) or time-varying so-called 'long-run risk' (Bansal and Yaron, 2005). We will no go into detail with these models. The main point is that if some aggregate risks that cannot be diversified away vary through time, e.g., the risk of a recession, then returns on risky assets might also be time-varying.

Before the checklist, it is important to point out that return predictability does not mean that we can make ourselves rich. Or, rather, at least not without taking on risk. Remember what the underlying explanation is. A recession is arriving, risk aversion goes up. How can you trade on this? You should be willing to take on more risk than the marginal investor at such points in time. E.g., when the recession is approaching, risks are increasing, and everybody is afraid, then you should be willing to invest in the risky stock market. If you are willing to do so, then you can generate higher expected returns. But, again, you do this at a time where everybody is shying away from stocks. You can only earn this extra return if you are different from everybody else. As Professor John Cochrane always reminds us: the average investor must hold the market (Cochrane, 1999). The conclusion is that there are periods where there is a higher likelihood that expected returns will be high, and vice versa, but there are good reasons: either risks or risk aversion are high during those periods.

16.3 Checklist

- Fifty years or so ago, during the 1960s and 1970s, the common belief was that stock returns were unpredictable. Stock prices incorporate all relevant information, and only unforeseen new information can cause stock prices to change. The best guess of tomorrow's stock return is today's return. Stock prices were believed to be determined as expected future dividends discounted to the present by a constant discount factor.

- Shiller (1981) showed that stock prices are far too volatile to be solely explained by the present value of dividends discounted by a constant discount rate.
- Initially, this result was interpreted as implying that capital markets are not efficient. Today, it is well-understood that markets can be efficient and discount rates time-varying.
- A huge body of research has confirmed that returns contain a small predictable component. This component is typically related to the macroeconomic situation, as the following chapters show.

17
Predicting short-to-medium horizon returns

We have discussed how the economy and the stock market are related. Stocks typically go up during expansions. Expansions last longer than recessions. Hence, stocks go up most of the time. We also know that stocks fall a lot during recessions. These insights help us understand the behaviour of stock markets. But can we go further and, for instance, say that given economic conditions today, stock returns will probably be high (or low) going forward? I.e., can we, using information today, say something about the future direction of the stock market? This is what this part of the book deals with.

A warning before getting started: It is very difficult to predict the future movements of the stock market. Every day, thousands of analysts, and millions of investors, try to predict the stock market, in order to increase their returns or reduce their losses. If it was straightforward to predict the stock market, they would all make a fortune. If we all knew that stocks would fall, we would all sell. But who would then be on the other side—who would buy the stocks? In order for trading to occur, investors must disagree on the outlook.[1]

The fact that it is difficult to forecast the stock market does not mean that we cannot say anything at all. This chapter lays out what we know about stock return predictability on the short-to-medium horizon. It recognizes that most of the fluctuations in the stock market are unpredictable, but characterizes those that are. Another important lesson of this chapter is that stock markets are very volatile in the short run but appears to be less so in the long run. Paradoxically, this implies that it looks as if we can say a little more about the future movements in the stock market when dealing with the longer run (several years). From today until tomorrow, or next week, we can say very little.

Before we begin, please remember that the mission of this chapter has not been fulfilled if you, after reading it, believe you can tell where the market is going in the short run with high probability. In contrast, if you believe that certain indicators contain a little bit of information about the short-run outlook for stocks, you have

[1] Some trading happens because somebody withdraw their savings from the stock market in order to increase consumption while others start saving. But this is not enough to account for the volume of trading. To generate lots of trading, information asymmetry must exist.

From Main Street to Wall Street. Jesper Rangvid, Oxford University Press (2021). © Jesper Rangvid.
DOI: 10.1093/oso/9780198866404.003.0017

understood the message. Importantly, however, even a little bit of predictability can have important economic implications.

17.1 Movements in the short and the long run

Before we start discussing indicators that tell us something about the future path of the stock market, it is useful to understand the difference between short-term and long-term fluctuations in stocks and what this means for our possibilities of saying something useful about their future movements.

Think about the weather. The day-to-day change in the temperature is difficult to predict. Will tomorrow be warmer than today? The likelihood that you will get this right is low. The change in temperature from winter to summer is easier to predict. A guess that it is warmer in July than in January (in the Northern Hemisphere) is a very good guess.

The stock market behaves to some extent similarly. Chapter 3 showed that during the last 147 years, 31% of the years (45 years) saw a negative real return. Over ten-year periods, the probability of negative average annual returns is only 12%. Similarly, whether stock prices are higher or lower tomorrow is very difficult to predict. But saying that stock prices in ten years will be higher than they are today is a pretty good guess. This chapter deals with shorter-horizon predictions. Next chapters deal with longer horizons.

17.2 Short-run (daily) predictability

The way economists think about stock-return predictability is that some economic indicator might say something about the outlook for stocks. For this to be possible, an indicator needs to be available in the first place. If studying high-frequency returns, such as daily return, we cannot really rely on individual macroeconomic variables, as most of these are simply not available on a short-term basis. For instance, GDP is available at the quarterly frequency and industrial production at the monthly.[2] Hence, for very short-term predictability, economists use data from financial markets themselves. Financial-market variables are stock returns, interest rates, and other asset prices.

[2] Individual macroeconomic variables are released once a month or once a quarter. There are, however, many different variables and they are released on different days during the month. By combining several macroeconomic variables, released on different days, into an index, economists can create real-time indicators, as Chapter 15 discussed. The point in the text is that we cannot use individual macroeconomic time series in isolation when studying daily/weekly returns.

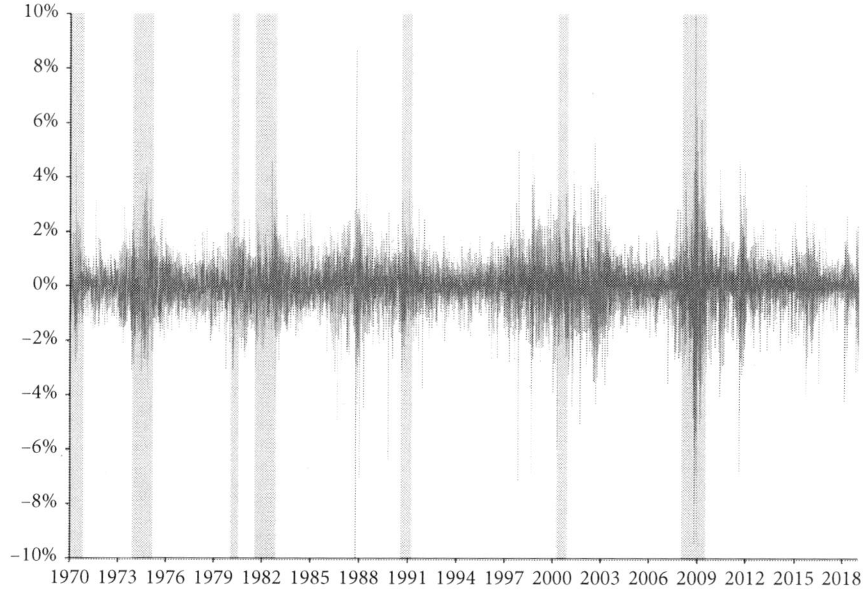

Figure 17.1 Daily percentage changes in the S&P 500. NBER-defined recession periods indicated by shading.
Data source: Datastream.

Let us first look at past short-run stock returns as predictors of future short-run stock returns. Figure 17.1 shows daily percentage changes in the S&P 500 since 1970. Inflation is important in the longer run, but inflation moves slowly. Hence, inflation does not impact daily changes in stock prices to any material degree. The same goes for dividends. They move slowly, too. I.e., the important determinant of short-run returns is short-run changes in stock prices.[3]

Figure 17.1 shows that there is a lot of volatility in the stock market in the short run. A couple of statistics are useful to illustrate this. The average daily price change since 1970, i.e. over the last app. fifty years, is 0.03%. The standard deviation of daily price changes is 1.03%, i.e. almost 33 times larger than the average price change. This means that there is a 95% probability that daily stock-price changes are somewhere between minus two percent and plus two percent. On average, the daily price change is only 0.03%, however. In statistical terms, we cannot reject the hypothesis that the daily price change is zero, i.e. unpredictable. Another relevant statistic is that almost half of all daily changes (45%) are negative. The probability that the stock market goes up tomorrow is almost as large as the probability that it goes down.

[3] Figure 17.1 excludes Black Monday (October 19, 1987), as the S&P 500 that single day lost a whopping 23%. It is the largest single-day drop in the index ever. Including it in Figure 17.1 would make it difficult to see anything else.

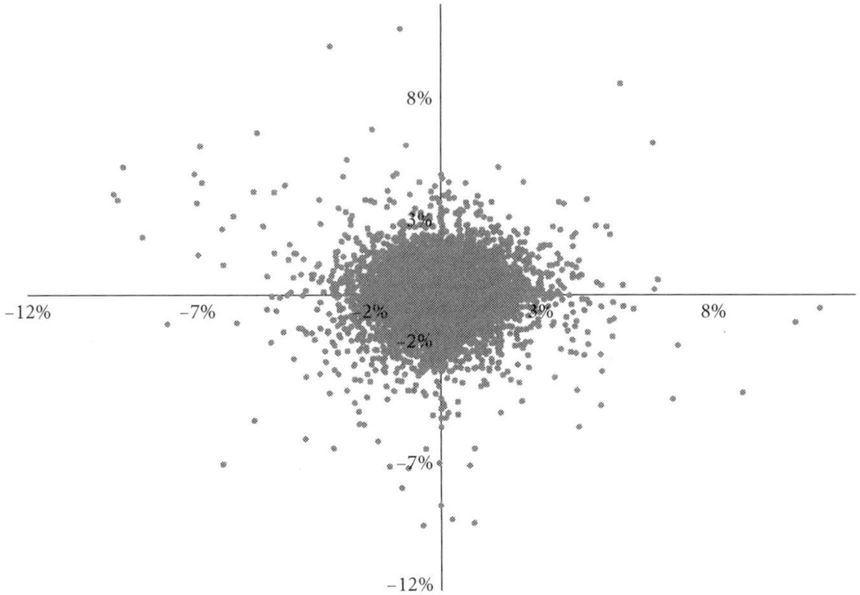

Figure 17.2 Scatter plot of capital gains on the S&P500 the previous day (horizontal axis) against capital gains today (vertical axis).
Data source: Datastream.

Even when there is almost the same number of positive and negative returns, it might be that they are lumped together such that a string of negative price changes follows a string of positive price changes. If so, there should be some relationship between price changes yesterday and today. We can check that. We can plot yesterday's price change against today's price change. This is in Figure 17.2.

If positive (negative) price changes were followed by positive (negative) price changes, at least for a couple of days, there would be some tendency for price changes to be scattered around a 45-degree line. This is certainly not the case. Price changes are scattered around a cloud centered at zero. One can in statistical terms check whether there is a systematic relation between price changes yesterday and today. Such a statistical test reveals that the likelihood that there is no systematic linear relation between price changes today and tomorrow is high. The point estimate of the correlation is positive, but the evidence is so weak that it is for all practical purposes non-existing.[4] In conclusion, observing price changes today tells us very little about price changes tomorrow.

[4] The likelihood that the coefficient relating yesterday's returns to today's return is equal to zero in a statistical sense is 40%. Economists view a relationship as systematic, i.e. statistically significant, if this likelihood is below 5% or 10%.

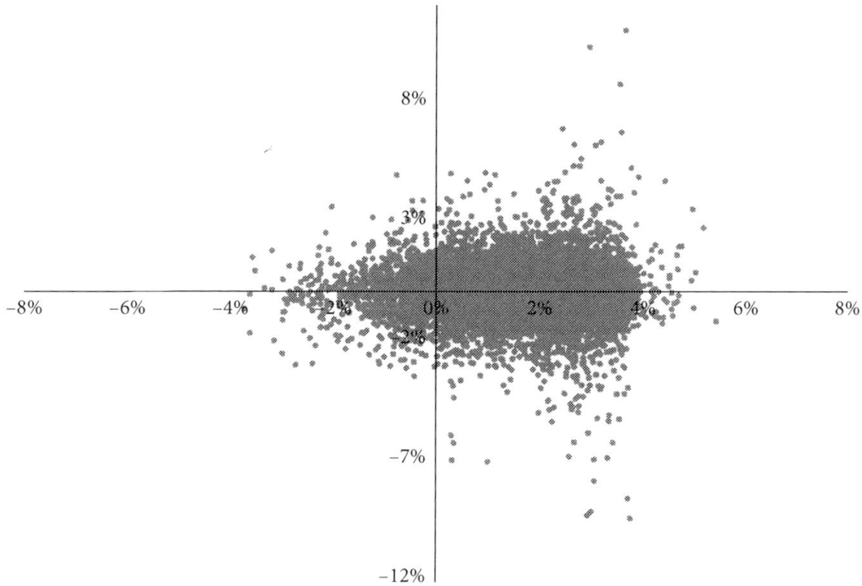

Figure 17.3 Daily US term spread (horizontal axis) versus capital gains on the SP500 the following day (vertical axis).
Data source: Datastream.

The fact that daily returns are noisy also indicates that it is difficult to predict daily returns using underlying economic fundamentals. We noticed in Chapter 15 that the term spread (the difference between yields on a short-term and a long-term government bond) is correlated with the arrival of a recession. The term spread is available at high frequency, e.g. daily. When daily stock returns are scattered all around, and the term spread follows a business cycle pattern, then daily stock returns and the term spread do not line up. This appears from Figure 17.3. There is a tendency for large term spreads to be associated with relatively large movements in stock prices the following day, but a large term spread is associated with both large increases and large drops over the coming day. A large term spread, thus, does not indicate the direction of the stock market, only that there will be a relatively large change in the stock market. When estimating the statistical relationship between the term spread today and movements in stock prices over the next day, the relationship is statistically insignificant.

The conclusion is that day-to-day movements in stock prices are difficult to relate systematically to underlying fundamental indicators and to past stock prices themselves in easily interpretable ways.

17.2.1 Reaction to macroeconomic announcements

Using advanced research techniques, researchers have established that stock prices react to announcements of macroeconomic news (Andersen, Bollerslev, Diebold, and Vega, 2003 and Boyd, Hu, and Jagannathan, 2005). If the latest information about GDP indicates that the economy is growing by more than what was expected, stock prices react instantly, sometimes within seconds or minutes. This means that there might be some sophisticated traders out there who use highly advanced and complex statistical techniques to identify information about the common underlying path of economic activity from the plethora of economic indicators that are published every day, and use this to say something about future short-run returns. Beber, Brandt, and Luisi (2015) provide an interesting example. Their findings indicate that one can predict short-run returns to some extent by releases of macroeconomic news. This means that even when daily stock-price movements seem to behave almost randomly, there is an underlying relation to the macroeconomy. But it is a short-lived one, and one that it difficult to capture out. For most of us, i.e. for longer-term investors, the reasonable working hypothesis is that daily returns are close to being unpredictable, and we should stop speculating whether returns will be higher or lower tomorrow. The more interesting question for most of us is what we can say about returns over the medium and long horizon.

17.3 Medium-frequency predictability

Daily returns are noisy. The signal-to-noise ratio, i.e. the clarity with which we can observe the underlying movements in expected returns, is low at the daily frequency. When reducing the frequency with which we observe returns, the signal-to-noise ratio improves. We begin to see patterns in monthly, quarterly, and annual returns. At the same time, at lower frequencies, we have macroeconomic series. This means we can investigate the extent to which macroeconomic variables relate to expected future returns.

Let us start getting a feeling for the noise in returns at low frequency, compared to the noise in high-frequency returns. Figures 17.4 through 17.7 show, respectively, daily, monthly, quarterly, and annual returns from the S&P 500 since 1970.

There are of course fewer and fewer observations in each graph, but it also becomes easier to see the general pattern. The fact that capital gains tend to be positive overall, and in particular during expansions, is easier to see when the frequency is lower. At the annual frequency, in Figure 17.7, almost all capital gains are positive in non-recession years. At the daily frequency, Figure 17.4, there are many days with negative capital gains even in non-recession months. This is also verified in the numbers. Remember from the analysis in the previous section that

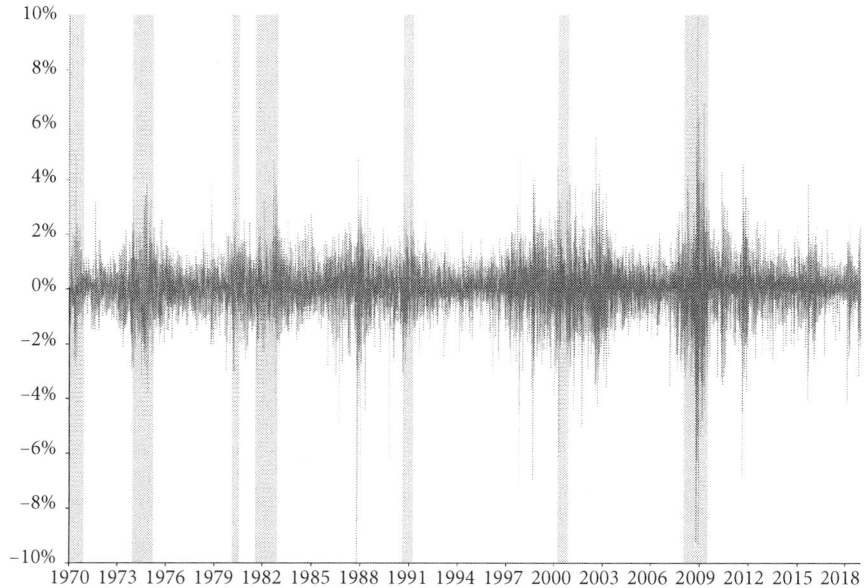

Figure 17.4 Daily capital gains.

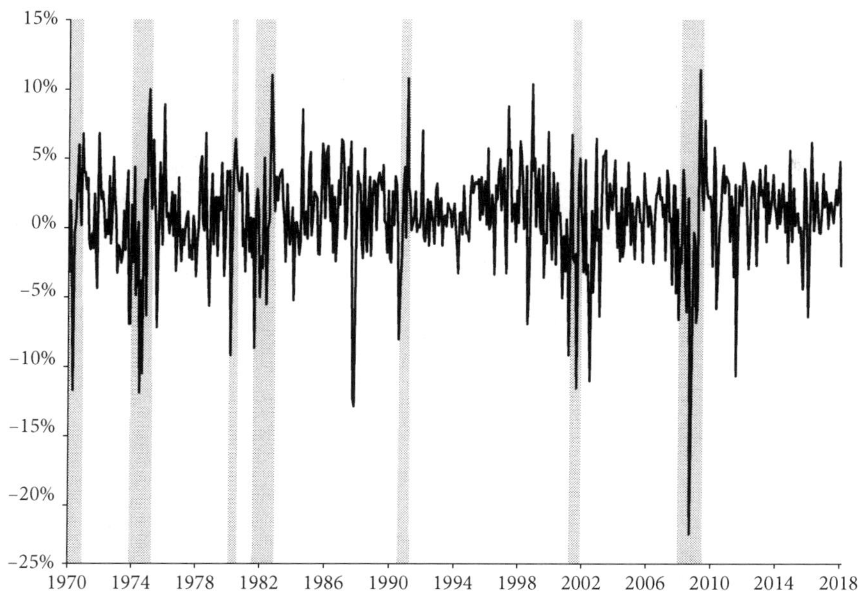

Figure 17.5 Monthly capital gains.

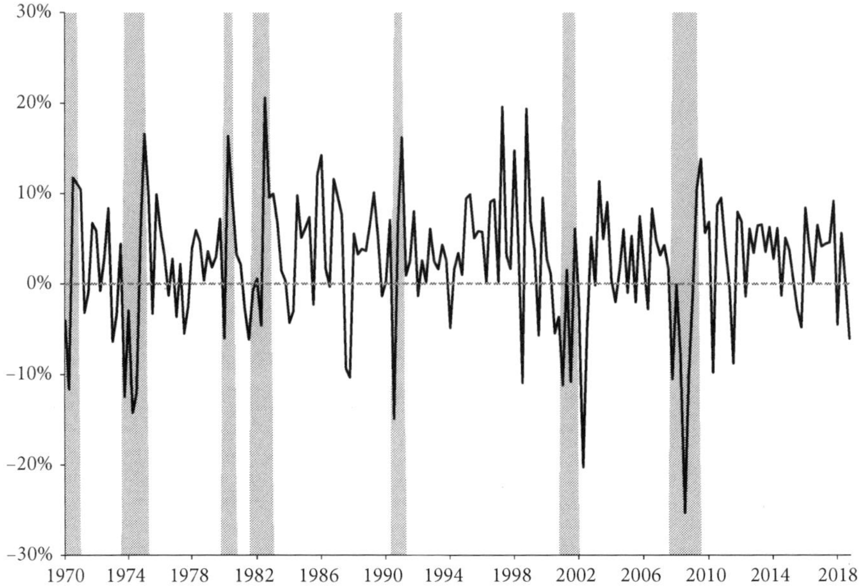

Figure 17.6 Quarterly capital gains.

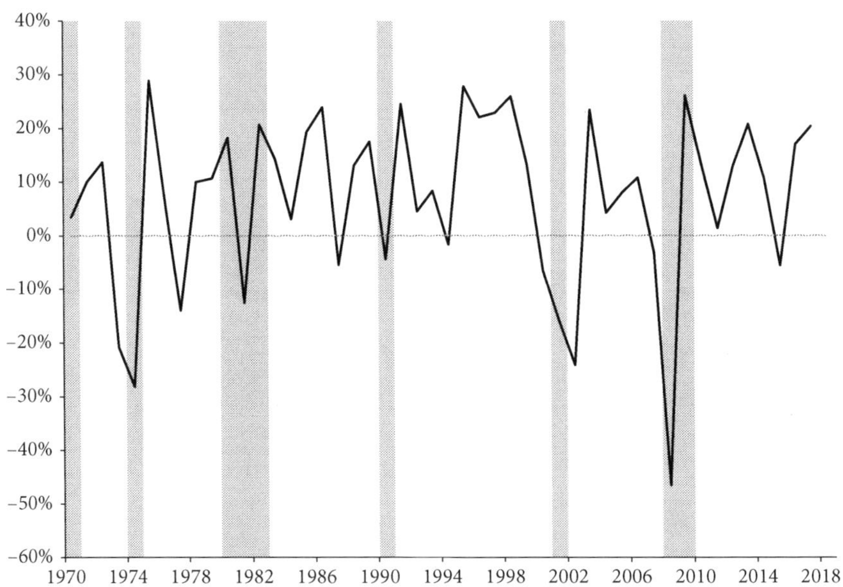

Figure 17.7 Annual capital gains.

Data source: Datastream and Figure 3.1.

45% of trading days during 1970–2018 saw negative capital gains. At the monthly frequency, 38% are negative. At the quarterly, 35%. And, at the annual frequency, 27% of the individual years from 1970–2018 saw negative capital gains. I.e., it is not only that there are fewer observations in the graphs. With less frequent measurements, short-run noise is reduced.

In the previous section, Section 17.2, we saw that the average daily price change was 0.03%. The standard deviation was 1.03, i.e. 33 times the average. The average monthly price change is 0.59% and the associated standard deviation is 3.65%, i.e. six times larger. The average quarterly stock-price change is 1.8% and the standard deviation 7.1%, i.e. 4 times larger. And, for annual frequency, the average price change is 7.2% and the standard deviation 16.2%, i.e. 2.3 times larger. The signal-to-noise ratio tends to be higher at a lower frequency.[5]

17.4 Macroeconomic variables and future returns

'Last month's level of industrial production has just been published. Industry has increased production. The latest figure for consumer-price inflation showed a large fall. GDP last quarter jumped.' These are economic news we read all the time. What do they imply for future stock returns? Is there any relation between variables measuring and forecasting the business cycle and future stock returns? Researchers have devoted a lot of their attention to this important question. Their conclusion is that there is some predictability: macroeconomic activity does seem to influence future stock returns. This is a very important conclusion.

Economists use statistical tools, such as regressions, to investigate relations between economic indicators and future stock returns. A regression gives an estimate of the average relation between future stock returns and the economic variable(s) we look at. Regressions can also be used to say something about the likelihood with which the average relation we establish really is there or whether it is a fluke. Economists proceed as follows. We look at data for stock returns and economic variables during a relatively long historical period. Preferably, the period we look at should include different business cycles, and not just the last couple of years. If finding a relation during the last couple of years only, one would be concerned if the relation persists when the business cycle changes. If the relation

[5] This is not because there are fewer observations when using quarterly price changes compared to, e.g., monthly. There are app. 200 quarters from 1970 to 2018. Using monthly data, we can estimate standard deviation and average returns from January 1970 and 200 months forward (i.e. using the same number of observations as there are quarters from 1970 to 2018), then do it again from February 1970 and 200 months forward, from March 1970 and 200 months forward, etc. We end up with a string of standard deviations and averages, all based on 200 months. We can then calculate the average of ratios of standard deviations to average price changes. The result is that the standard deviation is app. six times larger than the average, like when calculating the ratio at the monthly frequency over the full sample.

persists over the last fifty years or so, we feel on safer ground that it might also persist in the future.

The previous two sections looked at changes in nominal stock prices—we simply wanted to see how stock prices move around. When saying something about whether an economic variable predicts stock returns, we are often interested in all components of returns, i.e. both changes in stock prices and the dividend yield. And, we are interested in returns after taking account of inflation, i.e. real returns.

When picking indicators, we start by asking the obvious question why would you expect a relation between an economic variable and future stock returns in the first place? We know that stock returns are strongly influenced by the business cycle: When the economy is doing badly, stocks do badly. Hence, we are interested in variables that tell us something about future economic conditions. Luckily, this was exactly what we examined in Chapter 15. Chapter 15 studied variables that tell us something about future economic conditions.

17.4.1 Illustrating with the term spread

Chapter 15 concluded that the term spread—the difference between the yield on a long (ten year) and a short (three months) government bond—forecasts the business cycle and is available back in time. Furthermore, interest rates are readily available, i.e. do not have to be estimated. For these reasons, economists have a tradition of using the term spread, or the short interest rate itself, when trying to capture future stock-market fluctuations.[6]

We saw in the previous section that it is difficult to say anything at the daily frequency. Let us now ask whether there is a relationship between this month's term spread and next month's stock return. Chapter 15 noted that the Fed pegged the short interest rate until the Treasury-Federal Reserve Accord of 1951, i.e. it is after 1952 that the short interest rate and the term spread relate to economic activity. Before 1952, the term spread does not track recessions, as mentioned in Chapter 15.

We proceed as follows. We look at the term spread in January 1952 and returns during February 1952, then, next, what was the term spread in February 1952 and returns during March, etc. We do this for all months, and we ask what has been the average relation. Figure 17.8 shows the relation between the term spread in one month (on the horizontal axis) and real returns on the S&P500 during the next month (vertical axis). The term spread ranges from app. minus three percent

[6] The academic literature started analysing the short interest rate and the term spread as predictors of stock markets in the 1980s, see for instance Campbell (1987) and Campbell & Shiller (1988a, 1988b).

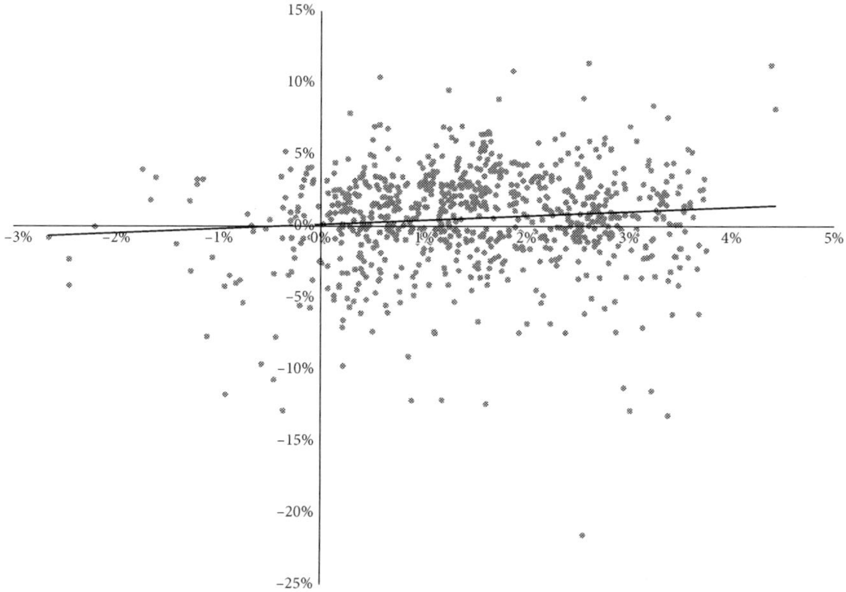

Figure 17.8 Scatter plot of the term spread in a month (horizontal axis) and real return on the S&P500 the following month (vertical axis). 1952–2018.
Data source: FRED and Figure 3.1.

to app. five percent, with most observations being positive. This is what Chapter 15 told us. Most of the time, the term spread is positive, but turns negative when a recession is approaching. There are two main conclusions from Figure 17.8. First, there is a weak positive average relation between the size of the term spread in one month and real stock returns during the next month, as indicated by the inserted trend line. Second, there is a lot of noise around the average relation. Is everything noise or is there a systematic relation? A regression analysis reveals that the probability that there is no systematic relation between the term spread this month and returns next month is lower than one percent. In other words, there is a systematic statistical relation between the term spread in one month and stock returns next month. So, Section 17.2 told us that the term spread today does not tell us much (= anything) about returns tomorrow. This section tells us that this month's term spread tells us something about next month's return.

What is the size of the relationship? On average, during the period from 1952 to 2018, when the term spread increases by one percentage point, e.g., goes from one percent to two percent, expected stock returns tend to increase by 0.3% next month. Over the 1952–2018 period, average monthly real stock returns are around 0.85%. A move of 0.3% is a large effect.

The relationship is positive, as also indicated by the trendline in Figure 17.8: when the term spread this month decreases (increases), stock returns go down (up) next month. This is intuitive. The term spread is high during early phases of expansions, where stocks are performing well, but drops when recessions are approaching, i.e. when stocks start to do poorly. So, the drop in the term spread indicates a recession is approaching, and stocks start doing badly. There is another way of saying this: most of the changes in the term spread are driven by changes in the short rate (the short rate is more volatile than the long rate), as Chapter 11 explained. In fact, the term spread and the short rate follow each other rather closely, with opposite signs. When the short rate goes up, the term spread goes down. This is illustrated in Figure 17.9. When the Fed tightens monetary policy, i.e. increases the short interest rate, the term spread drops. Given a positive relation between the term spread and returns next month, we would expect a negative relation between the short interest rate this month and stock returns next month. This is what we find. When the Fed tightens monetary policy, i.e. increases the short-term interest rate, the term spread increases, and stock returns suffer the following month. Chapter 11 hinted at such a relation. Here, we present the evidence.

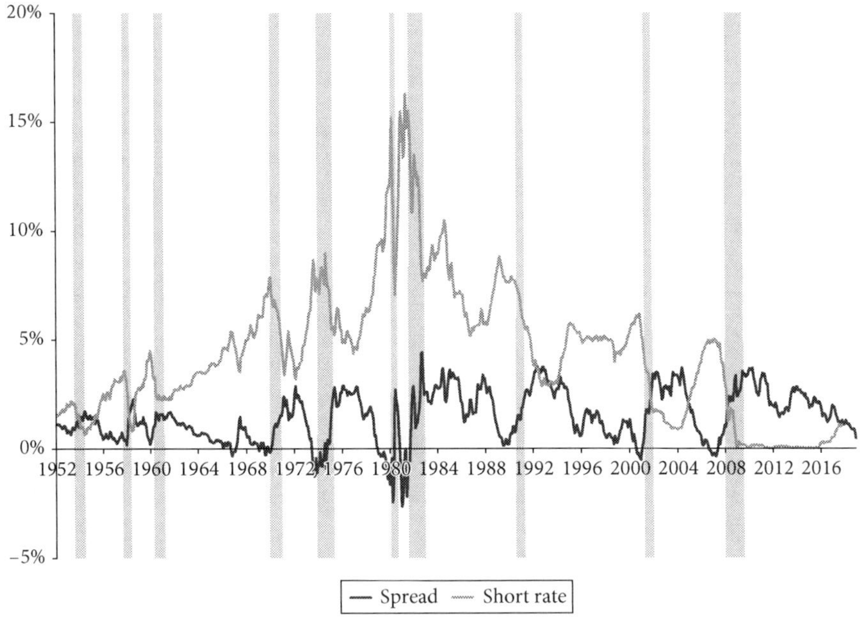

Figure 17.9 The term spread and the short interest rate. NBER-defined recessions indicated by shading.

Data source: FRED.

These relations between monetary policy, the term spread, the business cycle, and future stock returns are intuitive and make sense. There is uncertainty around this average relation, though, as Figure 17.8 also makes clear. Fluctuations in the term spread only account for a small part of fluctuations in stock returns next month. Only around 1% of stock-return fluctuations are due to fluctuations in the term spread. The remaining 99% of monthly stock market fluctuations are due to something else. So, we can detect a relation, but it is a noisy one.

The predictive relation established for real returns holds for nominal returns, too. It also holds for the equity premium, i.e. the excess return the stock market provides over and above a short interest rate. Results are the same as for nominal and real stock returns. The equity premium drops when the term spread drops. The relationship is statistically significant, too. However, most of the variation in the equity premium remains unexplained by the term spread.

17.4.2 Other macroeconomic variables

The term spread is one of the more successful predictive variables out there. The term spread forecasts recessions, and the performance of stocks depends on the business cycle. When the term spread forecasts recessions and stock returns, one would expect other variables related to recessions to forecast returns. In turns out that this is true, i.e. those variables that forecast recessions also relate to future returns. Table 17.1 summarizes the information some of the variables examined in Chapter 15 contain about future returns.

The table presents the results from a number of regression analyses relating the different predictive variables (term spread, short rate, etc.) to nominal returns, real returns, and the equity premium one-by-one on a monthly basis. A regression, as explained, estimates the average relation between the explanatory variable and returns. For each regression, three numbers are reported in Table 17.1: The relation between the variables, the probability of no relation, and the explained fraction. The 'Relation' gives the size of the estimated relation. For instance, Table 17.1 shows that the estimated relation between the term spread and real returns next month is 0.3, as also mentioned above. When the term spread increases by one percentage point, next month's stock return on average goes up by 0.3% percentage points. The 'Prob. of no relation' is the probability that the estimated relation is zero, taking into account uncertainty surrounding the estimated relationship. Economists typically assume that when the probability of no relation is smaller than five percent, there is a robust relation. The probability that there is no relation between the term spread and real returns is 0.6%, as Table 17.1 shows. This is a very low probability. We reject the hypothesis that there is no relation. Or, in plain language, there is a statistically robust relation between the term spread this month

Table 17.1 Results from predictive regressions. Predictive relations between variables and S&P500 returns the next month. Samples run from the year mentioned under the heading of each variable (row 'From') to 2018

	Term spread	**Short rate**	**Lead. indi.**	**PMI**	**Confidence**	**Indu. Prod.**
From:	1952	1952	1959	1950	1978	1934
Nominal returns						
Relation	0.22	−0.04	0.08	0.00	0.00	0.01
Prob. of no relation	4.0%	26.8%	7.9%	6.8%	75.3%	89.8%
Explained fraction	0.5%	0.2%	0.4%	0.4%	0.0%	0.0%
Real returns						
Relation	0.30	−0.10	0.10	0.00	0.00	−0.03
Prob. of no relation	0.6%	1.5%	3.1%	4.9%	91.8%	68.3%
Explained fraction	1.0%	0.7%	0.7%	0.5%	0.0%	0.0%
Equity premium						
Relation	0.30	−0.13	0.03	0.00	0.00	0.02
Prob. of no relation	0.4%	0.1%	3.1%	12.3%	81.7%	78.1%
Explained fraction	1.0%	1.3%	0.7%	0.3%	0.0%	0.0%

and real returns next month. Finally, the 'Explained fraction' is the fraction of variation in returns captured by variation in the explanatory variable. This is also called the 'R^2' by economists. Variation in the term spread explains 1.0% of the monthly variation in real returns.

Main conclusions from Chapter 15 were that the term spread, the short interest rate, and the six-month change in the composite leading indicator signaled turning points in the business cycle. Table 17.1 reveals that these variables also relate systematically to future returns, particularly real returns and the equity premium. These variables also have the intuitive sign: when the indicators indicate that a recession is approaching—when the term spread decreases, the short rate increases, and the composite leading indicator decreases—next month's stock return is lower. This holds for nominal, real, and excess returns. The variables capture around 1% of movements in monthly stock returns ('Explained fraction' in Table 17.1). Most of the fluctuations in the stock market are unpredictable, but a small fraction is predictable.

Chapter 15 noted that the PMI and in particular consumer confidence were noisy indicators of recessions. The statistical evidence that these variables systematically relate to future returns is weak, too.[7] And, for the sake of it, Table 17.1

[7] In Møller, Nørholm, and Rangvid (2014), we explicitly examine whether consumer confidence and/or the business cycle (as measured by the output gap) predict stock returns. We find that consumer confidence and the output gap both predict returns. Consumer confidence and the output gap are highly correlated, though. Controlling for this correlation, we find that consumer confidence does

also looks at monthly changes in industrial production, in order to see whether economic activity in itself influences next month's returns. It does not. This is not strange. Industrial production is the business cycle, i.e. when the economy is in recession, stock are already declining. We are interested in variables that forecast returns. Growth in industrial production is not one of them.

17.5 Stock-market variables and future returns

When academics investigate return predictability, they typically look at variables such as those mentioned in Section 17.4, but they also look at variables derived from stocks themselves, such as the dividend yield, the earnings yield, etc. For the S&P500, earnings and dividends have been available on a quarterly basis since 1871, but can be interpolated to monthly figures. Table 17.2 reveals how these variables predict next month's return on the S&P500. The table shows for each regression, the estimated relation, the probability of no relation, and the explained fraction, as in Table 17.1.

Since 1945, both the earnings yield and the dividend yield have been significant predictors of returns. An increase in the dividends/earnings yield this month has historically been associated with higher returns next month, whether we look at nominal, real, or excess returns. It is intuitive that the relation is positive. As explained in Chapters 4 and 5, dividends/earnings are long-run drivers of stock prices, i.e. stock prices and dividends/earnings tend to follow each other in

Table 17.2 Using the dividend yield (dy) and the earnings yield (ey) to predict next month's return on the S&P500

	1871–2018		1871–1945		1946–2018	
	dy	ey	dy	ey	dy	ey
Nominal returns						
Relation	0.02	0.07	−0.05	0.05	0.23	0.11
Prob. of no relation	79.4%	6.4%	67.0%	51.5%	0.9%	1.5%
Explained fraction	0.0%	0.2%	0.0%	0.0%	0.8%	0.7%
Real returns						
Relation	0.08	0.03	0.05	−0.03	0.18	0.07
Prob. of no relation	20.3%	40.2%	66.8%	68.4%	5.0%	10.0%
Explained fraction	0.1%	0.0%	0.0%	0.0%	0.4%	0.3%

not contain independent information about future stock returns over and above information already contained by the business cycle. The business cycle (measured by the output gap) independently predicts returns, on the other hand.

the long run. We mentioned in Chapters 4 and 5 that stock prices mean-revert towards dividends/earnings. If stock prices this month are, e.g., low relative to dividends/earnings this month, i.e. the earnings/dividend yield is high, there is a tendency for stock prices to increase over time, such that stock prices return to the growth path of dividends/earnings. This means higher future returns. So, the dividend yield and the earnings yield predict returns with a positive sign. Like the macroeconomic variables, the fraction of stock return volatility captured by the earnings and dividend yield is low at the monthly frequency, around 1%.

Another interesting conclusion from Table 17.2 is the lack of forecasting power of the dividend/earnings yield before 1945. Before 1945, fluctuations in the dividend/earnings yield did not translate into return fluctuations ('Prob. of no relation' is higher than 5% prior to 1945). Something has to give when dividend yields move, though. Per construction, movements in dividend yield must reflect movements in either expected discount rates or expected growth in dividends. Campbell & Shiller (1988a, 1988b) first described this important insight, as mentioned in the previous chapter. When dividend yields and earnings yields do not predict returns before 1945, one would expect that they predict movements in dividend growth. Chen (2009) and Golez & Koudijs (2018) show that this is the case. Since 1945, however, dividend yields have predicted returns.

17.6 Short-run predictability accumulates

One conclusion until now is that the degree of predictability at the monthly horizon is statistically significant, but low, around one percent. One might wonder whether it is so small that it negligible. It is not. The reason is that if you can predict a little this month, a little next month, and a little the month after, it adds up. The small degree of predictability we see at the monthly frequency becomes economically relevant over time.

Consider using the dividend yield today to forecast real returns over the next month, next quarter, next half year, next year, the next three years, and the next six years. In order to investigate whether the dividend yield predicts returns over the next month, next quarter, etc., we correlate (run a regression) the dividend yield this month with returns next month, then we correlate the dividend yield this month with returns over the next three months, then correlate the dividend yield this month with returns over the next six months, etc. Table 17.3 shows the fractions of future return variation over different horizons captured by the dividend yield (the R^2).

Table 17.3 Forecasting real stock returns over longer horizons. Explained fractions shown. 1871–2018

1 month	0.3%
3 months	1.2%
6 months	2.8%
12 months	5.7%
36 months	24.0%
72 months	22.4%

Table 17.3 reveals that the dividend yield this month on average has captured around 0.3% of the variation in real return over the following month, as already mentioned. The relationship is statistically significant, i.e. historically there has been a non-random relation between the dividend yield this month and real returns next month, but the relation has been tiny. In fact, 99.7% of variation in returns next month has been caused by something else.

The effect is persistent, though. I.e., the effect from a change in the dividend yield this month continues, so to say, month after month. The predictive power builds up with the horizon. From Table 17.3, this appears as an increase in the fraction of future return variation that a change in the dividend yield this month predicts. For instance, a change in the dividend yield this month, has captured almost a quarter (22.4%) of the variation in returns over the following six years. It seems that the dividend yield contains a small degree of information about returns next month but more information about stock returns over the next several years.

Compare Figures 17.10 and 17.11. The relationship between dividend yields this month and returns over the next month is visualized in Figure 17.10. There seems to be a weak relation only. Figure 17.11 shows the relation between dividend yields today and returns over the next six years. Here, there clearly is a relation. When dividend yields are high today, returns over the next six years have typically been high, too. Of course, the relationship is not perfect, there is uncertainty, but there is a clear tendency that higher dividend yields today have been followed by higher real returns over the next six years.

It was Eugene Fama and Kenneth French who, in the late 1980s, first published results such as these, i.e. evidence that the predictive power seems to build up with the horizon. Financial economists were excited. It seems there is a lot of return predictability on the long horizon, even when it appears small on the short horizon. Today, some economists are sceptical whether returns can in fact

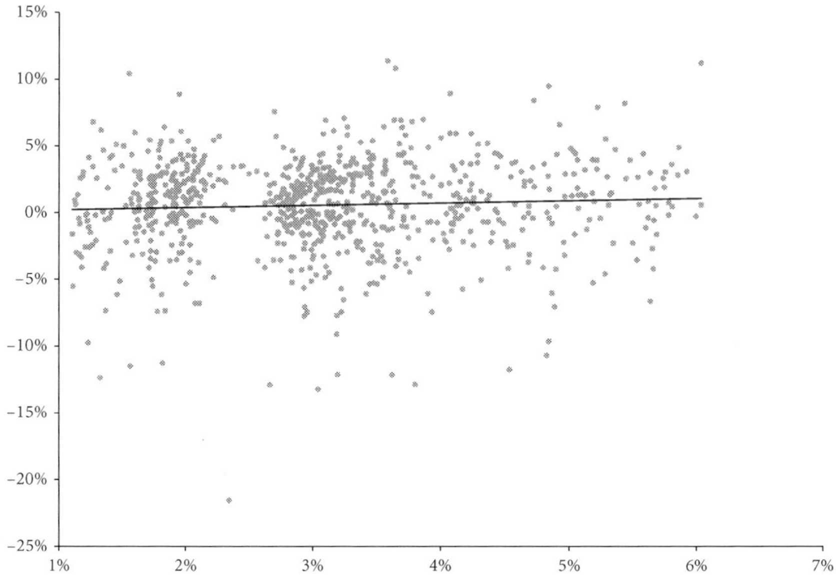

Figure 17.10 Dividend yield this month (horizontal axis) versus returns during the next month (vertical axis).

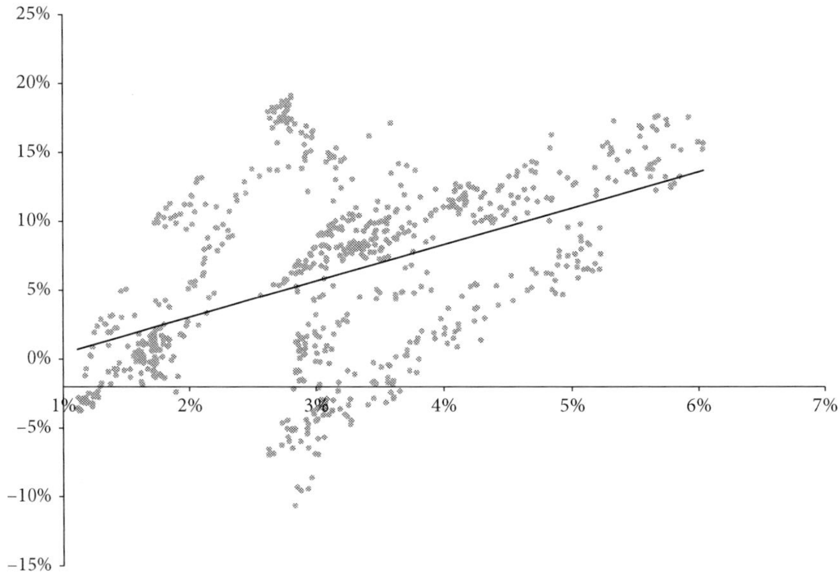

Figure 17.11 Dividend yield this month (horizontal axis) versus average annual returns during the next six years (vertical axis).

Data source: See Figure 3.1.

be better explained in the long run.[8] What is clear, though, is that we better visualize the relation between the dividend yield and future returns when we study long-horizon returns. And, this is important in itself. It gives us a better feeling for how important return predictability is. We conclude that long-horizon predictions illustrate the long-run economic importance of what looks like a miniscule fraction of returns that can be captured at the shorter (e.g., monthly) frequency. Or, in other words, even if there seems to be only little predictability at the short horizon, if one continues to exploit this month by month, it builds up and thereby becomes economically important.

17.7 Further topics

The upshot of the previous sections is that economic variables that relate to the business cycle contain information about future returns. This is useful information for investors. This section touches upon a number of aspects that investors should be aware of, too.

17.7.1 Many macroeconomic variables

Section 17.4 examines a handful of macroeconomic variables. There are many other macroeconomic variables out there. Probably to no big surprise, academics have studied a very large number of macroeconomic variables. These are variables such as the money supply, inflation, credit extension, all kinds of interest rates, exchange rates, housing starts, unemployment, employment, hours worked, the output gap, investment growth, consumption growth, export growth, etc. There are so many variables that it is difficult to keep track of them all. As a consequence, some economists have started combining variables into a few 'factors' that then

[8] The argument is technical, but basically goes as follows. Remember what we do here. We ask whether the dividend yield in, e.g., January 1952 can be used to explain returns from February 1952 through January 1958. We then go one month ahead and ask whether the dividend yield in February 1952 can be used to explain returns from March 1952 through February 1958. And so on. This means that 72 (= 6 times 12 months) of the return observations we use in the first prediction are overlapping with returns we forecast in the next prediction. And, when the dividend yield does not change much from month to month, which it does not, we create what economists call a spurious relation. In fact, from January 1952 through December 2017 (our sample period), there are 792 observations. But, when we use six-year returns (created from monthly observations), there are only 792/72 = 11 independent observations. The consequence is that it looks as if we get a better fit from the analysis relating six-year returns to dividend yields on a monthly basis, but statistically we might not. Researchers have come up with all sorts of statistical procedures that can be used to examine whether the statistical evidence for multi-period returns is superior to that of single-period returns. This is for statistical *feinsmeckers* and beyond the scope of this book. The conclusion from all this research is that predictability is sometimes stronger in the long run, but not always.

capture common movements in a high number of underlying variables (Ludvigson and Ng, 2009). Research into ways to combine and extract information from many macroeconomic variables is currently an active research area.

As Chapter 15 and Table 17.1 demonstrate, some variables are more useful than others in capturing the business cycle and hence returns. When analysing many variables, one runs the risk that one also includes variables that contain so much noise that it blurs the useful signals contained by more powerful variables. Researcher try to come up with clever ways to distinguish noise from signals in these large datasets. It is a fair conclusion that it is unclear how much value is really added by using a high number of variables that needs to be combined in complicated ways compared to keeping track of a few variables that then, on the other hand, are useful when it comes to their interpretation and what they contain. For most investors, it is more useful to pay attention to variables that have a robust relation to the business cycle instead of getting confused about the many other variables out there.

17.7.2 Can investors trade on this?

This chapter has shown that several variables contain information about future stock returns. The chapter has also shown that most of the variation in stock returns is caused by something else, i.e. predictability is present, but it is small on the short horizon. This makes one wonder whether investors can trade on this and increase their expected returns? Amit Goyal and Ivo Welsh published a now famous article on this issue in 2008. Their point is the following. When looking at the relation between a variable—say the term spread—and return, as in Table 15.2, then one can in 2018 see/estimate that historically there has been a tendency that when the term spread has gone up by one percentage point, returns have gone up by 0.3% next month. In 2018, we can estimated the average relation over the 1952–2018 period. But, in, e.g., 1970, an investor would not know that the best relation over the 1952–2018 period is 0.3. In 1970, an investor would probably look at the relation over the period 1952 to 1970 and use this as his/her best guess of the future relation. When estimating the relation between the term spread and next month returns from 1952 to 1970, this yields an estimate of 1.4. This is obviously very different from 0.3. In other words, one thing is that we know the best relation in the past, but will this also be the best relation in the future? And, if not, do we gain anything from using these past relations when predicting future returns?

Goyal & Welsh investigated variables such as those investigated here, i.e. the short interest rate, the dividend yield, etc. to see how investors would have performed in real time. Goyal & Welsh concluded that variables shown to predict returns over historical samples fail to generate significant 'out-of-sample' significance, i.e. would not have helped the investor in real time. This was a rather shocking result. It implied that estimation uncertainty is so large that historical relations do not really help investors in the real world.

Since the Goyal-Welsh results, a number of researchers have reexamined this. It turns out that the Goyal-Welsh result was probably too pessimistic. Using other variables than Goyal-Welsh, different techniques, different settings, etc. many researchers have shown that returns do in fact contain a predictable component that can be used in real time, see for instance Campbell & Thompson (2008), Ferreira & Santa-Clara (2011), Møller & Rangvid (2015, 2018) and others. Rapach & Zhou (2013) survey the literature.

17.7.3 International evidence

Many of the variables shown to predict returns in the US also predict returns in other countries. Rangvid et al. (2005) conducted a large international study of what macroeconomic variables predict returns around the world and concluded that interest-rate related variables contain information about future returns around the world. Rangvid et al. (2005) also consider the Goyal & Welsh critique, i.e. Rangvid et al. (2005) analyse out-of-sample predictions, too, showing that return predictability by interest-rate related variables is present also for real-time investors in many countries. Many of the academic articles on return predictability presented in recent years typically investigate non-US data, too, and conclude that stock returns are predictable by variables related to future business-cycle conditions also outside the US, see, e.g., Cooper & Priestley (2009, 2013), Møller & Rangvid (2018), and others.

17.8 Checklist

This chapter has demonstrated that:

- Daily stock returns move around in ways that are for most practical purposes unpredictable. There is so much noise in daily stock returns that it is difficult to identify systematic patterns. If we really scrutinize the data, we might be able to tease out a tiny degree of predictability, but most investors are better off not trying to predict movements in stock returns from one day to the next.
- With monthly returns, it becomes possible to see systematic patterns.
- Macroeconomic variables that contain information about business-cycle turning points also contain information about future returns. For instance, the term spread tends to decrease when a recession is approaching, as shown

in Chapter 15. As a consequence, a decrease in the term spread is associated with a drop in stock returns over the following month. Or, to put it more directly, the term spread forecasts stock returns.

- The term spread, the short interest rate, the composite leading indicator, etc., i.e. variables that forecast recessions, forecast stock returns. The academic literature has confirmed these insights for many countries, for nominal, real, and excess returns, for short- and long-horizon returns, etc.
- It is important to know that some macroeconomic variables forecast stock returns, but it is also important to be humble and realistic. The degree of predictability is low on the short horizon. Typically, on a monthly basis, the explanatory power is around 1%–2%. This means that around 99% of fluctuations in stock returns are unpredictable.
- The fact that it is difficult to predict stock returns, and that one should be humble, does not mean that it is impossible and that we should not try. The point of this chapter is that investors who are willing to behave differently from the rest of us and take on risk when others are scaling back, such as when a recession is approaching, can potentially improve their relative performance by timing the market.
- The degree of predictability is low on the short run, but if you can predict a little this month, a little next month, and a little the month after, it all adds up. The next chapter studies return predictability at longer horizons.

18
Predicting long-horizon returns

The previous chapter explained how variables that contain information about the future business cycle also tell us something—not a lot, but something—about stock returns over shorter horizons, such as a month, quarter, or a year or two.

This chapter deals with expectations for stock returns over longer horizons, e.g. over the next decade. The approach will be different from the approach in the previous chapter. The previous chapter linked expected stock returns to the business cycle. Whether a recession is approaching or not matters a lot for stocks on the short and medium horizon. This chapter looks at longer horizons. Here, business-cycle fluctuations matter relatively less, as longer horizons typically span at least one, potential several, business cycles.

The chapter starts out providing an overview of how academics analyse the long-run outlook for stocks. It then turns to the empirical evidence. It also presents a specific approach one can use to gauge the outlook for stocks in the long run.

Academics and investment houses typically model returns over the next decade when dealing with 'the long run'. This chapter does the same. There is nothing special about a decade. We could equally well have looked at the next seven years or the next thirteen years, and conclusions would be practically the same. The point is that we in this chapter look beyond a month or a year, and we do not look at 20, 30, or 50 years. Ten years is a natural candidate—easy to focus on. In the next chapter, we discuss very long-term outlooks, such as multiple decades.

18.1 How to back out expected long-horizon returns?

Chapter 4 decomposed stock returns into their underlying drivers. The chapter showed that stock returns are given by the sum of three components:

$$\begin{gathered}\text{Stock returns}\\=\\\text{The dividend yield}\\+\\\text{Growth in fundamentals}\\+\\\text{Growth in the stock-price multiple.}\end{gathered}$$

From Main Street to Wall Street. Jesper Rangvid, Oxford University Press (2021). © Jesper Rangvid.
DOI: 10.1093/oso/9780198866404.003.0018

Dividend yield is dividends paid out during the investment period in relation to the price paid for the stock at the beginning of the investment period. The 'fundamental' can be any variable that stock prices are expected to mean-revert towards, such as earnings, dividends, GDP, or similar. The stock-price multiple is the ratio of stock prices to the fundamental, such as the stock price-earnings multiple, stock price-dividend multiple, etc.

Recognizing that the sum of the dividend yield, growth in fundamentals, and growth in the stock-price multiple defines stock returns provides a consistent way to understand the drivers of stock returns. Consequently, it also provides a consistent way to forecast returns: to forecast stock returns, one has to forecast the dividend yield, growth in fundamentals, and growth in the stock-price multiple. As an example, if the dividend yield is 2% per year, growth in dividends per share also 2% per year, and stock market valuations are at neutral levels, so that no changes in stock-price multiples are expected, expected future annual returns are 2% + 2% + 0% = 4%. Similarly, a pessimistic investor who believes that the stock price-dividend multiple is high and market valuations consequently have to come down by, say, 4% per year, will expect a return of 0% per annum over the investment horizon, if the dividend yield and dividend growth rate are both expected to be 2% (2% + 2% − 4% = 0%).

But how should we come up with forecasts of growth rates? And how should we judge whether multiples are likely to expand or contract over the coming decade? The procedures used in the academic literature can be classified into the following forecasting approaches:

- Forecast stock returns based on the dividend yield.
- Forecast stock returns based on the dividend yield and growth in fundamentals.
- Forecast stock returns based on the dividend yield, growth in fundamentals, and growth in stock-price multiples, i.e. all three components.

18.1.1 Dividend yield and other valuation ratios

A large academic literature, starting with Fama & French (1988), who even refer back to Dow (1920), uses the dividend yield on its own to forecast stock returns. Instead of looking at all three drivers of returns (dividend yield, growth in fundamentals, and growth in stock-price multiples), Fama & French (1988) focused on the dividend yield only.[1] The initial reaction to the study of Fama & French

[1] Fama & French (1988) wrote: 'The hypothesis that D/P forecasts returns has a long tradition among practitioners and academics [for example, Dow (1920) and Ball (1978)]. The intuition of the 'efficient

(1988) was that it provided strong evidence in favour of long-horizon return predictability by the dividend-yield, as also discussed in the previous chapter. Subsequent research has reexamined this interpretation. For instance, dividends might be smoothed, or firms might return profits to shareholders via buy-backs instead of outright dividends. These corporate decisions could cause the dividend yield to send imprecise signals about future returns (Straehl & Ibbotson, 2017). As an alternative to the dividend yield, researchers have looked at other stock-price valuation ratios when forecasting the return on a broad portfolio, such as the share-price to GDP ratio (Rangvid, 2006), the share-price to consumption ratio (Menzly, Santos & Veronesi, 2004), the consumption-asset wealth ratio (Lettau & Ludvigson, 2001), etc. Still, the dividend yield plays an important role in the academic literature, not least due to the fact that the dynamic Gordon-model directly links the dividend yield to expected returns, as mentioned in Chapter 17.

In addition to the dividend yield, another valuation ratio plays a particularly prominent role when it comes to predicting long-term real stock returns: the Cyclical-Adjusted Price-Earnings (CAPE) ratio of Shiller (Campbell & Shiller, 1988a). This is the current share price divided by the average of earnings over the last ten years. There is a good reason why CAPE has played a prominent role when forecasting real returns. By themselves, earnings yields should proxy for expected real returns on stocks, as Siegel (2014) and Pedersen (2015) show.

18.1.2 Dividend yield and growth in fundamentals

Fama & French (2002), Arnott & Bernstein (2002), Ferreira & Santa-Clara (2011), and Asness & Ilmanen (2012) forecast returns by combining current dividend yields with expectations for growth in dividends or earnings. But how to estimate these growth rates? When forecasting returns over long periods—such as ten years—some researchers simply assume a growth rate, say 1.5% per year (Asness & Ilmanen, 2012). An often-used alternative is to forecast growth rates by a rolling window of historical growth rates of dividends per share or earnings per share, i.e. use the historical growth rate as an estimate of future growth in fundamentals. For instance, if the average growth rate of dividends has been 2% per year during the last, e.g., 20 years, expect dividends to grow by 2% per year over the next ten years. Bogle (1991a, 1991b) uses a 30-year moving average to forecast growth, Ferreira & Santa-Clara (2011) a 20-year moving average, while Bogle & Nolan

markets' version of the hypothesis is that stock prices are low relative to dividends when discount rates and expected returns are high, and vice versa, so that D/P varies with expected returns.' Campbell & Shiller (1988b) formally showed why the dividend yield contains information about expected returns and growth rates of dividends, as discussed in Chapter 17.

(2015) use a 10-year moving average. As an alternative to growth in earnings or dividends, some researchers use GDP growth when predicting returns on the aggregate market portfolio. Grinold & Kroner (2002), for example, estimate growth in fundamentals based on an assumed long-run relation between GDP and dividends/earnings, such that growth in dividends/earnings per share is estimated by growth in GDP.

We know that the decomposition of stock returns says that stock returns consist of three components. When basing stock-return predictions on the dividend yield and growth in a fundamental only, one a priori assumes zero expected change in future stock-price multiples. For instance, Arnott & Bernstein (2002), Ferreira & Santa-Clara (2011), and Asness & Ilmanen (2012) recognize that one should in principle include expected stock-price multiple changes in a return decomposition/-prediction, but they argue that rational investors should not expect changes in valuations, as valuations cannot grow or fall indefinitely. For this reason, they a priori disregard expectations of changes in stock-price multiples when forecasting returns.

18.1.3 Dividend-yields, growth in fundamentals, and changes in stock-price multiples

Valuation changes matter, as we saw in Chapter 4. For instance, if stocks currently trade at a high valuation, a forecaster might expect the stock-price multiple to contract, dragging down returns. And, vice versa for low stock-price valuations. Shiller's famous CAPE is built around this idea. Shiller expects stocks to perform poorly when CAPE is high.

There is a tension here. On the one hand, some researchers (e.g., Arnott & Bernstein, 2002; Ferreira & Santa-Clara, 2011; and Asness & Ilmanen, 2012) a priori rule out expectations of changes in stock-price multiples, as just mentioned. On the other hand, others (e.g., Shiller) mainly base their stock-market expectations on implied changes in stock-price multiples. Chapter 4 showed that stock-price multiples tend to revert slowly towards their means. Over very long periods, several decades, valuation changes cancel out. Chapter 4 also showed, however, that over ten-year periods, valuation changes account for a large fraction of movements in stock returns. This book believes that it adds to the predictive power when including expected mean-reversion in stock-price multiples when forecasting ten-year returns.[2] But how to forecast changes in stock-price multiples? Chapter 4 showed that valuation ratios are mean-reverting. Based on this, e.g.,

[2] This contrasts to forecasting over the very long run, such as several decades, as expected valuation growth is negligible over the very long run, as the next chapter explains. Basically, the forecasting horizon matters. Over the short run, the business cycle is important (previous chapter). Over a decade

Bogle (1991a, 1991b) and Bogle & Nolan (2015) assume that the value of the price-earnings ratio at the end of their ten-year forecast horizon equals its historical average of the preceding three decades. I.e., if the stock price-earnings multiple today is 10% higher than its historical average, expect it to come down with 1% per year over the next years ten years. So, if the annual dividend yield is 2%, annual growth also 2% per annum, but valuation change subtracts 1% per year, expected annual returns are 3%.

18.2 CAPE

Different researchers/practitioners use different approaches, as explained in the previous section. This section illustrates some of the different approaches and what they imply when it comes to forecasting US long-horizon returns.

18.2.1 CAPE and dividend yield

Among academics, the most widely used variable to predict stock returns is probably the dividend yield. Among practitioners, the dividend yield is used as well, but the CAPE ratio of Robert Shiller is probably even more famous. The dividend yield and CAPE rely on the same underlying ideas, even when there are some important differences. Let us review what CAPE is, see how it can be used to say something about expected returns, and finally how it compares to the dividend yield.

CAPE is the 'Cyclically-adjusted price-earnings ratio'. Start with the 'price-earnings' part. CAPE takes the share price and relates it to earnings-per-share. Shiller constructs it as follows. At the annual frequency, he takes the value of the S&P500 at the beginning of the year, specifically the average of daily closing prices of the S&P500 in January. He relates this to earnings per share during the preceding year. For instance, in January 2019, the S&P500 stood at 2607.4. Earnings per share for companies in the S&P500 throughout 2018, i.e. the year before, were 132.4. The price-earnings ratio was 2607.4/132.4 = 19.7. In January 2019, you had to pay app. 20 times earnings for the S&P500. Now take the 'Cyclically-adjusted' part. Shiller observed that earnings are volatile over the business cycle. A large one-year drop in earnings can cause the price-earnings ratio to jump about wildly. For instance, earnings dropped dramatically during 2008, as we return to below. Shiller wants to get an overall feeling for the valuation of the stock market. He does not want it to be impacted too much by short-term sudden movements in earnings. He thus smooths out cyclical fluctuations in earnings. Based on his 1988

or so (this chapter), valuation growth is important. Over the very long run (next chapter), economic growth is key.

academic paper with coauthor John Campbell that concluded that 'a long moving average of real earnings helps to forecast future real dividends', Shiller proposes to scale current stock prices by average earnings over the past ten years, adjusted for inflation. So, the cyclical-adjusted price-earnings ratio, CAPE, takes the current real stock price and scales it by the average of real earnings per share over the last ten years. As an illustration, in January 2019, the average of the last ten years of earnings (measured in January 2019 prices, i.e. in real terms) was 91.9. In January 2019, CAPE thus stood at 2607.4/91.9 = 28.4. In January 2019, cyclically adjusting earnings increases the valuation of the S&P500 by app. 50%, from 19.7 to 28.4.

Shiller points out that CAPE is mean-reverting, i.e. has a tendency to come down from high levels, and up from low. Figure 18.1 shows CAPE from 1881 through 2019 together with its average.[3] Average CAPE is around 17, i.e. on average over the last app. 150 years, investors have paid USD 17 for one USD 1 of earnings. CAPE has a tendency, perhaps particularly pronounced before the turn of the millennium, to fluctuate around this mean. Sometimes CAPE is above its mean, then it comes down. Sometimes below, then it comes up. Mean-reversion means that CAPE tells us something about the future direction of the stock market. When CAPE is high, expect stocks to come down, i.e. expect low returns. Shiller used this insight to famously call the burst of the dot-com bubble at the turn of the millennium (Shiller, 2000). Since the turn of the millennium, however, CAPE has been elevated, only briefly coming down in 2008–2009 during the financial crisis. This has fuelled discussion whether the natural long-run level of CAPE has increased. We return to this discussion below.

There is another way of looking at the implication of CAPE. Say CAPE is 20, i.e. investors are willing to pay USD 20 for earnings of USD 1 per share. This means that the earnings yield—earnings as a percentage of price—is 1/20 = 5%. As already mentioned, under certain conditions, the earnings yield is itself a measure of the expected real return on stocks (Siegel, 2014 and Pedersen, 2015). This means that the earnings yield can be used as an estimator of expected real stock returns. Usually, it is viewed as an estimator of the stable return from stocks, i.e. a long-horizon return. Figure 18.2 shows CAPE expressed as a yield together with average (geometric) annual real return over future ten-year periods.[4] Using the very first observation in the figure to explain, the interpretation of the figure is as follows: At the start of 1891, CAPE predicted an average annual return over the next decade of 6.2%, the first point of the 'CAPE as a yield' series to the left in the graph. The realized annualized real return over the ten-year period 1891–1901 turned out to

[3] The figure starts in 1881 because we use the first ten years, from 1871 to 1881, to calculate cyclically-adjusted earnings.

[4] To be precise, the figure shows log real returns and the log of the earnings yield, i.e. CAPE as a yield is calculated as $\ln(1 + 1/20) = 4.9\%$ when CAPE itself is 20.

Figure 18.1 CAPE.
Data source: See Figure 3.1.

be 8.1%, the first point of the '10y return' series to the left in the graph. And so on, year by year.

Figure 18.2 leaves the impression that CAPE captures the underlying slow-moving patterns in realized returns to some extent. When CAPE is trending upwards, such as during the early 20th century, the 1940s, the 1970s, and in the beginning of the 2000s, subsequent realized returns also trend upwards, and vice versa when CAPE is trending downwards, such as during the 1920s, 1950s, and 1980s and 1990s. At the same time, realized returns are more volatile than CAPE, i.e. there are some clear outliers, such as the period during the first world war and the 1960s, as well as the decade after 1999.

The decade after 1999 included both the burst of the dot-com bubble at the turn of the millennium and the 2008 financial crisis. On average, every year from 1999 through 2008, stocks returned a negative 5% per year on average, after inflation. This was the worst decade historically, as Figure 18.2 also shows. CAPE did not predict the magnitude of the fall in the stock market, but it did predict low returns. In 1999, CAPE predicted the lowest return ever. CAPE, thus, did well in the sense that it predicted historically low returns in 1999, but it did not fully capture the magnitude of the combined effect on subsequent returns from the burst of the dot-com bubble and the financial crisis.

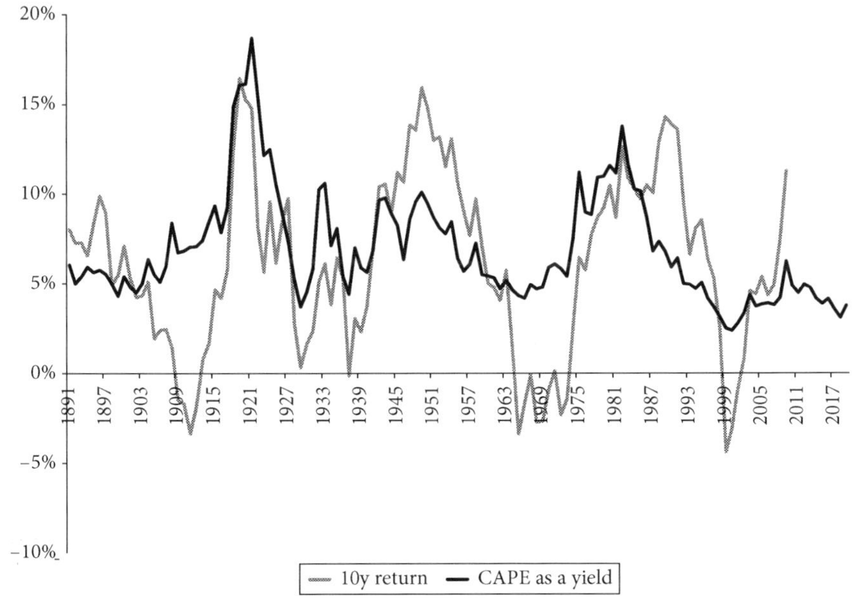

Figure 18.2 CAPE expressed as an earnings yield together with average annual real returns during subsequent decades.
Data source: See Figure 3.1.

Since the financial crisis, there has been discussion whether CAPE has become 'too elevated', and whether CAPE as a result predicts too low returns. Siegel (2016) argues that reported S&P500 earnings are 'too low', pushing up the CAPE 'too much', and thereby causing expected returns based on CAPE to be 'too low'. The reason, Siegel argues, has its roots in changes to accounting practices since 1990 that cause earnings to be lower during downturns than has been the historical norm. If so, the fall in earnings during the financial crisis of 2008–2009 has pushed up CAPE more than it should, compared to earlier otherwise similar experiences. Siegel (2016) finds that, as of January 2015, expected real returns from the S&P500 are 2.8% per year over the next decade based on CAPE but 5.3% when based on earnings from the National Income and Products Account (NIPA).

18.2.2 Dividend yield

The dividend yield has a special role in academic studies of return predictability, as mentioned. The dividend yield is not, however, a direct measure of expected

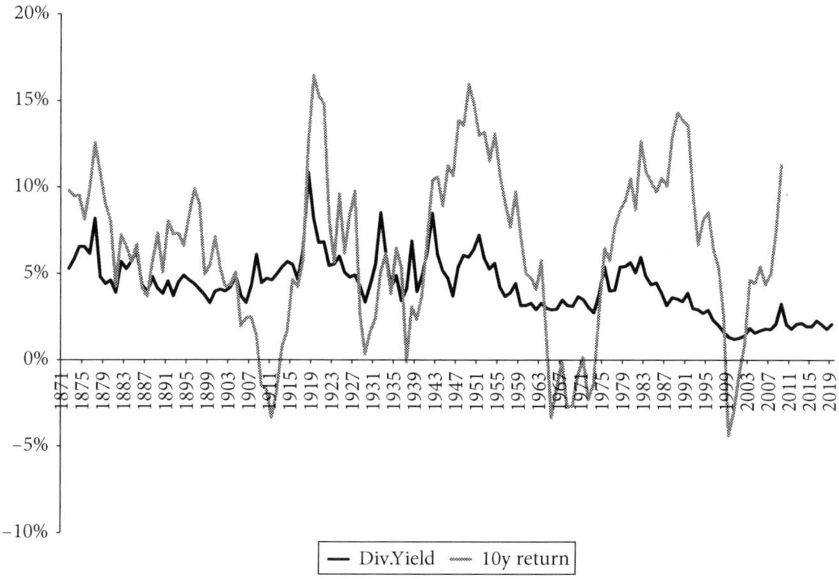

Figure 18.3 Dividend yield and average annual real returns during subsequent decades.

Data source: See Figure 3.1.

real returns, like the earnings yield. The dividend yield is only part of returns. Our stock-return decomposition tells us that returns are the sum of the dividend yield, growth, and multiple changes. This means that if the dividend yield increases by one percent, our best guess is not necessarily that expected returns increase by one percent, as expected returns also depend on expectations of economic growth and price-multiples. In other words, when relating the dividend yield to real returns, we need an estimate of how much expected real returns move when dividend yields move.

Figure 18.3 plots the dividend yield together with future ten-year real returns. The graph can be directly compared to Figure 18.2 that showed CAPE together with future ten-year real returns. The fit in Figure 18.2 is better. CAPE captures long-run returns better than the dividend yield.

CAPE and the dividend yield are correlated, though, as Figure 18.4 reveals and Chapter 4 discussed. When CAPE increases, there is a tendency for the dividend yield to increase as well, and vice versa. The dividend yield is generally lower than the earnings yield, though, and thus generally lower than average real returns, in particular since the 1960s or so. CAPE is also somewhat more volatile than the dividend yield. For these reasons, CAPE lines up somewhat better with future long-horizon real returns than does the dividend yield.

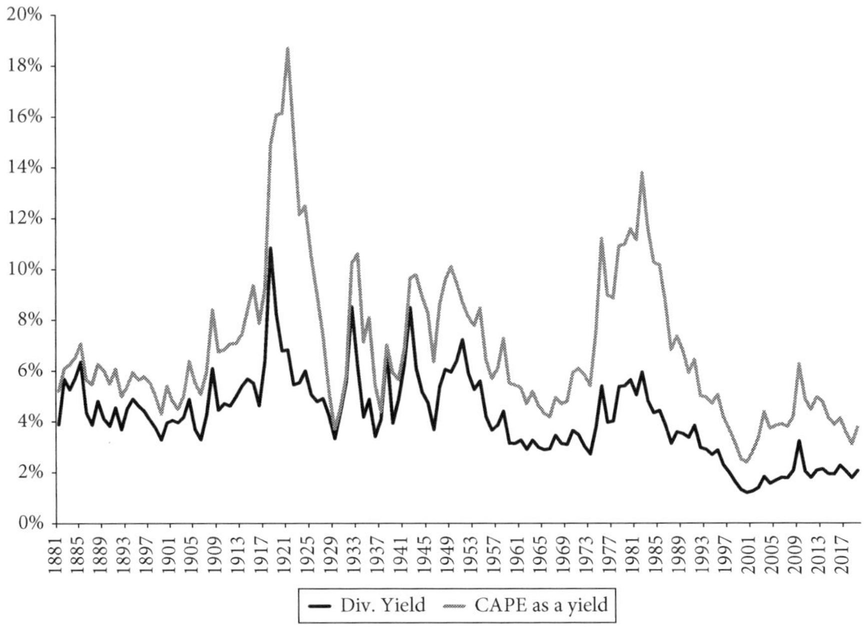

Figure 18.4 Dividend yield and CAPE.
Data source: See Figure 3.1.

18.3 Sum of the parts

Returns are the sum of the dividend yield, growth in a fundamental, and the change in the stock-price-to-fundamental multiple. Another way to forecast returns, thus, is to rely on forecasts of the dividend yield, growth, and multiple change, and then sum these to get an estimate for expected returns. This is the 'sum of the parts' approach.[5] This procedure is often used by practitioners. Box 18.1 contains examples.

When using the sum-of-the-parts approach, one has to come up with estimates of the dividend yield, growth, and change in valuation/stock-price multiple. There are several ways to do this. You need to decide upon the fundamental to use, and you have to determine the method used for forecasting expected growth in this fundamental. Similarly, you have to choose your method for forecasting the

[5] As mentioned, some researchers exclude the change in valuation ratios a priori and look at dividend yield plus growth. In the next chapter, we return to this assumption.

Box 18.1. Examples of practitioners' long-term equity forecasts

J.P. Morgan Asset Management in their 'Long-term capital market assumptions for 2019' expects US large-cap equities to return 3.25% per year (in real terms) over the next decade, based on the following sum-of-the-part calculation:[a]

$$3.25\% \approx \underbrace{2.0\%}_{\text{Dividend yield}} + \underbrace{2.5\%}_{\text{Earnings growth}} - \underbrace{1.4\%}_{\text{Change in price-earnings multiple}}$$

Mercer in their 'Capital market outlook for 2019' expect US large cap equities to return 4.4% per year (in real terms) over the next decade, based on the following sum-of-the-part calculation:[b]

$$4.4\% \approx \underbrace{2.5\%}_{\text{Dividend yield}} + \underbrace{2.3\%}_{\text{GDP growth}} - \underbrace{0.4\%}_{\text{Change in price-GDP multiple}}$$

Notice that JPM uses growth in earnings per share whereas Mercer uses growth in GDP. Consequently, J.P. Morgan uses the expected change in the price-earnings multiple whereas Mercer uses the expected change in the price-GDP multiple. Mercer uses growth in GDP, as they believe that 'growth in earnings per share (EPS) for US equities is strongly related to GDP growth'.

[a] J.P. Morgan rounds off to the nearest quarter percentage point, in this case 3.25%.

[b] J.P. Morgan and Mercer present expectations for nominal returns. In the calculations here, a two percent rate of inflation is assumed to calculate real growth, and hence real returns.

expected change in the stock-price multiple. There is no single 'correct' choice here. But given the choice of fundamental, you implicitly define your choice of stock-price multiple, as Chapter 4 showed. If you decide to look at earnings growth, you should estimate the change in the stock-price to earnings ratio. If you decide to look at GDP growth, you should estimate the change in the stock-price to GDP ratio. Etc.

18.4 An example of how to forecast stock returns

This book has shown that GDP is a long-run attractor of earnings and dividends. We now illustrate how one can use the 'sum-of-the-parts' approach to forecast stock returns, using GDP as the fundamental. Rangvid (2017) provides a more detailed description of this way of forecasting ten-year returns.

When looking at GDP growth, the relevant valuation ratio is the stock-price to GDP ratio. Using the 'sum-of-the-parts' approach, we need estimates of the dividend yield, GDP growth, and changes in the stock-price to GDP ratio.

Dividend yield: The dividend yield is persistent, as Chapter 4 showed. A reasonable estimate of the dividend yield during the next decade is the current level of the dividend yield.

Growth: As mentioned in Section 18.1, typically expected growth is measured by the historical average. One could, for instance, use average annual growth in GDP over the preceding two decades as a forecast of the average annual growth in GDP over the coming decade.

Valuation change: Chapter 4 showed that stock-price multiples revert to their mean. With a ten-year forecast horizon, it seems natural to expect the stock-price multiple to revert from its current value to its historical mean over the next 10 years. The historical mean is calculated as the mean during the past 20 years.[6]

Box 18.2 shows how to calculate expected returns.

Box 18.2. Calculating expected returns

Imagine that a researcher in January 2019 is asked to calculate expected average annual real log-return over the next decade. He/she could do as follows:

- In January 2019, the SP500 stood at 2,607.4. Dividends per share during 2018 were 53.8, so the log dividend yield is $\ln\left(1 + \frac{53.8}{2{,}580}\right) = 2.1\%$.
- Real GDP (log) growth averaged 2.2% per year over the last twenty years.
- In January 2019, the stock price-GDP multiple was 19% above its average over the last 20 years. Changes in the stock price-GDP multiple over the next ten years reduce expected returns by $[\ln(1 - 0.19)]\,/10 = -2.1\%$ per year.

Expected average annual real stock returns over the next ten years is:

$$2.2\% = \underbrace{2.1\%}_{\text{Dividend yield}} + \underbrace{2.2\%}_{\text{GDP growth}} - \underbrace{2.1\%}_{\text{Change in price-GDP multiple}}$$

[6] Earnings and dividends are measured 'per share', and are thus directly related to the index of share prices. GDP measures aggregate activity in the economy. Hence, the basis of earnings/dividends and GDP is different. This is not a problem here, as we are interested in time-series fluctuations of the ratios of stock prices to dividends, earnings, and GDP. In other words, if stock prices and GDP mean-revert towards each other, the stock price-GDP ratio will be mean reverting, even if stock prices and GDP are measured on a different basis. For more on this, see Rangvid (2006).

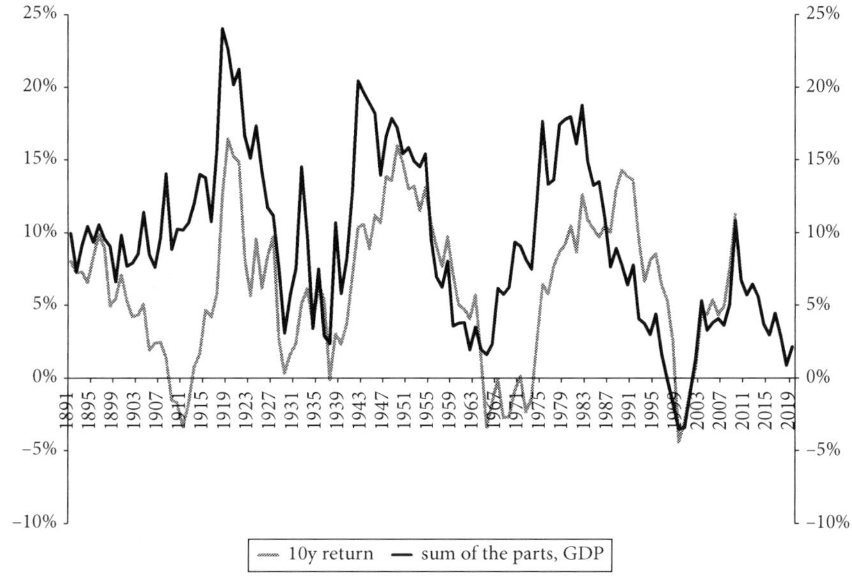

Figure 18.5 Sum of the parts (dividend yield + GDP growth + change in stock-price to GDP multiple) together with real returns during the following decade.
Data source: See Figures 2.1 and 3.1.

We can calculate expected real return every year using this procedure. The result is plotted in Figure 18.5 together with realized ten-year returns. This way of forecasting ten-year real returns has done a good job historically.

18.4.1 Growth in fundamentals

As mentioned, the sum of the parts approach is much used among practitioners. Differences between forecasters arise when it comes to the specific ways of calculating the individual parts of the sum. For instance, what measure of growth should be used? How should one estimate mean-reversion in valuation ratios? To illustrate the playing field, it might be useful to discuss a couple of alternatives to the procedure outlined in this section.

In the example in Section 18.4, GDP growth is estimated to be 2.2% per year over the next decade. One could use historical growth in real dividends or earnings as an alternative to real GDP growth. From 1998 to 2018, the twenty years preceding 2019, earnings grew faster than GDP (2.9% per year versus 2.2%). The estimate for expected returns would thus increase by 0.7%-points (= 2.9% − 2.2%) if using historical growth in real earnings instead of real GDP.

One could also look at other estimates for GDP growth. For instance, one could look at long-run projections from the OECD. OECD (2016) expects US real GDP to grow by 2.7% per year on average during the 2016–2025 period. The Congressional Budget Office (2016) is a little more pessimistic with real GDP expected to grow by 2% per annum from 2016–2026. So, there is room for interpretation. Forecasting is not an exact science.

18.4.2 Mean-reversion in stock-price multiples

In January 2019, reversion of the stock price-GDP multiple to its past 20-years average subtracts 2.1% from expected returns per year. Two alternative price-multiples immediately come to mind; the price-dividend multiple and CAPE. Remember from the decomposition of stock returns in Chapter 4 that if one uses the stock price-earnings multiple, one should calculate expected returns as the sum of the dividend yield, earnings growth, and growth in the stock price-earnings ratio.

Earnings growth, as mentioned, has been 2.9% per year. In 2019, CAPE is 20% above its historical average. Mean reversion of CAPE would thus subtract 2.0% from expected returns per year. Expected returns using the sum-of-the-parts approach, with earnings and CAPE instead of GDP and the stock price-GDP ratio, would imply that expected returns are:

$$3\% = \underbrace{2.1\%}_{\text{Dividend yield}} + \underbrace{2.9\%}_{\text{Earnings growth}} - \underbrace{2.0\%}_{\text{Change in CAPE}}$$

per year on average over the subsequent decade.

These small calculations illustrate why analysts disagree on the outlook for the stock market. If one relies on GDP as the fundamental, one (in 2018) expects stocks to return 2.2% per year on average over the next ten years in real terms. If one relies on earnings and CAPE, the forecast for annual real stock returns is 3%. Different analysts can have different views on the outlook for stocks. Table 18.1 collects the different forecasts for average annual real returns from US large-cap equities, as of 2019, presented in this section.

18.4.3 Combining CAPE and 'sum of the parts'

Figure 18.2 shows expected average annual real returns over the next ten years, as of every individual year, based on CAPE expressed as a yield together with realized real returns over the next ten year. Figure 18.5 does the same, but using

Table 18.1 Different procedures to forecast US real equity returns. Average annual real return over the next decade as of 2019

	Expected return	Building blocks		
		Dividend yield	Growth	Valuation change
J.P. Morgan	3.3%	2.0%	2.5%	−1.4%
Mercer	4.4%	2.5%	2.3%	−0.4%
SoP, GDP	2.2%	2.1%	2.2%	−2.1%
SoP, earnings	3.0%	2.1%	2.9%	−2.0%

the 'sum-of-the-parts', based on GDP. Comparing Figures 18.2 and 18.5, it appears that both predictors capture many of the overall movements in realized ten-years ahead returns: The increase in returns during the 1910s, the drops during the 1950s and 1960s, the increases during the 1970s, and the drops during the 1990s. There are, however, also some important differences. First, the 'sum of the parts, GDP' is more volatile than 'CAPE as a yield'. This means that there are some spikes and troughs that the 'sum-of-the-parts' captures but 'CAPE as a yield' does not. For instance, the drop in returns during the 1950s is better captured by the 'sum-of-the-parts, GDP'. Similarly, the 'sum-of-the-parts, GDP' more or less captures spot-on the low returns going forward from 1999. On the other hand, there are some volatile spikes in the 'sum-of-the-parts, GDP', such as the 15% annualized return predicted in 1932; stocks returned 'only' 5% per annum during 1932–1942. For reasons such as these, some analysts argue that it might improve forecasts if combining different procedures, see, for instance, Rapach, Strauss & Zhou (2010) and Asness & Ilmanen (2012). The idea is that by combining forecasts, some of the idiosyncrasies of individual forecasts would be averaged out. A simple way to combine forecasts would be to take the average of the different individual forecasts. In this case, to illustrate, the average of 'CAPE as a yield' and the 'sum-of-the-parts, GDP'. The result is presented in Figure 18.6. It turns out that this generates slightly better predictions than if using the individual predictors on their own. In 2019, this predicts an expected average annual real stock return of 3% per year over the next ten years.

Figure 18.7 presents an alternative way of illustrating the strong predictive power of the average of 'CAPE as a yield' and the 'sum of the parts, GDP'. The figure shows the average annual realized real return over subsequent decades for those years when the predictive variable (the average of 'CAPE as a yield' and the 'sum-of-the-parts, GDP') was lower than 5%, when it was between 5% and 10%, between 10% and 15%, and when it was above 15%. The figure is constructed as follows. First, collect years when future returns were expected to be low, defined as those years when the predictive variable predicted lower returns than 5%. For instance,

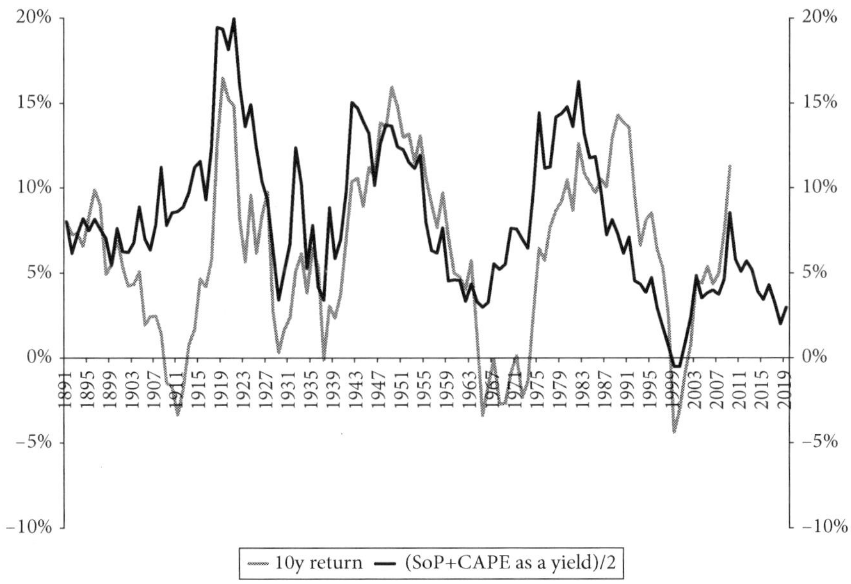

Figure 18.6 Average of CAPE expressed as a yield ('CAPE as a yield') and the 'sum of the parts' (dividend yield + GDP growth + change in stock-price to GDP multiple), called SoP, together with average annual real returns during the following decade.
Data source: See Figures 2.1 and 3.1.

in year 2000, the average of 'CAPE as a yield' and the 'sum-of-the-parts, GDP' predicted an average annual real return over the subsequent decade of −0.5%, in 1999 it predicted 0.5%, in 1965 it predicted 3%, and so on. Then, for each of these years, collect the average annual *realized* return over the respective subsequent ten-year periods. E.g., from 2000 to 2010, the average annual realized return turned out to be −3.1%. From 1999–2009, it was −4.4%. From 1965–1975, it turned out to be −3.4%. Etc. Finally, take the average of these realized average returns.

Figure 18.7 sends a clear message. Following years when the predictive variable (the average of 'CAPE as a yield' and the 'sum-of-the-parts, GDP') was low, subsequent realized returns have been low, too. When high returns were predicted, subsequent realized returns turned out to be high. For instance, the average annual realized return over ten-year periods following years when returns were predicted to be lower than 5% is 3.6%. On the other hand, in those years when returns were predicted to be high, above 15%, returns subsequently turned out to be high, at 13%. The conclusion is that the average of 'CAPE as a yield' and the 'sum of the parts, GDP' has predicted returns over subsequent decades. The fit is impressive.[7]

[7] Figure 18.7 is constructed by looking at realized returns following years when returns were expected to be low (below 5%), between 5% and 10%, between 10% and 15%, and high (above 15%).

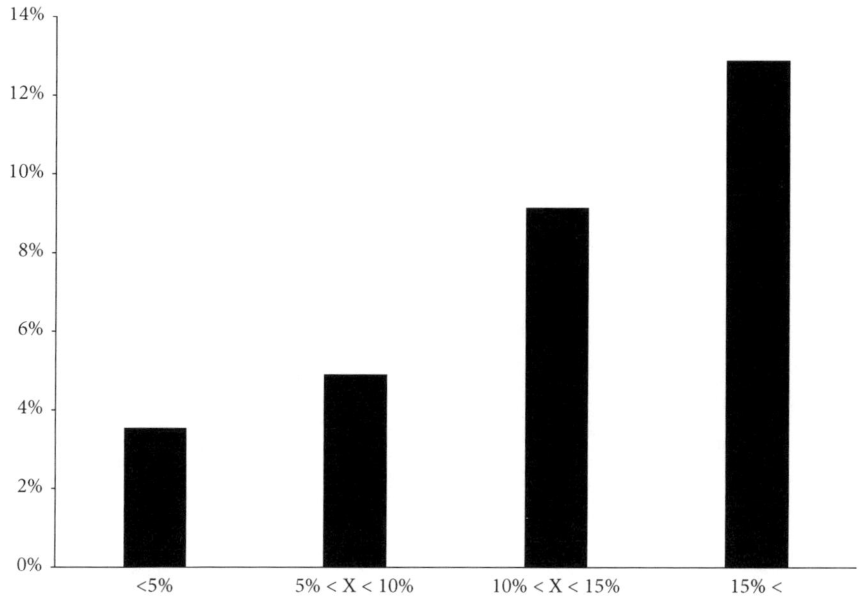

Figure 18.7 Average annual real US stock returns over subsequent decades when low returns (less than 5%), slightly higher (between 5% and 10%), even higher (between 5% and 10%), and very high (above 15%) returns were expected ex ante.
Data source: See Figures 2.1 and 3.1.

The fit is not perfect, of course. Figure 18.8 provides one way of illustrating this. It shows intervals within which half of subsequent realized returns fell when returns below 5% were expected ex ante, when returns between 5% and 10% were expected, between 10% and 15%, and above 15%. For instance, when low returns (less than 5% per annum) were expected, subsequently half of realized returns have been in the 0.4% to 6.2% interval. Similarly, when high returns (above 15% per annum) were expected, subsequent realized returns have been within the 10.4% to 15.3% interval. The figure again shows that there is information in return predictions. When low returns were expected, the range within which subsequent realized returns fell were lower than the range within which they fell when higher returns were expected. The figure also shows, however, that there is

This way of constructing the intervals implies that there is a different number of years in each interval. As an alternative, one could divide the sample into those 25% of years when predicted returns were the lowest and so on, until the fourth interval containing the 25% of years when returns were predicted to be the highest, i.e. the same number of years in each interval. If doing so, the conclusion is the same as the one drawn from Figure 18.7, i.e. subsequent realized returns turned out to be low when low returns were expected ex ante, and high when high returns were expected. Thus, the conclusion from Figure 18.7 is not sensitive to the specific choice of intervals.

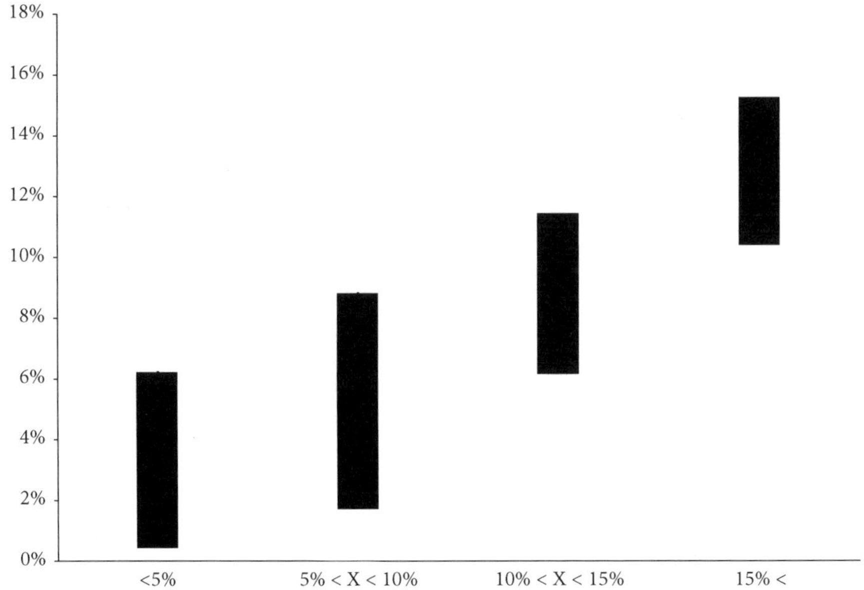

Figure 18.8 Ranges within which half of average annual real US stock returns over subsequent decades fell when low returns (less than 5%), slightly higher (between 5% and 10%), even higher (between 5% and 10%), and very high (above 15%) returns were expected ex ante.

Data source: See Figures 2.1 and 3.1.

uncertainty surrounding return forecasts. When low returns were expected (below 5%), the average of subsequent realized returns is 3.6% (Figure 18.7), but a quarter of subsequent realized returns have been below 0.4% and a quarter above 6.2% (Figure 18.8). Similarly, when high returns were expected (above 15%), the average of subsequent realized returns is 13% (Figure 18.7), but a quarter of realized returns has been below 10.4% and a quarter above 15.3%. We can estimate expected returns, but uncertainty surrounds them.

18.5 Checklist

This chapter has demonstrated that:

- Stock returns are given by the sum of the dividend yield, growth in a fundamental, and mean reversion in the stock price-fundamental multiple. To forecast stock returns, we forecast each of the components.

- In the academic literature, some researchers forecast stock returns over the next decade by the dividend yield only, others by the dividend yield plus growth in fundamentals, and some by the sum of all three components.
- Over the last 150 years or so, real stock returns over the next decade have been well captured by (i) Nobel laureate Robert Shiller's cyclical-adjusted price-earnings ratio (CAPE) inverted to become a yield and (ii) the sum of the dividend yield, growth in GDP, and mean-reversion in the stock price-GDP multiple.
- Uncertainty surrounds estimates of expected returns. Remember this when forming return expectations.

19

Predicting returns over several decades

Chapter 17 dealt with expectations of stock returns over short horizons. Given that stocks perform well during expansions but poorly during recessions, the key was to look for variables containing information about business-cycle turning points. Changes in the business cycle also affect the short interest rate, as central banks set the monetary policy rate based on business-cycle movements in economic activity. Changes in the short interest rate affect long interest rates. At the short horizon, the business cycle is a main determinant of asset prices.

Chapter 18, the previous chapter, dealt with expected stock returns over multi-year horizons, such as a decade or so. The chapter argued that the stock-price multiple (i.e. the stock price in relation to a fundamental long-run determinant of stock prices, such as dividends, earnings, or GDP) contains information about multi-year returns, together with yield and growth. When stocks trade at a high multiple, history shows that stock prices subsequently revert to the mean of the multiple. Multiples can remain elevated/low for several years, i.e. multiples contain only a little information about short-horizon returns, but are important for multi-year return expectations.

This chapter now closes the circle and looks at expectations of returns several decades out. This is obviously a difficult task, as fundamental economic structures might change over such long periods. But we need multi-decade forecasts in certain situations. When a young person saves for retirement, there might be 40 years until retirement and 20 years during retirement. To calculate expected retirement income, we need in this example expected returns 60 years out. So, sometimes, we need expectations about the very long run, even when it feels like reading tea leaves.

One conclusion of this chapter is that we must look beyond variables that predict turning points in the business cycle and stock-price multiples when we deal with the very long run. Over multiple decades, we will live through multiple business cycles. Variables that predict the next business cycle will not be particularly informative about the returns we expect over many decades. Similarly, in the very long run, stock prices follow underlying fundamentals, i.e. expected changes in stock-price multiples will be negligible. We have highlighted this already in Chapters 4 and 5. For these reasons, we turn in this chapter to the deep underlying drivers of long-run returns, primarily expectations to long-run economic activity.

From Main Street to Wall Street. Jesper Rangvid, Oxford University Press (2021). © Jesper Rangvid.
DOI: 10.1093/oso/9780198866404.003.0019

In the chapter, we thus utilize the conclusions from Chapter 14 that discussed the outlook for long-run economic growth.

Stock returns are given as the sum of the dividend yield, growth, and valuation changes. In the very long term, valuation changes cancel out, however, as just mentioned, and stock returns will be determined by yield plus growth. Given that dividend yields are low, and long-run economic growth is expected to be lower than what we have historically been used to, as Chapter 14 concluded, stock returns will most likely be lower going forward than we have been used to in the past.

The chapter also looks at expected long run interest rates. In the long run, interest rates are determined by economic growth. As growth is expected to be lower (than historically) going forward, we conclude that the likely scenario is one where yields remain low for an extended period of time, though perhaps not quiet as low as today.

19.1 Stock returns

Stock returns are given by the sum of the dividend yield, growth in fundamentals, and valuation growth.

Stock prices are the discounted value of future dividends. It is difficult to imagine that stock prices in the very long run can drift far away from the level implied by dividends. Dividends, in turn, will in the very long run be related to their fundamental determinants, earnings and GDP. In the short run, stock prices might wander away from underlying fundamentals, but in the long run, the only reasonable assumption is that stock prices and fundamentals share the same underlying long-run growth trend.

Chapters 4 and 5 discussed the long-run relation between stock prices, earnings, dividends, and GDP. The conclusion was that they all follow each other in the long run. When stock prices follow underlying fundamentals, valuation changes cancel out. This has an important implication. In the previous chapter, which dealt with multi-year forecasts, changes in stock-price multiples played an important role. For multi-decade forecasts, they do not. This means that when we forecast returns over the next decade or so (as in the previous chapter), we include valuation changes. When we forecast returns over multiple decades, we do not. We can summarize this as follows:

$$\text{Expected returns over a decade or shorter horizons} =$$
$$\text{Expected dividend yield} + \text{expected growth} + \text{expected valuation change.}$$

When we deal with the very long run, we disregard valuation changes:

$$\text{Expected returns over the next several decades} =$$
$$\text{Expected dividend yield} + \text{expected growth.}$$

This generates a useful way to determine expected returns in the very long run. We want to estimate the average return over many periods, not the variation in expected returns from year to year. Together with the assumption that valuation changes cancel out in the long run, this implies that we can work under the assumption that dividend growth rates and returns are constant, i.e. we are back at the Gordon growth model of Chapter 3:

$$\frac{\text{Stock price}}{\text{Current dividends}} = \frac{1}{\text{Expected stock returns} - \text{Expected dividend growth}}. \tag{19.1}$$

The Gordon growth model can be rearranged such that it provides an expression for expected stock returns:

$$\text{Expected stock returns} = \underbrace{\frac{\text{Current dividends}}{\text{Stock price}}}_{= \text{Current dividend yield}} + \text{Expected dividend growth}. \tag{19.2}$$

Current dividends divided by the current stock price is the current dividend yield. Expected dividend growth will in the long run be determined by expected economic growth. This means that we can estimate expected long-run stock returns as the current dividend yield plus economic growth.

Notice that this is a different approach to predicting stock returns compared to the approach in the previous chapter. The previous chapter used the fact that stock returns are defined as yield + growth + valuation change. No assumptions are involved, as it is a definition. When we evaluate expected returns as in Eq. (19.2), we assume constant growth and returns, and no valuation change. This is sensible when we deal with the very long run. The gain we obtain by imposing these assumptions is that we obtain a simple model for determining expected returns: the current dividend yield plus growth.

19.1.1 Growth, dividend yield, and expected stock returns

Chapter 14 dealt with the outlook for long-run economic growth. A main conclusion was that we should expect lower GDP growth going forward, compared to the historical experience. This, in itself, reduces expected returns. Lower expected growth is due to low or no population growth and a decline in productivity growth.

In Chapter 14, we mentioned that a reasonable estimate of the expected long-run average annual real per capita economic growth in advanced economies is around 1.5%, see Figure 14.9. For emerging economies, expected growth is somewhat higher, at around three percent per year. In the very long run, we expect real per capita economic growth, growth in real earnings per share, growth in real dividends per share, and real capital gains (growth in real share prices) to line up. Reasonable expectations of long-run growth in earnings, dividends, and stock prices are thus also around 1.5% for advanced economies.

Dividend yields move slowly. During the last couple of decades, the dividend yield has been slowly trending down, as Chapter 4 described. Currently, the US dividend yield is below, but close to, 2%.

If growth is 1.5% per year and the current dividend yield is around two percent, the Gordon growth model tells us that expected real US stock returns are 3.5% per year.

19.1.2 Share buybacks

Dividend yields in the US have been low since the mid-1980s, in particular, see Figure 4.2. Since the mid-1980s, at the same time, share buybacks have increased in the US, as Chapter 5 discussed. This means that firms have shifted from paying out dividends to buying back shares. As discussed in Chapter 5, in theory, expected shareholder return should be unaffected, as share buybacks should increase share prices, generating returns to share holders via capital gains instead of dividends.

Historical realized returns are what they are, however: realized dividends and realized capital gains. Share buybacks are not directly part of the return investors receive but influence returns via their potential influence on capital gains. This has implications for how to think of expected versus realized returns. The increasing use of share buybacks and the resulting drop in dividends might imply that the current dividend yield provides a too pessimistic outlook for future stock returns. Straehl & Ibbotson (2017) deal with these issues in some detail. They propose to adjust expected stock returns for share buybacks in one of two ways:

1. Adjust the dividend yield to include the buyback yield (add the buyback yield to the dividend yield). This provides a total payout yield. Then add growth in earnings per share or dividends per share.
2. Keep the dividend yield (i.e., do not adjust for share buybacks), but adjust growth to include an aggregate measure of growth, i.e. growth in total earnings or GDP.

Figure 19.1 Dividend yields dividend by 'CAPE as a yield'. US data. 1881–2018.
Data source: See Figure 3.1.

Share buybacks are volatile. Straehl & Ibbotson (2017) propose to use a cyclically adjusted total payout yield, similar to CAPE, i.e. take the average of the last ten years of the payout yield.[1]

Fundamentally, this discussion has its roots in corporate decisions on the channels through which to pay out that part of earnings corporations decide to return to shareholders; as dividends or as share buybacks. In other words, given a certain level of earnings, and thus a certain earnings yield, corporations decide how much to return to shareholders via dividends and how much via buybacks: how large should the dividend yield be compared to the earnings yield? Figure 19.1 shows the ratio of the dividend yield to the earnings yield, using cyclically-adjusted earnings, i.e. 'CAPE as a yield'. Until the 1970s, the dividend yield was on average around 70% of the earnings yield. Since then, the dividend yield has hovered around 50% of the earnings yield. Another way to incorporate the shift in payout policies of firms, thus, is to estimate the long-run total payout yield (dividend yield

[1] There has been discussion of these conclusions. Arnott & Bernstein (2018) argue that Straehl & Ibbotson (2017) in their analysis do not look at the entire US stock market, but only a subset of stocks, and that the outstanding pool of shares of the total stock market is not shrinking, as it should be if all companies buy back shares. Straehl & Ibbotson (2018) reply that even when looking at the entire stock market, the outstanding pool of shares is shrinking due to buybacks.

Figure 19.2 Global dividend yield. Equal-weighted average of dividend yields in 15 advanced economies. 1900–2016.

Data source: Jordà, Knoll, Kuvshinov, Schularick and Taylor (2019).

plus buyback yield) as the fraction of the dividend yield to the earnings yield before the change in payout policy, i.e. as 70% of the current earnings yield.

As the previous chapter showed, CAPE as a yield is currently around 3.5%. 70% of this is 2.5%. This is an estimate of the cyclically-adjusted total payout yield. Together with a per capita growth rate of 1.5%, this yields an estimate of the expected annual real long-run stock return of 4% in the US.

19.1.3 Other countries

The issue of share buybacks is particularly pronounced for the US. Even if share buybacks have increased in some countries, the extent to which this has happened is lower than in the US, as Chapter 5 discussed.

Figure 19.2 shows the development in the global dividend yield since 1900. It is calculated as the average of the dividend yields of the advanced economies studied in Chapter 6.[2] Global dividend yields are lower today than 100 years ago, like in the

[2] There are some missing observations in the dividend yield series, i.e. not all countries are represented for the total sample from 1900–2016.

US, but the drop is smaller. Average global dividend yields fluctuated around 4.5% before 1950 and have fluctuated around 3.5% since then. Since the 1980s, global dividend yields have been around 3%, dropping during the 1980–2000 period and increasing since then.

With current global dividend yields at 3% and an expected growth rate of real GDP per capita of 1.5% in advanced countries, expected long-run real stock returns in advanced countries are 4.5% per year.

The main message is that long-run stock returns are given by the current dividend yield plus expected long-run economic growth. Countries expected to grow faster are also expected to deliver higher stock returns, for a given dividend yield.[3] Emerging markets are expected to grow by around 3% in the long run, as Chapter 14 showed. With a dividend yield of 3% in emerging markets, too, expected long-run returns in emerging markets are 6% per annum.

So, to summarize, as of 2020, expected annual real stock returns for the very long run are 4% in the US, 4.5% across developed economies, and 6% across emerging markets.

The historical annual real return from stocks has been around 7% in the US. Going forward, we expect it to be around 4%. Stocks are thus expected to provide lower returns going forward, compared to the historical experience. The next section discusses whether the situation is different for bonds.

19.2 Interest rates

Interest rates have been falling since the early 1980s. Figure 19.3 shows nominal yields on ten-year government bonds from a number of large countries. The picture tells a clear story: interest rates were rising during the 1960 and 1970s. Since then, i.e. for the last 40 years or so, interest rates have been constantly falling. The fact that interest rates have behaved more or less in the same way in all countries indicates that global common factors have been driving interest rates around the world.

Figure 19.4 shows that there is a good reason why nominal interest rates spiked during the 1970s, and have been falling ever since: inflation rates increased dramatically during the 1970s, but have come under control since the mid-1990s. When inflation rates fall, nominal interest rates fall, too, all else equal. Why did inflation rise during the 1970s? One important reason was that oil prices rose,

[3] All countries do not face the same dividend yield, however. This is why there is no simple linear relation between historical growth rates and stock returns across countries, as discussed in Chapter 6. For instance, in the text, we use a current dividend yield of 2.5% in the US and 3% across advanced economies. For a given dividend yield, however, higher growth will lead to higher returns.

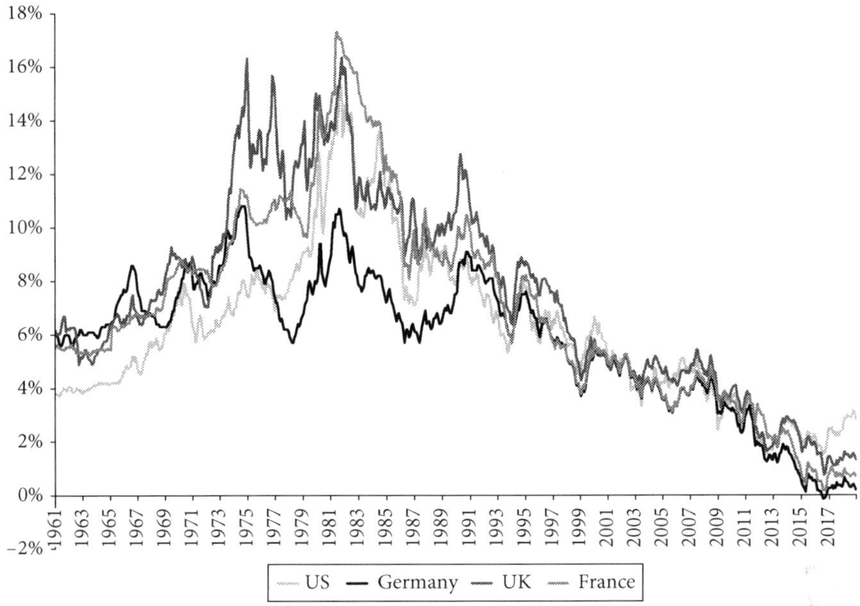

Figure 19.3 Nominal yields on ten-year government bonds in selected countries.

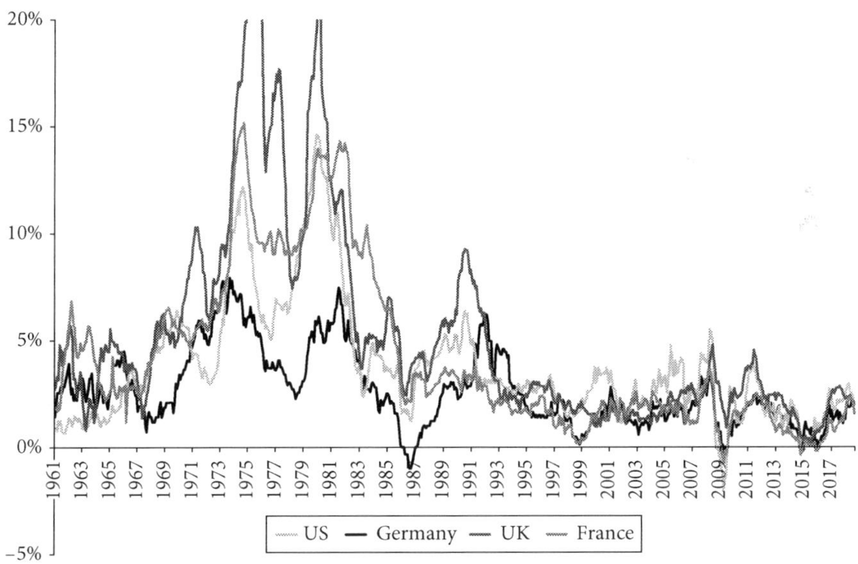

Figure 19.4 Inflation rates in selected countries.
Data source: FRED.

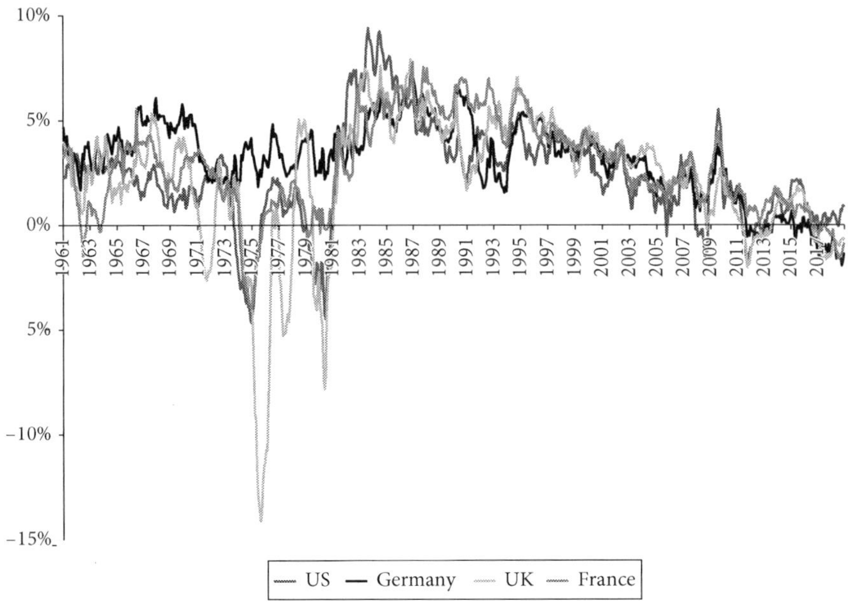

Figure 19.5 Real interest rates on ten-year government bonds in the US, Germany, UK, and France.
Data source: FRED.

causing other prices to rise, i.e., a supply-side shock. In addition, monetary policy was not focused enough on keeping inflation low. Central banks started focusing squarely on inflation in the 1980s. Since then, inflation has been low and stable, fluctuating within a 0% – 3% band.

Figure 19.5 shows real interest rates, calculated as nominal interest rates minus inflation. During the 1970s, real interest rates were negative in several countries, eroded by high rates of inflation. Real yields have been on a declining path since the mid-1990s. Today, real yields are very low, in many cases negative.

From a long-term perspective, current interest rates really are historically low. Figure 19.6, shows the path of the Bank of England central policy rate since the Bank was founded in 1694. This is an impressing long data series of monetary policy rates. It covers more than three centuries. Figure 19.6 reveals that the policy rate has never been as low as it has been since the 2008 financial crisis.

Furthermore, from a very long-term historical perspective, Figures 19.7 and 19.8 show global nominal (Figure 19.7) and real (Figure 19.8) interest rates extending all the way back to 1320. The figures reveal that nominal and real interest rates have basically been falling for seven hundred years. There are two noteworthy exceptions to this secular decline in rates. During the period from

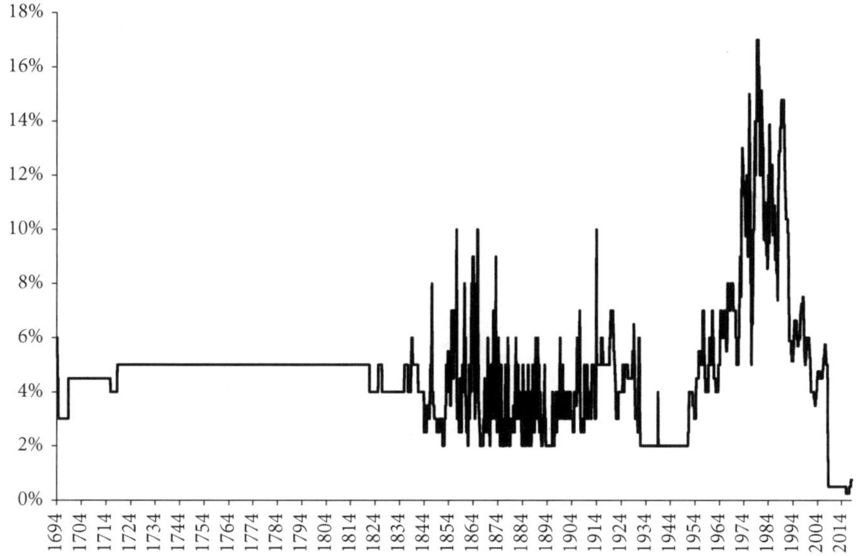

Figure 19.6 The central policy rate of the Bank of England, since the inception of the Bank in 1694.

Data source: Bank of England.

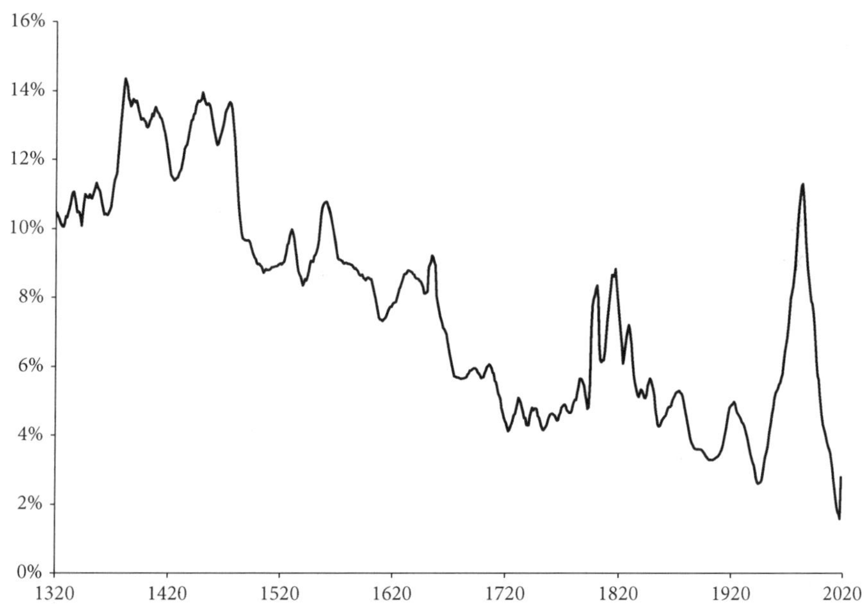

Figure 19.7 Nominal global interest rate since 1320.

Data source: Schmelzing (2020).

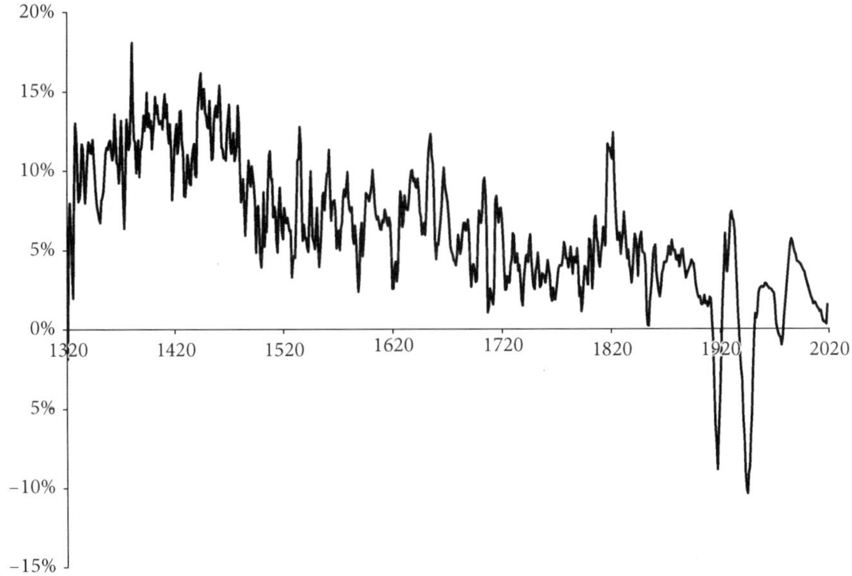

Figure 19.8 Real global interest rate since 1320.
Data source: Schmelzing (2020).

1945 through 2010, nominal rates rose from 1945 to 1980, only to fall since then. Furthermore, real rates dropped dramatically during the first and the second world war when inflation rates rose, eroding nominal rates of returns. Apart from these episodes, interest rates have been falling for almost seven hundred years.

The question is what will happen from here. To address this, we need some theory for what influences interest rates in the long run.

19.2.1 Why have interest rates come down?

The interest rate equates supply of savings and demand for investments. Imagine you have money you do not want to spend today. You can save it in financial assets, such as bonds. The higher the return you get on your savings, i.e. the higher is the interest rate, the more you would like to save, and supply of savings increases. Alternatively, you can use your money to invest in real capital that produces goods. The lower is the interest rate, the more likely it is that your investment will be profitable (for an investment to be profitable, its return should exceed the alternative costs, e.g. the interest rate). In other words, the lower is the interest rate, the higher is demand for investments. The equilibrium real interest rate is the one that equates demand for investments and supply of savings. Figure 19.9

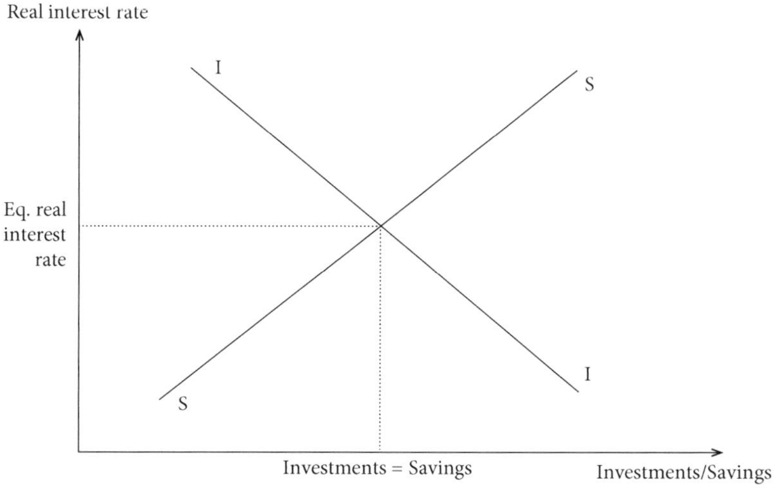

Figure 19.9 The equilibrium real interest rate.

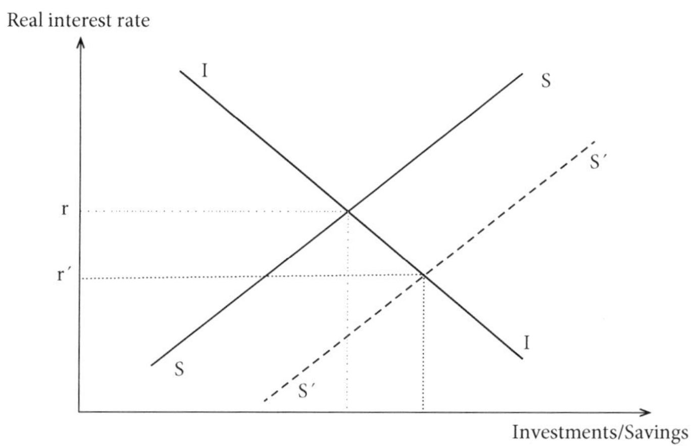

Figure 19.10 The equilibrium real interest rate after an increase in the supply of savings.

illustrates how the equilibrium interest rate is determined. The II line illustrates that investments are higher when the real interest rate is lower. The SS line illustrates that savings are higher when the real interest rate is higher.

This simple framework can be used to understand what moves the equilibrium interest rate. If more people want to save at a given level of the interest rate, the SS line moves to the right, see Figure 19.10. Supply of savings increases at each level of the interest rate. The interest rate must fall (from r to r' in Figure 19.10) to equate saving and investments. Similarly, if more people want to make investments at a given level of the interest rate, the II line moves to the right. The interest rate must rise to equate supply of savings and demand for investments. To gauge the long-run outlook for yields, we must thus think about the underlying long-run determinants of demand for investments and supply of savings.

There are two schools of thought. One believes that real interest rates have declined over the past 40 years primarily because the global supply of savings has increased, not least due to demographic developments. A prominent figure behind this theory is former Princeton Professor and Fed Chairman Ben Bernanke. He developed these thoughts in an important speech in 2005. He called it 'The Global Savings Glut'. When savings increase, interest rates come down, as in Figure 19.10. According to this theory, the future direction of yields will not least depend on future developments in demographics, as these will influence developments in global savings.

The second school believes that the world has gone through a period with a steady decline in profitable investment opportunities, leading to a reduction in demand for investments. Low demand for investments push down interest rates. Advocates of this school expect profitable investment opportunities to remain depressed in the years to come, i.e. interest rates will remain low. A prominent figure in this debate is Lawrence Summers, professor at Harvard University. This school of thought goes under the heading of 'Secular Stagnation'.

19.2.1.1 Higher savings propensity

Saving for retirement and saving during retirement both affect savings patterns. Saving for retirement increases the supply of savings. This pushes down interest rates. During retirement, we dissave, i.e. rely on savings accumulated during our working age. When we dissave, we sell assets. When many people sell bonds, prices drop. This pushes up interest rates. Shifts in the relative fraction of people who save for retirement versus people in retirement have implications for overall savings rates. It turns out that such shifts in global population structures line up with movements in real interest rates.

Figure 19.11 shows developments in the fraction of people saving for retirement (age 40–65) to the fraction of population retired (above age 65), globally. The figure reveals that the number of middle-aged individuals (as a fraction of the total population) has increased relative to the number of old individuals since the 1990s. The difference between the two (called 'Difference' in Figure 19.11) has been increasing during the 1990 to 2015 period. This means that the number of people saving for retirement has increased relative to the number of people in retirement. Global savings have gone up, and yields have come down.[4] On the other hand, up

[4] The situation has been particularly pronounced in China. Working age population, i.e. those who save for retirement, doubled from around 20% of the Chinese population in 1980 to around 40% of the population in 2015.

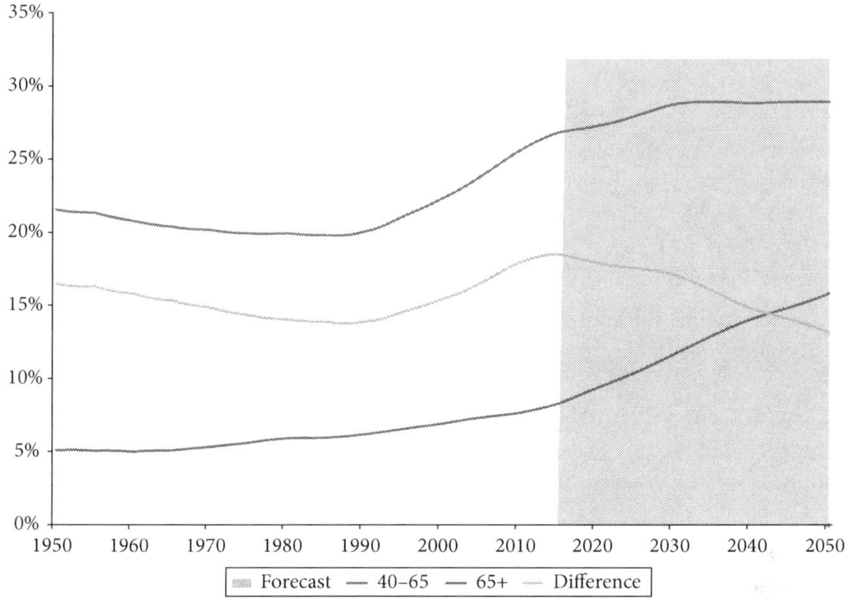

Figure 19.11 Middle-to-old age ratio.
Data source: World Population Prospects, The United Nations.

until 1980, the fraction of old individuals to middle-aged individuals increased, illustrated by the decline in the 'Difference' in Figure 19.11 during the 1950 to 1980 period. Less people saving should push up yields. And, indeed, yields increased during the 1960s, 1970s, and early 1980s, see Figure 19.3.

Ben Bernanke's Global Savings Glut paid special attention to the role of savings in China and other emerging economies. Bernanke's argument was that these savings were channelled to the US and other advanced economies, influencing yields in advanced economies, pushing yields up until app. 1980 and pushing them down afterwards.

19.2.1.2 Lower investments propensity

Lower real rates can also be caused by lower demand for investments (lower demand for investments shifts the II curve to the left in Figure 19.9, causing the interest rate to drop). The 'Secular Stagnation' theory describes why demand for investments is low. The theory originates back to the economist Alvin Hansen who used it in his Presidential address to the American Economic Association in 1938 (Hansen, 1939). Hansen argued that slow population growth and a decline in innovation would cause a drop in profitable investment opportunities. This would lead to a reduction in aggregate demand for investments, and consequently an excess of supply of savings. Equilibrium interest rates would fall.

Lawrence Summers brought attention to these ideas after the financial crisis (Summers, 2014). Summers argues, similar to Hansen in the 1930s, that productivity growth has stalled, leading to a reduction in demand for investments. Summers also argues that demand for savings has increased, for the same reasons as those emphasized in the 'Global Savings Glut' hypothesis outlined in the previous section, i.e. changes in population structures. Summers concludes that the reduction in demand for investments and increase in supply of savings has caused the equilibrium interest rate to turn negative, i.e. very low.

This has a number of implications. If monetary policy is constrained by the zero lower bound (the monetary policy rate cannot go much below zero), but the equilibrium interest rate that equates demand for investments and supply of savings is negative, then the prevailing interest rate will be higher than the equilibrium rate. With too high interest rates (compared to the equilibrium interest rate), demand for investments will be low. With too few investments, economic growth will suffer and unemployment will increase, Summers argues. With hysteresis effects,[5] this will have persistent negative consequences for productivity and economic activity going forward. In addition, when the equilibrium interest rate is very low, central banks need to keep policy rates very low, too, in order not to depress demand for investments too much. But very low monetary policy rates can cause financial instability, as investors will 'search for yield', pushing up assets prices, thereby potentially creating asset bubbles. Second, Summers argues, low equilibrium interest rates justify expansionary fiscal policy. When monetary policy is constrained by the zero lower bound, fiscal policy should take over and help to increase aggregate demand, Summers believes.

19.2.1.3 Other explanations for low interest rates

Many countries have experienced increasing inequality during the previous decades, as mentioned in Chapter 2. Higher inequality means that a larger fraction of income and wealth is concentrated in the hands of the already wealthy. Wealthy individuals have a higher tendency to save. Higher inequality, coupled with the wealthy having a higher savings rate, can help explaining why the supply of savings have increased. Higher supply of savings push yields lower. Rising inequality may be a contributing factor to the reduction in real rates since the 1980s.

[5] Hysteresis refers to persistent movements in unemployment. When you become unemployment, you lose skills, in particular if you are unemployed for longer. When you have less skills, it becomes even more difficult to find a job, i.e. you will remain unemployed for longer. Summers developed the theory of hysteresis in the mid-1980s together with Olivier Blanchard, see Blanchard and Summers (1986).

Another explanation relates to the financial crisis. As argued in Chapter 12, one reason behind the financial crisis was a rise in household indebtedness. After the financial crisis, many households have reversed gear. Shocked by the dramatic consequences of indebtedness, households have reduced their demand for borrowing, i.e. increased supply of savings. This cannot explain why real rates started falling in the 1980s, but it can explain what have kept rates low.

Finally, since the financial crisis, monetary policy has been unusually expansionary in many countries, as argued in Chapter 12. Expansionary monetary policy has helped push down interest rates.

In total, there are a number of factors that have pushed down interest rates during the last decades. The question is whether some of these factors will reverse going forward, tending to push up interest rates, or whether they will persist such that interest rates will stay low in the foreseeable future.

19.2.2 The long-run outlook for interest rates

Interest rates are currently (in 2020) very low. In nominal terms, in real terms, and in historically terms. Given that nominal yields are close to zero, it is difficult to imagine that they can fall much further. There are for all practical purposes only two possibilities: either interest rates stay low for many years or they increase.

19.2.2.1 Demand for savings

Section 19.2.1 argued that changes in demographics have increased the supply of savings since the 1980s, causing a fall in interest rates. Going forward, there is reason to expect these patterns to reverse somewhat. Figure 19.11 indicates expected changes in global populations until 2050. These are the expectations of the United Nations. The figure reveals that the share of middle-aged individuals (as a fraction of the total population) is expected to remain flat whereas the share of those above 65 is expected to increase. If this holds true, the fraction of the population that dissaves will increase relative to the fraction that saves. The consequence will be a fall in the supply of savings. Interest rates should increase.

Why do we expect these changes in population structures? We live longer, and life expectancy is expected to increase. In addition, fertility rates trend down, as discussed in Chapter 14. This lowers the relative number of young individuals. All in all, expected changes in population structures might exert an upward pressure on interest rates going forward.

19.2.2.2 Demand for investments

The underlying idea in the Secular Stagnation hypothesis is that lower productivity will result in fewer profitable investment opportunities, and thus, in the end, low

Table 19.1 The difficulties in foreseeing the impact of innovations

"Heavier-than-air flying machines are impossible." (Lord Kelvin, President of the Royal Society, 1895)
"Everything that can be invented has been invented." (Charles Duell, Commissioner, US Office of Patents, 1899)
"The wireless music box has no imaginable commercial value. Who would pay for a message sent to nobody in particular?" (David Sarnoff Associates, 1920s)
"Who the hell wants to hear actors talk?" (Head of Warner Brothers, 1927)
"I think there is a world market for maybe five computers." (Thomas Watson, Chairman of IBM, 1943)
"There is no reason anyone would want a computer in their home." (Ken Olsen, Chairman of DEC, 1977)

Source: Bean, Broda, Ito, and Kroszner (2015)

demand for investments and low interest rates. The central question, thus, is what to expect about future productivity growth? Chapter 14 concluded that it is likely that productivity growth will be lower going forward than it has been during the last 100–150 years. Chapter 14 also concluded that we should not be too gloomy either.

As mentioned, the Secular Stagnation idea was originally developed by Hansen in the late 1930s. This was right after the Great Depression and views were gloomy. Hansen expected low growth going forward. How did things develop during the 1950s and 1960s? The advanced world saw massive improvements in productivity. The predictions of the original Secular Stagnation were wrong. Will it be better this time? Bean, Broda, Ito, and Kroszner (2015) have a fascinating collection of calls by clever people that turned out to be wrong, and far too pessimistic, see Table 19.1.

On the other hand, we should also not fool ourselves into believing that the most likely scenario is one where productivity growth returns to levels seen during the 1960s. Chapter 14 concluded that we should expect lower rates of productivity growth going forward. This will keep rates low.

19.2.2.3 Concluding on the outlook for yields

Based on likely developments in population structures, we might expect an upward pressure on interest rates. Similarly, when monetary policy is normalized, interest rates might be lifted somewhat. On the other hand, productivity growth will most likely be lower than we have been used to historically. Advocates of the secular stagnation hypothesis expect low interest rates going forward for this reason. It is difficult to weigh these different theories against each other, as they do not make precise predictions. On balance, they indicate somewhat higher interest rates than currently, but not as high rates as historically.

If we want a number, a good rule of thumb is that the real interest rate relates to the rate of real per capita consumption growth which, in turn, equals the rate of productivity growth and per capita economic growth.[6] As discussed in Chapter 14, we expect productivity growth to be lower going forward. This should keep a lid on interest rates. If one expects long-run productivity growth of 1.5%, this could be a good guess of the long-run equilibrium real interest rate. This is higher than today but lower than the historical average.

19.3 Equity risk premium

The equity risk premium is the difference between the returns on stocks and bonds, i.e. the compensation investors require for holding risky assets.

In the preceding sections of this chapter, we have concluded that a reasonable estimate of long-run real stock returns is 4.5% per annum in advanced economies. We have also concluded that a reasonable estimate of the long-run real interest rate, i.e. the long-run real return on bonds, is 1.5%. This means that a reasonable estimate of the equity risk premium in advanced economies is around 3% per annum.

Chapter 6 concluded that the historical risk premium in advanced countries has been around 3% per annum on average. The expected future risk premium, thus, does not seem to differ much from the historical risk premium across advanced countries.

The situation is different for the US. Chapters 3 and 6 concluded that the historical risk premium in the US has been around 5%. If expected future long-run real stock returns are around 4% in the US, and the expected long-run real interest rate 1.5%, the expected equity risk premium will be around 2.5% per annum in the long run, considerably below the historical US risk premium.

19.4 Implications of low returns

Future interest rates are expected to be lower than historically. Stock returns are expected to be lower, too. We live in a world of low expected returns.

[6] Chapter 6 described how economic growth relates to the level of the interest rate.

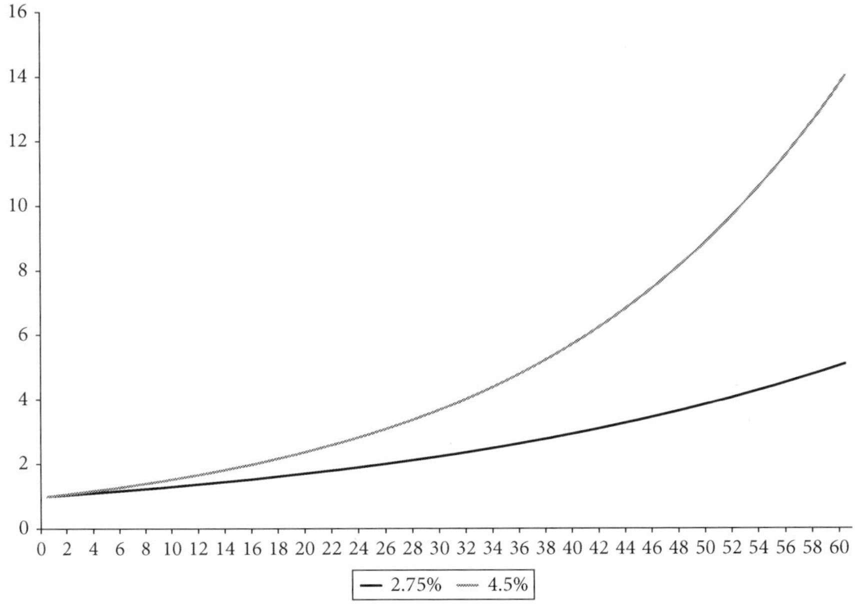

Figure 19.12 Accumulation of wealth over 60 years for different levels of annual returns.

US real stock returns have historically been around 7% per year while interest rates have been around 2%. This implies that a 50%/50% stock/bond portfolio has historically delivered around 4.5% year in real terms. Going forward, we expect US stocks to return around 4% per annum in real terms while we expect the long-run real interest rate to be around 1.5%. A 50%/50% stock/bond portfolio is expected to return around 2.75% per year.

Does it matter whether long-run returns are 2.75% or 4.5% per year? Seems like minor differences. It is hugely important! We are talking long-run expectations here. Figure 19.12 illustrates the consequences for the accumulation of wealth if returns are respectively 2.75% and 4.5% per year, and the investor saves for 60 years.

If savings grow by 2.75% per year, the value of one dollar saved today will have grown to 5.1 dollars after 60 years. If savings increase by 4.5% per year, as historically, one dollar increases to 14 dollars over 60 years. 4.5% is 63% higher than 2.75% (0.045/0.0275 = 1.63). 14 dollars is almost 200% higher than 5.1 dollars. This is the effect of compounding. Even small differences in annual returns become hugely important when we talk about expected wealth after many years.

This discussion is not least relevant for people saving for retirement. If an individual starts working at 25 and retires at 65, then savings accumulate for

40 years. If the person lives until he/she is 85, wealth will still accumulate during retirement. We will be talking 60 years of accumulation. It really hurts if returns are low over long periods of time.

19.5 Checklist

This chapter has demonstrated that:

- Expectations for stock returns in the very long run, such as several decades, are best formed by making reasonable judgements about the current dividend yield and future long-run growth rates of economic activity and dividends.
- Dividend yields have been trending down during the last several decades. Currently, in the US, the dividend yield is below but close to 2%.
- Chapter 14 was devoted to analysing the likely path of future long-run economic growth. The main conclusion was that long-run growth in real per capita economic activity in advanced countries will most likely be around 1.5% per year.
- As the US dividend yield is around 2% and a reasonable estimate of long-run real economic growth is 1.5%, a reasonable estimate of long-run US stock returns is something like 3.5% per annum in real terms.
- Perhaps 2% dividend yield is a little low, however, given that US firms have started using share buybacks as a means to return earnings to shareholders. A sensible estimate of the total payout yield is 2.5%. This gives an estimate of annual real returns from US stocks of 4% (2.5% + 1.5%).
- In other parts of the world, the dividend yield is higher. The global dividend yield is currently around 3%. As expected growth is 1.5% in advanced economies, expected stock returns in advanced economies are 4.5%. Because expected growth is 3% in emerging economies, expected stock returns in emerging markets are 6% per year. For a given dividend yield, countries expected to grow faster are expected to deliver higher returns.
- Real interest rates are determined by supply of savings and demand for investments. Supply of savings have come down since the early 1980s due to population shifts. Demand for investments has come down due to fewer profitable investment opportunities (resulting from low productivity growth). Real interest rates are historically low at the time of writing.
- Going forward, extraordinarily expansionary monetary policy should be normalized. This should tend to increase interest rates. Global savings patterns might reverse going forward, too. This could decrease global savings, pushing up interest rates. On the other hand, productivity growth will remain lower

than we have been used to historically, as Chapter 14 argued. This keeps a lid on interest rates.

- All in all, interest rates might increase somewhat compared to their currently very depressed levels, but will most likely remain lower than historically. A reasonable estimate of the long-run real interest rate is 1.5% in advanced economies.
- The equity risk premium is estimated to be around 3% in advanced economies. This is in line with the historical risk premium in advanced economies, though considerably lower than the historical premium in the US.
- When saving for many years, it is of first-order importance whether we expect something like 2.75% annual return on our portfolio or something like 4.5%. It might seem like a small difference, but we are talking long-run return expectations here. Small differences in expected returns have dramatic implications for the accumulation of wealth.

PART VI

PRACTICAL INVESTMENT ADVICE

20
Building and maintaining investment portfolios

The goal of this book is to explain and examine the relation between the economy and the stock markets in order to help investors navigate financial markets. To further this goal, this last chapter provides research-based perspectives on a number of challenges investors face when building and maintaining investment portfolios.

20.1 Diversification

There are few 'free lunches' on financial markets. If any, a good candidate is 'diversification'. Diversification means spreading savings across many types of assets. This implies holding different stocks, from different sectors, from different countries, together with bonds of different maturities issued by both domestic and foreign corporations and governments, and of high and low credit quality. If you can get access to private equity funds and other so-called 'alternative investment', these should be included in your portfolio as well. Basically, you should spread your investments over as many less-than-perfectly-correlated asset classes as possible.

The number of asset classes you can spread your investment across depends on whether you are an individual investor or a professional. Some types of investments are simply difficult to get access to as an individual investor. This is true not least for so-called 'alternative investment'.[1] If you as a retail investor cannot get access to these types of investments, you can still get far if spreading your investments across traditional asset classes.

It is important to understand exactly what the benefits of diversification are. They are not about generating higher expected returns per se. Rather, diversification helps generating higher expected returns for a given level of risk. Or,

[1] These include investments in things like private equity, forestry, farming, wind mills, roads, bridges, buildings, hospitals, and the like. These investments are often large (hundreds of millions of dollars) and difficult to get out of when first having made them, i.e. they are illiquid. Some mutual funds and Exchange Traded Funds (ETFs) provide indirect access to some of these asset classes, though.

From Main Street to Wall Street. Jesper Rangvid, Oxford University Press (2021). © Jesper Rangvid.
DOI: 10.1093/oso/9780198866404.003.0020

alternatively, diversification helps reduce the risk of your portfolio, without sacrificing expected returns. As diversification lowers risks without sacrificing expected returns, it is almost 'a free lunch'.

Risk refers to fluctuations in the value of your portfolio. Most investors are risk averse, i.e. do not like risk. We would like to reduce risk as much as possible for any given level of expected returns.

> **Lesson 1**. The first lesson to remember when building an investment portfolio is to secure a high level of diversification across the assets in your portfolio, i.e. holding many different assets.

20.2 Individual securities or portfolios of securities?

Holding one stock exposes you to all the idiosyncrasies of the firm that has issued that stock. Adding an additional stock to your portfolio, lowers the risk of your portfolio if the two stocks do not move in tandem. That is diversification.

Even when many investors have probably heard about the benefits of diversification, the majority of individual investors do not diversify their portfolios to an extent that comes even close to eliminating unnecessary (so-called idiosyncratic) risks. In fact, when looking at the actual portfolios of individual investors, it turns out that they are grossly underdiversified.

I coauthored a study where we looked at the stock holdings of all the individual investors in a country, Denmark (Florentsen, Nielsson, Raahauge, and Rangvid, 2019). We found that the average number of different stocks investors hold is less than two. Two thirds of all investors hold stocks issued by one company only. It is great if the single stock you hold performs well, but not so great if it does not. Alas, we found that investors need a considerable amount of luck to find that single stock (or two) that performs better than a broad diversified portfolio. Most investors seem to have forgotten the benefits of diversification.

Other researchers have conducted similar studies using data from other countries, though based on smaller subsamples of investors. Results are typically similar to those we found for the total Danish population. For instance, Barber & Odean (2000) and Goetzmann & Kumar (2008) study subsamples of US individual investors. They find that the typical investor holds very few stocks, typically less than three stocks. The conclusion is that individual investors show a strong inclination to buy very few individual stocks. This hurts investors' performance. This is why we stress the benefits of diversification.

How many stocks are needed to build a diversified portfolio? This depends on the period we look at (correlations can differ across time), the market we talk about, etc. Research shows that at least ten stocks are necessary, and, to be on the safe side, thirty-to-fifty stocks is a better answer, see Campbell Lettau, Malkiel & Xu (2001), Domian, Louton, & Racine (2007), and Florentsen, Nielsson, Raahauge, and Rangvid (2019). But which stocks should I buy? How should I evaluate their relative performance? And, how should I rebalance my portfolio?

When the number of stocks needed to secure diversification is high, when it is cumbersome to keep track of many different stocks, and, most importantly, when we can see in the data that there is a strong tendency for individual investors to underdiversify, it seems that many investors would be better off buying mutual funds. Mutual funds invest in a high number of underlying assets. It is easier to buy and keep track of one mutual fund (that then takes care of investments in a high number of underlying securities and thereby secures diversification) than investing in a high number of individual securities yourself.

Lesson 2. Many individual investors basically do not diversify their stock portfolios. It seems that many investors would be better off buying mutual funds than buying a few individual stocks.

Many investors have preferences for stocks from their own country. This is called home bias. A rule-of-thumb is that the fraction of your equity exposure to one country should be the share of that country in the world market portfolio. I.e., if the US accounts for 40% of the world's stock market capitalization, 40% of equity holdings should be in US stocks. A simple way of achieving such diversification is to buy a global equity mutual fund.

20.3 Passive or active mutual funds?

Mutual funds help investors diversify. In addition, mutual funds secure that the underlying portfolio is balanced, reinvest dividends, and, in some countries, help the individual investor with relevant reports to tax authorities. In short, mutual funds secure diversification and help investors administer their savings. Mutual fund must be compensated for these services, i.e. investors pay fees for investing via mutual funds. That is the disadvantage of saving via mutual funds.

The fee you pay a mutual fund covers the cost of running the fund as well as the profits the fund makes. One important determinant of the size of this cost is whether the mutual fund invests in a 'passive' or an 'active' way. A passive mutual fund tracks an index. Imagine that you want to invest in the S&P500. You can buy a fund that tracks the S&P500 very closely. The only objective of the fund is to mirror the S&P500, not to think about whether some stocks within the S&P500 universe will do better than others. Replicating the index is a relatively easy task. Stocks are bought according to their proportional weight within the

S&P500. A computer can take care of this. The costs are low, sometimes a few basispoints only.

As an alternative, consider a mutual fund where you want to get exposed to the S&P500, but you want a portfolio manager who selects stocks he/she believes will outperform the S&P500 index. In this case, the mutual fund manager must actively overweight/underweight certain stocks. This is an active mutual fund. The costs of running such an active mutual fund are higher. Consequently, the fees paid for active management are higher than fees paid for passive. And—ceteris paribus—fees reduce your return.

A complicating factor here is that fees often depend on the size of your investment, in particular for active funds. This means that professional investors, such as banks or pension funds, who invest large amounts of money, typically pay lower fees than individual investors. This also means that the likelihood that an active fund—all else equal—delivers outperformance is higher for an investor who pays a low fee, such as a professional investor, than for an investor who pays higher fees, such as retail investors.

Should you buy active or passive funds? This is a heated debate. There are academics out there who fiercely recommend buying passive funds, while others fiercely recommend active. When a debate is heated, it is most often because the answer is not straightforward. Based on voluminous academic research on the relative merits of active and passive investments, a couple of conclusions stand out, though.

US equity funds on average perform as well or better than their index *before* fees, but, *after* fees, most active equity funds underperform (Fama & French, 2010). There is a small group of funds that perform well, also after fees (Fama & French, 2010 and Kosowski, Timmermann, Wermers, and White, 2006). These funds are difficult to find a priori but tend to be small-cap funds and growth funds (Grinblatt and Titman, 1989), funds that deviate significantly from their benchmark (Cremers and Petajisto, 2009), and funds that invest in asset classes that are less followed, such as fixed income funds or equity funds from smaller markets (Berk and Binsbergen, 2015). The reason these managers do well is that they acquire skills regarding investments in firms in specific industries (Kacperczyk, Sialm, and Zheng, 2005) or geographical locations (Coval and Moskowitz, 2001), and are able to pick the right stocks in expansions and time the market in recessions (Kacperczyk, van Nieuwerburgh, and Laura Veldkamp, 2015).

Lesson 3. You should pay attention to the size of fees. Active funds charge higher fees than passive funds. Most active funds underperform their index after fees, but there is a small group of active funds that tend to outperform.

Given that many active managers underperform after fees, it is not all too surprising that passive funds have gained in popularity during recent years. In the US, for instance, passive funds account for 36% of assets under management by mutual funds in 2018, up from 18% ten years earlier (ICI, 2019).

The active/passive discussion has a certain element of philosophical thinking to it. For prices to exist, trading is needed. It is only when a trade happens that a price is determined. For prices to adjust, someone must make an active decision. But, if everybody is passive, who sets the price? Who distinguishes good firms from bad firms? Basically, if everybody turns passive, who makes sure that capital markets function? This has an interesting implication: the more passive investors there are, the easier it is for active investors to outperform. If few investors follow firms, it becomes relatively easier to gain informational advantages as an active investor, and thus also relatively easier to outperform. Pastor & Stambaugh (2012) were first to articulate this. So, when active managers struggle to demonstrate value-for-money, there are good reasons why more and more investors become passive. On the other hand, the more is invested passively, the higher is the likelihood that an active manager will outperform.

> **Lesson 4**. It is difficult to find outperforming active mutual funds. Hence, many investors are turning passive. The more passive investors there are, however, the easier it should be for active investors to outperform.

20.4 What fraction should I invest in stocks?

How should you divide your savings between risky and safe assets? This is an important decision, as the book has demonstrated that stocks are expected to yield higher returns than bonds, but are also more risky. This means that you can increase your expected returns if you allocate more of your savings to stocks, but risk then also increases. There is no single 'right' asset allocation, as it depends on individual characteristics, but there are some concepts and characteristics that one should reflect upon when determining the allocation between risky and safe assets.

20.4.1 Risk aversion

The most important determinant of how much you want to invest in risky assets is your tolerance towards risk: how much can you loose before you start feeling bad? If you feel very bad about taking on risk, i.e. your risk aversion is high, you should invest a smaller proportion in stocks. If you are OK with accepting some risk, at the gain of hopefully getting a higher return in the end, you can invest a higher fraction of your wealth in risky assets.

> **Lesson 5**. The higher is your aversion towards risk, the less you should invest in risky assets.

20.4.2 Investment horizon

If you invest a higher fraction of your wealth in risky assets, the expected return on your investment will increase, but the uncertainty surrounding your expected return will also increase. Most economists believe that in the short run, the risk-return trade-off is more or less constant. This means that if you increase the fraction of your wealth invested in risky assets, risk and return increase in the same proportion, leaving the risk-return ratio unaffected. You increase expected return but you increase expected risk as much.

This might change if you have a longer horizon, such as several years or even decades. In this case, there is an argument for increasing the fraction of your wealth invested in risky assets. If returns on risky assets are mean-reverting, i.e. have a tendency to increase in the future if they have been low in the past, then these returns are 'less risky' in the long run. Mean-reverting returns also means that returns contain a predictable component, as we have explained.

One key point in this book is that stock returns contain a small predictable component. Over longer horizons, we can say something about expected stock returns. It is difficult and noisy, but we can say more than nothing. This means that when you have a long horizon, you can allow yourself to increase the fraction you invest in stocks. So, if you invest for retirement, i.e. your horizon is long, you should invest more in stocks than if you invest for next year's vacation.

There is a famous rule of thumb: invest 'one hundred minus your age' in stocks. I.e., if you are 20 years old and invest for retirement, invest 80% (100—20) in stocks and 20% in bonds. If you are close to retirement, for instance you are 65 years old, invest 35% (100—65) in stocks and 65% in bonds. It is simple, and there are lots of qualifications, but it works as a guiding principle. One qualification is that this is an old rule, and life expectancy has increased during recent decades. For this reason, perhaps the rule today should rather be '110 minus your age', or '120 minus age'. In any case, the general point is that investors with a long horizon, such as pension funds, endowment funds, young individuals saving for retirement, etc., should – all else equal – invest more in risky assets than investors with a short horizon (firms that have surplus liquidity that they need to invest, investors who expect to use the savings within a not too distant future, etc.).

Lesson 6. The longer is your investment horizon, the more you can allocate to risky assets.

20.4.3 Rebalancing

When you have found the right mix between stocks and bonds, you need to think about your reactions to changes in that mix resulting from changes in the market value of your investment. An example illustrates. Imagine you have USD 100 to invest and you want a fifty-fifty portfolio of stocks and bonds. Imagine now that stocks return 10% over the coming year and bonds 2%. After one year, the value of your stock investment is 50·(1.10) = 55 and the value of your bond investment 50·(1.02) = 51. Your allocation is no a fifty-fifty portfolio, as stocks now make up 55/106 = 52% of your portfolio and bonds 51/106 = 48%. Given your preference for a fifty-fifty portfolio, you might start thinking about selling some stocks and buying some bonds. You should not rebalance every day, but from time to time. This could for instance be every quarter or every year, or when you deviate from your benchmark allocation by more than a certain threshold, for instance, when you deviate by more than x percentage points.

An advantage of this rebalancing strategy, at the same time, is that you reduce your exposure to the stock market after the stock market has increased, and increase it after a stock market fall. If stocks are mean reverting, which this book believes, you thereby manage your risk, as you secure that you do not have too much at stake after a stock-market boom, or too little after a crash. When stocks are mean-reverting, they increase after a fall. If stocks have fallen in value, and you have not rebalanced, your allocation to stocks is less than 50%. When stocks rebound after the crash, you do not gain the full benefit that your fifty-fifty strategy otherwise would have allowed you.

Lesson 7. Make sure to rebalance your portfolio from time to time such that it remains aligned with your attitude towards risk.

20.4.4 Your labour income profile

Risk aversion and investment horizon are the most important aspects to evaluate when thinking about the asset-allocation decision, i.e. how much to invest in risky assets. The sophisticated investor recognizes that other things might matter for the asset-allocation decision. For instance, when you invest for the long run, whether you have a stable labour-income profile or one that fluctuates considerably.

Think about it in the following way. The reason why you should include both risky and safe assets in your portfolio is that safe assets provide a stable stream of income whereas risky assets provide you with a higher, but also more risky, expected return. If your risky assets take a hit, then, at least, you still have your safe assets. Thus, you should not invest more in risky assets than you can afford to lose without panicking (your risk aversion determines this).

Now, if your labour income is stable and reasonably secure, it will embed some of the properties that characterize a safe asset. Your total portfolio includes the safe financial assets, the risky financial assets, and your labour income. This means that you implicitly have a higher exposure to safe assets in your total portfolio if your labour income is relatively safe. All else equal, with such a labour profile, you can allow yourself to take on more financial risk when you invest for the long run, i.e. increase the fraction of your savings invested in risky assets, compared to a person with a volatile labour-income process. So, all else equal, a finance professor with tenure whose income process is reasonably stable might increase his/her allocation to risky assets, relative to a self-employed entrepreneur starting a company in a volatile industry.

> **Lesson 8.** If your labour income process is relatively safe, you can allocate a larger fraction of your savings to risky assets when you invest for the long run.

20.5 The economic environment and asset allocation

Risky assets tend to perform well during economic expansions, and less well during economic contractions, as this book has demonstrated. During economic contractions, safe assets perform relatively better than risky assets. The book has shown that it is difficult to forecast turning points in the business cycle, but predictability is not zero. This means that there is a potential for increasing expected return if increasing allocations to risky assets at the late stages of recessions, when the business cycle is improving, and reducing allocations to risky assets when the economic upswing starts to look tired. You should not make dramatic portfolio adjustments, as it is difficult to predict business cycle turning points, but small adjustments might pay off.

> **Lesson 9.** Over the shorter horizon, the stance of the business cycle should be taken into account when determining your asset allocation. If you increase the allocation to stocks at the bottom of a recession, you improve performance.

20.6 Checklist

This chapter has argued that the following key points are useful when building investment portfolios:

- Strive for maximum diversification. If your portfolio contains risks that can be diversified away, it will only add to the risk of your portfolio, not to your return. You can only expect to be compensated for bearing risk that cannot be diversified away. Diversification is necessary for successful portfolio construction.
- Most private investors either (i) do not know/understand the importance of diversification or (ii) disregard it. Individual investors who invest directly in stocks typically invest in a very low number of different stocks, one or two only. A one- and a two-stock portfolio is grossly underdiversified.
- Diversification means spreading your investments across a high number of individual securities, different asset classes, and different countries. With mutual funds, it is easier to invest in foreign countries, different kinds of stocks (large-cap, small-cap, growth, value), and different kinds of bonds (government bonds, corporate bonds, bonds from different countries, etc.).
- Pay attention to the size of fees if you invest via mutual funds. A passive mutual fund secures diversification at low costs. An active mutual fund charges higher fees, but allows for the possibility that you outperform (or underperform) the index. Most active mutual funds underperform their index after fees but a minority outperforms. The debate between advocates of passive and active investing is heated.
- Stocks are expected to yield a higher, but also more uncertain, return than bonds. The asset allocation decision is thus important for your expected performance.
- The fraction of your portfolio that you should invest in risky assets depends first and foremost on your risk aversion. If you cannot stand the thought that your portfolio looses value, you should hold fewer risky assets.
- The investment horizon is also important. Stocks have a tendency to mean-revert in the long run. This means that if you invest for the long run, you can allow yourself to invest relatively more in risky assets.
- The book has shown that economic activity has a profound influence on financial assets. This means that you should increase your allocation to stocks when the economy is expected to do well, and reduce it when you think the business cycle is about to change for the worse. You should not make dramatic adjustments, as it is difficult to time the market, but small adjustments might improve performance.

Bibliography

ALESINA, A., AND L. H. SUMMERS (1993): 'Central Bank independence and macroeconomic performance: Some comparative evidence,' *Journal of Money, Credit, and Banking*, 25(2), 151–162.

ANDERSEN, T. G., T. BOLLERSLEV, F. X. DIEBOLD, AND C. VEGA (2003): 'Micro effects of macro announcements: Real-time price discovery in foreign exchange,' *American Economic Review*, 93(1), 38–62.

ARNOTT, R. D., AND P. L. BERNSTEIN (2002): 'What risk premium is normal?,' *Financial Analysts Journal*, 58, 64–84.

ARNOTT, R. D., AND P. L. BERNSTEIN (2018): 'The long-run drivers of stock returns: Total payouts and the real economy: A comment,' *Financial Analysts Journal*, 74, 8–9.

ASNESS, C., AND A. ILMANEN (2012): *The 5 percent solution*. Institutional Investor Magazine.

BALKE, N. S., AND R. J. GORDON (1989): 'The estimation of prewar gross national product: Methodology and new evidence,' *Journal of Political Economy*, 97(1), 38–92.

BANSAL, R., AND A. YARON (2005): 'Risks for the long run: A potential resolution of asset pricing puzzles,' *Journal of Finance*, 59(4), 1481–1509.

BANZ, R. W. (1981): 'The relationship between return and market value of common stocks,' *Journal of Financial Economics*, 9, 3–18.

BARBER, B. M., AND T. ODEAN (2000): 'Trading is hazardous to your wealth: The common stock investment performance of individual investors,' *Journal of Finance*, 55, 773–806.

BARRO, R. J. (2006): 'Rare disasters and asset markets in the twentieth century,' *Quarterly Journal of Economics*, 121(3), 823–866.

BARRO, R. J., AND D. B. GORDON (1983): 'Rules, discretion and reputation in a model of monetary policy,' *Journal of Monetary Economics*, 12, 101–121.

BARRO, R. J., AND J. F. URSUA (2008): 'Macroeconomic crises since 1870,' *Brookings Papers on Economic Activity*, Spring 2008, 255–335.

BEAN, C. A., C. BRODA, T. ITO, AND R. KROSZNER (2015): 'Low for long? Causes and consequences of persistently low interest rates,' *Geneva Report on the World Economy 17*.

BEBER, A., M. W. BRANDT, AND M. LUISI (2015): 'Distilling the macroeconomic news flow,' *Journal of Financial Economics*, 117, 489–507.

BERK, J. B., AND J. VAN BINSBERGEN (2015): 'Measuring skill in the mutual fund industry,' *Journal of Financial Economics*, 118, 1–20.

BERNANKE, B. S. (2005): 'The global saving glut and the U.S. current account deficit,' Speech, At the Sandridge Lecture, Virginia Association of Economists, Richmond, Virginia.

BERNANKE, B. S. (2006): 'Monetary aggregates and monetary policy at the federal reserve: A historical perspective,' Available at https://www.federalreserve.gov/newsevents/speech/bernanke20061110a.htm.

BERNANKE, B. S. (2010): 'Monetary policy and the housing bubble,' Speech, Annual Meeting of the American Economic Association.

BERNANKE, B. S., AND K. K. KUTTNER (2005): 'What explains the stock market's reaction to Federal Reserve policy?,' *Journal of Finance*, 60(3), 1221–1257.

Bernstein, W. J., and R. D. Arnott (2003): 'Earnings growth: The two percent dilution,' *Financial Analysts Journal*, 59(5), 47–55.

Beshears, J., J. J. Choi, D. Laibson, and B. C. Madrian (2018): 'Behavioral Household Finance,' in *Handbook of Behavioral Economics—Foundations and Applications 1*, ed. by B. D. Bernheim, S. DellaVigna, and D. Laibson. Elsevier.

Blanchard, O. J., and S. Fisher (1989): *Lectures on Macroeconomics*. MIT Press.

Blanchard, O. J., and L. H. Summers (1986): 'Hysteresis and the European unemployment problem,' *NBER Macroeconomics Annual*, 1, 15–77.

Bogle, J. C. (1991a): 'Investing in the 1990s,' *Journal of Portfolio Management*, 17, 5–14.

Bogle, J. C. (1991b): 'Investing in the 1990s: Occams razor revisited,' *Journal of Portfolio Management*, 18, 88–91.

Bogle, J. C., and M. W. Nolan (2015): 'Occams razor redux: Establishing reasonable expectations for financial market returns,' *Journal of Portfolio Management*, 42, 119–134.

Boyd, J., J. Hu, and R. Jagannathan (2005): 'The stock markets reaction to unemployment news: Why bad news may some times be good for stocks?' *Journal of Finance*, 62, 649–672.

Brynjolfsson, E., and A. McAfee (2011): *Race Against the Machine*. Lexington: Digital Frontier Press.

Buraschi, A., and P. Whelan (2016): 'Bond markets and monetary policy,' in *Handbook of Fixed-Income Securities*, ed. by P. Veronesi, pp. 77–92. Wiley.

Burns, A. F., and W. C. Mitchell (1946): *Measuring Business Cycles*. NBER.

Campbell, J. Y. (1987): 'Stock returns and the term structure,' *Journal of Financial Economics*, 18, 373–399.

Campbell, J. Y., and J. H. Cochrane (1999): 'By force of habit: A consumption-based explanation of aggregate stock market behavior,' *Journal of Political Economy*, 107(2), 205–251.

Campbell, J. Y., M. Lettau, B. Malkiel, and Y. Xu (2001): 'Have individual stocks become more volatile? An empirical exploration of idiosyncratic risk,' *Journal of Finance*, 56, 1–43.

Campbell, J. Y., A. W. Lo, and A. C. MacKinlay (1996): *The Econometrics of Financial Markets*. Princeton University Press.

Campbell, J. Y., and R. J. Shiller (1988a): 'The dividend-price ratio and expectations of future dividends and discount factors,' *Review of Financial Studies*, 1, 195–228.

Campbell, J. Y., and R. J. Shiller (1988b): 'Stock prices, earnings, and expected dividends,' *Journal of Finance*, 43, 661–676.

Campbell, J. Y., and S. B. Thompson (2008): 'Predicting excess stock returns out of sample: Can anything beat the historical average?,' *Review of Financial Studies*, 21, 1509–1531.

Chen, L. (2008): 'On the reversal of dividend and return predictability: A tale of two periods,' *Journal of Financial Economics*, 92, 128–151.

Clarida, R., J. Gali, and M. Gertler (1998): 'Monetary policy rules in practice: Some international evidence,' *European Economic Review*, 42, 1033–1067.

Cochrane, J. H. (1992): 'Explaining the variance of price-dividend ratios,' *Review of Financial Studies*, 5, 243–280.

Cochrane, J. H. (1999): 'Portfolio advice for a multi-factor world,' *Federal Reserve Bank of Chicago Economic Perspectives*, 22, 59–78.

Cochrane, J. H. (2008a): 'The dog that did not bark: A defense of return predictability,' *Review of Financial Studies*, 21, 1533–1575.

COCHRANE, J. H. (2008b): 'Financial Markets and the Real Economy,' in *Handbook of the Equity Risk Premium*, ed. by R. Mehra, pp. 237–325. Elsevier.

COOPER, I., AND R. PRIESTLEY (2009): 'Time-varying risk premiums and the output gap,' *Review of Financial Studies*, 22, 2801–2833.

COOPER, I., AND R. PRIESTLEY (2013): 'The world business cycle and expected return,' *Review of Finance*, 17, 1029–1064.

COVAL, J. D., J. W. JUREK, AND E. STAFFORD (2009): 'The economics of structured finance,' *Journal of Economic Perspectives*, 23(1), 3–25.

COVAL, J. D., AND T. J. MOSKOWITZ (2001): 'The geography of investment: Informed trading and asset prices,' *Journal of Political Economy*, 109, 811–841.

CREMERS, M., AND A. PETAJISTO (2009): 'How active is your fund manager? A new measure that predicts performance,' *Review of Financial Studies*, 22, 3329–3365.

CROWE, C., AND E. E. MEADE (2007): 'The evolution of central bank governance around the world,' *Journal of Economic Perspectives*, 21(4), 69–90.

CUKIERMAN, A. (2008): 'Central bank independence and monetary policymaking institutions—past, present and future,' *European Journal of Political Economy*, 24, 722–736.

DOMIAN, D. L., D. A. LOUTON, AND M. D. RACINE (2007): 'Diversification in portfolios of individual stocks: 100 stocks are not enough,' *Financial Review*, 42, 557–570.

DOW, C. H. (1920): *Scientific stock speculation*. The Magazine of Wall Street, New York.

EASTERLIN, R. A. (1974): 'Does economic growth improve the human lot? Some empirical evidence,' in *Nations and Households in Economic Growth: Essays in Honor of Moses Abramovitz*, ed. by R. David, and R. Reder, pp. 89–125, New York. Academic Press.

ESTRELLA, A., AND M. R. TRUBIN (2006): 'The yield curve as a leading indicator: Some practical issues,' *Current Issues in Economics and Finance*, July/August 2006 Volume 12, Number 5, Federal reserve bank of New York.

FAMA, E. F. (1970): 'Efficient capital markets: A review of theory and empirical work,' *Journal of Finance*, 25, 383–417.

FAMA, E. F. (1991): 'Efficient capital markets: II,' *Journal of Finance*, 46, 1575–1617.

FAMA, E. F., AND K. R. FRENCH (1988): 'Dividend yields and expected stock returns,' *Journal of Financial Economics*, 22, 3–25.

FAMA, E. F., AND K. R. FRENCH (1989): 'Business conditions and expected returns on stocks and bonds,' *Journal of Financial Economics*, 25, 23–49.

FAMA, E. F., AND K. R. FRENCH (1992): 'The Cross?Section of Expected Stock Returns,' *Journal of Finance*, 47, 427–465.

FAMA, E. F., AND K. R. FRENCH (1993): 'Common risk factors in the returns on stocks and bonds,' *Journal of Financial Economics*, 33, 3–56.

FAMA, E. F., AND K. R. FRENCH (2002): 'The equity premium,' *Journal of Finance*, 57, 637–659.

FAMA, E. F., AND K. R. FRENCH (2010): 'Luck versus Skill in the Cross?Section of Mutual Fund Returns,' *Journal of Finance*, 65, 1915–1947.

FED (2009): 'Where should I look to find statistics on the share of subprime mortgages to total mortgages?,' Available at http://www.frbsf.org/education/publications/doctor-econ/2009/december/subprime-mortgage-statistics/.

FED (2013): 'Assessing the costs and consequences of the 2007–09 financial crisis and its aftermath,' *Federal Reserve Bank of Dallas Economic Letters*, 8, 9.

FED (2019): 'Which leading indicators have done better at signaling past recessions?,' *Federal Reserve Bank of Chicago Fed Letters. No. 9.*

FERNALD, J. G., AND C. I. JONES (2014): 'The future of US economic growth,' *American Economic Review: Papers and Proceeding*, 104, 44–49.

FERREIRA, M., AND P. SANTA-CLARA (2011): 'Forecasting stock market returns: The sum of the parts is more than the whole,' *Journal of Financial Economics*, 100, 514–537.

FLORENTSEN, B., U. NIELSSON, P. RAAHAUGE, AND J. RANGVID (2019): 'The aggregate cost of equity underdiversification,' *Financial Review*, 54, 833–856.

FREEMAN, R. B. (2009): 'What does global expansion of higher education mean for the U.S.?' NBER WP 14962.

GOETZMANN, W. N., AND A. KUMAR (2008): 'Equity portfolio diversification,' *Review of Finance*, 12, 433–463.

GOLEZ, B., AND P. KOUDIJS (2018): 'Four centuries of return predictability,' *Journal of Financial Economics*, 127, 248–263.

GORDON, R. J. (2012): 'Is U.S. economic growth over? Faltering innovation confronts the six headwinds,' NBER WP 18315.

GORDON, R. J. (2014): 'The demise of U.S. economic growth: Restatement, rebuttal, and reflections,' NBER WP 19895.

GORDON, R. J. (2016): *The rise and fall of American growth: The US standard of living since the civil war*. Princeton University Press.

GOYAL, A., AND I. WELCH (2008): 'A comprehensive look at the empirical performance of equity premium prediction,' *Review of Financial Studies*, 21, 1455–1508.

GRAHAM, B., AND D. DODD (1934): *Security Analysis*. McGraw-Hill.

GREENWALD, D. L., M. LETTAU, AND S. C. LUDVIGSON (2019): 'How the wealth was won: Factor shares as market fundamentals,' Manuscript.

GRINBLATT, M., AND S. TITMAN (1989): 'An analysis of quarterly portfolio holdings,' *Journal of Business*, 62, 393–416.

GRINOLD, R., AND K. KRONER (2002): 'The equity risk premium: Analyzing the long-run prospects for the stock market,' *Investment Insight*, 5, 7–3.

GRUBER, J. W., AND S. KAMIN (2017): 'Corporate buybacks and capital investment : An international perspective,' *IFDP Notes*. Washington: Board of Governors of the Federal Reserve System.

HAMILTON, J. D., E. S. HARRIS, J. HATZIUS, AND K. D. WEST (2015): 'The equilibrium real funds rate: Past, present and future,' *NBER WP No. 21476* .

HANKE, S. H., AND A. K. KWOK (2009): 'On the measurement of Zimbabwes Hyperinflation,' *Cato Journal*, 29(2), 353–364.

HANSEN, A. H. (1939): 'Economic progress and declining population growth,' *American Economic Review*, 29, 1–15.

HARVEY, C. R. (1988): 'The real term structure and consumption growth,' *Journal of Financial Economics*, 22, 305–333.

IBBOTSON, R. G., AND P. CHEN (2003): 'Long-run stock returns: Participating in the real economy,' *Financial Analysts Journal*, 59(3), 88–98.

ICI (2019): *2019 Investment Company Fact Book*. Investment Company Institute.

INGLEHART, R., AND H.-D. KLINGEMANN (2000): 'Genes, culture, democracy, and happiness,' in *Culture and subjective well-being*, ed. by E. Diener, and E. Suh, pp. 165–183. MIT Press.

JONES, C. I. (2016): 'The facts of economic growth,' in *Handbook of Macroeconomics*, ed. by J. B. Taylor, and H. Uhlig, pp. 3–69. Elsevier.

JORDA, O., K. KNOLL, D. KUVSHINOV, M. SCHULARICK, AND A. M. TAYLOR (2019): 'The rate of return on everything, 1870–2015,' *Quarterly Journal of Economics*, 134(3), 1225–1298.

Kacperczyk, M., C. Sialm, and L. Zheng (2005): 'On the industry concentration of actively managed equity mutual funds,' *Journal of Finance*, 60(4), 1983–2012.

Kacperczyk, M., S. van Nieuwerburgh, and L. Veldkamp (2016): 'A rational theory of mutual funds' attention allocation,' *Econometrica*, 84(2), 571–626.

Kocherlakota, N. R. (1996): 'The equity premium: It's still a puzzle,' *Journal of Economic Literature*, 34, 42–71.

Kosowski, R., A. Timmermann, R. Wermers, and H. White (2006): 'Can mutual fund 'stars' really pick stocks? New evidence from a bootstrap analysis,' *Journal of Finance*, 61, 2551–2595.

Krishnamurthy, A., S. Nagel, and A. Vissing-Jørgensen (2015): 'ECB policies involving government bond purchases: Impacts and channels,' *Review of Finance*, 22, 1–44.

Krishnamurthy, A., and A. Vissing-Jørgensen (2011): 'The effects of quantitative easing on long-term interest rates,' *Brookings Papers on Economic Activity*, 21, 215–287.

Kroencke, T. A. (2019): 'Recessions and the stock market,' Unpublished.

Lettau, M., and S. C. Ludvigson (2001): 'Consumption, aggregate wealth, and expected stock returns,' *Journal of Finance*, 56, 815–849.

Lucas, R. E. (1988): 'On the mechanics of economic development,' *Journal of Monetary Economics*, 22(1), 3–42.

Ludvigson, S. C., and S. Ng (2009): 'Macro factors in bond risk premia,' *Review of Financial Studies*, 22, 5027–5067.

Lueven, L., and H. Tong (2012): 'U.S. monetary shocks and global stock prices,' *Journal of Financial Intermediation*, 21, 530–547.

Mehra, R., and E. C. Prescott (1985): 'The equity premium. A puzzle,' *Journal of Monetary Economics*, 15, 145–161.

Menzly, L., T. Santos, and P. Veronesi (2004): 'Understanding predictability,' *Journal of Political Economy*, 112, 1–47.

Miron, J. A., and C. D. Romer (1990): 'A new monthly index of industrial production, 1884–1940,' *Journal of Economic History*, 50, 321–337.

Møller, S. V., H. Nøholm, and J. Rangvid (2014): 'Consumer confidence or the business cycle: What matters more for European expected returns?,' *Journal of Empirical Finance*, 28, 230–248.

Møller, S. V., and J. Rangvid (2015): 'End-of-the-year economic growth and time-varying expected returns,' *Journal of Financial Economics*, 115, 136–154.

Møller, S. V., and J. Rangvid (2018): 'The end-of-the-year effect. Global economic growth and expected returns around the world,' *Management Science*, 64, 573–591.

Moody's (2009): 'Moody's: Corporate Default and Recovery Rates, 1920-2008,' Moody's Investors service.

Muir, T. (2017): 'Financial crises and risk premia,' *Quarterly Journal of Economics*, 132, 765–809.

Neuhierl, A., and M. Weber (2019): 'Monetary policy communication, policy slope, and the stock market,' Journal of Monetary Economics, Forthcoming.

Nordhaus, W. D. (2015): 'Are we approaching an economic singularity? Information technology and the future of economic growth,' NBER WP 21547.

Obstfeld, M., and K. Rogoff (1996): *Foundations of International Macroeconomics*. MIT Press.

OECD (2015): 'In It Together: Why less inequality benefits all,' OECD Report.

PASTOR, L., AND R. F. STAMBAUGH (2012): 'Are stocks really less volatile in the long run?,' *Journal of Finance*, 67, 431–478.

PATELIS, A. D. (1997): 'Stock return predictability and the role of monetary policy,' *Journal of Finance*, 52, 1951–1972.

PEDERSEN, L. H. (2015): *Efficiently inefficient. How smart money invests and market prices are determined*. Princeton University Press.

PIKETTY, T. (2014): *Capital in the Twenty-First Century*. Harvard University Press.

PIKETTY, T., AND G. ZUCMAN (2014): 'Capital is back: Wealth-income ratios in rich countries 1700–2010,' *Quarterly Journal of Economics*, 129(3), 1255–1310.

PWC (2017): 'The world in 2050,' PWC Report.

RANGVID, AND OTHERS (2013): *The Financial Crisis in Denmark - Causes, Consequences, and Lessons*. Danish Ministry of Industry, Business and Financial Affairs.

RANGVID, J. (2006): 'Output and expected returns,' *Journal of Financial Economics*, 81(3), 595–624.

RANGVID, J. (2017): 'What rate of return can we expect over the next decade?,' Unpublished manuscript.

RANGVID, J., D. E. RAPACH, AND M. E. WOHAR (2005): 'Macro variables and international stock return predictability,' *International Journal of Forecasting*, 21(1), 137–166.

RANGVID, J., M. SCHMELING, AND A. SCHRIMPF (2014): 'Dividend predictability around the world,' *Journal of Financial and Quantitative Analysis*, 49(15–6), 1255–1277.

RAPACH, D., J. K. STRAUSS, AND G. ZHOU (2010): 'Out-of-Sample Equity Premium Prediction: Combination Forecasts and Links to the Real Economy,' *Review of Financial Studies*, 23(2), 821–862.

RAPACH, D., AND G. ZHOU (2013): 'Forecasting Stock Returns,' in *Handbook of Economic Forecasting*, ed. by G. Elliott, and A. Timmermann, pp. 328–383. Elsevier.

RIETZ, T. (1988): 'The equity premium: A solution,' *Journal of Monetary Economics*, 22(1), 117–131.

RIGOBON, R., AND B. SACK (2004): 'The impact of monetary policy on asset prices,' *Journal of Monetary Economics*, 51(8), 1553–1575.

RITTER, J. R. (2012): 'Is economic growth good for investors?,' *Journal of Applied Corporate Finance*, 24(2), 8–18.

ROMER, C. D. (1989): 'The prewar business cycle reconsidered: New estimates of gross national product, 1869-1908,' *Journal of Political Economy*, 97(1), 1–37.

ROMER, C. D. (1994): 'Remeasuring Business Cycles,' *Journal of Economic History*, 54, 573–609.

ROMER, C. D. (1999): 'Changes in business cycles: Evidence and explanations,' *Journal of Economic Perspectives*, 13(2), 23–44.

ROMER, P. M. (1990): 'Endogenous technological change,' *Journal of Political Economy*, 98(5), S71–S102.

SAEZ, E., AND G. ZUCMAN (2016): 'Wealth inequality in the United States since 1913: Evidence from capitalized income tax data,' *Quarterly Journal of Economics*, 131(2), 519–578.

SCHMELING, M., AND C. WAGNER (2019): 'Does central bank tone move asset prices?,' Unpublished manuscript.

SCHNEIDER, F. (2007): 'Eight centuries of global real interest rates, RG, and the suprasecular decline, 1311–2018,' *Bank of England Staff Working Paper 845*.

SCHNEIDER, F. (2007): 'Shadow economies and corruption all over the world: New estimates for 145 countries,' *The Open-Access, Open-Assessment E-Journal*, 1(2007–9), 1–47.

SHILLER, R. J. (1981): 'Do stock prices move too much to be justified by subsequent changes in dividends?,' *American Economic Review*, 71(3), 421–436.

SHILLER, R. J. (2000): *Irrational Exuberance*. Princeton University Press.

SIEGEL, J. J. (2014): *Stocks for the long Run: the definitive guide to financial market returns and long-term investment strategies*. McGraw-Hill Publishers.

SIEGEL, J. J. (2016): 'The Shiller CAPE ratio: A new look,' *Financial Analysts Journal*, 72(3), 41–50.

STRAEHL, P. U., AND R. G. IBBOTSON (2017): 'The long-run drivers of stock returns: Total payouts and the real economy,' *Financial Analysts Journal*, 59(1), 88–98.

STRAEHL, P. U., AND R. G. IBBOTSON (2018): 'The long-run drivers of stock returns: Total payouts and the real economy: Author response,' *Financial Analysts Journal*, 74(1), 9–10.

SUMMERS, L. H. (2014): 'US economic prospects: Secular stagnation, hysteresis, and the zero lower bound,' Speech, National Association of Business Economics.

TAYLOR, J. B. (1993): 'Discretion versus policy rules in practice,' *Carnegie-Rochester Conference Series on Public Policy*, 39, 195–214.

WEIL, P. (1989): 'The equity premium puzzle and the risk-free rate puzzle,' *Journal of Monetary Economics*, 24(3), 401–421.

Index

9 780198 866404

Made in the USA
Las Vegas, NV
19 September 2026

04212443-fd02-4911-81d0-467d7d02aaceR01